REDISCOVERING THE DEAD SEA SCROLLS

Rediscovering the Dead Sea Scrolls

An Assessment of Old and New
Approaches and Methods

Edited by

Maxine L. Grossman

WILLIAM B. EERDMANS PUBLISHING COMPANY

GRAND RAPIDS, MICHIGAN / CAMBRIDGE, U.K.

Published 2010 by
Wm. B. Eerdmans Publishing Co.
2140 Oak Industrial Drive N.E., Grand Rapids, Michigan 49505 /
P.O. Box 163, Cambridge CB3 9PU U.K.

Printed in the United States of America

15 14 13 12 11 10   7 6 5 4 3 2 1

Library of Congress Cataloging-in-Publication Data

Rediscovering the Dead Sea scrolls:
    An assessment of old and new approaches and methods /
    edited by Maxine L. Grossman.
        p.   cm.
    Includes bibliographical references.
      ISBN 978-0-8028-4009-7 (pbk.: alk. paper)
      1. Dead Sea scrolls.   I. Grossman, Maxine L.

    BM487.M445   2010
    296.1'55 — dc22

                                    2010005263

www.eerdmans.com

To Florentino García Martínez,

with our gratitude

Contents

Contributors

MARTIN G. ABEGG, JR. is Professor of Religious Studies at Trinity Western University, Langley, BC, Canada.

JAMES R. DAVILA is Professor in Early Jewish Studies at the University of St. Andrews, Scotland.

STEVE DELAMARTER is Professor of Old Testament at George Fox Evangelical Seminary, a graduate school of George Fox University, in Portland, OR.

MAXINE L. GROSSMAN is Associate Professor in the Joseph and Rebecca Meyerhoff Center for Jewish Studies at the University of Maryland.

CHARLOTTE HEMPEL is a Senior Research Fellow in Second Temple Judaism in the School of Philosophy, Theology and Religion at the University of Birmingham, UK.

JUTTA JOKIRANTA is University Lecturer in Old Testament/Hebrew Bible Studies at the University of Helsinki.

JONATHAN KLAWANS is Associate Professor of Religion at Boston University.

ROBERT KUGLER is the Paul S. Wright Professor of Christian Studies at Lewis & Clark College in Portland, OR.

HAYIM LAPIN is Professor in the Department of History and the Joseph and Rebecca Meyerhoff Center for Jewish Studies at the University of Maryland.

JODI MAGNESS is the Kenan Distinguished Professor for Teaching Excellence in Early Judaism in the Department of Religious Studies at the University of North Carolina at Chapel Hill.

SARIANNA METSO is Associate Professor in the Department of Near and Middle Eastern Civilizations and the Department of Historical Studies at the University of Toronto.

CAROL A. NEWSOM is the Charles Howard Candler Professor of Old Testament/Hebrew Bible at the Candler School of Theology, Emory University.

EIBERT TIGCHELAAR is BOF Research Professor in the Faculty of Religion at the Katholieke Universiteit Leuven, Belgium.

EUGENE ULRICH is John A. O'Brien Professor of Hebrew Scriptures at the University of Notre Dame.

BRUCE ZUCKERMAN is Professor of Religion at the University of Southern California and Director of the West Semitic Research and InscriptiFact Projects, which create, preserve and distribute high resolution images of ancient Near Eastern texts.

Abbreviations

AB	Anchor Bible
ABD	*Anchor Bible Dictionary,* ed. David Noel Freedman
ABRL	Anchor Bible Reference Library
AGJU	Arbeiten zur Geschichte des antiken Judentums und des Urchristentums
BA	*Biblical Archaeologist*
BASOR	*Bulletin of the American Schools of Oriental Research*
BETL	Bibliotheca ephemeridum theologicarum lovaniensium
BH	Biblical Hebrew
BHS	*Biblia Hebraica Stuttgartensia*
BibOr	*Biblica et orientalia*
CahRB	Cahiers de la Revue biblique
CC	Continental Commentaries
CQS	Companion to the Qumran Scrolls
DJD	Discoveries in the Judaean Desert
DSD	*Dead Sea Discoveries*
DSS	Dead Sea Scrolls
EDSS	*Encyclopedia of the Dead Sea Scrolls,* ed. Lawrence H. Schiffman and James C. VanderKam
ER	*Encyclopedia of Religion,* ed. Mircea Eliade
EstBib	*Estudios bíblicos*
EVV	English versions

FRLANT	Forschungen zur Religion und Literatur des Alten und Neuen Testaments
HAT	Handkommentar zum Alten Testament
HDSS	Elisha Qimron, *The Hebrew of the Dead Sea Scrolls*
HSS	Harvard Semitic Studies
HTR	*Harvard Theological Review*
HUCA	*Hebrew Union College Annual*
IEJ	*Israel Exploration Journal*
IOS	Israel Oriental Studies
ISFDA	InscriptiFact Image Database Application
JAAR	*Journal of the American Academy of Religion*
JBL	*Journal of Biblical Literature*
JECS	*Journal of Early Christian Studies*
JFSR	*Journal of Feminist Studies in Religion*
JJS	*Journal of Jewish Studies*
JNES	*Journal of Near Eastern Studies*
JQR	*Jewish Quarterly Review*
JSJSup	Journal for the Study of Judaism: Supplement Series
JSNTSup	Journal for the Study of the New Testament: Supplement Series
JSOTSup	Journal for the Study of the Old Testament: Supplement Series
JSPSup	Journal for the Study of the Pseudepigrapha: Supplement Series
JSS	*Journal of Semitic Studies*
LBH	Late Biblical Hebrew
LHB/OTS	Library of Hebrew Bible/Old Testament Studies
LSTS	Library of Second Temple Studies
LXX	Septuagint
MT	Masoretic Text
NEA	*Near Eastern Archaeology*
NEchtB	Neue Echter Bibel
NovT	*Novum Testamentum*
NovTSup	Novum Testamentum Supplements
NRSV	New Revised Standard Version
NTOA	Novum Testamentum et Orbis Antiquus
OCP	*Orientalia christiana periodica*
OEANE	*The Oxford Encyclopedia of Archaeology in the Near East,* ed. Eric M. Meyers

PAM	Palestine Archaeological Museum
PEQ	*Palestine Exploration Quarterly*
PTSDSSP	Princeton Theological Seminary Dead Sea Scrolls Project
RB	*Revue biblique*
RBL	*Review of Biblical Literature*
RevQ	*Revue de Qumran*
SBLBSNA	Society of Biblical Literature Biblical Studies in North America
SBLDS	Society of Biblical Literature Dissertation Series
SBLEJL	Society of Biblical Literature Early Judaism and Its Literature
SBLMS	Society of Biblical Literature Monograph Series
SBLPS	Society of Biblical Literature Pseudepigrapha Series
SBLRBS	Society of Biblical Literature Resources for Biblical Study
SBLSCS	Society of Biblical Literature Septuagint and Cognate Studies
SBLTT	Society of Biblical Literature Texts and Translations
ScrHier	Scripta hierosolymitana
SDSSRL	Studies in the Dead Sea Scrolls and Related Literature
SHR	Studies in the History of Religions
SJLA	Studies in Judaism in Late Antiquity
SP	Samaritan Pentateuch
SSN	Studia semitica neerlandica
STDJ	Studies on the Texts of the Desert of Judah
StPB	Studia post-biblica
SUNT	Studien zur Umwelt des Neuen Testaments
TSAJ	Texte und Studien zum antiken Judentum
VT	*Vetus Testamentum*
VTSup	Supplements to Vetus Testamentum
WMANT	Wissenschaftliche Monographien zum Alten und Neuen Testament
WSRP	West Semitic Research Project
WUNT	Wissenschaftliche Untersuchungen zum Neuen Testament
ZTK	*Zeitschrift für Theologie und Kirche*

Introduction: Tools for Our Work

The study of the Dead Sea Scrolls is, at its most basic, an interdisciplinary endeavor. In identifying, reconstructing, translating, and interpreting the texts from Qumran — not to mention assigning meaning to them in the larger contexts of ancient Judaism, early Christianity, and biblical studies — scrolls scholars range widely through the fields of philology, literary analysis, ancient history, and beyond. The fragmentary state of the evidence makes such interdisciplinary work a necessity. But interdisciplinarity is also an opportunity — to contextualize the evidence in new ways, introduce new modes of analysis, and potentially reconfigure the larger picture of the world of the Dead Sea Scrolls.

The purpose of this volume on methods and theories in the study of these texts is to bring together a range of diverse perspectives on and scholarly approaches to the scrolls, some addressing issues that are foundational to the field, and some exploring avenues that lead in untested or experimental directions. In formulating their contributions, authors were asked to provide not only an introduction to a given approach to the scrolls, but also a more self-reflective assessment of the limits of their approaches and the potential pitfalls associated with them. Contributors were also invited to focus on a single example or a cluster of related examples, in the interest of providing readers with a concrete and vivid sense of how their approaches work in actual practice.

Interest in questions of method has ebbed and flowed over the course of the history of scrolls scholarship, but the current moment — in which full editions of the scrolls and helpful electronic tools are available to students and scholars with diverse backgrounds and areas of expertise — is one in which methodological pursuits are particularly apt. Several conferences have been devoted to the subject of *how* the scrolls are studied, and these have generated conference volumes that serve as important resources in the field.[1] A number of comprehensive treatments of the scrolls also incorporate discussions of scholarly approaches to the texts, material culture, and contexts of the scrolls,[2] and the fiftieth anniversary of their discovery generated a significant burst of publications a decade ago, reflecting similar interests.[3]

This volume attempts to do something a bit different from these more comprehensive scholarly resources. First, the essays collected here are purposely *introductory.* Contributors have been careful to define their terms and outline their questions in ways that will be inviting to new readers without being off-putting to those with more scrolls experience. Ideally, these essays will be of use to established scholars and senior graduate students, but they are equally designed to be accessible to serious undergraduate students in courses on the scrolls, and to those whose interest in the scrolls comes out of their work in other areas of study. At the same time, this volume purposely is *not* an introduction, in the sense of a comprehensive treatment of approaches to the scrolls as such. Although interest in a certain degree of coverage can be seen in the topics addressed here, the real focus of this volume is on the overlap and intersection of interests that reflect the current state of scholarship in the field, as well as its potential for future development. Thus, some topics — scribal practices, Scripture and its transmission, the nature of the rule texts — have necessarily received attention from multiple authors, while other topics — the calendar texts, Josephus's treatment of fate and free will — have received the more focused attention of individual contributors.

There are probably as many definitions of "method" or "methodol-

---

1. See esp. M. O. Wise, N. Golb, J. J. Collins, and D. G. Pardee, eds., *Methods of Investigation of the Dead Sea Scrolls and the Khirbet Qumran Site;* and now J. G. Campbell, W. J. Lyons, and L. K. Pietersen, eds., *New Directions in Qumran Studies.*

2. See, esp., P. W. Flint and J. C. VanderKam, eds., *The Dead Sea Scrolls after Fifty Years;* see also L. H. Schiffman and J. C. VanderKam, eds., *Encyclopedia of the Dead Sea Scrolls.*

3. See, in addition to the above, S. E. Porter and C. A. Evans, eds., *The Scrolls and the Scriptures;* R. A. Kugler and E. Schuller, eds., *The Dead Sea Scrolls at Fifty;* and L. H. Schiffman, E. Tov, and J. C. VanderKam, eds., *The Dead Sea Scrolls Fifty Years After their Discovery.*

ogy" as there are scholars with methodological concerns. My own understanding of *method* includes attention to particular approaches to scholarship and an awareness of the academic tasks that they entail. Attention to method leads us to the most basic epistemological questions, beginning with our understanding of the evidence. Different fields (or subfields) will have different understandings of what counts as legitimate evidence, how that evidence can be linked together (including what interpretive leaps are, or are not, permissible), and what sort of finished picture the evidence can be made to support. To say that conclusions vary when we move from one approach to another implies not only that different approaches may yield different results but that they may reach entirely different *kinds* of results, and that they may disagree on the degree of certainty that is desirable or, indeed, possible with respect to any given conclusion.

In the process of describing their chosen methods, the authors of these chapters have also worked at the meta-level, by thinking in explicitly *methodological* ways. Methodology, the analysis or study of a given approach within a discipline, provides a kind of contextualizing discourse within which an actual method can be understood. The point of methodology is not only to understand the pragmatics of a method or approach, but more fully to make sense of its underlying logics, to identify (and query) its assumptions, and to push for a better understanding of its limitations, biases, and potential contributions to the field. As such, thinking methodologically gives us the opportunity to foreground the *process* of our work, rather than focusing primarily on its outcome. One consequence of this approach is that it provides a better sense of what we are arguing and why. A perhaps even more significant consequence is that we are better able to communicate that sense, and to understand the arguments of other people, whose assumptions, definitions, and logics may be different from our own.

At least in the contemporary study of religion, "methods" tend to go hand-in-hand with "theories," and it makes sense in a methodological project to think of "methods and theories" together. But this latter term is somewhat ambiguous and deserves attention of its own. A theory, of course, is a particular argument or claim with regard to the subject in question (the Essene Hypothesis, for example, offers a theory of the origins and identity of the community associated with the scrolls). Scientists use the term theory in a different way, to refer to a basic principle or premise that can be used to predict future outcomes. More relevant for our own discussion is a notion of *theory* as the conceptual underpinning for larger scholarly claims. In this sense, the theory offers the conceptual framing, and the method is the academic practice that takes place in light of it. Theory can also be shorthand for "critical theory," the literary and cultural critiques that form the basis for contemporary cultural studies.[4]

To speak of "methods and theories" in the study of the Dead Sea Scrolls, consequently, is once again to identify a visibly intersectional practice, potentially incorporating everything from the most material carbon 14 analysis of a leather manuscript to the most "high theory" of cultural critiques of the definitions of "history." Not every approach will be mutually compatible with every other, but precisely in the lines of tension between approaches we may find opportunities for new views on familiar topics, as well as a provocation to reconsider our starting assumptions. At stake here is the opportunity to rethink the familiar image from the *Damascus Document,* in which the leader of the covenant community is imagined as an interpreter of Torah, who "takes out a tool for his work" (מוציא כלי למעשיהו).[5] In place of one authoritative approach or strategy, a single "tool for our work," this volume offers a variety, some overlapping, and some that stand alone.

The chapters in this volume are the products of a process that has been unusually collaborative, thanks to the enthusiasm and engagement of all those involved. Participants shared drafts with one another, consulted by telephone and email, and met in person (in ways formal and informal) at two successive Annual Meetings of the Society of Biblical Literature. Some of this collaboration is visible in the footnotes of the chapters that follow, but even more of it is present in the basic fabric of the work. As such, these chapters do indeed reflect a collective development of technical tools and collective explorations into their potentialities.

Both within and outside the field of Qumran scholarship, the study of the scrolls is sometimes treated as a rather specialized closed shop. By encouraging interdisciplinary and self-consciously methodological discussions, this volume intends to open that shop and invite new conversations across lines of interest, discipline, and scholarly subfield.

The volume opens with a methodological reflection by Sarianna Metso. Her primary question is one that lies at the starting point of any

---

4. On both "theory" and theories, see esp. M. C. Taylor, ed., *Critical Terms for Religious Studies;* and A. K. M. Adam, ed., *Handbook of Postmodern Biblical Interpretation.*

5. CD 6:3-8, quoting Isa 54:16. For text, translation, and notes, see J. M. Baumgarten and D. R. Schwartz, "Damascus Document (CD)," 22-23.

methodological study: how does new evidence force us to reconsider both our picture of a field and our approach to the study of it? In her exploration of the significance of the scrolls for our study of ancient Judaism, Metso considers three examples that will prove relevant throughout the volume: the concept of biblical texts, the formation of halakhah, again in conceptual terms, and the problem of historical reconstruction on the basis of the evidence of the scrolls.

The next three chapters focus particularly on the material evidence of the manuscripts of the Dead Sea Scrolls. Eibert Tigchelaar begins with the question of how scholars understand the concept of "manuscript" and how they go about grouping fragments and assigning them to their larger manuscript contexts. He discusses the process both in theory and through a single example, that of 4Q184, *The Wiles of the Wicked Woman.* His assessment of the material evidence and the literary content of the fragments highlights the details of the process, points out a few notable pitfalls, and ultimately provides us with a new interpretation of this significant text.

Martin G. Abegg, Jr., follows with a chapter on Hebrew paleography, orthography, morphology, phonology, and syntax — the basic building-blocks that are necessary for understanding the process of reading the Hebrew of the scrolls. What he describes as a "primer on linguistic analysis" is in fact an explanation not only of the highly technical elements that make up philological study but also of their implications for our understanding of the development of the Hebrew language. The subject of "scribal practice" plays a central role in Abegg's discussions of both biblical and nonbiblical Dead Sea Scrolls, as it will in several of the other chapters that follow.

Bruce Zuckerman completes this cluster of chapters, with a discussion of the "high-tech" options for visual reproduction and manipulation of scrolls fragments. While providing an update of his earlier work on the subject, Zuckerman also deals extensively with the methodological implications of new technology for scrolls preservation and future research. Alternating closely-focused examples with programmatic discussions, he provides both pixel-by-pixel analysis and also a most necessary assessment of the current state of the field.

The three chapters that follow form another cluster, in perhaps unexpected ways. These begin with Jodi Magness's discussion of the archaeology of Qumran, which provides a bridge from material analysis to some rather more theoretical questions of social and historical reconstruction. Magness paints a clear and striking picture of how archaeology is done, from the digging of trenches to the academic "bequeathing" of archaeological finds. Her discussion of theories of archaeology, the practical evidence from Qumran, and the present-day state of the field offers readers insights into what is perhaps the most highly contested aspect of Dead Sea Scrolls studies today. In the process she argues for a particular interpretation of the site of Qumran, one enmeshed with an understanding of the community associated with the site and the purity needs of that community.

Hayim Lapin's discussion of social history provides a nice foil to Jodi Magness's chapter, and indeed the two are in conversation on a number of key points. Lapin addresses not merely the historical claims that can be made in light of the Qumran scrolls, but rather the question of what a social historian would do with the evidence of the scrolls and the site of Qumran. By shifting focus to such material realia as the architectural fragments and coin evidence from the site, the material costs implicit in scrolls production, and the geographic origins of clay jars found at the site and in the scrolls caves, Lapin pushes for a more concrete reading of the historical picture of the scrolls sectarians, and a more radical one as well.

In his own contribution to the reframing of history in the scrolls, James R. Davila introduces the concept of counterfactual history. Long a staple of fantasy and science fiction, and more recently a significant element in contemporary economic theory, counterfactual or alternate history reconsiders our understanding of past events by imagining an alternate framing in which entirely different events took place. Davila's own experiment in this field is to imagine the transmission of a manuscript of the *Hodayot,* the Qumran *Thanksgiving Hymns,* through a sequence of translations into first Greek, and then Syriac. He then asks how a modern scholar would interpret the resulting manuscript evidence. His reading both recontextualizes our understanding of the scrolls and serves to underscore some of the problems implicit in contemporary study of Jewish and Christian Pseudepigrapha.

The next cluster of chapters turns again to a textual analysis of the scrolls. Eugene Ulrich explores the methodological issues implicit in modern treatments of ancient Scripture, including modern biases with regard to canon and textual forms. Ulrich begins by defining the key terms of authoritative literature and Scripture, before turning to a discussion of the canonical process. He then addresses some of the key theoretical issues at stake in our treatment of ancient evidence for Scripture, including the problems associated with distinguishing between biblical and "parabiblical" texts, classifying Qumran texts in terms of particular text forms, and otherwise making claims about ancient scriptural traditions in light of modern assumptions.

Charlotte Hempel follows with a chapter on source and redaction criticism in the scrolls. Using biblical studies as a foil, Hempel argues for an approach to the scrolls that acknowledges their ongoing development and recognizes the possibility that some texts were *never* present in fixed "final" forms. With attention to recent work by Emanuel Tov on scribal practice and George Brooke on the need to break down the divide between source and textual criticism, Hempel examines the Qumran rule texts and finds in them significant evidence for ongoing growth and textual development. Her readings push us to rethink the relationships between these central sectarian texts and, even more so, the dynamics that underlay their production and use.

Steve Delamarter offers another perspective on Qumran scribal practice, this time from an explicitly external and experimental angle. Working comparatively, in light of sociological theory and examples from modern Ethiopian scribal traditions, Delamarter formulates a model of scribal practice as the privilege of priestly "deep insiders" within a religious community. His exploration of the visual cues and "paratextual" aspects of manuscripts leads him to argue that distinct scribal practices are closely associated with particular communities, and that the presence of widely divergent manuscripts most likely indicates a diversity of source communities. His treatment of the Paleo-Hebrew scriptural manuscripts in light of these sociological arguments allows him to argue for a specific social context for the origin of these texts.

From the sociology of scribal practice, we turn next to a series of chapters that address rhetoric, ritual, and other theoretical frames for consideration of the significance of the scrolls. Carol Newsom provides an introduction to the field of rhetorical theory, which shows how texts or authors effect change in the world through their use of language. As Newsom demonstrates, in readings of the rule texts from Qumran and the *Thanksgiving Hymns,* this approach is well-suited to the study of sectarian texts, whose most central agenda involves breaking down an individual's existing identity structures and re-forming them within the context of a new, ideal sectarian participant. An examination of the shared and divergent rhetorical choices of these texts allows Newsom to clarify the picture of the social and religious world in which they were composed and experienced.

Robert Kugler takes on the challenge of sorting out a set of calendrical texts, focusing here less on their technical temporal details and more on the conceptual question of why a given calendrical text might continue to be copied long after it had been superseded by a later manuscript tradition. Kugler finds a context for considering this question within the field of ritual studies, and especially the theories of Michael Chwe, who argues that collective ritual practice is grounded in participants' shared knowledge, and their knowledge *of* that shared knowledge. To the extent that texts reflect this reverberating sense of common knowledge, they provide for and undergird collective identity and memory.

My own chapter considers the issue of gender in the scrolls and explores in particular the question of what it meant to be "a man" in a sectarian community associated with the scrolls. The chapter revisits a familiar, and much contested, reading of a passage from the *Rule of the Congregation,* which appears to assert that women were expected to testify before their group's leader(s) about their husbands' private marital behaviors. Close attention to the androcentric nature of this text, in light of two other rule texts from Qumran, allows for an evaluation of the history of interpretations of this passage and also for an explanation of why early scholars found it so provocative and challenging.

Sociological approaches to the scrolls are treated by Jutta Jokiranta in a chapter that addresses such central issues as the definition(s) of sectarianism and the treatment of this concept in scholarship on the scrolls; the problematic question of when and how to label a text "sectarian"; and the even more fraught question of how to draw historical information from a sectarian textual tradition. Jokiranta then follows up with an exploration of social identity theory, showing how a social identity approach provides new opportunities for thinking in critical terms about the scrolls and their world.

Jonathan Klawans concludes the volume with an examination of Josephus's treatment of ancient Jewish sectarian attitudes toward fate and free will that contextualizes the ancient sources in terms of contemporary religious studies theory and practice. Klawans offers new insights into just what Josephus is trying to achieve (working with the analogy of the introductory religious studies classroom), in the process of untangling the vexed question of just how predestinarian ancient Judaism was. His examination of compatibilism, predestination, and divine election takes advantage of comparative readings of later Christian theological conflicts, and in the process he successfully delineates the range of these theological views and their limits in both the scrolls and Josephus. The result is simultaneously an exploration of methodological study and a demonstration of its usefulness in ways both general and particular.

The origins of this book lie in an electronic "guest lecture" that Jim Davila invited me to give to his honors seminar on the Dead Sea Scrolls at the University of St. Andrews in the spring of 2005.[6] Our email correspondence about that essay led to this project, and I am grateful for his insights and those of Eibert Tigchelaar, through the course of the project.

I am grateful to all the contributors to this volume, whose enthusiasm and hard work made my job so easy. Chapter authors were patient through multiple rounds of editing and were generous in sharing their work and critiques with one another. The result is a record of ongoing conversation with many shared touchpoints as well as differences of opinion or perspective. Additional thanks go to Charlotte Hempel, for suggesting that we think in terms of "tools for our work."

Participants benefited from a round of in-person conversations, in a working group meeting immediately prior to the 2006 Annual Meeting of the Society of Biblical Literature in Washington, DC. I wish to thank the Joseph and Rebecca Meyerhoff Center for Jewish Studies at the University of Maryland, which underwrote this meeting, and the Office of International Programs at the University, which contributed to the presence of a number of our international participants. I am grateful to Charlotte Hempel and Sarianna Metso for their participation in a public lecture the night before our work meeting.

A session on methodology and the scrolls at the 2007 Annual Meeting of the Society of Biblical Literature enabled us to think about these ideas again, at a later stage in the process. Thanks are due to the speakers in that session, who included Jonathan Klawans, Jim Davila, and Eyal Regev (whose contribution is in publication elsewhere), and Ross Kraemer, who served as respondent.

I would particularly like to thank Hayim Lapin for his contribution, which was the result of an almost-eleventh-hour request. In agreeing to replace a contributor who had to drop out of the project, and more generally in offering support and thoughtful engagement throughout the process, he has given of his time and his insights. I thank him and our sons Ben and Elli for sharing this path with me.

The editors at Eerdmans have been enthusiastic and supportive

---

6. See "From Text to History: Some Methodological Observations."

through this project, and I thank them for their guidance and assistance. Thanks go especially to Jon Pott for accepting the original proposal and to Linda Bieze and Allen Myers for their help throughout the process.

Nearly half of the contributors to this volume have published monographs in the Studies on the Texts of the Desert of Judah series edited by Florentino García Martínez. Certainly all of us have benefited from his scholarship, his collegiality, and his intellectual generosity over the years. We dedicate this volume to him in appreciation of his constant encouragement of new scholars and new approaches to the scrolls.

When the Evidence Does Not Fit:
Method, Theory, and the Dead Sea Scrolls

Sarianna Metso

In theory, scholars agree that the data and clues embedded within a text should be the controlling guide to understanding and describing that text and to drawing historical conclusions from it. In practice, however, the general tendency is to interpret new data according to the current state of accumulated knowledge. But what if the new data does not conform to the patterns of the traditional mode of understanding? Fresh analysis is required to determine whether the new data is being misinterpreted or whether the old patterns of understanding need to be revised.

The Dead Sea Scrolls present a new phenomenon in Jewish literature. They uniquely offer information about the thought world and practices of a specific community, produced by the group itself in an era that predates any other similar literature. Before the discovery of the scrolls, there were very few writings — either "scriptural" texts or sectarian manuscripts — in the original language extant from the closing centuries of the Second Temple period. The texts or manuscript copies that were used as the basis for writing the history of that period were often centuries or even millennia later than the events they attempted to reconstruct. The possibility, and the challenge, that the much earlier documentary evidence of the scrolls offers is to interpret accurately the information they provide and to avoid anachronistic interpretation.

Now that the first stage of scholarship — the full publication of the scrolls — has been accomplished, the next stage is for scholars to conceptualize and synthesize the information contained in the complete corpus. Initial attempts at such conceptual work began to take shape even in the early years following the discoveries, and new and more comprehensive formulations have continued to emerge. In the face of our new evidence, however, some of our widely-held ideas or ways of conceptualizing the data have proven to be problematic. But again, is the problem in the data, or is it in the traditional concepts and criteria that scholarship had constructed? In this chapter, I would like to focus on three notions in particular — although I cannot claim expertise in all of them — and make some general observations about the current state of Qumran research. I will discuss first, the concept of biblical texts, mainly as a template for further exploration of nonbiblical texts; second, the concept of halakhah; and third, the feasibility of historical reconstruction on the basis of the Dead Sea Scrolls. I intend my remarks as an invitation to discussion rather than as a full-fledged analysis.

The Concept of Biblical Texts

Although my work has not focused as much on the biblical texts, I have been struck by the numerous and diverse ways that the biblical scrolls have challenged reigning suppositions of what constitutes a biblical or scriptural text.[1] I bring up this topic in part because the discussion that has taken place with regard to scriptural texts in my view anticipates the questions that are now beginning to be asked about the nonscriptural material, including the halakhic texts that will be subject for discussion below.

The *Great Psalms Scroll* from Cave 11 brought the problem to the fore as early as 1965.[2] Soon after the publication of this manuscript by James Sanders, a fierce debate ensued, in which his classification of this manuscript as biblical was disputed, primarily on the basis of five features: (1) its liturgical nature, (2) the presence of "nonbiblical" passages, (3) the tetragrammaton in Palaeo-Hebrew, (4) a prose passage called "David's Compositions," and (5) the order of some Psalms at variance with the Masoretic

---

1. The term "biblical" is part of the problem. It is not my purpose here to engage in semantics, but I do recognize that the term "biblical" itself is hugely problematic in the context of the Second Temple period, and many scholars prefer to use "scriptural texts" or "authoritative texts" instead. The term "biblical texts," however, continues to be used as a label, e.g., in the DJD Index volume (E. Tov et al., DJD 39). For further discussion, see the contribution by Eugene Ulrich in this volume.

2. J. A. Sanders, DJD 4.

order.[3] Major scholars classified the manuscript as a secondary liturgical collection rather than as a biblical manuscript.

Progress in the analysis of other scriptural scrolls has demonstrated that all of these features, which originally were considered unique to 11QPs[a], turned out to be characteristic of well-known scriptural manuscripts, including the Greek and Syriac Psalters, other Psalm manuscripts from Qumran, or even the Masoretic Psalter itself.[4] New evidence, and reconsideration of previously known evidence, has demonstrated in short that neither in content nor in scribal practice does 11QPs[a] display features that would distinguish it from other acknowledged scriptural manuscripts. Thus, it has seriously challenged the position of the Masoretic Text as the dominant standard for judging "the biblical text," and it has illuminated our understanding of the canonical process.

The so-called "Reworked Pentateuch" (4Q364-367) has also evoked calls for reconsideration. In a much quoted passage, the editors of the manuscript state:

> This composition contained a running text of the Pentateuch interspersed with exegetical additions and omissions. The greater part of the preserved fragments follows the biblical text closely, but many small . . . elements are added, while other elements are omitted, or, in other cases, their sequence altered.[5]

As long as the MT was viewed as the "standard" for a biblical text, such variation tended to deny biblical status to these texts. But again, as subsequent commentators have pointed out, the editors' characterization here is applicable to just about any scriptural text in the Second Temple period. Eugene Ulrich puts it succinctly: "small additions, omissions, and altered sequences are *characteristic* of the biblical text in this compositional period," and "these are *indicators* of a biblical text, not features that would disqualify it from scriptural status." The variants in 4QRP, he argues, "seem to be classifiable in the same categories as the variants between Exodus and Deuteronomy or between MT and SP." In his view, 4QRP may "constitute simply a variant literary edition of the Torah, alongside the MT and the SP."[6]

---

3. See E. Ulrich, *The Dead Sea Scrolls and the Origins of the Bible*, 115-16.

4. Ulrich, *The Dead Sea Scrolls and the Origins of the Bible*, 116-17.

5. E. Tov and S. White, "4QReworked Pentateuch," DJD 13, 187, 191.

6. E. Ulrich, "The Text of the Hebrew Scriptures at the Time of Hillel and Jesus," esp. 102-103. See also his contribution in this volume.

James VanderKam, too, while commenting on Emanuel Tov's classification of this manuscript as a Rewritten Bible text, remarks, "if that is the proper classification the accent would have to fall on the word *Bible*, not on *Rewritten*. It is not easy to see how the Reworked Pentateuch differs in character from, say, the earlier layer of the Samaritan Pentateuch." He points out that "in a number of comments Tov acknowledges this state of affairs."[7] In fact, Tov now has in a recent article revised his earlier view and considers that at least some Jews regarded it as a scriptural text.[8]

What are the methodological implications of observations such as these? George Brooke, while somewhat more hesitant to place 4QRP in the group of biblical texts, argues that texts such as 4QRP have implications for the practice of textual criticism. In his view, "the rewritten scriptural texts need to become much more explicitly part of the arsenal of the text critic, playing their full part in the description of the fluid transmission of the texts." There should be "a shift away from a sole concern with the quest for the original form of the text" and "a more neutral set of terms for describing what is attested in the manuscript evidence," so that a variant is not seen "principally in terms of scribal error." The rewritten scriptural compositions, in his view, are "primary evidence for how authoritative traditions were appropriated and managed in particular communities in the late Second Temple period" and "must not be prevented on the basis of anachronistic reasoning from taking their proper place."[9]

The authority of the Masoretic Text had initially led to a perception that divergences in the Qumran scriptural material must have reflected variants from an established norm. Attention to the new evidence as such, however, has led to a new understanding of the entire picture of scriptural development.

The Concept of Halakhah

The situation was somewhat similar for the early scholarly analysis of the legal texts in the scrolls. A rather firm dichotomy was erected between the laws recorded in the *Damascus Document* and those recorded in the *Com-*

---

7. J. C. VanderKam, "The Wording of Biblical Citations in Some Rewritten Scriptural Works," esp. 45.

8. E. Tov, "The Many Forms of Scripture." I want to thank Professor Tov for kindly sending me an advance copy of his article.

9. G. J. Brooke, "The Rewritten Law, Prophets and Psalms," esp. 38.

munity Rule, with the legal material in the *Damascus Document* generally described in terms of halakhah and the material in the *Community Rule* classified in such terms as "constitutional," "communal," or "organizational" rules. I have recently questioned whether this common dichotomy between "halakhic texts" and "community rules" is justified, or whether it needs to be reconsidered in light of the evidence.[10]

A key to the issues underlying this topic is the matter of how the legal traditions in the Essene community were generated. Some have argued that the sole source for Qumran legal traditions was scriptural exegesis.[11] Others have wondered whether different communities generated their legal traditions in different ways, with scriptural exegesis as the source for legal traditions in the community that used the *Damascus Document* and some other source as the basis for the community that used the *Community Rule.*[12] Yet another possibility is that communities may have operated in multiple ways, deriving rules regarding the covenant from the Torah, but rules for social organization from the lived experience of the community members.[13]

I have studied a handful of cases in which quotations from the book of Leviticus function as explicit or implicit proof-texts for establishing community discipline and cohesion both in CD and in 1QS, as well as in other texts. The cases deal with the topics of

10. See my "Creating Community Halakhah." The term "halakhah" itself, of course, is an anachronism; as a *terminus technicus* it is used nowhere in the scrolls. See J. P. Meier, "Is There *Halaka* (the Noun) at Qumran?"

11. L. H. Schiffman, *The Halakhah at Qumran,* 19-21, 75-76. See, e.g., the introduction to the book: "We can state with certainty . . . that the Qumran legal traditions are derived exclusively through exegesis" (19), and the summary of ch. 1: "All necessary guidance in matters of *halakhah* came from biblical exegesis" (76). Schiffman presents a reformulated view in "Legal Texts and Codification in the Dead Sea Scrolls."

12. P. R. Davies, "Halakhah at Qumran." Davies argues: ". . . some Qumran law is halakhah (in my sense) and some not. . . . The distinction between scripturally-derived and non-scripturally-derived law is either explicit or implicit in the Qumran literature and not a scholarly rationalization, and . . . the distinction is of fundamental importance in Qumran research" (38). Referring to the communities behind CD and 1QS, Davies writes: ". . . I want to suggest that the legal (and indeed, social) basis of each community is constituted rather differently, and that the term 'halakhah' is appropriate to the one and not to the other" (39).

13. M. Weinfeld, *The Organizational Pattern and the Penal Code of the Qumran Sect,* 71-76. See esp. p. 71: ". . . the *organizational* rules of the Qumran sect have nothing to do with specific Jewish ideals. They rather reflect the way guilds and religious associations of the Hellenistic period used to structure their regulations of order . . . similar rules in the Qumran sect cannot be seen as the result of the concept of purity in Qumran, as Schiffman contends" (216).

(1) separation from outsiders (CD 6:14-21 [Lev 10:10]; 1QS 5:14-15 [Lev 22:16]);

(2) rebuke of transgressors (4QRebukes Reported by the Overseer; CD 9:2-4 [Lev 19:17]; 1QS 5:24–6:1 [Lev 19:18]; 4QBerakhot (4Q288) [Lev 19:17-18]);

(3) destiny of a traitor (CD 9:1 [Lev 27:29]);

(4) painting of apostates as those ruled by the spirits of Belial (CD 12:2b-3a/4QD^f 5 i 18-19 [Lev 20:27]); and

(5) picturing insiders as those to be saved by Melchizedek (11QMelchizedek (11Q132:2, 25) [Lev 25:13; 25:9]).

In these cases, the laws of Leviticus have been used creatively to address issues unique to the separatist and esoteric community of the Essenes living in the environment of hellenized Palestine. The rules are practical in orientation, and a comparison between different copies of single documents indicates that rather than being derived from scriptural exegesis, these rules originated in the exigencies of community life; only at a secondary stage was a scriptural basis added to provide explicit authority. Thus, in some cases the scriptural "exegetical hooks" discernible in the ancient writers' halakhic discourse turn out to be the end result, not the starting point of the process.

We have space only for a single example: A case addressing separation from outsiders is recorded in the *Community Rule* (1QS 5:14-15 [Lev 22:16]). 1QS 5 contains a collection of rules for community life, including a passage about the oath pronounced by initiates as they join the community. The oath stipulates that they must bind themselves to the law of Moses (1QS 5:7b-10a) and separate from the men of injustice, i.e., from the outsiders (1QS 5:10b-20a). A major clue emerges through a comparison of the *Serekh* texts from Cave 4 and 1QS. The texts display redactional development in this passage: Whereas the Cave 4 manuscripts contain no scriptural quotations or even clear allusions to serve as proof-texts for their rulings, the Cave 1 manuscripts apparently have added precisely such supporting documentation.[14]

The passage begins by discussing an "outsider," that is, either a person who is not a member of the group or a member whose conversion is insincere and thus should be considered an outsider:

14. I have discussed the redactional development of S more fully in *The Textual Development of the Qumran Community Rule,* and more recently in *The Serekh Texts,* 15-20.

4QS[b,d]

1QS

He shall not touch the purity of the men of holiness, and he shall not eat with him in the community.

He shall not enter the waters in order to touch the purity of the men of holiness, for men are not purified (14) unless they turn from their evil; for he remains unclean amongst all the transgressors of his word. No one shall join with him with regard to his work or his wealth *lest he burden him* (15) *with iniquity and guilt* (Lev 22:16). But he shall keep away from him in everything, for thus it is written, *You shall keep away from everything false* (Ex 23:7). No one of the men

No one of the men of the community shall answer to their authority with regard to any law or decision. He shall not be united [with him with regard to wealth and work(?).] No man of holiness shall eat [anything of their property, or take anything at all from their hand.]

of the community shall answer (16) to their authority with regard to any law or decision. No one shall eat or drink anything of their property, or take anything at all from their hand, (17) except for payment, as it is written, *Have no more to do with man in whose nostrils is breath, for what is he worth?* (Isa 2:22). For (18) all those who are not counted in his covenant, they and everything that belongs to them are to be kept separate. No man of holiness shall rely on

They shall not rely on [any dee]ds of vanity, for vanity are all those who do not know his covenant. He will destroy from the earth all those who spurn his word: all their deeds are impure before him, and al[l their wealth unclean.]

any deeds (19) of vanity, for vanity are all those who do not know his covenant. He will destroy from the earth all those who spurn his word: all their deeds are impure (20) before him, and all their wealth unclean.

In this passage the basic statement of the oath to separate oneself from outsiders is clarified and confirmed in 1QS with biblical proof-texts — Lev 22:16 and Exod 23:7. The former, "lest he burden him with iniquity and guilt," is cited implicitly (cf. Lev 22:15-16, ולא . . . והשיאו אותם עון אשמה), whereas the latter is a direct quotation. The quote in Lev 22:16 comes from the Holiness Code, where it refers to the prohibition against allowing ordinary Israelites to partake in eating sacred donations set aside for priests. The thought behind this idiom, השיאו עון אשמה, is that when a priest transgresses, the entire community will carry his punishment.[15] In other words, the community that is in contact with the transgressor will be contaminated by that transgression, even when the community has not had complicity in the act itself.

The way this idiom is used in 1QS is interesting, for it both connects with the context of Leviticus and departs from it. It connects with Leviticus in the sense that both texts are concerned with guarding the purity of the community when holy food is consumed. The phrase "the purity of the men of holiness" (טהרת אנשי הקודש), used in various places in the scrolls, should likely be interpreted as a reference to the common meal of the community.[16] Just as the sacred donations in ancient Israel were available only to the priests, so was the participation in the common meal of the Essenes permitted only for the full members of the community who had undergone a lengthy period of probation and could be considered "men of holiness" who were obligated to the priestly rules of the Torah. Novices or nonfull members in the Essene community, like laypeople in the Israelite community, were excluded from partaking in holy food.[17]

In the context of the *Community Rule,* however, the notion of impurity that can make the entire community bear guilt is expanded to include matters that seemingly have little to do with cultic offering, namely matters of work and property, which had a high potential of bringing the members of the community in contact with outsiders. This would place in jeopardy the community's ritual purity, based as it was on priestly and Levitical ideals of Torah. The purity of correct scriptural interpretation also needed to be protected, for the "secrets" or "hidden things" *(nistarot)* could not be revealed to outsiders, and neither could the community's interpretation be tainted by outsider opinions. Both versions of the text state: "No one of the men of the community shall answer to their authority with regard to any law or decision."

The two redactional developments in 1QS beyond the earlier version in the 4QS manuscripts appear to have different reasons: One development was apparently responding to the need to provide justification for the strict rule of separation, perhaps in response to challenges to the rule

15. This idiom is a hapax in the Hebrew Bible. On the meaning and different possibilities of translating the idiom, see J. Milgrom, *Leviticus 17–22,* 1869-70.

16. Thus already S. Lieberman, "The Discipline in the So-called Dead Sea Manual of Discipline," esp. 203.

17. Exclusion from partaking in holy food was also used as a punishment for offenses by members; see, e.g, 1QS 6:24-25 and 7:2-3.

by members who considered the separation excessive. Here the justification provided was based on the highest authority possible: the Torah. The second development was apparently responding to the need to temper the rigidity of the rule with a concession — "except for payment." Pragmatic necessity may have forced this concession upon the isolated community as it experienced the attempt to live apart in the desert. With these two redactional developments the *Serekh* community forged the compromise between its high ideals of purity and its practical requirements of living: justification through Scripture of its separation in general and pragmatic exception in a specific case.

Scriptural exegesis was, of course, a resource for creating halakhah in many instances. But the exigencies of communal life also functioned as a source for creating legal traditions, and the subsequent appeal to the authority of the Torah was employed to provide the solid foundation for practices that were considered necessary to preserve the holiness of the community. Thus, we can agree with Lawrence Schiffman and those who have demonstrated that halakhic exegesis was a basis of the group's praxis, but we may also stress that the opposite was the case: the exigencies of the community's lived experience also functioned as a source for creating fresh halakhah.

Since we have had space to present only a single example, it is important at least to mention other examples and to inquire whether the community believed that the community regulations based on practical experience held the same authority as the rules based on the Torah. The penal codes provide the evidence: in certain cases the punishment for violating community regulations is identical to that for violating the law of Moses. For example, the offenses of "slandering the rabbim" (1QS 7:16-17, par. 4QD^e 1:6-7), "making complaints about the authority of the community" (1QS 7:17), and "deviating from the fundamental principles of the community" after ten years of membership (1QS 7:18-25) elicit the punishment of permanent expulsion — the same punishment as meted out for "transgressing a word from the law of Moses presumptuously or negligently" (1QS 8:21-23).

The Cave 4 *Serekh* manuscripts show community regulations that originated in the exigencies of community life, without appeal to the authority of the Torah. At a secondary stage, visible in 1QS, a scriptural basis was sometimes added to provide explicit authority. This raises the question whether, at the original stage, the community regulations were consciously considered on the same level with halakhah derived from Scripture. From what we can deduce from the above examples in the penal code, it appears that the two kinds were *treated* equally, but the intentionality is not disclosed. It is difficult to tell whether the community leaders *reflected* on this issue and *consciously affirmed* that the level of authority was equal for the two kinds. Thus far, I have not found a way to penetrate further. It may well have been, however, that conscious reflection on the issue was that catalyst that initiated the secondary development. That is, it may have been that individual members' challenges piqued the leaders' reflection, resulting in the conviction that the two kinds were on the same level.

These findings suggest that we should continue inquiring into various aspects of halakhah to determine whether our operating assumptions are accurate. One aspect is the addressee: is halakhah addressed to "all Israel" or only to a specific group within Israel?

Moshe Weinfeld distinguishes between commands in the Torah, which are addressed to all Israel, and community regulations which apply only to the specific group that produces them and volunteers to live by them.[18] Charlotte Hempel appears to make a similar kind of distinction, when she describes halakhah as "legislation that is general in its formulation and application and which does not refer to a particular organized community."[19] It seems to me, however, that an essential feature of the self-understanding of the Yahad was the absolute conviction that their community alone was the true Israel that lived according to the law of the Torah. For the Essenes, their way of life was the proper fulfillment of the Torah, which outsiders had failed to follow. Imbedded in the concept of halakhah, then, is the notion of universality, although in practice the setting of halakhah is particularistic; halakhah is created and applied within a specific group. In its intentionality, the halakhah of the Essenes was no dif-

---

18. Weinfeld, *The Organizational Pattern and the Penal Code of the Qumran Sect;* see esp. 72: "One must distinguish between divine commands sanctified by the Torah which belong to the sphere of the covenant between God and Israel, and the regulations of the sect which relate to the social organization of the sect, and as such do not apply to the people of Israel as a whole but to a specific group which is bound by rules accepted voluntarily by its members."

19. Hempel, in *The Laws of the Damascus Document,* uses this term mainly as a *terminus technicus* to distinguish between the different redactional strata in the *Damascus Document,* and in doing so she expresses some ambivalence: "I have retained the standard terminology after some consideration mainly because of my dissatisfaction with alternatives I considered" (25).

ferent from that of the Pharisees or any other Jewish group: each group considered their own rules as correct and valid for true Israel.

Thus, like the concept of biblical texts, which in recent years has been subject to reconsideration in light of the new textual evidence from Qumran, existing understandings of halakhah are challenged by the scrolls. Both in our study of the halakhic content and in our further examination of the processes of development of halakhah in the scrolls, this new evidence provides methodological challenges and opportunities for new avenues of research.

Feasibility of Historical Reconstruction

A final question that looms ever more important as scholars attempt to synthesize the many literary and historical aspects of the scrolls is whether the legal texts can be used as direct evidence for historical reconstruction of the community and its practices.

After so much earlier work based on Cave 1 manuscripts, the appearance of multiple manuscript copies in Cave 4 both illuminates and complicates the situation. The various manuscripts contain different types of variants, some indicating the presence of parallel editions and others the development of redactional levels. If we can assume a direct relationship between literary texts and the historical situations that the texts describe, then these variants may possibly aid us in detecting and describing the historical developments experienced by the specific groups which formulated and copied the manuscripts. But the literary analysis of these texts exposes, even in the earliest compositional and editorial stages, various passages that originated in different groups at different times. If the specific group that copied a composite text is not the same group that first produced it, how can we use the text as a reliable source to reconstruct the history, beliefs, and practices of the later group?

Let us consider a representative example. A passage from the Treatise on the Two Spirits in 1QS is quoted in another manuscript, titled *A Ritual of Marriage* (4Q502).[20] The latter has posed problems for interpreters primarily because of its fragmentary state, and not surprisingly, different scholars have offered different interpretations. Maurice Baillet, its editor,

20. I have discussed this and three additional examples more fully in "Methodological Problems in Reconstructing History from Qumran Rule Texts."

originally considered it a liturgy for a ritual of marriage and gave it that title.[21] Joseph Baumgarten, in contrast, viewed it as a ritual for the Golden
Age to be celebrated at the time of Sukkot. explicitly making the parallel
with the "sacred vigil" of the Therapeutae.[22] Michael L. Satlow also saw it
as a festival text but thought that the festival was related to the New Year.[23]
I agree with Baumgarten's observation that the ritual involved is explicitly
termed "a festival"[24] and thus is connected with some Jewish festival, but
further specification still eludes me. I think it is important to point out,
however, that the extant 4Q502 fragments contain more than ten references to women and family life.

The differences in interpretation do not end there. On the one hand,
Baumgarten thinks that 4Q502 relates specifically to the Qumran community.[25] On the other hand, Johann Maier thinks that the text is "nonsectarian" and "probably remains of a pre-Qumranic liturgical tradition."[26]
We need not settle the question of the specific character of 4Q502 here, but
may instead focus on one aspect of the text. Fragment 16, with only eight
words preserved and some only partially, appears to be a parallel to 1QS 4:4-
6, part of the Treatise on the Two Spirits. The parallel passage comes from a
list of virtues induced by the spirit of light, and reads as follows:

> a spirit of his knowledge with regard to every plan of action, zeal for
> the precepts of righteousness, a holy purpose with a constant mind,
> abundant kindness towards all the sons of truth, a glorious purity
> which loathes all the impure idols, circumspection linked to discern-
> ment in all things, and concealment of the truth of the mysteries of
> knowledge. These are the counsels of the spirit for the sons of truth in
> the world. The visitation of all those who walk in it . . . (1QS 4:4-6;
> transl. Michael A. Knibb).

21. M. Baillet, DJD 7, 81-105. See also Tov et al., DJD 39, 71.

22. J. M. Baumgarten, "4Q502, Marriage or Golden Age Ritual?"

23. M. L. Satlow, "4Q502 A New Year Festival?"

24. Baumgarten, "4Q502," 128-29.

25. DJD 18, 144: "It is now known from 4Q502 that women were evaluated within the
Qumran community in accordance with their 'intelligence and understanding' as 'daughters
of truth.' The Essenes who married did so not only after determining their future wives'
probable fecundity, but after three years of probation (Josephus B.J. 2.161). The latter . . . may
have been intended as a pre-marital demonstration of good character, analogous to the pro-
bationary period for male candidates to the order."

26. J. Maier, "Ritual of Marriage," 783.

It seems improbable that the whole of the Treatise in 1QS 3:13–4:26 would have formed part of 4Q502. Something like the list of spiritual virtues may once have been an independent text,[27] and in fact, ethical lists were commonplace in Hellenistic and early Jewish and Christian writings.[28]

But this does not yet resolve the questions of the relationship between 4Q502 and 1QS. A number of interesting possibilities open up: Is the text of 4Q502 literarily dependent on the *Community Rule* in the passage overlapping with 1QS 4:4-6, or should we assume a common source behind the two texts? From a socio-historical point of view, was the text of 4Q502 created by an Essene scribe quoting another Essene text (the *Community Rule*), or was the text of 4Q502 created outside of Essene circles, with no knowledge of the *Community Rule* and/or the Treatise on the Two Spirits? In other words, should we read this passage from 4Q502 without reference to the Treatise on the Two Spirits, presuming that what is quoted there is merely an independently existing list of virtues that only happened to be incorporated also in the *Community Rule*? Or is the passage from 4Q502 actually quoting the Treatise on the Two Spirits, at a time when it was independent and not yet incorporated into the *Community Rule* of Qumran?

Depending on our textual analysis of these two texts and of their mutual relationship, we may end up with very different historical scenarios.[29] Rather than moving directly from the surface meaning of the text into historical reconstructions, then, we must take account of the various possibilities for explaining the sociological or editorial relationships between them.

From this discussion we can see parallel editions of texts, development of texts through editorial revision, and borrowing of earlier texts by

27. Several scholars have denied that the Treatise forms a literary unity, but to my knowledge, no one has suggested that the list of virtues, of the spirit of light and the spirit of darkness respectively, originally formed separate units within the Treatise. For the redactional features of the Treatise, see P. von der Osten-Sacken, *Gott und Belial*, 17-26; J. Duhaime, "L'instruction sur les deux esprits et les interpolations dualistes à Qumran"; A. Lange, *Weisheit und Prädestination*, 128; J. J. Collins, *Apocalypticism in the Dead Sea Scrolls*, 38-42, esp. 39.

28. See, e.g., Aristophanes *Batr.* 5.145; Andronicus *Stoicorum Veterum Fragmenta* 3.64; Virgil *Aen.* 6.732; Horace *Ep.* 1.1.33-40; Philo *Sacr.* 20-27; *Leg.* 1.19.26; 2.23.24; Wis 14:25-26; 2 Cor 6:6-8; Gal 5:22-23; 2 Pet 1:5-7.

29. Eibert Tigchelaar resolves these questions by arguing that Baillet's inclusion of frag. 16 in 4Q502 is simply false and that the fragment belongs to 4QS^c instead. See "'These are the names of the spirits of . . .'"

newer formulations. But there is an additional source of complexity for our pursuit of the historical realities behind these texts, in that the texts themselves testify to the importance of orality as a major factor in the transmission of legal traditions. When judicial decision-making is described in the *Community Rule,* there is no mention of written rules; the text stipulates instead that the authority for judicial decisions rests with the *rabbim* (1QS 6:8-13) or the sons of Aaron (1QS 9:7).

The reliance on oral tradition, as Martin Jaffee notes, does not preclude the presence of literacy or the availability of written texts, but it does complicate the picture.[30] Thus, it is important to reexamine the term "lawbook" or "rulebook," especially in relation to the *Community Rule* and similar texts. The modern term "rulebook" routinely denotes a normative, legally binding set of written regulations that determine behavior. That is, the written law is established beforehand, and when subsequent cases arise, they are adjucated in accordance with the previously written and known law. What if, however, the Essene community's authoritative form for decision-making were oral, as opposed to written? It is indeed plausible that the rabbim decided judicial cases (as the scrolls attest), and then records of the decisions by the rabbim were consigned to writing in the form of "community rules." The possibility that texts like the *Community Rule* were subsequent written records of diverse oral judicial decisions, rather than already established prescriptions for conduct, also helps explain the fact of contradictory regulations in the texts.

The texts recording previous decisions by the rabbim concerning cases or problems that might later confront a neophyte would, of course, have been of great significance for educating new members of the community. Such a concern for neophyte education can be seen in the rules of admission into the community, which emphasize study as a prerequisite for participation in community decision-making (e.g., 1QS 6:13-15, 21-23; see

---

30. M. S. Jaffee, *Torah in the Mouth,* 8 and 38. See also M. LeFebvre, *Collections, Codes, and Torah.* LeFebvre argues that the prescriptivization of the Torah did not happen until the Hellenistic era; until then, the nature of Israel's law collections was descriptive rather than prescriptive, idyllic rather than actual. In regard to sectarian developments of the Second Temple period, he writes that they "may involve more than competing interpretations of Torah prescriptions, but different views of what Torah is, how it functions, and how (or whether) received traditions need to be harmonized with received texts. Though the recharacterization of Torah was evidently widespread from the Hellenistic period, it cannot be assumed that all Judaic circles embraced it. The actual history of Torah's recasting as a legal source remains to be worked out on a case-by-case, sect-by-sect basis" (265).

also 1QS 3:13; 9:18-21). Given this examination, then, the community's rule texts may not have been what we think of as rulebooks (i.e., prescriptive texts) but rather after-the-fact recordings of decisions by the rabbim later used as educational texts for neophytes.

The relationship of text to history is thus complicated by the evidence provided by the Qumran legal texts. The presence of parallel editions, developing redactional stages, and evidence for borrowing and cross-influence between different documents opens the door to methodological challenges that may reshape the field. This evidence demands that scholars who attempt historical reconstruction on the basis of the rule texts consider a broader range of possibilities. The way these texts functioned in the life of the Essenes must be studied before the connection between text and historical reconstruction can be convincingly made.

The new evidence provided by the Dead Sea Scrolls provides a unique challenge to scrolls scholars. It raises a broad range of methodological and theoretical questions, and an even broader range of not-yet-asked questions must be raised in our attempt to understand the treasury of documents illuminating Second Temple Judaism. Such questions have the potential of making us rethink even our most basic understandings of what such central concepts as Scripture, halakhah, and history mean in this period. The assumptions that so well served previous generations of scholars who had to work with only post-70 C.E. data need now to be reassessed in light of the new pre-70 data. With a larger amount of evidence, we are also in a better position to create a methodologically more solid foundation for our analyses. This will result in ruling out certain hypotheses, while at the same time demonstrating the accuracy of others.

Constructing, Deconstructing and Reconstructing Fragmentary Manuscripts: Illustrated by a Study of 4Q184 (4QWiles of the Wicked Woman)

Eibert Tigchelaar

In this chapter we begin with a well-known but important observation. The finds of Qumran Cave 4 consist of a hodgepodge of at least fifteen thousand (but possibly as many as forty thousand) fragments. These have largely been sorted and assembled into slightly fewer than seven hundred manuscripts, which provide the basic categorization used in editions, research tools, and scrolls studies. However, whereas fragments are discrete physical entities, manuscripts are scholarly constructs. This chapter will comment on the concept of manuscripts, the historical process of sorting and assembling manuscripts, and the need to critically approach and if necessary deconstruct the editors' construction of manuscripts, as well as the possibilities and methods for reconstructing manuscripts. It would be possible to give many illustrative examples, but this chapter will go back and forth between general observations and the exemplary discussion of one particular manuscript, 4Q184. Right from the outset, it should be stated that one can benefit fully from reading this chapter only if one also examines the publicly available images of the fragments.

What Is a Manuscript?

The word "manuscript" as used in Dead Sea Scrolls studies has several different meanings. First, virtually every discrete piece of inscribed skin or papyrus is a part of an originally larger inscribed object (for a possible exception cf. 4Q341, "4QExercitium Calami C," previously called

"4QTherapeia" or "4QList of Proper Names"). We may refer to this pre-supposed original whole as the original "manuscript" from which one or more extant fragments remain. More often, "manuscript" is used in a second sense, namely as the sum and tentative assemblage of all the fragments and only those fragments that are hypothesized to originate from one and the same original whole. A third use of "manuscript" refers to the tentative scholarly reconstruction of the original whole on the basis of the extant evidence. One often finds different terms used interchangeably with "manuscript," such as "scroll," "document," or "text." I use the word "scroll" only for those manuscripts that have been rolled; generally "document" is now used for a particular category of writings, including deeds and other administrative writings; I distinguish "manuscript" as a real or reconstructed physical object from "text" as that which is inscribed in a manuscript or part of a manuscript. Also, "text" is often used as a synonym of "composition."

On the whole, the Qumran inventory numbers correspond to the term "manuscript" in the second meaning — hence "inventory number" and "manuscript" are often used interchangeably. Exceptions are those inventory numbers that refer to collections of unclassified fragments (1Q68-70; 2Q33; 3Q14; 4Q172; 4Q178; 4Q385c; 4Q490; 4Q516-520; 5Q25; 6Q31; 11Q30) or to collections of fragments that have not been identified as belonging to other manuscripts (4Q281a-f; 4Q282a-t; 4Q468m-bb, cc-dd). In other cases multiple inventory numbers may refer to different parts of a manuscript, for example where recto and verso (front and back) of a manuscript have different numbers, where different compositions within one manuscript have different numbers (1QS, 1QSa, 1QSb; 4Q259, 4Q319), or in other diverse cases (4Q203 and 4Q204; 4Q392 and 4Q393).

In this chapter, the term "construction" of a manuscript refers to the process of sorting out, assembling, and arranging fragments into groups that are believed to stem from a single original manuscript. Most of this work was carried out from 1953 to 1960 by the original team of editors, although subsequent editors have often refined their constructions. The term "reconstruction" refers to the application of an ensemble of methods in order to determine the original place of fragments in the manuscript and to identify other characteristics (such as width, height, etc.) of the original physical manuscript. Already in DJD 1, J. T. Milik combined construction and reconstruction. However, Hartmut Stegemann and his students, notably Annette Steudel, have developed material reconstruction as a method. I use the term "deconstruction" somewhat playfully for the critical and methodical questioning of the plausibility of the constructions and reconstructions of manuscripts by editors.

The aim of this chapter is to further the reader's understanding and awareness of the methods and considerations used in the construction and reconstruction processes, in order that students and scholars might critically assess these. Additionally, it is hoped that this chapter may stimulate some readers to engage in these procedures themselves.

Tools

One cannot assess the constructions and reconstructions of manuscripts on the basis of transcriptions. One must turn to images of the fragments, and sometimes to the fragments themselves. Although some aspects of the fragments (e.g., thickness, quality of the leather) are difficult to see in photographs and are sometimes not described by editors, the available photographs often provide enough information for first provisional hypotheses. In fact, an inexperienced and untrained scholar will rarely gain useful information from an examination of the actual fragments. Those interested in the reconstruction of manuscripts should ideally have access to the following tools.

1. The DJD series.[1] The following elements of the volumes are of prime interest:
   • the plates, displaying which fragments have been assembled and constructed as a manuscript;
   • the general introduction and physical description of the fragments, providing information not visible in the photographs;
   • the references to the PAM (Palestine Archaeological Museum) photographs in which the fragments can be found (although these references are rarely complete).
2. Collections of PAM photographs, available in the unofficial ("bootlegged") Biblical Archaeology Society facsimile edition[2] and the two authorized Brill editions: the Microfiche Facsimile edition[3] and *The*

---

1. Oxford: Clarendon, 1955-.
2. R. H. Eisenman and J. M. Robinson, eds., *A Facsimile Edition of the Dead Sea Scrolls.*
3. E. Tov, ed., with the collaboration of S. J. Pfann, *The Dead Sea Scrolls on Microfiche.*

Dead Sea Scrolls Electronic Reference Library, volume 1 (the publisher has provided a patch so that it can be used with Windows XP).[4] Each of these editions has its shortcomings and drawbacks (missing photographs, often mediocre quality, incorrect numbers), but taken together they give an unprecedented access to the PAM archive of scrolls photographs. Note that the quality of the photographs of *The Dead Sea Scrolls Electronic Reference Library,* volume 3, is superior, but that this volume contains only a portion of the PAM photographs: like the DJD Plates, it usually presents only the latest photographs.

3. Catalogues that list correspondences between manuscripts, inventory numbers, and PAM photographs. An ideal combination is the Stephen Reed *Dead Sea Scrolls Catalogue* (since it gives not only overviews, but indirectly also insight into the historical processes of construction),[5] supplemented with the official list of manuscripts in DJD 39.[6] The *Companion Volume to The Dead Sea Scrolls Microfiche Edition* is based on Reed's catalogue but gives in addition the dates of the PAM photographs.[7]

4. Electronic search tools that allow one to search not only for words, but also for sequences of letters. For me, the most useful are Martin Abegg's modules, together with the Accordance program.[8]

5. Organized overviews of characteristics of scrolls. The reader is referred to Hartmut Stegemann's brief article,[9] but especially to Emanuel Tov's extensive and systematic work on scribal features found in the scrolls.[10]

---

4. T. H. Lim, ed., in consultation with P. S. Alexander, *The Dead Sea Scrolls Electronic Reference Library,* 3 vols.

5. S. A. Reed, M. J. Lundberg, with the collaboration of M. B. Phelps, *The Dead Sea Scrolls Catalogue.*

6. E. Tov, et al., DJD 39. See now Tov, *Revised Lists.*

7. E. Tov, ed., with the collaboration of S. J. Pfann, *Companion Volume to The Dead Sea Scrolls Microfiche Edition.*

8. M. G. Abegg, Jr., Qumran Sectarian Manuscripts: Qumran text and grammatical tags © 1999-2006. Version 2.8. (Accordance module). For Accordance, cf. www.accordancebible .com.

9. H. Stegemann, "Methods for the Reconstruction of Scrolls from Scattered Fragments."

10. E. Tov, *Scribal Practices and Approaches Reflected in the Texts Found in the Judean Desert.*

Constructing Scrolls

The first step toward the construction of scrolls was the sorting of the at least fifteen thousand fragments from Cave 4. Steudel summarizes the criteria used by the editors to group the fragments as follows:

> the general appearance of the leather, its colour, the thickness and the preparation of the skin, the dimensions of the manuscript, the columns, the margins and the rulings, the ink, the trace of the pen, the hand (i.e. handwriting), the carefulness or carelessness of the scribe, the orthography, the language, the content and the genre.[11]

This early process of sorting out fragments and constructing manuscripts is recorded briefly and in general terms in the provisional reports *(travails d'édition)* and in the photographic records of the Palestine Archaeological Museum (the PAM photographs). The DJD editions usually use the last photographs taken of a manuscript, but the earlier ones show intermediate stages of the process, sometimes clearly demonstrating the editors' uncertainties about specific fragments, which might be moved from one plate to another (and back again).

In spite of all the criteria to differentiate among fragments, a definite construction of manuscripts is in many cases not possible. First, a large number of fragments are simply too small to assign to any manuscript with certainty (cf. the thousands of unidentified fragments published in DJD 33). Second, examination of the few large scrolls from Caves 1 and 11 demonstrates that within one manuscript there can be differences of hand, leather, rulings, care, orthography, genre, and even composition. The original editors followed the rule that manuscripts should not be multiplied beyond necessity and grouped fragments together on the basis of shared features, even though they were well aware of some differences. Hence, only rarely did later editors join manuscripts that the earlier editors distinguished; more often the opposite is the case, namely that later editors concluded that fragments brought together by the original team of editors stemmed not from one, but from two or even more distinct manuscripts. Such differences of judgment should be distinguished from the relatively rare erroneous assignments of fragments to manuscripts. Most mistakes have been found in DJD 5 (the Allegro

---

11. A. Steudel, "Assembling and Reconstructing Manuscripts," 519.

volume) and some in DJD 7 (the Baillet volume) with its many papyrus fragments.

How can the inexperienced scholar assess an editor's assignment of fragments to manuscripts? To begin, one must pay attention to the red flags given by the editors, or provided by the photographs. Some editors such as J. T. Milik, John Strugnell, and Maurice Baillet explicitly refer to uncertainties and alternative assignments. A second red flag is indicated if inventory numbers have a letter in addition to the figure (such as 4Q214a and 4Q214b). This usually indicates that later editors have subdivided an older inventory number (in this case 4Q214) into different manuscripts (4Q214, 4Q214a, and 4Q214b). One should try to understand why the earlier editors grouped those fragments but later editors separated them. A third red flag appears if, in the series of PAM photographs, some fragments move from one plate to another or disappear from the manuscript where they were originally placed. In all such cases, one should turn to all the available materials, including the older PAM photographs.

The "Manuscript" 4Q184

In 1964 John Allegro published in the *Palestine Exploration Quarterly* a "text," which he called "The Wiles of the Wicked Woman," together with a plate showing the fragments of this "document."[12] In 1968 Allegro published in DJD 5 the manuscript 4Q184,[13] without any specific name, consisting of frag. 1 (the "text" published in the *PEQ*), as well as five more fragments, numbered 2-6. Ever since, the manuscript has been referred to as 4Q184 (4QWiles of the Wicked Woman). Most readers will know that the DJD 5 volume suffers from serious flaws, many of which were discussed in the lengthy review by Strugnell, which ever since has served as an indispensable complement to the DJD volume.[14]

The publication in two stages immediately created confusions. The published text and plate in the *PEQ* edition give the impression of a one-page, rectangular, almost square piece of leather, containing a poem from beginning to end. Hence, Jean Carmignac compared the manuscript to

12. J. M. Allegro, "'The Wiles of the Wicked Woman.'"
13. J. M. Allegro, with the collaboration of A. A. Anderson, DJD 5.
14. J. Strugnell, "Notes en marge du volume V des 'Discoveries in the Judaean Desert of Jordan.'"

4Q175 (4QTestimonia), another one-page composition.[15] However, the DJD publication of five additional fragments that could not be placed in the same sheet apparently invalidated this suggestion. The DJD edition implies that 4Q184 consists of fragments stemming from several columns of a scroll. In his review, Strugnell hesitated, acknowledging that the hand and appearance of the other fragments were similar to frag. 1, but also suggesting that frag. 1 belonged to a manuscript of no more than one page and that the other fragments might belong to other documents. To my knowledge, after Strugnell, no one has discussed this issue. Now that virtually all of the Cave 4 materials have been published, we may return to 4Q184 and use it as the case study of this chapter.

The PAM Photographs

My starting point is that manuscripts, as published by editors, are scholarly constructs, and that it can be instructive to retrace the scholarly process of sorting and assembling the fragments into manuscripts. This can be done in part by studying the PAM photographs. Allegro gives no references, but Reed and the later lists give the following PAM photograph numbers (for the DJD volumes published before 1994, Reed's catalogue is especially useful, since he usually mentions exactly which published fragments are on which photograph): PAM 40.607, 40.612, 40.613, 41.323, 41.815, 42.621, 42.640, 43.432. Ideally, the reader should take time to examine the photographs. I will go through the photographs, commenting on each of them.

PAM 40.607: In the earliest photographs, fragments usually are not yet assembled. This photograph shows the bottom right piece of frag. 1 joined to the large left piece in lines 16 and 17, but it is not clear whether the fragments were found together or were joined at the Museum. PAM 40.612 shows the middle piece (now in lines 9-13), and PAM 40.613 the large upper right piece, but without its top portion. These three photographs were made in May 1953. In PAM 41.323, from October 1954, these pieces are brought together, along with the piece from the top center and the left end of lines 14-16. In this photograph the separate pieces have not yet been joined. Joining of fragments is attested first in PAM 41.815, from September 1955, where all but two of the pieces of frag. 1 are joined as in

15. J. Carmignac, "Poème allégorique sur la secte rivale."

the later Allegro publications. The exceptions are the top center piece with the top margin and line 1]**תשח[א תועות** and the bottom left piece with the bottom margin and]**בני איש**[. The latter is found lower in the photograph, along with frags. 3, 4a (the upper left piece of frag. 4), 4b (the rest of frag. 4), and a small fragment with two letters (*beth-yod/ waw*) and the bottom margin. This photograph also has a small tag mentioning "4QWisd[a] 14 JMA." The next photograph, PAM 42.621, from July 1958 (see the Microfiche edition), finally has all the pieces of frag. 1 (the bottom left part is still not joined), frags. 3, 5 and 6, as well as frag. 4a and a tiny fragment with remnants of letters. Frag. 4b is found on PAM 42.640, together with many unidentified fragments. Finally, in PAM 43.432 of April 1960 we have frags. 1, 3-6 as published in DJD 5, including all the joins (fig. 1).

The first thing we observe is that frag. 2 is not on any PAM photograph. The catalogues indicate that the fragment is in the Oriental Institute Museum of the University of Chicago, which also provided the photograph for the DJD volume (fig. 2). The identification of frag. 2 as belonging to 4Q184 was therefore based on the photograph of frag. 2. Further, we can observe that initially (in PAM 41.323) only pieces of frag. 1 were assembled, but that later, in PAM 41.815 frags. 3, 4a, and 4b and in PAM 42.261 frags. 5 and 6 were added, probably by Allegro. The temporary removal of frag. 4b to another plate with unidentified fragments (PAM 42.640) indicates that its assignment to 4Q184 was not considered certain. The search through the PAM photographs also sheds light — and this is important for the study of all other manuscripts — on the question of which pieces were found together and which were joined. Thus, the photographs show that 4Q184 frag. 4 consists of two pieces (frags. 4a and 4b) and also that the join is physically and paleographically suspect.

One may wonder where frags. 3-6 were located before they were added to 4Q184. It is possible that some of these fragments can be found on early photographs not listed by Reed or the other catalogues.

Assessing the Sorting of the Fragments

Scholars do not usually begin with a review of the grouping of the fragments, but such a review can be helpful here in several ways. The questions one has to pose are why the editors brought certain fragments together and to what extent each grouping is definite, plausible, possible, or even un-

Figure 1. PAM 43.432, frags. 1 and 3-6 of 4Q184 (4QWiles of the Wicked Woman) (different scale from Figure 2)   (Courtesy Israel Antiquities Authority)

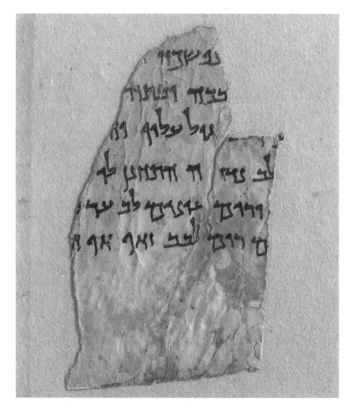

Figure 2. Frag. 2 of 4Q184 (4QWiles of the Wicked Woman)
(Courtesy of the Oriental Institute of the University of Chicago)

likely. Also, one may ask whether the editors may have overlooked fragments. The last question should not concern us here. Statistically, it is likely that there are a few fragments belonging to this manuscript amidst the thousands of unidentified fragments (cf. e.g., DJD 33), but most of those fragments are tiny, and finding an identification on the basis of a photograph is very difficult.

The identification and placement of most pieces of frag. 1 are unproblematic, based on the physical and textual joins. However, in view of the hesitation with regard to frag. 4b, and Strugnell's uncertainty, one should ask about the reasons for adding frags. 2 through 6 to 4Q184, and to what extent one can assess their assignment.

Above, I quoted Steudel's description of the many different criteria for grouping fragments. We should now discuss some of these in greater detail and apply them to 4Q184. Normally, the general appearance of the leather cannot with any certainty be checked on the photographs. The same goes for the criteria of color, thickness, and preparation of the skin. Normally one should trust the judgments of editors in this respect. However, in many cases those general features are not enough to sort fragments. Fragments of similar appearance may belong to different manuscripts, and also vice versa. Also, within a manuscript (a scroll), there may be some differences of color or preparation from sheet to sheet. As for 4Q184, all the fragments seem to be somewhat crumpled and are light with darker areas.

On the whole, scrolls tend to be written with more or less the same dimensions. A fixed dimension in a scroll is the total height of the sheets and columns. In carefully written scrolls there is usually little or no variation in the height of the writing blocks, the dimensions of the margins, the distance between the lines, or the number of lines per column. Differences do sometimes occur from sheet to sheet, for example, in the *Isaiah Scroll* where the number of lines per column varies by sheet.

Large dimensions can be measured with a ruler, although one should be aware of the fact that photographs of fragments may be inexact, due to distortions of the skin or because fragments may have been taken from photographs that do not have precisely the same scale. As an often indispensable help, one should make a transparent photocopy of the DJD plate or trace the fragments on tracing paper. This makes it possible to place the transparency of one fragment on top of another, and so compare, e.g., the distance between the lines or possible corresponding damages.

Dimensions

In 4Q184 one can only compare the bottom margins and the distances between the lines. Among the fragments attributed to 4Q184, there are some differences of dimension. This is most obvious in the case of the bottom margins that are preserved in frags. 1 through 4. In frags. 1 and 3 the margin is smaller, 1.7-1.8 cm, as opposed to 2.0-2.1 cm in frag. 4, and 2.4-2.6 cm in frag. 2. It is more difficult to measure the distance between the lines on the fragments, and one can more easily compare these by using transparencies or tracing paper. In this way one can see that the interlinear space is slightly larger at the bottom of frag. 1 than at its top, though that may be because the leather is crumpled or has shrunk. One can place frag. 3 over the bottom lines of frag. 1 and observe that the distance between the lines in frags. 1 and 3 is identical. The same goes for frags. 5 and 6. The lines neatly overlap. On the other hand, the same method shows that the distance between the lines in frag. 2 is uneven and clearly larger. The evidence of frag. 4 is uncertain, also because the join of 4a and 4b is problematic. The lines do not correspond exactly to those of either frag. 1 or frag. 2.

Since such differences in dimensions virtually never occur within columns of the same sheet, and only rarely between sheets of the same scroll, one may preliminarily conclude that it is virtually impossible that all these fragments stem from the same sheet, and unlikely, though not impossible, that they all stem from the same scroll.

Hand

"Hand" is an important criterion for classifying fragments, but those who read the editors' paleographical descriptions should be aware that some scholars use "hand" as a reference to an individual's handwriting, and others (for example Strugnell) more generally as a reference to a style or type of handwriting.

The hand of the fragments of 4Q184 is fairly consistent, in a style that Strugnell called "Rustic Semiformal." However, the hand of 4Q184 departs in several respects from that style, and Strugnell characterized it as a relatively old example of the rustic semiformal series (cf., e.g., the long and narrow *kap*).[16] One may also note some signature features of this specific hand, as opposed to other rustic semiformal hands, such as the wedged head of the *lamed,* which is found in almost all *lamed*s in the fragments (but not in the one *lamed* in frag. 4; the wedge in frag. 6 is not exactly the same). The slightly smaller letters in most of frag. 1 and the thicker letters in frag. 3 might distract from the common features, but an assignment of frags. 1-3, and probably 5, to the same hand would seem very likely to me. One difference between frag. 2 and frag. 1 is the profusely curved *nun*s in frag. 2 lines 4 (נדכה) and 5 (עינים), a feature that is rare in the other fragments (but see frag. 1 line 6 באישני).

I am more hesitant with regard to frag. 4b, which belongs to the same type of hand but has several letters that are different in form from those in

---

16. On scribal hands, see also Abegg's contribution to this volume.

frag. 1 (not only the *lamed,* but also the *šin*). Frag. 4a might have the same hand as frags. 1-3, but the letter samples are too limited to state this with any certainty. In sum, with regard to both hand and dimensions, frag. 4b is somewhat different from the other fragments.

How important are these features? Within a manuscript, different variations are sometimes found (and even for the forms of the letters of frag. 4b there are relatively close parallels in frag. 1). One would expect the same dimensions and hand, but there are several attested examples where one scribe took over from another (1QpHab; 1QH[a]) or where the writing of the same scribe varies (4Q176). However, in grouping fragments one should proceed from the expectation of the regular, and not from the exception. From this point of view, one may provisionally conclude that up to now nothing challenges the attribution of frags. 3 and 5 (and 6?) to the same manuscript as 4Q184, but that there may be some doubts with regard to frag. 2, and some more with regard to frag. 4b.

Steudel also mentions the criterion of orthography, the spelling used by a scribe. This criterion is of little help here, in view of the small samples of frags. 2-6. Note, however, that both frags. 2 and 3 have the not-uncommon long form of the second person masculine singular suffix.[17]

Content and Genre

In many cases, editorial interpretations of content and genre have played a role in the grouping of fragments. One may note a few idiomatic correspondences. Frag. 3 line 5 uses the words אישון and פחז, words that are rare in the scrolls, but which both are found in frag. 1. The correspondences עינים in frag. 2 and אשמות in frag. 4 are more general, whereas the occurrence of the word רחובות in frag. 6 may have been the reason to assign it to 4Q184. The third person singular feminine suffix in frag. 5 may be associated with frag. 1, which abounds with these suffixes.

More interesting than isolated words are features of style and genre. Frag. 1 is poetic, describing the behavior of a seductress. The other fragments have an obviously different style. Frags. 2 and 3, though fragmentary, clearly address a second person masculine singular, use imperatives (2 4 התחנן; 3 2 הבר), and probably refer to God. Frags. 5 and 6 seem to have jussives, again suggesting a different style. Frag. 4b, finally, defies an

---

17. For a discussion of this grammatical point, again see Abegg's chapter in this volume.

easy classification, but nothing suggests that it is either descriptive of a seductress or instructive.

Arguments about content, style, and genre are problematic when
dealing with fragments. Compositions often consist of sections with different styles, and style or content alone should not be decisive in determining whether fragments belong together or should be attributed to different
manuscripts. In the case of 4Q184, we are challenged to determine what
kind of composition could have contained both the famous poem of frag. 1
and a series of specific instructions to a second person singular addressee.

The only thing we may conclude with great likelihood is that apart
from a general correspondence of hand, frag. 4b does not correspond in
any other respect (dimensions, details of hand, or style) to the other fragments. It should be removed from 4Q184.

Reconstructing

In scrolls studies the term "reconstruction" can refer either to the reconstruction of text or to the reconstruction of manuscripts. The two are usually
distinct. The reconstruction of text relates to the tentative textual restoration
of lost parts of words, lines, and sometimes columns that have been partially
preserved. Most editors restore words that are partially broken or small gaps
in between preserved words; in the case of copies of compositions that are
known, one can complete entire lines on the basis of parallel texts.

The reconstruction of manuscripts aims at determining (approximately or precisely) the original place of fragments in the manuscript (most
often a scroll), as well as other physical aspects of the manuscript. Sometimes reconstruction is based on knowledge of the text of the composition
copied in the manuscript, enabling us to arrange the fragments in the correct
order and to calculate the amount of text missing between fragments. In the
case of previously unknown compositions, reconstruction may be based on
textual overlaps with other fragmentary copies of the same composition, on
material reconstruction, or some combination of the two (a good example is
the reconstruction of 4Q405, "4QSongs of the Sabbath Sacrifice[f]").

Many material reconstructions are based on the physical nature of
the most common kind of manuscript: the scroll.[18] When one rolls a scroll,
each subsequent revolution is slightly longer than the previous one: the

---

18. Again, see Stegemann, "Methods for the Reconstruction of Scrolls."

smallest revolutions are on the inside, the largest on the outside of the scroll. Most kinds of damage to a scroll will appear on consecutive revolutions, and patterns of damage may appear in fragments that stem from the same section of a scroll. Hence, specific damage patterns in fragments indicate that they come from the same section of a scroll, and sometimes one can calculate the distance between fragments. In addition, patterns of damages in a large fragment can, e.g., indicate whether the fragment comes from the inside, middle, or end of the scroll. If a damage pattern repeats after 4 cm, the fragment will be from the inside of the scroll, while a repetition of the damage pattern after 10 cm indicates that the fragment stemmed from the middle of a large scroll, or the outside of a smaller one. Such reconstructions can have consequences for the interpretation of fragments or a manuscript. Sometimes, damage patterns and the conclusions that one should draw are obvious. More often, the discerning of possible damage patterns demands training and can be subjective. It is helpful to make transparent copies of the fragments that one studies, or to draw the important features of a fragment on tracing paper, and to place the copy on top of other fragments.

Considering 4Q184 Fragment 1

Due to the crumpling and distortion of the leather, the pieces of frag. 1 do not join nicely anymore and the plate in the DJD edition should be used with caution. For example, one can easily see that the bottom left piece is not joined properly, and that there is a lacuna between line 17 בחלקות[and]בני איש[(one should follow Strugnell's suggestion to read]בני איש[בחלקות[כול). Similarly, the bottom right piece should join in lines 16, 17, and the bottom margin to the central piece.

It is not easy to interpret the damage patterns of the pieces in frag. 1. The large left piece of frag. 1 has a width of ca. 6.5 cm at its top, and there are some rough correspondences of shape with the left sides of some other pieces. Thus, the left side of the central piece (the piece that has דרכי מות in line 9 and עיניה הנה in line 13) roughly corresponds to the left side of the left fragment in the same lines. However, these broad similarities of shape are not found systematically in the pieces of frag. 1, and the supposition that in this fragment we had a revolution of the scroll of ca. 6.5 cm can at best be a hypothesis,

In this particular case, we should also consider the suggestions of

Carmignac and Strugnell that frag. 1 may represent a one-page manuscript. This suggestion is based on a combination of physical and literary evidence. The joined pieces of frag. 1 preserve the top margin, almost all of the right and bottom margins, and in some lines the left end of the page or column. The right side of the fragment with the right margin has neither traces of a previous column, nor of stitching, and could therefore represent the right edge of the manuscript. The fact that almost an entire page/column has been preserved, without any remnants of other columns, supports the likelihood of a one-page sheet. From a literary perspective, the text of this fragment has often been regarded as an independent poem, starting in line 1, and ending in line 17. The hypothesis is that the first word, of which only the final *he* remains, identified the protagonist of the poem ("the harlot"? "folly"?), and that the text ended with כול בני איש. The assumption that we have here a self-contained poem also underlines several poetic analyses, which regard for example the hemistich in line 8, "she is the beginning of all the ways of perversity," as the central statement of a symmetrically balanced poem.

This assumption is entirely possible but not necessary. It is on the basis of the physical features that one assumes that the complete poem coincides with the preserved seventeen lines. The beginning is too damaged to determine whether the poem started here or earlier. Also, there seem to be no literary arguments indicating that the poem ended at the end of this column or page.

Reconstructing 4Q184

Above, I have argued that 4Q184 frag. 4b should be removed from the grouping of the 4Q184 fragments and stated that it is uncertain whether frag. 2 belongs to that grouping. Of the remaining fragments, frag. 3 is the most interesting since it is the largest of the remaining fragments and preserves the bottom margin.

One can place a transparent copy or drawing of frag. 3 on top of frag. 1, which shows that both the distance between the lines and the dimensions of the bottom margin correspond. Since frag. 3 does not fit in the same column as frag. 1, one must assume that it comes from another, possibly adjacent column of the same scroll. One may compare the shape of frag. 3 to that of frag. 1 by placing the transparent copy of the fragment on top of frag. 1 and shifting it until one finds a resemblance. The presence of the bottom margin on both fragments facilitates the comparison. In this case, the agreement of shape is not difficult to find: the left part of frag. 3 corresponds closely to the left part of the large left piece of frag. 1, without the small fragments that were joined later (the letters מיד of תמיד in 3 2 should cover ישר of ישרים of 1 14; and 3 5 עם should cover 1 17 בד of בדרכי). If one were to remove the small half loose piece with פתות in 1 17, then the entire left side and the bottom of frag. 3 would agree with that of frag. 1, while the upper part of frag. 3 would correspond to a crease in frag. 1. One may therefore assume that frag. 3 was exactly one (or more) revolutions distant from that section of frag. 1, and one may hypothetically place frag. 3 in the column before or after frag. 1.

A hypothetical placement in the preceding column would imply that the last line of frag. 3 immediately preceded the first line of frag. 1. Indeed, the phrase עם אישני פחז "with eye-pupils of insolence," reminds one of the poem of frag. 1 which uses פחז twice (1 13, 15) or three times (perhaps also 1 2). In fact, אישני is also attested in 1 6 but with a different meaning. One might even hypothesize that the poem of frag. 1 began in this line, first describing the eyes of the woman, before turning to her mouth (a description *a capite ad calcem*). However, the preceding lines of frag. 3 are addressed to a second person masculine singular, which would mean that the poem would have begun at the very bottom line of a column. Also, the words of 3 5 are without context, and it is not clear that this is a description of a woman. Placing frag. 3 at the bottom of the column preceding frag. 1 would indicate that at this point the revolution of the scroll was at least ca. 12 cm (the distance between the left side of the piece of frag. 1 and the corresponding left side of frag. 3). This is by no means impossible, but it implies a rather long scroll.

Alternatively, frag. 3 can be placed in the column after frag. 1. Allowing a minimal margin of 1 cm between the columns, and placing frag. 3 close to the right margin, one would have to posit at least 8.5 cm between the revolutions. This rough calculation would change, however, if one assumes the loss of one layer or revolution between the fragments. In that case frag. 3 would have originated from the left part of the column, and one might allow for a smaller revolution of e.g. 6.5 cm.

Regardless of whether one places frag. 3 before or after frag. 1, the evidence would indicate that the poem of frag. 1 is part of a manuscript that also contains an address to a second person masculine singular. Frag. 3 lines 2 אליו כ]פיכה תמיד הבר אליו כ]פיכה (with uncertain *kap* at the end), perhaps "always purify for him [your] h[ands(?)]," and 3 פ]רוש אליו כפיכה

בתפ]לה, "[s]tretch out your hands towards him in pra[yer(?)]" seem to be admonitions, perhaps followed by צו]ה/י[סיר ממכה עול צו, "[he will (?)] remove from you wickedness." The use of עול, which appears no fewer than four times in frag. 1, may be important. The remnants of frags. 4a, 5, and 6 are even more meager, but the two jussive forms in 5 3 and 6 2 again suggest an admonition of a second person singular.

The implications of the assignment of frag. 3 to 4Q184, and the material correspondence with a piece of frag. 1, have import on their interpretation. One must conclude that 4Q184 frag. 1 is not the remains of a single-page sheet, but part of a larger scroll that also contained some kind of direct-speech admonitions. This does not of necessity imply that the poem of the wicked woman was written as a part of the composition as a whole. It is conceivable that a once-independent poem was incorporated in the original or in a revised form into a larger composition. It is also possible that different compositions were collected in one manuscript.

The rough and uncertain hypothesis that we have a width of a revolution of ca. 6.5 cm in frag. 1 is not of much help, since we do not know whether the scroll was rolled with the end in the inside, or the other way around, nor whether the scroll was rolled tightly or not.

4Q184 Frag. 2

Even though the hand of 4Q184 frag. 2 is identical with or very similar to that of 4Q184, the size of its writing and the dimension of the bottom margin are different (and the different dimensions according to the plate are not likely to be due to a different scale in the photograph provided by the Oriental Institute, since the measurements in the DJD plate concur exactly with the data given by the OIM site).[19] The dimensions of the bottom margins differ relatively significantly, from 1.8 cm for frags. 1 and 3, to 2.5 cm in frag. 2. One should assess whether this is reason for attributing the fragment to a different scroll. Such questions should be considered in light of the physical characteristics attested in other scrolls. Fortunately, we now have at our disposal an indispensable collection of data gathered by Tov, who also gives data on the dimensions of the top and bottom margins.[20] The things one should in general make sure when measuring bottom margins are:

---

19. Cf. http://oi.uchicago.edu/museum/highlights/palestine.html, image 4 of 13.
20. Tov, *Scribal Practices and Approaches*, 100-103.

- Is the entire unwritten section of the fragment a bottom margin? In some cases, a scribe may not have inscribed the last line of a column, suggesting a larger bottom margin. Or, if there are no visible horizontal guiding lines, an empty line may sometimes be mistaken for a bottom margin.
- Is the unwritten section of the fragment the entire bottom margin? If a fragment with an unwritten bottom section has a more or less straight horizontal edge, one is tempted to regard this as the bottom of the scroll. However, in the case of small fragments this is not always certain.

For the 4Q184 fragments the bottom margin seems indeed to be the entire bottom margin. With regard to 4Q184 frag. 2, one may consider the possibility that its last line was not inscribed. One can check this most easily by placing the transparency of frag. 2 on top of frags. 1 or 3. Such a check shows that in this case also the bottom margins differ. Tov's data indicate that only rarely does a single manuscript display such significant differences in the dimensions of the bottom margin (and some of those few examples, such as 4Q418, are questionable; since many of Tov's data depend on those given by the editors, one cannot trust every single detail). Here, we must add that in 4Q184 2 there is not only a difference in the size of the margins but also in the size of the letters and of the interlinear space. These differences strongly suggest, but do not prove, that 4Q184 2 came from a different scroll.

Should one assign 4Q184 2 to any other existing manuscript — that is, to one of the other Cave 4 inventory numbers? One may approach this question by paying attention both to physical and to textual features. From a textual perspective, the terminological correspondences between frag. 2 lines 4-6 and the text of the *Barkhi Nafshi* manuscripts, especially 4Q436 1 ii 2-4, are striking. Cf.

4Q184 2 4	לב נדכה	לב נדכה	4Q436 1 i 1; ii 4
4Q184 2 5	רום עינים	רום עינים	4Q436 1 ii 3
4Q184 2 6	זאף[21 אף	זעף אף	4Q436 1 ii 2
4Q184 2 6	רום לבב	גבה לב	4Q436 1 ii 3

21. Allegro read ואף, but Strugnell correctly noted that the fragment reads זאף, apparently an error for זעף.

Also, the same motif of removal of evil (or apotropaic prayer: התחנן לו) may be present. However, the genre here is different (admonition to pray in 4Q184 frag. 2), there is no textual overlap with the *Barkhi Nafshi* manuscripts, nor does the hand correspond to any of the *Barkhi Nafshi* manuscripts. Nonetheless, the text of the *Barkhi Nafshi* manuscripts does suggest one possible relation between the fragmentary lines of 4Q184 2, namely that the addressee should pray to God (line 4) that the vices mentioned in lines 5-6 be removed from him. That again may also be the meaning of 4Q184 3, that the addressee should entreat God to remove wickedness from him.

The question whether the hand of 4Q184 2 might suggest its appurtenance to another manuscript can only be answered by comparing all the other published manuscripts. I have done this by going through all the plates in the DJD volumes, but I did not find any positive match. In the end, one has to conclude that frag. 2 is either the sole survivor of a manuscript now lost to us, written in the same style or even by the same scribe as 4Q184, or a fragment of 4Q184, but from a different sheet than 4Q184 1 and 3.

4Q184 Frag. 4b

In the case of 4Q184 frag. 4b, the assignment to 4Q184 is much more problematic. Apart from a general agreement in type of hand (but with letters that do not conform to the most common forms in frag. 1), the presence of a bottom margin (but a larger one), and the use of the word אשמות (frag. 1 lines 3 and 10; frag. 4b bottom line) there is little that connects it to 4Q184.

The few textual remains in the fragment do not give enough clues with regard to the contents or genre. The phrase בן אדם is quite rare in the texts from Qumran. Apart from a few occurrences in the *Pseudo-Ezekiel* texts, where the prophet Ezekiel is called בן אדם, the phrase is only attested twice in the *Hodayot* (1QH[a] XII 31 and XVIII 30), and in 4Q418 frag. 55 line 11 (4Q382 frag. 40 line 1 is uncertain). It is not clear how the following ורוחו is related to בן אדם. (Strugnell therefore emended the phrase to ב>י<ן אדם ורוחו, "between a man and his spirit.") In the next line the phrase (ב)אשמות מעו]ל, "(in) guilty transgressions," is even more rare. Outside this fragment, the phrase is only attested (in the singular) three times in the *Hodayot*. Coincidentally, 1QH[a] XII 31 has in one line both באשמת מעל and בן אדם, and one is inclined to argue that with regard to idiom the fragment stands closest to the *Hodayot*. However, the hand of the fragments is not even close to that of any of the Cave 4 *Hodayot* manuscripts, and the fragment cannot be attributed either to an already identified manuscript, or to a specific composition.

Conclusions with Regard to 4Q184

The study of the fragments above has shown that it is by no means certain that all the fragments assigned to 4Q184 really belonged to one and the same manuscript. This especially holds true for frags. 2 and 4b. Unfortunately, I have not succeeded in finding an alternative assignment for those fragments, even though their terminology is reminiscent of the *Barkhi Nafshi* texts and the *Hodayot,* respectively. More important than these negative conclusions is the discussion of the evidence of frag. 3, which shows that it did belong to the same scroll, and possibly the same sheet, as 4Q184 frag. 1. As I have stated above, this positive assignment has consequence for the interpretation of the scroll and for the poem in frag. 1. It is the challenge for future study to interpret the poem while taking account of frag. 3.[22]

Final Reflections

For beginners in the field of Dead Sea Scrolls studies, such constructions, reconstructions and deconstructions may be too technical. In addition, they require an investment of time without any promise of success. And then, many readers may not even have access to all the tools one should ideally put to use. But the most important thing for all students and scholars who work with the scrolls is to gain an awareness of the nature of the material we are working on. All too often, students, and even scholars, confuse fragment and text, manuscript, scroll, and composition, betraying a lack of differentiation between physical evidence and scholarly interpretation. Students of the scrolls should be encouraged or trained to examine and interpret the plates in the DJD editions or the photographs in the CD-

---

22. After the completion of this chapter, I went one step further and considered the possibility that 4Q184 and 4Q525 were copies of one and the same sapiential composition. Cf. my "Lady Folly and Her House in Three Qumran Manuscripts." E. Qimron, "Improving the Editions of the Dead Sea Scrolls," 138, was the first to have discussed this possibility.

Roms. It is useful to learn how to read the fragments, but one should also consider the questions of how and why editors assembled specific fragments into manuscripts. This kind of examination will help one to assess the degrees of certainty, plausibility, or sometimes unlikelihood of these scholarly constructs.

The Linguistic Analysis of the Dead Sea Scrolls: More Than (Initially) Meets the Eye

Martin G. Abegg, Jr.

Introduction

This chapter is in essence a primer on linguistic analysis in the editions of the Dead Sea Scrolls. It describes those components we have come to expect in any complete *editio princeps* (first printed edition) of an ancient text: discussions of paleography, orthography, morphology, phonology, and syntax. Although it is tempting to skip through such introductory paragraphs to get to the transcriptions of the text, there is much to be gained from their thoughtful examination. Critical dating issues are still best determined from paleography; important clues concerning provenance have been linked closely to orthography and morphology. Phonology and syntax also have key roles to play for understanding the practice of ancient scribes, in addition to their obvious worth to studies of the development of the Hebrew language.

This introduction to the "tools of the trade" provides an opportunity to survey the linguistic nature of the corpus of the DSS as a whole. Starting first with discussions of a better-known subject, the nonbiblical Qumran manuscripts, we will then turn to the lesser known: the biblical DSS manuscripts.[1] Finally, by way of application, we will turn our attention to an ongoing debate concerning scribal schools and provenance.

---

1. The distinction in the description of these two groups of manuscripts is important. "Biblical" refers to those texts that comprise the corpus of the Hebrew Bible *(Tanakh)* or Protestant Old Testament. "Qumran" refers only to those manuscripts that were preserved in the eleven caves near the ruins at Qumran. "DSS," on the other hand,

Paleography

Paleography is the study of handwriting and is of primary importance for the dating of ancient manuscripts. Although to the uninitiated it might seem rather bold to claim that a date accurate within fifty years can be obtained from examining letter forms, a few moments' reflection on the development of handwriting styles in modern times — from the period of our grandparents to our children — should prove helpful. My grandmother's beautiful hand is many light years from the scratches that my older daughter produces. Quite clearly, handwriting evolves.

The seminal work in the field of Qumran paleography, which has provided the basis of nearly all dating decisions since, was published by Nahman Avigad and Frank M. Cross.[2] As recently as 1991 and 1996, two groups of manuscripts were tested by modern radiocarbon methods, in Zurich and Tucson, respectively.[3] These tests were in relative agreement with the results reached by paleographic methods and serve as an independent verification for paleographic studies. As an augment to the alphabetic table provided by Cross and Avigad (see page 50), the chart on page 51 presents the Qumran manuscripts that were dated by radiocarbon means and provides a visual aid for the discussion that follows.[4] Given Cross's assertion that "while the radiocarbon method gives a fairly broad range of dates, paleographical analysis is more precise, often narrowing the range of dates to a half century,"[5] I have followed his lead in organizing the table and the accompanying chart chronologically by paleographic dates.

Before we take a closer look at the details of paleography, several elements of the radiocarbon data require some explanation so as to be meaningful to those of us who are not nuclear physicists.

---

indicates manuscripts from any of the Judean Desert sites: Qumran, Murabbaʿat, Masada, etc.

2. N. Avigad, "The Palaeography of the Dead Sea Scrolls and Related Documents"; and F. M. Cross, "The Development of the Jewish Scripts."

3. The following discussion and data from these tests come from an article by G. Doudna, "Dating the Scrolls on the Basis of Radiocarbon Analysis."

4. This table is the work of my graduate assistant Nathaniel Dykstra, who meticulously traced from the digital photographs of the documents contained in T. Lim, ed., in consultation with P. S. Alexander, *The Dead Sea Scrolls Electronic Reference Library.*

5. F. M. Cross, "Palaeography and the Dead Sea Scrolls," 385.

	4Q208	1QIsaᵃ cols. 37-38	4Q542	4Q521	4Q53	1QS	4Q266	4Q213	4Q365	1QHᵃ cols. 9-10	4Q258	4Q267	1QApGen	11Q19 cols. 60-66	1QpHab	4Q171
א																
ב																
ג																
ד																
ה																
ו																
ז																
ח																
ט																
י																
כ																
ל																
מ																
ס																
נ																
ז																
ס																
ע																
פ																
צ																
ק																
ר																
ש																
ת																

a. The interval of ± *one sigma* (1σ) indicates a time interval that has a 68 percent probability of including the true date of the test subject.

b. Two ranges are given in 4 cases (1QIsaᵃ, 4Q542, 1QS, 4Q365) due to ancient variations in the amount of carbon 14 in the atmosphere. A calibration curve has been created based on tree ring studies and is used to account for these variations. For example, the present calibration data for this time period shows a rise in carbon 14 in the first half of the second century B.C.E. and a subsequent dip in the second half. Thus samples from either early or late in the second century would retain the same amount of carbon 14 today. Given the nature of the dates determined for the other manuscripts, as well as the paleographic data, the second result (in bold) is to be preferred.

Text	Radiocarbon Dates 1-σ 1997 decadal calibration	Paleographic Date
4Q208 Astronomical Enoch[a]	167-53 B.C.E.	225-175 B.C.E.
1QIsa[a]	341-325 B.C.E. or **202-114 B.C.E.**	125-100 B.C.E.
4Q542 Testament of Qahat ar	385-349 B.C.E. or **317-208 B.C.E.**	125-100 B.C.E.
4Q521 Messianic Apocalypse	39 B.C.E.–66 C.E.	125-75 B.C.E.
4Q53 Samuel[c]	196-47 B.C.E.	150-30 B.C.E.
1QS Community Rule	164-144 B.C.E. or **116 B.C.E.–50 C.E.**	100-50 B.C.E.
4Q266 Damascus Document[a]	4-82 C.E.	100-50 B.C.E.
4Q213 Levi[a] ar	197-105 B.C.E.	50-25 B.C.E.
4Q365 Reworked Pentateuch[c]	339-327 B.C.E. or **202-112 B.C.E.**	50-25 B.C.E.
1QH[a] Hodayot	37 B.C.E.–68 C.E.	30-1 B.C.E.
4Q258 Community Rule	36 B.C.E.–81 C.E.	30-1 B.C.E.
4Q267 Damascus Document[b]	168-51 B.C.E.	30-1 B.C.E.
1QapGen Genesis Apocryphon ar	47 B.C.E.–48 C.E.	30 B.C.E.–68 C.E.
11Q19 Temple Scroll	53 B.C.E.–21 C.E.	1-30 C.E.
1QpHab Habakkuk Commentary	88-2 B.C.E.	1-50 C.E.
4Q171 Psalms Commentary[a]	29-81 C.E.	not given

c. Test subjects that lie outside the expected date range (250 B.C.E.–68 C.E.) are likely contaminated with a foreign substance that results in a false age. For example, 4Q542 (Qahat) is unexpectedly old. The fact that a sample tested before cleaning gave an even older date suggests that some contaminant remains that continues to skew the results. On the other hand, the unexpectedly young results for 4Q171 (Psalms Commentary[a]) are best explained by the presence of modern contaminants.

The time span under discussion is divided into three general periods corresponding to changes in scribal style: Archaic (250-150 B.C.E.), Hasmonean (150-30 B.C.E.), and Herodian (30 B.C.E.–68 C.E.). These three ranges are subdivided in the editions with combinations of such qualifiers as "early, mid and late." So, for example, 11Q19 is described as mid-Herodian.

A complete letter-by-letter paleographic discussion would require much more space than this context allows, but a few salient points should help prepare our eyes for the more technical fare of Cross and the discussions contained in the editions. *Aleph:* as is clear from 4Q208, the archaic *aleph* is often very similar to an X. By the end of the Herodian period the left leg had migrated upward, forming an inverted V, and the overall impression of the letter is more along the lines of an N. The letter *he* is a very important letter for dating, as its development reveals three distinct forms roughly paralleling the three periods. In the archaic period the right leg was drawn first, the horizontal stroke then began below the top, and finally the left leg was penned downward from near the middle of the horizontal. In the Hasmonean period the horizontal was shortened and the left leg was drawn as a loop from top to bottom. Finally, in the Herodian period a form was adopted that was similar in construction to the archaic figure, but was distinguished by the bold horizontal that began nearer the top of the right leg. The *samekh* began as an open letter in the Archaic script and closed by the mid-late Hasmonean period. Finally, the *ayin* in the Archaic period had an almost vertical stance that noticeably rotated clockwise with the passage of time.

Orthography

Orthography is, simply stated, the study of the way words are spelled. In modern English, rules govern the distinct spelling conventions of Canadian, British, and American forms of expression and the "scribal practices" that follow. Words ending in *-our* in Canada and Britain are usually modified to *-or* in American English (honour/honor), while American convention prefers an *-er* ending to words ending with *-re* in Canada and Britain (theatre/theater). Grey days are quite frequent in winter in British Columbia, while across the border in Washington State the same weather is gray. In similar fashion, we can describe the spelling conventions that distinguish Biblical Hebrew, DSS Hebrew, Mishnaic Hebrew, and Modern Hebrew from one another.

In this and the following two sections of this chapter, Elisha Qimron's *The Hebrew of the Dead Sea Scrolls* (hereafter, *HDSS*) is the standard reference.[6] Although published in 1986, and thus before the recent flood of new publications, it captures the key issues that will demand our attention here. We will sample a few, but by no means all, of the more important of Qimron's discussions.

a. The most notable characteristic of DSS Hebrew, and of Qumran Hebrew in particular, is the use of the letters *waw* and *yod* to indicate vowels. The technical term for this phenomenon is *mater lectionis* (pl. *matres lectionis*), Latin for "mother of reading." This function is most especially noticeable with the *waw*, as this letter regularly represents the o/ō and often the u/ū of Biblical Hebrew (BH). Nearly two hundred words could be used to illustrate this feature. The following table presents the most fre-

6. HSS 29 (Atlanta: Scholars, 1986).

quent and representative examples.[7] The middle columns of the table document all the nonbiblical manuscripts from the eleven caves at Qumran.[8] It is now possible to produce the same list with results for the DSS biblical manuscripts, which are found in the columns on the right side of the table.

	BH	DSSH	Meaning	Nonbiblical mss from Qumran			DSS Biblical mss		
				Plene words	Total words	percent Plene	Plene words	Total words	percent Plene
1.	אדני	אדוני	Lord	53	71	75	59	92	64
2.	אלהים	אלוהים	God	258	336	77	262	625	42
3.	את	אות	DO w/suffix[9]	94	100	94	100	194	52
4.	זאת	זאות, זות, זואת	this (f.)	58	75	77	63	143	44
5.	חדש	חודש	month	91	105	87	11	43	26
6.	חכמה	חוכמה	wisdom	22	55	40	2	11	18
7.	חק	חוק	statute	129	136	95	30	49	61
8.	חשך	חושך	dark	72	79	91	15	27	64
9.	כהן	כוהן	priest	199	214	93	23	72	29
10.	כח	כוח	strength	83	98	85	16	31	51
11.	כל	כול	all	2088	2476	84	499	1061	47
12.	לא	לוא	not	960	1308	73	688	1305	53
13.	משה	מושה	Moses	75	95	79	42	184	23
14.	עון	עוון	iniquity	81	112	72	32	65	49
15.	קדש	קודש	holy	411	446	92	44	109	40
16.	ראש	ראוש, רואש, רוש	head	67	86	78	35	73	48
17.	שלש(ה)	שלוש(ה)	three	129	136	95	10	29	34

7. All of the data and Hebrew text presented in this chapter were produced by Accordance Bible software using the QUMRAN module (M. G. Abegg, Jr., Qumran Sectarian Manuscripts: Qumran text and grammatical tags © 1999-2006. Version 2.8) for the nonbiblical corpus as well as the yet unreleased DSSBIB module for the biblical corpus. The latter is in final stages of development and should be available close to the time of the publication of this volume. I owe a debt of deep gratitude to Roy Brown who with OakTree Software has been unflagging in his support of the development and retrieval of data for serious scholarship.

8. This is an update of a table I included in "The Hebrew of the Dead Sea Scrolls," 329. For a complete list of the documents that form the basis of this present study, see E. Tov, et al., DJD 39, 29-89, 165-76, and 182-83. The Damascus Document from the Cairo Genizah is not included in the figures.

9. Except with the second masculine plural suffix (אֶתְכֶם) which is everywhere without the waw.

Whereas the middle columns indicate the consistent tendency to fuller spellings among the nonbiblical Qumran scrolls, the right-hand columns suggest that something quite different is afoot among the DSS biblical manuscripts. These reflect a consistently higher number of *plene* forms than are found in BH (less than one percent in the MT) but only half the number of *plene* forms as in the nonbiblical Qumran manuscripts. This phenomenon suggests a more conservative approach to the copying of Scripture even as Hebrew of the Second Temple period was developing a fuller form of expression. It also encourages us to "look inside the numbers" by examining individual manuscripts. In the two tables that follow, our 17 words are plotted in the top 25 manuscripts (by size), first for the nonbiblical Qumran manuscripts and then for DSS Bible manuscripts.

Nonbiblical Manuscripts from Qumran

MS	Words	Full Orthography	Mixed	Defective
1. 11Q19	10,006	אלהים, את, חדש, חק, כהן, כל, לא, קדש, ראש, שלש	זאת, עון	
2. 1QH^a Hand A	7475	אדני, את, חק, חשך, משה, קדש	חכמה, כח, כל, לא, עון	זאת
3. 1QM	5414	אדני, אלהים, חדש, חכמה, חק, חשך, כהן, כח, כל, לא, משה, קדש, שלש	ראש	
4. 1QS	5441	אלהים, את, זאת, חדש, חק, חשך, כהן, כח, כל, לא, משה, קדש, ראש, שלש	עון	חכמה
5. 4Q418	3124	את, עון, קדש	זאת, חכמה, חק, כח, כל, לא, ראש	משה
6. 4Q266	2225	את, חדש, חק, כח, משה, קדש	כהן, כל, לא, עון ראש, שלש	
7. 1QH^a Hand B	1756	אדני, זאת, חק, חשך, כח, כל, עון, קדש	לא	
8. 4Q365	1697	אלהים, את, חדש, חק, חשך, כהן, כח, כל, משה, קדש, ראש, שלש	לא	חכמה
9. 1QpHab	1624	חק, כהן, כח, לא, קדש	כל, עון	
10. 4Q511	1474	את, חשך, כהן, כח, כל, לא, עון, קדש, ראש	אלהים	
11. 4Q381	1431		חק, לא	אלהים, את, חדש, חכמה כח, כל, עון, קדש, ראש

MS	Words	Full Orthography	Mixed	Defective
12. 4Q405	1362	אלהים, חדש, חק, כהן, כל, לא, ראש	קדש	
13. 4Q491	1359	אלהים, זאת, חשך, כהן, כח, כל, לא, קדש, ראש, שלש		
14. 4Q504	1337	את, זאת, חק, כהן, כח, כל, לא, משה, עון, קדש	אדני	
15. 4Q503	1213	אלהים, את, חדש, חשך, כל, לא, קדש, ראש, שלש		
16. 11Q5	1111	אלהים, חדש, חכמה, כח, כל, לא, עון, קדש, שלש		
17. 4Q364	1077	אלהים, את, זאת, משה, ראש, שלש	כל, לא	קדש
18. 3Q15	1067	כהן	ראש, שלש	כל
19. 4Q270	1037	חק	כהן, כל, קדש	חדש, לא, משה
20. 4Q502	1031	חק, כל, עון, קדש		
21. 4Q299	1017	חק, חשך, כהן, כח, קדש	חכמה, כל, לא	משה
22. 4Q525	1001	אלהים, זאת, חכמה, חק, כהן, כל, לא	עון, ראש	
23. 4Q403	967	אלהים, חדש, כהן, כח, קדש, ראש, שלש	כל	
24. 4Q258	935	כהן	חק, כל, קדש	לא, משה,
25. 4Q417	930	חק	כל, לא	חכמה, כח

The partial list produced here is suggestive of a classification of manuscripts according to scribal school.[10] At one end of the spectrum is 4Q381, which is highly defective (it regularly uses shorter spellings). At the other extreme are manuscripts such as 1QM, 1QS, 1QpHab, 4Q491, 4Q511, and 4Q503, which are characterized by a consistent *scriptio plena* or fuller approach to spellings. Although most documents from Qumran fall somewhere between these two extremes, the corpus on the whole is generally nearer the *scriptio plena* end of the spectrum. Emanuel Tov has noted that almost all the "sectarian" documents are written *plene,* whereas nonsectarian manuscripts — including 4Q381 (4Q Non-Canonical Psalms B) — are normally written defectively.[11] This factor would suggest that perhaps the con-

10. E. Tov, "The Orthography and Language of the Hebrew Scrolls Found at Qumran and the Origin of These Scrolls," and most recently, *Scribal Practices and Approaches Reflected in the Texts Found in the Judean Desert.*

11. Tov, *Scribal Practices and Approaches,* 261.

vention of fuller spellings is a local, or Qumran, practice. Our table demonstrates that this view is not without its problems, however: 4Q258 (4QS^d) and 4Q270 (4QD^e) are certainly to be classified as sectarian documents but are less firmly *plene*. The following table of the top twenty-five biblical manuscripts may aid our understanding of this critical discussion.

Biblical Manuscripts from Qumran

Ms	Words	Full	Mixed	Defective
1. 1QIsa^a	22687	אדני, אלהים, את, זאת, חדש, חק, חשך, כהן, כח, לא, משה, שלש	כל, עון, קדש, ראש	חכמה
2. 1Q8	4476		לא	אדני, אלהים, את, זאת, חדש, חכמה, חשך, כהן, כח, כל, משה, עון, קדש, ראש
3. 4Q51	3656	כהן	אלהים ,את, חדש, כל, לא, שלש	זאת, ראש
4. 11Q5	3280	אדני, אלהים, זאת, חכמה, חק, חשך, כהן, כל, לא, עון, קדש, ראש		
5. 4Q22	2566	את, כח, עון, קדש	חק, לא	אלהים, זאת, חדש, כהן, כל, משה, שלש
6. 4Q27	1971	אלהים, את, חדש, כהן, כל, לא, משה, קדש, ראש, שלש		
7. 4Q23	1452			את, כהן, כל, לא, משה, עון, קדש, ראש, שלש
8. 11Q1	1336			אלהים, את, זאת, חדש, חק, כהן, כח, כל, לא, משה, קדש, ראש
9. 4Q56	1287			אלהים, את, זאת, כהן, כל, לא, משה, עון ,קדש, ראש, שלש
10. 4Q1	1247			אלהים, את, זאת, כח, כל, לא, משה, שלש
11. 4Q82	1114	אלהים, את, חשך, עון, קדש, שלש	אדני, כל, לא	ראש
12. 4Q11	1086			אלהים, את, זאת, חדש, חק, כל, לא, משה, קדש, ראש
13. 4Q57	1083	אדני, אלהים, זאת, חק, חשך, כל, לא, עון	כהן, קדש	

Ms	Words	Full	Mixed	Defective
14. 4Q14	1009		כל	אדני, אלהים, את, זאת, כח, לא, משה
15. 4Q70	927		את, לא	אלהים, זאת, חכמה, כל, עון, ראש
16. 4Q112	794			אלהים, כח, לא
17. 4Q24	773		את	אלהים, חדש, כהן, כל, לא, משה, קדש, ראש
18. 4Q72	771			אלהים, זאת, כהן, כל, לא, ראש
19. 4Q30	695	את		אלהים, זאת, חק, כל, לא
20. 4Q41	685	אלהים, את, זאת, חק, חשך, עון	כל, לא	משה
21. 4Q84	606			אלהים, זאת, חשך, כהן, כח, כל, לא, עון, קדש
22. 4Q58	571		כל, לא	אלהים, את, זאת, חשך, קדש, ראש
23. 4Q33	526			אלהים, את, זאת, כל, לא
24. 4Q13	525	אלהים, את, כהן, משה	כל, לא	
25. 4Q78	521	אדני, אלהים, כח, כל, לא		

This table of biblical manuscripts from the Judean Desert reveals all the more clearly that DSS documents distinguish themselves — except possibly for the borderline cases 4Q22 and 4Q51 — as either *plene* or defective. This appears broadly reflective of two distinct approaches to the text. The fact that the defective group is patterned after Classical BH norms whereas the *plene* group is noticeably similar to the nonbiblical texts from the Qumran caves is striking and suggestive.

b. The letter *yod* is commonly used to indicate the vowels $\bar{\imath}$ (*HDSS* §100.32) and $\bar{e}$ (*HDSS* §100.33) but with considerable less frequency than the use of the *waw* for $o/\bar{o}$ and $u/\bar{u}$. As examples, note the Qumran Hebrew spellings of בנימין (1QM 1:2, BH: בְּנִמְן), רישון/ריאשון/ראישון (1QM 6:1, BH: רִאשׁוֹן), and שרירות (1QS 1:6, BH: שְׁרִרוּת).

The examples of $\bar{e}$ indicated by *yod* (*HDSS* §100.33) tend toward the exception rather than the rule: וְרִאשִׁית (4Q252 1 iv 4, BH: וְרֵאשִׁית), המיאות (11QT 58:4, BH: הַמֵּאוֹת); העיד (11QT 61:9, BH: הָעֵד), and ריעיכה (11QT 54:20, BH: רֵעֶיךָ).

Nouns ending in *he* whose construct singular is vocalized with a *sere* are also occasionally spelled with a *yod,* producing a form that is identical to the plural construct: אשי ריח ניחוח (11QT 23:17; 28:02, 2, BH: אִשֵּׁה) and חזי התנופה (11QT 22:9, BH: חֲזֵה). For further discussion see *HDSS* §100.34.

As might be expected, these functions of the *yod* tend to occur in the same group of DSS manuscripts that also incorporates the *waw* as a *mater.* For example, the larger biblical manuscripts affected are consistently those which also exhibit a fuller spelling with *waw*: 1QIsaᵃ, 4Q27, 4Q78, 11Q5, and the borderline 4Q51.

c. The spellings of Jerusalem (ירושלים) and David (דויד) are mentioned together here as they have been identified as important indicators of Late Biblical Hebrew (hereafter, LBH; see *HDSS* §500.1). The plene spelling of Jerusalem occurs in 69 percent of all cases (33 of 48) in the nonbiblical Qumran manuscripts while the longer spelling of David is consistent (26x) without a single short spelling extant. These LBH indicators are similarly evident in the DSS biblical manuscripts occurring respectively in 50 percent and 83 percent (53 in 4Q51 alone) of all cases. These spellings also tend to occur in manuscripts that incorporate the *waw* as a *mater*: 1QIsaᵃ, 4Q51, 4Q82, and 11Q5 represent the larger manuscripts in the table above.

d. The combination *yod-aleph* in the final position, evidenced frequently in the particle כיא, is well known (see *HDSS* §100.51) to students of the scrolls. This feature is called a *digraph,* two letters that are used to write one sound. The word כיא occurs 629 times of 1058 total occurrences (59 percent) in the Qumran nonbiblical manuscripts whereas in the MT the longer spelling does not occur even once in 4487 cases. In the biblical texts the longer form occurs 254 times of 1206 total instances (21 percent) revealing a clear influence of Qumran Hebrew on the scribal practice of these Second Temple biblical manuscripts. Among the larger DSS biblical manuscripts in our list above, this feature is again concentrated in those which also use *waw* as a vowel letter: 1QIsaᵃ, 4Q27, and 4Q57.

This review of orthographic variations in the DSS sets the stage for other such changes in phonology, morphology, and syntax. Together, these variations are indicative of changes in the Hebrew language that also clearly affected how some scribes copied Scripture in the Second Temple period.

Phonology

Phonology is the study of speech sounds in language. In modern writing, with the existence of dictionaries and spell checkers, sounds modified over time in daily speech are often pronounced contrary to their written form. For example, the "k" of the English word "knee" was vocalized until the seventeenth century and is still heard today in the German cognate, "knie." In antiquity such modifications occasionally caused misspellings that give a clue to ancient pronunciation patterns. An awareness of this phenomenon also provides an additional clue to scribal practice *and* saves the modern reader the trouble of locating a word that does not exist in the lexicons!

a. As has been noted (*HDSS* §200.11), the weakening of gutturals generates misspellings with some frequency in the scrolls. In the nonbiblical Qumran scrolls the tally is something just less than 200 words. By far the most common variation is the omission of the *aleph,* with more than 100 cases (e.g., נשיי for נשיאי at 11Q19 57:12).[12] There are 30 occasions where a *he* stands for an *aleph* (e.g., קורה for קורא at 1QS 7:1) and there are 28 instances where a *he* is omitted (e.g., יוריב for יהוריב at 4Q329 f2a-b 4). Rarer incidents are *aleph* for *ayin* (6x), *aleph* for *heth* (2x), *aleph* for *he* (2x), omission of *ayin* (2x), *he* for *ayin* (1x), *ayin* for *aleph* (1x). What perhaps has not been made clear up until now is the fact that the *heth* is hardly altered at all; it never stands instead of any other letter, is replaced by *aleph* on only two occasions, and is never omitted.[13]

Among the biblical DSS the instances of variation brought about by the weakening gutturals is unexpectedly a bit more pronounced, with approximately 175 occurrences in a smaller corpus. Aside from this, the picture is very similar: the omission of the *aleph* occurs more than 75 times, *he* stands for *aleph* in 49 instances, *he* is omitted in 10, *ayin* is omitted in 2, and *ayin* replaces *aleph* in 3. Two surprises appear, and both — with small exception — are found in 1QIsaᵃ. On 20 occasions, *aleph* replaces *he* in the biblical DSS, as compared to 2 in the nonbiblical Qumran scrolls. All but one of these — מא for מה at Exod 13:14 (XHev/Se5 1 6) — occur in 1QIsaᵃ. The *heth* also shows more variation in the biblical scrolls, twice in 11Q1 and

---

12. Figures here and in the following paragraph reflect "phonological" variations of the *aleph* and *he,* not "orthographic." E.g., the presence of *aleph* as a *mater* or as part of a digraph is orthographic; the absence of consonantal *aleph* is phonological.

13. An examination of corrections among the nonbiblical manuscripts does not greatly alter this picture and in fact suggests that errors of *he* for *heth* were normally spotted and fixed. Note 1QS 4:4 (מחשבת), 7:11 (וחנם), and 14 (ישחק).

9 times in 1QIsaᵃ: six times *heth* is replaced by a *he;* twice it stands for an *ayin;* and on one occasion each it is replaced by an *aleph,* an *ayin,* or is omitted.

b. The interchange between sibilants *samekh (s)* and *sin (ś)* is also well known (*HDSS* §200.15). There are 36 instances among the nonbiblical Qumran manuscripts where the shift is *sin* spelled with a *samekh* (22 in the *Copper Scroll* alone, see עסר for עשׂר at 3Q15 2:9) and 11 cases where words with lemmas with *samekh* are spelled with a *sin* (see מאשׁו for מאסו at 1QpHab 1:11). There are no clear cases where *shin* is involved as a variation (see, however, the possibility that יכחס = יכחשׁ at 1QS 7:3). Among the biblical DSS there are only 8 variants that are explained by a shift from *sin* spelled with a *samekh* but 14 of the reverse. Again, there are no instances where *shin* is involved as a variant. The simplest explanation that reflects all available data is that both the *samekh* and *sin* had come to be pronounced as *s* whereas *shin* remained distinct.

These phonetic changes, unlike those of orthography (see above) and morphology (discussed below), are dispersed among manuscripts of both Qumran and Classical Hebrew styles. Qimron's assessment of the distribution of the evidence for the weakening of gutturals also stands for the confusion of sibilants. They tend to be found "in non-formal manuscripts — and very occasionally in formal ones."[14] Of the 240 phonological variants described here, only 7 occur in formal manuscripts: 4Q11 (1x), 4Q14 (2x), and 4Q51 (4x). We must conclude that common scribes of Qumran and Classical Hebrew styles were equally poor spellers. In contrast, senior scribes who were responsible for deluxe biblical manuscripts did noticeably better.

Morphology

Morphology is concerned with the rules of word formation and the derivation of word elements. Especially important here is inflection, the marking of words to distinguish gender, number, and other factors. An example of an inflectional change in English is the expression of the Early Modern (King James) English second singular present tense verb "savest" as com-

---

14. Qimron, *HDSS,* 25. See Tov, *Scribal Practices and Approaches,* 126 for a list of formal *(deluxe)* editions. Among the 25 largest biblical manuscripts listed in the orthographic chart, 4Q11, 4Q14, 4Q22, 4Q51, and 4Q71 are considered deluxe manuscripts by Tov.

pared to the Modern English "save." The following five examples are concerned with inflectional paradigms common to Qumran Hebrew but either not found, or uncommon, in Classical BH.

a. The long form of the second person masculine singular perfect verb has long been recognized as a characteristic of Qumran Hebrew (*HDSS* §310.11).[15] The inflection ending in תה- is nearly the norm in the nonbiblical scrolls, occurring in 529 of 582 extant forms (91 percent). It shows up frequently in the biblical scrolls as well: 175 of 513 occurrences (34 percent). As the percentage in the MT is much smaller — 155 long to 1691 short (8 percent) — it is clear that Qumran Hebrew has influenced certain scribes as they copied biblical manuscripts. Of the large biblical scrolls evidencing the longer form, nearly all also exhibit the orthographic element *waw* as a *mater*: 1QIsaᵃ, 4Q13, 4Q22, 4Q27, 4Q41, 4Q78, 4Q82, and 11Q5. In only 2 instances — once each in 1Q8 and 4Q112 — does the longer ending appear in otherwise defective manuscripts. This feature is also echoed to a lesser degree in the longer second person masculine plural: תמה-, 50 percent of Qumran nonbiblical and 20 percent of DSS biblical manuscripts.

b. A significant sign of LBH and also Qumran Hebrew is the use of the so-called cohortative forms of the first person to denote the indicative (*HDSS* §310.122; see ונבואה at 4Q51 9e-i 16, whereas the MT of 1 Sam 10:14 has וַנָּבוֹא). There are 163 extant cohortative and 285 simple imperfect forms in the nonbiblical scrolls (36 percent). In comparison, cohortative forms make up only 19 percent of the MT (531 cohortative and 2293 first person imperfect forms). The Qumran biblical texts exhibit 197 cohortative of 769 first person imperfect forms (20 percent). This does not appear to be a significant increase, but fully 55 cases are at variance with the MT. Of the large manuscripts exhibiting this feature, with the notable exception of occurrences in 1Q8, all are also *plene*: 1QIsaᵃ, 4Q13, 11Q5, and the borderline 4Q51.

c. The so-called "pausal" forms of the *qal* imperfect make up 27 percent of possible cases in the nonbiblical Qumran texts (*HDSS* §311.13, and see יעבורו at 4Q27 65-71 7; the MT of Num 32:27 has יַעֲבְרוּ).[16] Whereas

15. I have followed Qimron by categorizing this as a morphological instead of orthographical phenomenon. This is reasonable as the *he* that appears with the afformative of the second person masculine plural verb (תמה-) is more readily explained as a morphological feature.

16. Weak verbs that have no o-form *qal* imperfect were excluded in the count: *lamed-he*, geminate, *ayin-waw/yod*, and *pe-aleph* verbs such as אמר.

the MT has only 11 *plene* pausal forms of 2829 possibilities (0.4 percent), the influence of Second Temple scribal style on the DSS biblical texts is clear: 88 variants of 752 possibilities (12 percent) are explained by this influence. Of the large biblical manuscripts which display these "pausal" imperfects, 1QIsaᵃ, 4Q27, 4Q41, 4Q57, and 11Q5 are all examples of *plene* manuscripts. The two borderline cases, 4Q22 and 4Q51, also display pausal inflections.

d. Likewise there exists in the Qumran manuscripts a "pausal" *qal* imperative in those forms with affixes or pronominal suffixes (*HDSS* §311.14, and see וְהִרְגוּ at 4Q22 38:29, whereas the MT of Exod 32:27 has וְהִרְגוּ). There are 10 instances out of 147 possibilities in the nonbiblical Qumran texts (7 percent), compared to five *plene* forms of 609 in the MT (0.7 percent). The phenomenon is curiously more pronounced in the DSS biblical texts with 38 instances of 274 possibilities (14 percent), or double the proportion found in the nonbiblical Qumran texts. Of the large biblical manuscripts displaying these "pausal" imperatives, 1QIsaᵃ, 4Q78, 4Q82, and 11Q5 are all examples of *plene* manuscripts. The two borderline cases, 4Q22 and 4Q51, again display "pausal" inflections.

e. The second masculine singular suffix כה- instead of the BH ךָ- has been noted for its prevalence in the Qumran nonbiblical manuscripts (*HDSS* §322.12).[17] Of 3464 extant cases, 2582 or 75 percent display the full spelling. The Hebrew Bible, representing a Classical Hebrew norm, has only 39 of 6918 instances, or less than 0.6 percent. It is thus an important gauge of the influence of Qumran style that the DSS biblical manuscripts display 798 full forms of a total of 2741 occurrences, or 29 percent. The largest of these — 4Q27, 4Q57, 4Q82, 11Q5 — are all *plene* examples in the table above. It is important to note that 1QIsaᵃ is uniquely mixed, having 231 long forms and 120 short. As 100 (83 percent) of the short forms are found in columns 1-27, and 212 (92 percent) of the long forms are in columns 28-54, this is an important factor in the discussion of multiple hands or sources for the *Great Isaiah Scroll*.

---

17. As with the form of the second person masculine singular perfect verb, I have followed Qimron by categorizing the *he* of this suffix as a morphological instead of orthographical phenomenon. Again, this is reasonable as the *he* that often appears in the second masculine plural (כמה-) and third masculine plural (המה-) suffixes is more readily explained as a morphological feature.

Syntax

Syntax is a study of how words work together in phrases, clauses, sentences, and beyond. Changes in syntax can be quite subtle and difficult to identify, especially for the non-native speaker or reader. An American in Canada would be struck by the fact that victims of a car crash are taken "to hospital" rather than "to the hospital." A native-born Korean, even after years of English study, would likely not notice the subtle difference. As there are no surviving native speakers of Second Temple Hebrew, it is not an overstatement to say that the study of the variations of syntax in the DSS is an especially difficult undertaking.

In general, the syntax of the nonbiblical Dead Sea Scrolls reveals a continued evolution of changes that had begun to be evident in LBH. However, given the influence of Qumran Hebrew that we have noted on the biblical manuscripts in the areas of orthography and morphology, it is intriguing to note how few biblical variants are solved by Qimron's twenty syntactic categories (*HDSS* §400). Other studies such as those published by Takamitsu Muraoka have proved to be more helpful.[18] Muraoka takes as his starting point the Qumran biblical texts and sets out to discover the nature of DSS Hebrew syntax by analyzing cases of syntactical variation. In essence this comparison solves the native speaker problem, since the native scribes give evidence of their own syntactic preferences as they make modifications in the Classical Biblical Hebrew texts. And, indeed, there are a considerable number of syntactical variants in the biblical texts from the Judean Desert.

One change that has come to light in an area where even Muraoka has not yet fully ventured — the syntax of the finite verb — provides a good example of syntactical change in the biblical manuscript corpus. Generally, even here the changes are modest. A global review reveals a total variation in the verbal system of a bit more than 2 percent of the whole. When compared to the overall number of real variants — approximately 6 percent — verbal syntax actually appears quite stable.[19] There are, how-

18. See esp., T. Muraoka, "An Approach to the Morphosyntax and Syntax of Qumran Hebrew."

19. A total of 386 variants involve aspect in the verbal system, with a total of 18,654 verbal forms. At this point in the preparation of the biblical data base we have accounted for 6,096 "real" variants in the corpus of 104,757 total words. This is an average of 5.8 percent. "Real" variant here refers to those that could affect the translation; this definition excludes orthographic, phonetic, and morphological variants.

ever, two areas that stand out for comment. On the one hand, given the fact that the use of the so-called *waw*-consecutive or preterite *(wayyiqtol)* was declining dramatically in this period — by the time of the Mishnah it is not used at all aside from biblical quotations — it is rather surprising that only 35 variants might be explained by this influence. This is a mere 2.2 percent reduction in the number of *waw* consecutives, certainly meaningful, but not of special significance. On the other hand, the increase in *waw* plus the imperfect *(wəyiqtol)* that has been noted among the Qumran nonbiblical texts[20] might explain the surprising 33 percent increase of this combination among the DSS biblical manuscripts.[21] This increase is likely to be accounted for by the sum of three factors: a slight decrease in the use of the perfect consecutive paralleling the decline of the imperfect consecutive, a diminished use of the *waw* with the simple imperfect to determine a telic sense, and the overall increase in the use of the conjunctive *waw* in general.

Similar to the distribution of phonological variations, the increase in *wəyiqtol* forms is fairly evenly evident in both *plene* (1QIsa^a, 4Q57, 4Q78, 11Q5, and the borderline 4Q51) and defective manuscripts (1Q8, 4Q14, 4Q56, 4Q58, and 4Q72). Again as noted with the results of the phonological evidence, the lion's share of variation occurs in nonformal manuscripts (115 cases), while three formal manuscripts show one variation each (4Q14, 4Q51, and 4Q72).

This discussion offers us much food for thought. Paleography has provided a means of dating the manuscripts of the Dead Sea Scrolls by handwriting style to the end of the Second Temple period (250 B.C.E. to 68 C.E.). Orthography and morphology reveal two groups of manuscripts, one consistent with Classical Hebrew norms and another that shows decided variance. For the sake of convenience we have adopted the designation "Qumran Hebrew" for the latter group, because the phenomena discussed are most prevalent in the manuscripts that come from the eleven caves at Qumran. Phonology and syntax also tend to delineate two groups of manuscripts. Here, however, the variations tend to occur in both Classical and Qumran Hebrew manuscripts but are generally not evident in the copying of deluxe scrolls.

---

20. Abegg, "The Hebrew of the Dead Sea Scrolls," 337.

21. The instances of *waw* plus the imperfect in the MT of passages paralleled by the DSS biblical scrolls are 353, to which 118 have been added by variation.

Application of Method

A host of the factors developed thus far in the description of paleography, orthography, phonology, morphology, and syntax play a significant role in a number of critical Scroll issues. In this concluding section these methodological components will be brought to bear on an important ongoing debate. I have no pretense to solve the problem with such brief discussion but rather only hope to add an additional element that has yet to be considered.

Most of the phenomena I have described in the discussions of orthography and morphology above have been seized upon by Emanuel Tov as components of a scribal system that he has termed "Qumran Scribal Practice."[22] And there is no doubt that he is right as to the "Scribal Practice" portion of the term. The fact that a good number of the nonbiblical manuscripts — including most of what might be termed sectarian texts — are written in this form of Hebrew *and* the fact that a smaller but significant number of biblical manuscripts exhibits the same practice might well point to a unique writing system among the Qumran sectarians. Critics of Tov's hypothesis have countered that the phenomenon might more accurately be termed "Second Temple Scribal Practice" since we do not have the benefit of several discoveries like Qumran from the same time period to clarify the extent of distribution. If Tov is to be vindicated, it would be helpful to demonstrate some additional factor that links the scribal practice displayed in the scrolls to the scribal community that many believe inhabited the ruins of Qumran.

A corpus of texts that have thus far only been examined in a limited fashion shows some promise to provide just such a link: *tefillin* (phylacteries), leather boxes worn by male Jews on the hand and forehead in obedience to Exod 13:9. The *tefillin* worn on the head consisted of a capsule with four compartments, containing — according to b. Menaḥ. 34b — four parchments with the biblical passages Exod 13:1–10, 11–16; Deut 6:4–9; and 11:13–21, respectively. The hand *tefillin* consisted of one compartment containing a single parchment inscribed with all four passages. Twenty-eight tefillin were found in Judean Desert sites, at least 20 of them coming from the caves at Qumran. What makes these tefillin especially interesting for the purpose of this study is the fact that they not only contain a mixture of parchments that conform to later Talmudic strictures

---

22. Tov, *Scribal Practices and Approaches*, 261.

and those that do not, but that some are written in an orthographical/ morphological system evidenced by so many of the Qumran manuscripts and others in a style that could be identified as Classical Biblical Hebrew. The obvious question is, do those written in what Tov has called "Qumran Scribal Practice" conform to the talmudic regulations, or do they reflect other scriptural selections?

Tov undertakes an examination of the *tefillin* parchments from Cave 4 and determines that A-B, J-Q "and probably also G and I"[23] were written in the fuller style exhibited by many of the Qumran manuscripts. My own study, in light of our discussion of orthography and morphology above, would agree with Tov's assessment of these manuscripts and would add H (4Q135) to the list as well. Every one of these thirteen *tefillin* also shares an important additional feature: each contains at least one nonconforming biblical passage. A, I, and M contain Exod 12:43-51; A, B, G, H, J, L, M, and O contain Deut 5:1–6:3; A, K, P, and Q contain Deut 10:12–11:12; and N alone contains Deut 32:14ff. Clearly standing apart from this first group, the conforming *tefillin* from Cave 4 — C-F, R-S[24] — also share the characteristic of having been written in a Classical Biblical Hebrew style. If this exhausted the available data we would have reason to conclude with Tov that "texts written in the Qumran practice and not reflecting the rabbinic prescriptions probably derived from the Qumranites themselves."[25] By extension we could also include all nonbiblical and biblical manuscripts written in this later style as well. One of the "holy grails" of Qumran study would then be found: "Which texts — biblical and nonbiblical — were actually copied by the sectarians themselves?" There are, however, additional *tefillin* from Caves 1 and 8, as well as six manuscripts which may all come from other Judean Desert sites. These parchments Tov did not include in his study.

Three of the extra-Qumran *tefillin* — 34Se1, Mur 4, and XHev/Se5 — were written in the more conservative scribal style, and each contains only rabbinically-prescribed portions. Two *tefillin* from Qumran Cave 8 show evidence of being written in the Qumran scribal style and also have the nonprescribed portions. Unfortunately, the exceptionally clear picture that has been emerging thus far clouds with an examination of the last pieces of evidence, 1Q13 and XQ1-3.

23. 4Q128-129, 4Q137-144 and probably 4Q134 and 4Q136.
24. 4Q130-133 and 4Q145-146.
25. Tov, *Scribal Practices and Approaches*, 271.

1Q13, published by Dominique Barthélemy in 1955,[26] exhibits no sign of the orthographic or morphological features that define the later scribal style, has surprisingly few variants, and yet unexpectedly has two of the nonprescribed passages: Deut 5:1–6:3 and 10:12–11:12. XQ1-3, published by Yigael Yadin in 1969,[27] have a rather dubious origin. They were bought by Yadin for the Shrine of the Book from an anonymous Jerusalem antiquities dealer. Yadin writes, "According to the dealer, the *tefillin* had been found in the Qumran caves — possibly cave 4 — but he did not know for certain." The fact that Cave 4 fragments fetched a premium brought several manuscripts of dubious provenance into the Qumran collection. XQ1-3 are thus just as likely to have come from another site in the Judean Desert.[28] A clue that might help establish provenance is paleography. A manuscript with a date after 70 C.E. would necessarily be extra-Qumran and less likely sectarian. Yet Yadin describes the handwriting as "formal" and the style as "Herodian" and posits a date from the first half of the first century C.E.[29] An examination of the handwriting leaves little doubt that he is correct. Whereas the *he* and *samekh* are arguably Hasmonean, the *aleph* and *ayin* are clearly of Herodian form.[30] Like 1Q13, XQ1-3 exhibit very little sign of the later scribal style, have few real variants, and yet preserve three of the four nonconforming passages: Exod 12:43-51; Deut 5:1–6:3; and Deut 10:12–11:12. One additional factor of interest entails phonology. Although the *tefillin* in general display a high degree of phonological variation — 10 of the 45 DSS biblical manuscripts that exhibit phonological variation are *tefillin* — XQ1-3 have none and 1Q13 contains but one instance, ירתם for יראתם at Deut 5:5. There are no syntactic variants at all.

Thus our review provides little help for Tov's hypothesis. 1Q13 and XQ1-3 cannot be aligned with the pattern seen among the other *tefillin*. In light of the presence of nonprescribed passages these *tefillin* appear sectarian, yet they are not written in Tov's "Qumran Scribal Practice." In addition, three of these "sectarian" parchments — XQ1-3 — quite possibly do not come from the Qumran caves at all. Finally, the phonological and syn-

26. D. Barthélemy and J. T. Milik, DJD 1, 72-76.

27. Y. Yadin, *Tefillin from Qumran.*

28. Weston Fields, who has thoroughly researched the early acquisitions, has told me in private correspondence that once the Palestinian Archaeological Museum adopted the policy of paying the Bedouin more for the valuable Cave 4 fragments, the inevitable happened: "everything was from Cave 4."

29. Yadin, *Tefillin from Qumran,* 22.

30. See the illustration of the script, Yadin, *Tefillin from Qumran,* 26.

tactical character of these documents suggest that they were written by senior scribes, well versed in Classical Hebrew style.

Conclusions

It has been my hope to establish these five components — paleography, orthography, phonology, morphology, and syntax — of what might be called, in broad strokes, linguistic analysis, as important elements for the study of the Dead Sea Scrolls. Certainly there is much more to be gained here for other Scroll disciplines than simply study for study's sake. In closing I will recount some of the important gains and challenges that all students of the scrolls must take into account for their own study.

a. There is incontrovertible evidence of a Second Temple scribal style exhibited by the nonbiblical Qumran manuscripts that can, in the first instance, be clearly seen by a review of the *waw* as *mater*. An examination of additional orthographic and morphological phenomena only serves to underline this important fact. Whether this style should be described with Tov as Qumran Scribal Practice seems quite possible, although a few sectarian manuscripts and nonconforming *tefillin* written in a classical style throw some doubt on this conclusion and will foster further study.

b. This scribal style has obviously affected a certain group of scribes copying biblical manuscripts in the Second Temple period. Every one of the twenty-five largest biblical manuscripts that shows consistent use of a *waw* as *mater* is documented repeatedly among the remainder of the orthographic and morphological discussions. Not one of the defective manuscripts can boast of even one such mention.

c. Initial research into phonology and syntax paints a rather different picture. Manuscripts showing a high degree of variation in these areas are evenly distributed among *plene* and classical groupings. Only deluxe biblical manuscripts are free of the variants brought about by the modifications in phonology and syntax that are evident among the DSS.

d. This study of syntax is still in its infancy and will likely become a focus of research now that the Dead Sea Scrolls corpus is fully available. Results here may aid in clarifying the discussion of scribal styles. Syntactical studies will most certainly promote a fuller understanding of the evolution of Hebrew at the end of the Second Temple period and its relationship to Mishnaic Hebrew, a form that makes its appearance less than two centuries later.

The Dynamics of Change in the
Computer Imaging of the Dead Sea Scrolls
and Other Ancient Inscriptions

Bruce Zuckerman

In the late 1990s I wrote and collaborated on a series of articles evaluating "the state of the art" for high resolution image documentation of the Dead Sea Scrolls and other ancient manuscripts. At the same time I considered how computer-imaging applications might be successfully applied to the analysis and decipherment of these texts.[1] What strikes me about all these studies, as I review them today, is how quickly they have gone completely out of date. Almost all of their technical information, delineating how our group of scholars and technologists[2] documented, analyzed, digitally manipulated, and distributed image data of the scrolls and other ancient texts is now woefully inadequate and even, to some extent, misleading. This certainly is not the expected norm for studies on ancient texts — or for our tried-and-true grammars, lexicons, and critical editions — which tend to have a decent "shelf life," especially in their documentation of primary data. But the impact of digital technologies is not only profound, it is also dynamic; indeed, it

1. B. Zuckerman, "Bringing the Dead Sea Scrolls Back to Life"; B. Zuckerman and K. Zuckerman, "Photography of Manuscripts"; "Photography and Computer Imaging"; see also B. Zuckerman, "Working with a Little More Data"; "Every Dot and Tiddle."

2. Primarily, two closely related research entities are involved, both headquartered in the College of Letters, Arts & Sciences at the University of Southern California. These are the West Semitic Research Project (WSRP; see http://www.usc.edu/dept/LAS/wsrp/), an image archive now encompassing more than 150,000 images of ancient texts and artifacts, and the InscriptiFact Image Database Application (ISFDA; see http://www.inscriptifact.com/), which currently distributes some 25,000 high-resolution images of ancient texts and artifacts to researchers in 35 countries with more being added on a continuing basis.

changes before our eyes. New tools and software applications, and new versions of existing applications, change the way we *see* ancient texts, sometimes quite drastically. Thus, practices that seemed sophisticated ten years ago seem now naïve, somewhat simplistic, and, at times, altogether unsatisfactory. I have no doubt that ten years from now this present discussion will almost certainly suffer from similar critical inadequacies.

The problem is this: every time a new piece of hardware becomes available (e.g., a better digital camera, a superior imaging array,[3] or a more powerful computer) or a software application is created or expanded that allows for manipulations previously not considered (e.g., a better way to catalogue and distribute image data with accompanying metadata, a more precise means for filtering and refining an image, or a more precise measurement and scaling application), these advances have profound *methodological* impact. That is, not only must we learn to master such tools, we also must rethink our overall approach to analyzing ancient texts in light of what they allow us to do.

Indeed, one might begin to wonder about the usefulness of printed illustrations altogether. Here we have a genuine dilemma: with digital data so dynamic and interactive, static illustrations constrained to the printed page simply will no longer do. The method of analysis — the central concern of this chapter and this volume — is inextricably bound to the dynamic dimensions of the illustrations, and conventional printing gives readers only a shadow of what is necessary to evaluate the relevant digital techniques and methodological concerns. With no optimal solution on the horizon, we have chosen to illustrate this chapter with a few key images, and to send readers to a website for further illustrations in a format as good as the internet allows.[4] No program on the web of which I am aware can meet the standards required to best illustrate this chapter,[5] but what

---

3. WSRP was slow to convert from conventional to digital photography. But digital is now clearly the only serious game in town, not least because specialized films (esp. infrared films so important to DSS imaging) have, one-by-one, ceased to be manufactured. Nevertheless, attention must be paid to the preservation and maintenance of already existing film negatives and transparencies and also to their digitization, since these glass and chemically based records often preserve important image data.

4. See http://www.usc.edu/dept/LAS/wsrp/information/DynamicsDSS.

5. For a preliminary example of an effort at electronic publication that endeavors to integrate images and text, see G. Barkay, M. Lundberg, A. Vaughn, B. Zuckerman, "The Amulets from Ketef Hinnom" (with an expanded version on CD-ROM). See also "The Challenges of Ketef Hinnom."

can be shown will have to do. In any case, although the specific tools and techniques presented here may soon go out of date, we may hope that the underlying approaches and methodological observations will have more enduring value.[6]

A good place to start is with what I term DSS digital "nip/tuck." The scrolls as reclaimed from antiquity have suffered much damage of the sort that calls out for repair. While a highly skilled conservator can protect a scroll from further deterioration or damage, in many (if not most) cases the prudent course of action is to take no concrete action at all. In the early days of DSS studies, scholars with direct access to the scrolls were in the habit of taking matters literally into their own hands. Sometimes this resulted in fairly crude physical "repairs" that did more harm than good. Other scholars worked indirectly, using scissors and tape to cut up and reassemble photographic prints or transparencies of scrolls.[7] Not surprisingly, direct or indirect repairs always lacked precision and, on occasion, even hid more information than they revealed.

The advent of high-resolution image data of the DSS has made facile "electronic repairs" of scrolls much easier to manage. Two complementary advantages inherent in the digital image data of DSS particularly facilitate these repairs. First, scrolls images are essentially two-dimensional; their third dimension is normally of minimal importance for imaging and image scaling/matching. This point has significant implications. With standard software programs to synchronize scale and resolution, images can easily be adjusted to match one another. Thus, for example, if an early photographic image is digitally scaled and adjusted to a more recent image, the two are almost always totally compatible. In contrast, this almost *never* applies for images of inscriptions that have significant depth (e.g., a stone stela or a cuneiform tablet). In this latter case the depth dimensions never quite seem to match, because it is difficult to keep the camera perfectly aligned horizontally to the surface (and indeed the inscribed surface itself

---

6. For the technical, scientific details on optimal imaging of DSS, see the studies cited in note 1 above. Our discussion here will assume access to the technically best available images obtainable at any given time.

7. I have encountered a notable early example of this in cutting-and-taping of early prints of the *Genesis Apocryphon,* apparently done by Nahman Avigad in preparation for the preliminary edition of the text he published with Yigael Yadin. For a number of years the original negatives of some of the interior columns of 1QapGen were lost, and these cut-up prints constituted the only known image data for this part of the text. Fortunately, many of the original negatives have since resurfaced.

may be variable in depth relative to the position of the camera).[8] But a camera mounted and stabilized on a professional copy stand can easily be adjusted for a targeted flat surface, like that of a scroll, so that it is correctly aligned. As a general rule, most of the existing image documentation of DSS reflects scrupulous care in keeping optimal camera alignment with scroll surfaces.

This can be highly useful for facilitating repairs, drawing upon image data recorded at different times and under differing circumstances. A recently-made high-resolution infrared image may reveal a good deal more information than an earlier picture. Meanwhile, an older though technically inferior picture may contain more data, because when that picture was made (perhaps some forty years ago) the scroll itself was in better condition. The facility of matching fragments in a two-dimensional referential framework makes this relatively easy to do.

The second advantage to digital images involves the ability to place various image components on separate image layers that can be made to appear or disappear with a single command click from a mouse or trackpad. This allows for precise comparisons that would be impractical with conventional photographic images. For example, one may superimpose an older image, showing a better-preserved section of a scroll that has subsequently deteriorated over time, over a more recent image that conveys better data but shows less of the scroll itself. Toggling the former layer off and on can reveal in fine detail how the scroll has changed over time, which in turn can help facilitate the process of electronic repair. It also allows conservators to track with greater accuracy the changes in a scroll surface over time.[9]

The layering of components of an image also facilitates the repair

8. Photogrammetric software (which has been extensively employed in, e.g., aerial mapping) may potentially provide a solution to this problem. One of the leaders in pioneering the application of photogrammetry to cultural heritage artifacts is Cultural Heritage Imaging (CHI), led by Mark Mudge and Carla Schroer; see http://www.c-h-i.org/. A collaborative project of WSRP, CHI, and others, funded by the Institute for Museum and Library Services, is currently exploring these possibilities.

9. This also applies to images photographed in visible light versus those photographed, more commonly, in the infrared spectrum. Infrared images typically reveal more textual information than visible-light images but are notoriously poor in resolution. A digital overlay of infrared and visible light images in separate layers thus can give the best sense of both text and physical condition. Present and future documentation of the DSS should include matching pictures in both the visible and the infrared spectrum. See B. Zuckerman, "Bringing the Dead Sea Scrolls Back to Life," 186-89, and note 25 below.

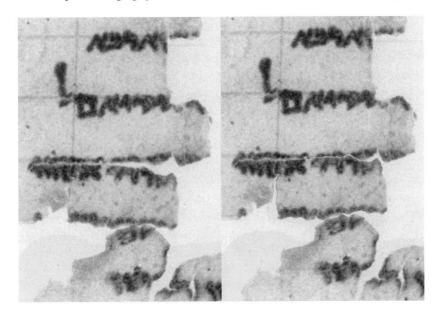

Figure 1. Detail of Column "Zero" from the Genesis Apocryphon,
illustrating a piece split off (left) and then electronically repaired (right).
(Photograph by Bruce and Kenneth Zuckerman, West Semitic Research. Courtesy
Department of Antiquities, Jordan. Computer enhancements by Bruce Zuckerman)

process itself. Consider the close-up image (see fig. 1) of a detail from a
fragment of the *Genesis Apocryphon*.[10] The left-hand picture shows an infrared image of the end of line 13 of the so-called "Column 0,"[11] essentially
in its existing physical condition when this picture was taken in 2001. As
can be seen, a small fragment has split away and rotated downward in a
clockwise direction. The right-hand picture shows the electronic repair.
The split-off piece has been electronically cut out, placed on a separate image layer and then rotated upward and counterclockwise to bring it back
into closer alignment with the surface from which it had separated. Note

10. The image is registered as AWS 43 and was made by myself and Marilyn Lundberg
at the Amman Citadel Museum in Jordan in 2001. A high resolution image is available on
ISFDA (see note 2 above) as ISF_DO_00665.

11. "Column Zero," so named by this writer, was largely reconstructed after cols. 1-22
had been collated and published. It was first presented in preliminary form by B. Zuckerman
and M. O. Wise in an unpublished paper, "A Re-study of the 1Q20 Fragments," at the SBL Annual Meeting in 1991. For a discussion of the readings of this column, see now, most conveniently, J. A. Fitzmyer, *The Genesis Apocryphon of Qumran Cave 1 (1Q20)*, esp. 64-65, 115, 117-19.

that no attempt has been made to make the repair appear seamless (although a number of techniques could have been employed to make the scroll look as good as new). From a methodological standpoint, it is important that a viewer see how the repair was done and be able to judge the validity of the operation.[12] In a dynamic image (as opposed to the "before-and-after" static image shown here) one could easily superimpose the repair over the original image, in separate layers, so that observers could toggle on or off and thus better judge the precision of the repair.

This case shows a fairly simple and straightforward repair. However, in some instances electronic repairs require more subtle measures. Consider, in this respect, fig. 2, another detail from the *Genesis Apocryphon* (col. 0, line 12).[13] As the infrared picture (left) shows, this part of the line has also split apart. However, the split here is uneven, being wider in the middle and narrower on either side.[14] Such unevenness is not unusual; the organic nature of scroll material means that pieces can warp, shrink, or expand inconsistently. In such cases, one cannot simply move the relevant components piecemeal. Another technique of electronic repair is preferable. Using this technique, which I have dubbed "patching,"[15] one cuts out and copies onto a separate layer a smaller section of the image, or patch (see fig. 2, middle). Then the layer with the patch is superimposed over the original image and adjusted so as to best clarify the reading. In this case (see fig. 2, right) the patch has been moved down to close the split. Once again, it is important that the seams be left visible so that an independent observer can judge whether the patchwork result is acceptable. This is especially important in a case like this, in which the manipulation of the image data could not be reproduced with the physical pieces of the scroll itself. A more aggressive procedure of this sort requires a higher critical profile.[16]

12. This issue is considered in greater detail below in reference to the concept of a "digital surrogate." For a preliminary discussion, see Zuckerman, "Every Dot and Tiddle," 194-95, n. 1.

13. The image is also based on AWS 43, see notes 10 and 11 above. This image and others that follow but are not included in this chapter are available on the website identified in note 4 above.

14. This is caused by the complexity of the split: the two sides have detached from each other on a horizontal plane but also open up with a significant third dimension, each side curling up and away from the other, like the petals of a flower as they open.

15. See, Zuckerman, "Every Dot and Tiddle," 189, n. 1.

16. I have elsewhere noted this distinction by contrasting "noninvasive" to "invasive" manipulations of digital imaging data. By noninvasive, I mean "manipulations that in no

A closely related procedure might be characterized as DSS "jigsaw puzzling." As anyone who has spent time poring over DSS fragments or images understands, the most labor-intensive aspect of the work is separating out the fragments of one manuscript (or related sets of manuscripts) and trying to piece them together. Of course, when the fragments (especially those of Cave 4) were first gathered together, this was done by eye and hand. A number of historical pictures today show table upon table of scrolls arrayed in plates like so many jigsaw puzzle pieces.[17]

The availability of digital versions of DSS fragments makes this procedure far more manageable and further allows anyone with access to high-resolution digital images to get into the game. A good example involves one of the first DSS to come to scholarly attention, 1Q72, or 1QDaniel[b].[18] Images of this text have been available for some time; recently, however, the use of improved infrared imaging has revealed a previously unknown fragment (see fig. 3), which has been recognized as part of 1Q72 (see fig. 4).[19] It only remained to determine where this newly-found piece of an old puzzle would fit. Making the match, as it turned out, was remarkably easy to do (see fig. 5), even though the actual join occurs across the downstroke of a single letter *kap*. The match can be further confirmed by the contextual

---

major manner physically alter the appearance of the assembled fragments *per se*." In contrast, an "invasive" procedure "significantly manipulates the data in a way that is somewhat false . . . [in that] one could not reproduce the procedure with the original skin itself." See Zuckerman, "Every Dot and Tiddle," 188-89.

17. Search "Dead Sea Scrolls" and "fragments" in Google images to find examples, such as are found, e.g., at http://advancement.sdsu.edu/marcomm/features/2007/scrolls.html.

18. See D. Barthélemy and J. T. Milik, DJD 1, 151, where the text was published, however, without accompanying photographic images; see also J. Trever, "Completion of the Publication of Some Fragments from Qumran Cave I"; note in particular Pl. 6 (JCT 105 in S. Reed, M. Lundberg, and M. Phelps, eds., *The Dead Sea Scrolls Catalogue;* unless otherwise noted, all inventory numbers and relevant abbreviations are cited according to this edition).

19. See M. Lundberg and B. Zuckerman, "New Aramaic Fragments from Qumran Cave One." The association with 1Q72 was based on the close similarity of the written hand in the two texts. The more recently recognized fragment was part of a plate of miscellaneous DSS materials, originally thought to be uninscribed, that were given to John Trever in 1949 by their owner, Athanasius Samuel, as a gift in thanks for the photographic work he had done on the scrolls. A WSRP team consisting of the present writer, Kenneth Zuckerman, and Marilyn Lundberg had the opportunity to photograph this fragment in 1995. The fragment is now in the possession of Martin Schøyen (designated in his collection as MS. 1926/4c). To the best of my knowledge, the principal pieces of 1Q72 remain in the possession of the Syrian Orthodox church archdiocese headquartered in Teaneck, NJ.

Figure 5. "Jigsaw puzzle" electronic match of two fragments of 1QDaniel[b].
(Original photograph of larger section by John C. Trever; photograph of smaller fragment by
Bruce Zuckerman and Marilyn Lundberg, West Semitic Research; courtesy M. Schøyen
Collection. Computer enhancements by Bruce Zuckerman)

compatibility of the surrounding text in both the line where the join has
been made and in the previous line. This match crosses a physical gap between the fragments but also a notable time gap, connecting a picture from
1949 with one taken in 1995.

Another useful example comes, once again, from Column o of the
Genesis Apocryphon.[20] In this case larger physical clues help enable a
match between two of the larger fragments (see figs. 6 and 7, for frags. 1
and 2). The key element that enables a probable match is the vertical rule
line, made by the ancient scribe to mark the end of Column o. Since both
fragments preserve clear, if faint, traces of this column-ending rule line, it
can be used as a control to line up the two fragments. When one does so,
the several letters of line 14, half of whose traces are on one side of the
break and half on the other, seem to match — specifically, in order, the let-

20. Based on the images cited in note 10 above (AWS 4a, ISF_DO_00661; see Reed,
Lundberg and Phelps, *The Dead Scrolls Catalog*).

ters *shin, mem,* and possibly *yod.*[21] While the context is too fragmentary to reconstruct a reliable running text in line 14, this match nonetheless serves the important function of locating these two larger fragments of Column o relative to one another.[22]

Not all "jigsaw" joins are made based on matching letters, rule lines, or other specifically scribal traces. On some occasions, the texture of the skin on which the text is written can supply the crucial clues. Consider the two fragments of 11Q10, the Cave 11 *Targum of Job* (11QtgJob) illustrated here (fig. 8). Although no clear join can be made by matching letters, a lighter discoloration of the mottled skin in each fragment suggests that they can be joined together.[23] Two other supporting clues guide and therefore reinforce this proposed join: first, the shapes of the fragments themselves fit together just where the lighter mottled areas on both sides of the join seem optimally matched; second, when the two fragments are put together in this fashion, their bottom lines are also properly aligned.

Finally, another crucial clue can be noted. The traces preserved of the second-to-last letter in the middle line of the upper, larger fragment must be the upper portions of an *ayin.*[24] Near the upper left corner of the smaller, lower fragment there also is a very small, dark "dot." Viewed in isolation, this "dot" would be discounted as insignificant, a mere variation in skin tone. However, when the two fragments are joined, this "dot" seems

21. See Fitzmyer, *The Genesis Apocryphon of Qumran Cave I,* 64-65; he accepts the first two letter readings but not the *yod.*

22. Another fragment ("fragment 3") was also placed at the top of the column by Zuckerman and Wise, "A Re-study of the 1Q20 Fragments." This fragment was so seriously deteriorated that the vertical column-ending rule line could no longer be seen. Nonetheless, the uneven placement of the final letters followed by blank spaces in the several lines preserved on this fragment indicate that the fragment preserved the end of a column. When one searches for a match by electronically sliding this fragment along the top of frag. 1, the traces of as many as six letters appear to line up (in order, *waw, mem,* final *nun,* [space], *he, waw, aleph*). These readings are now accepted by Fitzmyer in his reconstruction of line 5 of Column o; see *The Genesis Apocryphon of Qumran Cave I,* 64.

23. Images of these fragments are taken from PAM 44.114 (see Reed, Lundberg and Phelps, *The Dead Sea Scrolls Catalog,* 163, 396; the identification of these fragments as part of 11QtgJob was first made by Reed in this catalogue). The larger fragment is designated by the DJD editors of 11QtgJob as "A6" and the smaller fragment as "A8." "A6" was already tentatively associated with col. 17:3-5 by the DJD editors. See F. García Martínez, E. Tigchelaar, and A. S. van der Woude, eds., DJD 23, 120-21 and pls. XII, XXI. To my knowledge, the join proposed here has not been noted elsewhere. This and other readings in the *Job Targum* noted below are part of a commentary-in-progress being prepared by Bruce Zuckerman and Brent Strawn.

24. So read by the DJD editors; see García Martínez et al., DJD 23, 120.

better interpreted as a trace of ink from the barest tip of the diagonal base stroke of this letter.[25]

Further verification can be given by another valuable technique, "letter cloning" and matching.[26] This technique involves copying a clear and complete letter (or set of letters) from elsewhere in the manuscript onto a separate layer and then superimposing this "cloned" version over traces of an incomplete or unclear letter (or letters) to see if there is a compatible match. This technique can also prove useful for testing proposed restorations in *lacunae.* Such a direct comparison, using letter examples in the scribe's own hand, is highly effective for verifying the feasibility of a proposed reading or restoration. In this case an *ayin* was "cloned" from the first letter in 11QtgJob 18:8 and moved into position over the traces on the two fragments (see fig. 9). As can be seen, the match is remarkably close.[27]

The choice of letters for cloning and comparison is a significant methodological concern. In this case I chose the *ayin* in 18:8 to the exclusion of other *ayin*s from elsewhere in 11QtgJob, including, for example, those in 17:5 and 17:6. Two criteria guided this choice. The first, letter environment, considers the position of a letter in a word or phrase, as well as what comes before and after it. Scribes do not write their letters in isolation: the way they write a given letter changes, depending on its position in a word (especially initial and final position versus medial position) and what letter(s) or spaces come before and after.[28] The *ayin* under consideration here is the initial letter of a word, and the scribe of 11QtgJob tends to write a larger, more elongated *ayin* at the beginning of a word than, for example, in a medial position. Thus the use of the medial *ayin*s in 17:5 or 6 as clones for comparison with the traces under consideration would lead to a mismatch — with the cloned *ayin*s significantly smaller than the proposed form to which they would be compared. In contrast, the word-initial *ayin*

---

25. It is often difficult to distinguish ink traces from skin variations in black-and-white infrared pictures such as those in the PAM series. However, visible-light color images often mark these subtle color distinctions. Hence, color images should be consulted when possible to facilitate fragment matching.

26. A term first coined in Zuckerman, "Every Dot and Tiddle," 193.

27. A standard imaging tool permits diminishing the opacity of the cloned letters to about 60 percent, to make them semitransparent, which facilitates comparison by allowing the traces to show through the overall shape of the clone letter to which they are being matched (or mismatched).

28. For an extensive discussion of letter environment, see B. Zuckerman and L. Dodd, "Pots and Alphabets."

in 18:8 is, if anything, slightly longer than the postulated form of *ayin* that is reconstructed across the join.

The other criterion, letter proximity, works on the methodological assumption that, once letter environment has been taken into consideration, the best choice for cloning is a clear letter or letter combination that is in closest proximity to the traces under consideration. The reason for this also has to do with scribal tendencies and what one might characterize as scribal drift. While professional scribes strive for uniformity and consistency in writing their letter forms, nonetheless over a number of columns their writing will tend to drift, perhaps due to physical or mental fatigue and perhaps to interruptions in their work. From a methodological standpoint, it is therefore better to choose letters for cloning and comparison that are physically closer to the traces that one wishes to analyze rather than to traces from a more remote location. How serious scribal drift will be in a given manuscript has to be judged on a case-by-case basis. Typically, especially if the hand is that of a professional, the drift will be minor and subtle (as is the case in 11QtgJob). Hence, as a general rule, letter environment should be given precedent over letter proximity, since the former tends to have far more significant impact on the way letters are made.

Comparison through cloning not only has a significant positive function — of showing what letters could make a proper match — but it also can demonstrate the opposite. The case at hand is instructive. Just to the left of the *ayin* we have been discussing is a trace of ink, apparently the upper tip of the succeeding letter. The DJD editors read this letter very tentatively as a *mem* and restore, עם[לא], translated "afflic[tion]," presumably rendering something akin to the MT's עני.[29] However, a combination of word-initial *ayin* followed by medial *mem* (cloned from the form עמך in 6:3) superimposed over the existing traces (see fig. 10) shows that the traces are incompatible with the cloned template. On the other hand, when one superimposes the combination of initial *ayin,* followed in succession by *nun* and *yod* (cloned from עני in 25:4; see fig. 11), the match looks quite compatible. This in turn suggests that the translator opted for a rendering cognate to the underlying Hebrew form.

This leads to another methodological consideration regarding the optimal use of cloned letters. To wit: It is generally better to clone and compare combinations of letters, rather than to make clone/comparisons using a succession of single cloned letters. This necessarily follows from

---

29. See García Martínez et al., DJD 23, 120-21.

the considerations discussed above in regard to letter environment. In the instances just noted, for example, one could simply choose single letters to clone and compare. To be sure, there is nothing wrong in a comparison of this sort *per se;* it is simply not as methodologically thorough as the recommended procedure. Of course, the beauty of working dynamically with cloned letters is that there is no limit to the approaches that can be easily tried and assessed. One can put the various clones on separate layers and then test and verify letter environment *and* letter proximity, using both single-letter and letter-combination comparisons.

Another example shows how employing cloned letters can help in reconstructing a text — even when the text is no longer there. This case involves 11QtgJob 27:6. The beginning of this line has been scratched out, although slight traces of at least two to three letters appear to be visible, including fairly clear traces of a *waw* at the beginning of the line (see fig. 12). The scratched-out area — which is uneven and presumably follows the letter shapes that are erased — divides into two parts of approximately four and three letter spaces respectively, with the surface area in between unaffected. It seems likely that two words or phrases are involved here and that the text should reflect some part of Job 34:11b, since text clearly reflecting the end of 34:11a is preserved at the end of the previous line. The MT of 34:11b reads, וכארח איש ימצאנו, lit., "and according to a man's way, he makes him find." Clone matches of the likely Aramaic equivalent — namely, וכארח אנש — fit strikingly well with the scratched-out areas, both in letter spacing and in terms of the precise areas scratched out and the few remaining ink marks (see fig. 13). This suggests that the copyist committed an error of dittography — writing the phrase twice — and then realized his error and erased the first phrase.[30]

Of particular note here is the area at the end of the first scratched-out word (where the *resh* and the *heth* should be).[31] The scratched-out area of

---

30. Another possibility is וכארח גבר since גבר is also used in the Job Targum as a reflex of Hebrew איש (see 38:7, 8 = MT 42:11, 12). Since אנש is employed in 24:5 as an apparent reflex of Hebrew אדם in v. 11a, the translator may have wished to vary his translation in 11b by using the alternate synonym. A cloned version of גבר (taken from 24:3, directly above) in lieu of אנש fits essentially just as well.

31. Cloning the letter combination כארח from 23:6 results in a slight mismatch in the scratched-out space, because of the width of the *aleph* in the cloned form. On the other hand, the letter combination ארח from 6:2 produces a good match. This should serve to underline that cloning is *not* a precise tool for text reconstruction but is rather a relatively reliable guide to help control and verify (or exclude) readings and reconstructions.

the presumed third letter seems to follow the shape of a *resh* (roughly an upside-down right triangle whose vertical side is on the right). In this respect, *resh* is not only the obvious letter for the space but just about the only letter (outside of *dalet*) that fits the space perfectly. As the cloned form makes clear, there is also the slightest trace of a vertical mark where the initial leg of a *heth* would have to be positioned. Being able to use cloned letters for close comparisons of this nature makes the development of text reconstructions far less speculative than would otherwise be the case. Indeed, one would hesitate to put forward this reconstruction without the aid of cloned comparisons to back up an otherwise highly speculative interpretation.

Finally, let us consider one further area of digital analysis: the graphic representation of textual data. Let me mark a distinction here between "graphic representation" and "drawing," since they are not always the same thing — especially in a digital environment. In fact, the latter might best be considered a subgroup of the former. Consider in this regard fig. 14, a "before-and-after" enhancement of a detail, once again from the *Genesis Apocryphon* (here col. 0, line 8). The image on the right is relatively unenhanced and thus somewhat difficult to read. The image at left shows a "cleaned-up" version of this same area, improved by the application of selected imaging enhancement tools from a standard Photoshop toolbox. The resulting "improvements" look very impressive. But there is more here than meets the eye — a good deal more. The tools employed to gain this result are known respectively as the "dodge" and "burn" functions. The "dodge" tool allows one to selectively lighten any designated area of the image, indeed areas as small as a few pixels; the "burn" tool allows one to darken a designated area with the same precision. Using these tools in tandem I have engaged in image manipulation on a microscopic level, selectively darkening and lightening areas of the image a few pixels at a time. The image looks essentially seamless, with no evidence for the hundreds of individual manipulations I used to "sculpt" the image on the left. An unwitting observer might simply attribute its clarity to the "magic" of computer imaging enhancement and accept it uncritically as a legitimate representation not only of what the reading should be but what it actually *is*.

But this type of imaging enhancement, known as "pixel editing," is a highly subjective process. Different scholars employing these same "dodge" and "burn" tools would be no more likely to come up with the same depiction of a text than they would if they were making separate drawings. And that is just the point. Graphic representations of ancient inscriptions — no matter how realistic they appear to the eye — are no less and no more reliable than conventional scholarly drawings, nor should they carry more legitimate weight. The reliability of a given drawing depends on the talent of the researcher — what epigraphers call an eye for form. But while the eye for form can be judged against a standard of excellence, it *never* should be accepted as reflecting a standard of objectivity. A graphic representation is simply one scholar's opinion: no more, and no less.

Pixel editing a text in this fashion may have heuristic value. One could imagine assigning students in an epigraphy course to do individual reconstructions of a given scroll or scroll fragment by employing the "dodge/burn" functions. Not only would this exercise give students a tangible grasp of the form and shape of letters, it would also serve — as drawings were compared and contrasted — to demonstrate how subjective interpretation can be — that one eye for form usually does not jibe as much as one might expect with another.

One can help control the process of graphic representation by using cloning as a guide. Let us return to 1QDaniel[b] to illustrate the point. The line just above the מלכא join and just to the right clearly contains a *shin* and a *dalet,* followed by traces of two other letters. Context leads one to conclude that these letters are best identified as a *resh* followed by a final *kap* to be read "Shadrach" (see Dan 3:26). To create a graphic reconstruction of this form, one simply clones a nearby *resh* and a nearby final *kap* and superimposes them appropriately over the partially preserved traces (fig. 15a). With these cloned letters as guiding templates, one can draw a more precise rendition (fig. 15b), adjusting for slight differences as appropriate. In the case of the *resh* this adjustment is miniscule, but for the final *kap,* one must assume that the scribe employed a slightly more curving downstroke here than in the cloned template, as he picked up his pen in anticipation of the next letter. Of course, this is a subjective assumption, but that is precisely what a graphic representation should show: how a given scholar chooses to represent the form and shape of letters he or she wishes to analyze.

Such an approach can be especially useful in graphically representing a text such as the *Genesis Apocryphon,* where, even in the infrared, the letter forms are often far from clear. Consider fig. 16, again taken from col. 0. The top image represents a reading (from line 5) in a relatively unenhanced form, for which only the lower portion remains, the tops of the letters being lost at the break. The bottom image is a complex graphic

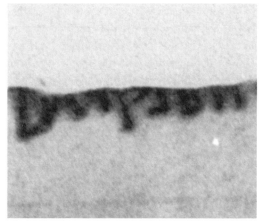

Figure 16. Detail from Column "Zero" of the Genesis Apocryphon. The image at top shows a relatively unenhanced form; the image below is a graphic representation of the same form made as the combination of a pixel-edited and drawn illustration.
(Photograph by Bruce and Kenneth Zuckerman, West Semitic Research. Courtesy Department of Antiquities, Jordan. Computer enhancements by Bruce Zuckerman)

representation: the preserved portion has been "cleaned up" through pixel editing, and the upper portion has been reconstructed as a drawing, using letter clones as templates. As long as the viewer knows that this reconstruction has been highly manipulated, it can serve a useful role in terms of presentation and analysis.

Note that I labeled the totally restored part of this reading a "drawing." As noted above, all drawings are graphic representations but not all graphic representations are drawings. To create a drawing, one actually makes specific lines delineating a representation. Before the advent of computer graphics, one conventionally did this rather painstakingly with pencils, pens, and paper — and to do this work well one had to have genuine talent as a scholar, epigrapher, and artist. With the advent of computer drawing, the first two prerequisites still apply, but the last becomes less essential. Indeed, anyone capable of digitally "connecting the dots" can do very sophisticated computer drawings that compare favorably with an artist's best work and, in terms of versatility, can do far more than even the best graphic artist could with traditional drawing tools.

The "paths" function in Photoshop and similar imaging programs provides the means of doing the best drawings in a digital environment. The paths "pen tool" permits a user to create control points over any part of an image. New points on the image are automatically connected in succession with straight or curved lines, which can be shaped and manipulated with great precision. Because these lines are mathematically-based vectors, they are unaffected by magnification, so one can use paths to do finely-detailed drawing and outlining, even at a microscopic level. Once a path or series of paths is created, it can be converted or rasterized with a wide variety of graphic functions into pixel-generated drawings and placed on separate layers, superimposed over an image. This makes paths the ideal tool for facilitating the illustration of letters in the DSS.

From a methodological standpoint, two uses of the paths function are most significant for illustrating letters: "stroking" and "outlining." Stroking works best for letter forms such as that found in fig. 17 (right), a detail of a letter *bet* from 3Q15, the *Copper Scroll*.[32] Because this letter is incised, presumably with a chisel or similar tool, its significant epigraphic and paleographic feature is the largely uniform fine line chiseled into the metal, equivalent to what Ada Yardeni has characterized as the "skeleton" of a letter; the width of the stroke does not add any significant material information.[33] In such a case, it is best to place a path so it will follow the fine chisel mark of the letter, delineating the skeleton, as it were, as shown in fig. 17 (middle). Once the path has been fine-tuned, the illustrator can "stroke" the image by instructing the program to make a line drawing of a given uniform width, with the path precisely in its middle (fig. 17, left). Note, by the way, that the the letter has been illustrated in red rather than in traditional "India ink" black. Photoshop and similar programs offer the illustrator a wide palette of easy-to-use colors. In a case like this the red

32. The *bet* is the initial letter of 8:10. The image comes from AWS 27, photographed by B. and K. Zuckerman in 1988. This specific image can be found in the InscriptiFact Image Database as ISF_DO_00803.

33. See A. Yardeni, *The Book of Hebrew Script*, 134. She notes: "the 'skeleton' . . . is the central line running through the strokes of the actual existing form."

stands out far more clearly against the background than black would; hence it is a better choice for purposes of illustration.[34]

Of course, most letters in DSS are inked on a flat animal skin surface, typically with a nibbed pen. In these instances, the width of the stroke does convey significant information, since it indicates how the pen was held in the scribe's hand and its angle to the writing surface as it was employed in the succession of strokes. The order and direction of strokes also convey essential information, since the movement of the pen in the scribe's hand — and how that movement changes over time — is the very essence of paleographic analysis.[35] Every letter tracks a movement that needs to be carefully considered, and the static presentation of a standard "pen-and-ink" drawing is simply incapable of conveying the dynamics of the pen's movement, the scribal *ductus*. In contrast, the utility, precision, and flexibility of digital drawing convey such information in a dynamic and intuitive fashion.

Here, the use of path outlines is particularly valuable. Instead of depicting the skeleton of the letter, one uses paths to delineate the outer edge of the individual strokes and then uses a command to fill in the space demarcated inside. Consider the paleo-Hebrew "parallel bar" *aleph* from 4Q22 paleoExodus^m (fig. 18).[36] One could illustrate this as in a pen-and-ink drawing, using paths to outline the letter shape and filling in with the traditional black. But such an illustration (see fig. 19) would convey only the most limited information about scribal *ductus* and, indeed, would not be much more useful than showing a detail of the letter itself. Instead, one might outline the three letter strokes of this *aleph* with individual paths and then fill in each stroke with contrasting colors — in this case, red for the first stroke made by the scribe, yellow for the second, and green for the third (see fig. 20). Put into separate layers, these strokes can be toggled on

---

34. Stroking is also generally preferable for characterizing the letters incised on stone stelas; here again one tries to place the path along the fine line of the chisel mark and then use a line approximately the average width of the incised line.

35. For further discussion, see, e.g., Yardeni, *The Book of Hebrew Script*, 157-61; and, more generally, Zuckerman and Dodd, "Pots and Alphabets."

36. The *aleph* is taken from the initial letter of אעלה from col. 38, line 33 (= Exodus 30:30). See P. Skehan, E. Ulrich, and J. Sanderson, eds., DJD 9, 125. The detail is taken from AWS 39, taken by B. and K. Zuckerman in 1988. It can be found on the InscriptiFact Image Database as ISF_DO_00708. The drawings that follow were originally created by the present writer to illustrate a study on the paleographic development of the Hebrew *aleph* in Zuckerman and Dodd, "Pots and Alphabets," 128, fig. 14d.

and off individually and superimposed in order, thus giving the viewer an intuitive grasp of how the illustrator reconstructs the stroke order (see fig. 21). The direction of the strokes can also be illustrated by drawing arrows (again, individually on separate layers) that indicate the motion of the pen as the illustrator interprets it. Since Photoshop and other similar programs have a custom command for making paths that depict arrows, their graphic representation is quite easy to do (see fig. 22).

In this fashion, one can convey considerable information about a scholar's interpretation of scribal *ductus*. An equivalent static drawing on paper would lack the facility of its digital counterpart: the ability to work dynamically and electronically to peel away any section at will; the option of building comparative script charts, by copying the forms and moving them to another electronic location; indeed, the possibility of superimposing a drawing directly over an image of a given letter, so that the reader can see with unrivaled precision how an epigrapher has read and interpreted its construction for purposes of paleographic analysis. The ability to document letters in this fashion has the potential to change entirely the way paleography is studied, for now the data can be made to reflect more precisely the dynamic motion of a scribal pen.

In concluding this study, I wish to make several points about the future direction of DSS scholarship in general and documentation in particular, in light of the dynamic opportunities that computer imaging offers for improving interpretation of these important texts. First, we need better image documentation of the DSS — much better documentation. The vast majority of our data is based on decades-old images, mostly from the "PAM" series. They are good for their time, but not really good enough on their own to allow scholars to take fullest advantage of the computer imaging techniques considered here. We need new images in the infrared spectrum, but also matching images in visible-light color and filtered visible-light black-and-white. Images also need to be done in far greater detail. How much detail varies, of course, depending on what scroll (or fragment) is being imaged. But, as a general rule, images should be sufficiently detailed so that the fine details (the order and direction of pen strokes, the follicle pattern on the skin, other subtle changes in texture) are clear. When feasible, images should be illuminated from the back as well as the front, since this is the only reliable means for distinguishing small cracks and holes that might otherwise be thrown into shadow and potentially confused with ink traces. When possible, both front and back of scrolls and scroll fragments must be documented. In other words, every effort should be focused on making the best image record possible.

A closely related point concerns leadership. In the documentation of the DSS, scholars — experts on the reading and decipherment of these texts — must be allowed to "call the shots." In the early history of scrolls study, scholars *were* the leaders of almost all the work physically done on the DSS, in particular, the team that worked on the scrolls originally housed at the Palestine Archaeological (later Rockefeller) Museum. They were the ones who opened them up and pieced them together. The magnitude of their collective scholarly accomplishment is now broadly acknowledged. However, it is also clear that the scrolls themselves suffered physically to some extent because conservators and preservationists were not involved as much as they should have been in the reconstructive work.

In more recent times, the pendulum has swung too far the other way. Today and in the more recent past, decisions and policies regarding the care and handling of the scrolls (e.g., how they are conserved, mounted, or prepared for display) have been and are being instituted with only the most limited consultation with the scholars who might actually wish to study and read them in the future. Such decisions have been driven by necessity in order to protect the documents. Nonetheless — and this cannot be emphasized too strongly — scholars need to be intimately involved in all decisions that may impact on the ability, now or in the future, to get the best image data from the DSS.

Of course, in order to be studied, these images must be properly distributed. It should be the policy of those charged with distributing DSS image data to make the best digital data available in high-resolution form to the scholars who need them in order to do their best work. Moreover, care must be taken to make sure that the image data has full and proper documentation. As we have seen above, digital data is all too easily manipulated so that images that look "authentic" may intentionally or unintentionally be skewed according to someone's subjective viewpoint.

In this respect, a distinction needs to be made between a "digital image" and what has come to be termed a "digital surrogate." The latter has sufficient documentation connected with it so that its user can properly track its "empirical provenance." As characterized, for example by Mark Mudge, Michael Ashley, and Carla Schroer, "Digital surrogates of our 'real world' cultural heritage can robustly communicate the empirical features of C[ultural]H[eritage] materials. When digital surrogates are built transparently, according to established scientific principles, authentic, reliable scientific representations can result."[37]

What is necessary for such "reliable scientific representations"? In the development of the image database InscriptiFact at the University of Southern California,[38] we have gone to great lengths to give detailed cataloguing information and extensive metadata on the inscriptions we distribute. These include the medium of the original image, the photographer, and where and when the image was made. If the image was originally on film, the metadata notes the kind of film, format, scanning method, resolution, and so on. Further manipulations to the image are noted as well. Without the support of careful and publicly accessible documentation of this nature, an image — especially in this digital age — could be made to show just about anything, with its user none the wiser.

There can be no doubt that the DSS have gained celebrity status; they are the "rock stars" of antiquity, especially in the public imagination. Yet we must never forget that the scrolls are more than simply the cultural icons they have become. They still have valuable information to reveal to us, and they are an essential, but far from fully exploited, resource for scholarship. It is entirely likely that, if they are properly documented, taking fullest advantage of the latest technologies, present and future, and if they are properly studied, taking fullest advantage of present and future digitally-driven analytic techniques, they will yet reveal a good deal more about the ancient world from which they have come.

37. M. Mudge, M. Ashley, and C. Schroer, "A Digital Future for Cultural Heritage," published online as http://www.c-h-i.org/events/CIPA_2007.pdf.
38. For further information on InscriptiFact, see http://www.inscriptifact.com/.

Methods and Theories in the Archaeology of Qumran

Jodi Magness

How does archaeology contribute to our understanding of the Dead Sea Scrolls? The answer to this question depends on one's interpretation of the site of Qumran. If, as some scholars claim, the scrolls were not deposited in the caves by the inhabitants of Qumran, they have no direct connection with the archaeological remains in the settlement. However, if one accepts (as I do) that the scrolls were deposited in the caves by the inhabitants of Qumran, archaeology can help us better understand the lifestyle and beliefs of this community. In fact, Qumran has numerous features that are unparalleled at other sites, which are best understood in light of sectarian halakhah and especially a concern with purity issues. Rarely, I believe, does archaeology so clearly reflect a system of religious beliefs and practices.[1]

The History of Qumran Archaeology

The site of Qumran attracted little scholarly and popular attention before the 1990s (see Fig. 1). Rising interest in Qumran archaeology since then is largely the result of increased public awareness of the Dead Sea Scrolls. During the 1980s, scandals surrounding delays due to alleged Vatican or scholarly conspiracies were widely publicized by the media. By the early 1990s, all of the Dead Sea Scrolls had been "freed" — that is, photographs

---

1. For a general overview and further discussion, see J. Magness, *The Archaeology of Qumran and the Dead Sea Scrolls.*

Figure 1. View of Qumran looking south.   (Courtesy of Jodi Magness)

of all of the scrolls, even those that were still unpublished, were made widely accessible to scholarly readers. This basically put an end to the conspiracy theories surrounding the scrolls, but the controversies surrounding Qumran were just beginning.

Until the 1980s, the interpretation proposed by Roland de Vaux (who directed the excavations at Qumran in the 1950s) was widely accepted among scholars. According to this interpretation, the site of Qumran was inhabited by the same community that deposited the scrolls in the caves. These people were members of a Jewish sect that de Vaux and others identified with the Essenes mentioned in ancient historical sources. This consensus was shaken by a pair of Belgian archaeologists, Robert Donceel and Pauline Donceel-Voûte. The Donceels had been invited by Jean-Baptiste Humbert, who is now the staff archaeologist at the Dominican Ecole Biblique et Archéologique Française (the French School of Biblical Studies and Archaeology in Jerusalem) to help prepare the material from de Vaux's excavations for publication. In a *Nova* television special about the Dead Sea Scrolls that was broadcast in 1991, the Donceels dropped a bombshell: in their opinion, Qumran was not a sectarian settlement as de Vaux believed, but a *villa rustica* — a country villa! Although the Donceels left the project without completing their study of the material, they published several articles with their interpretation.[2] Since then a number of scholars have proposed other interpretations, arguing that Qumran was a fort, a manor house, a pottery production center, or a commercial entrepôt.[3] Although none of these alternative theories has gained widespread acceptance, they have succeeded in calling into question the validity of de Vaux's interpretation.

One problem surrounding the archaeology of Qumran is that a full and final scientific report on de Vaux's excavations has never been published. Although he wrote several detailed preliminary reports (published in French), and a general overview of the archaeology of Qumran (translated into English), de Vaux died in 1971 without having published all of the material from his excavations.[4] In Israel, there is an unwritten but universally accepted custom that once a site is excavated, the material from that excavation (and sometimes even the site itself) "belongs" to the excavator. This means that the excavator has sole authority over the publication of and access to the material from the excavation. If the excavator dies without having published the material, it is "inherited" by the excavator's home institution. When Yigael Yadin died in 1984, for example, the unpublished material from his excavations was inherited by his home institution, the Hebrew University of Jerusalem. Together with the Israel Exploration Society, they divided the unpublished material from Yadin's excavations at Hazor and Masada among faculty members at the Hebrew University's Institute of Archaeology, who were put in charge of overseeing the publication process. This same procedure caused the delays in the publication of the Dead Sea Scrolls, which belonged to the members of the original team that de Vaux had assembled. These scholars had the right to reassign the publication of their material (for example, to their students) and grant or deny access to it.

In 1991, universal access to the Dead Sea Scrolls was made possible because the Huntington Library in San Marino, California, which has copies of all of the scrolls on microfiche, decided to make them universally available. This is not the case with the material from de Vaux's excavations at Qumran. No "copies" exist of the archaeological artifacts from Qumran, most of which are now stored in the basement of Jerusalem's Rockefeller

2. See, e.g., P. Donceel-Voûte, "Les ruines de Qumran réinterprétées."

3. See J. Magness, review of Y. Hirschfeld, *Qumran in Context;* review of K. Galor, J.-B. Humbert, and J. Zangenberg, eds., *Qumran: The Site of the Dead Sea Scrolls.*

4. For the English overview, see R. de Vaux, *Archaeology and the Dead Sea Scrolls.*

Museum. The unpublished artifacts and records from de Vaux's excavations are also inaccessible to anyone without Humbert's permission. Although we still await a final excavation report, in 1994 Humbert and Belgian archaeologist Alain Chambon published a large volume described as the first in a series.[5] This volume contains original photographs from the time of de Vaux's excavations, plans (line drawings) of the excavated areas, and de Vaux's original field notes. The original edition, in French, has been translated into German and English.[6] A second volume containing scientific studies (anthropology, physics, and chemistry) of some of the remains from Qumran was published in 2003.[7]

What is archaeology, and what excavation methods do archaeologists use?

The Oxford Companion to Archaeology defines archaeology as "the study of the past as evident in the material remains available to us."[8] In contrast, history is the study of the past based on information provided by written documents. In other words, although both archaeologists and historians study the past, they use different methods and different sources to obtain their information. These sources of information often provide different (although not necessarily mutually exclusive or conflicting) pictures of the past. For example, since many texts were written by or for the ruling classes (elites) of ancient societies, they tend to reflect their concerns, interests, and viewpoints. In contrast, although archaeologists often uncover the palaces and citadels of the ruling classes, they also dig up houses and workshops that belonged to the poorer classes of ancient societies. Archaeological evidence can be used to complement or supplement the information provided by written records, and in cases where we have no written records (such as in prehistoric societies), it is our only source of information.

Some ancient sites were occupied for only one brief period or phase. However, many sites in Palestine were occupied over longer periods. At such multiperiod sites, the buildings and debris from the successive phases of occupation accumulated, forming a series of levels, one above the other like a layer cake. In the case of many biblical sites in Israel, there can be twenty or more different occupation levels, forming an artificial mound

5. J.-B. Humbert and A. Chambon, eds., *Fouilles de Khirbet Qumrân et de Ain Feshkha I.*

6. For the English edition, see Humbert and Chambon, *The Excavations of Khirbet Qumran and Ain Feshkha;* also see a review of this volume by J. Magness.

7. J.-B. Humbert and J. Gunneweg, *Khirbet Qumran et 'Ain Feshkha II.*

8. B. M. Fagan, ed., *The Oxford Companion to Archaeology,* 42.

called in Hebrew a *tel* (Arabic *tell*). Archaeologists refer to these occupation levels as strata (sing. stratum) and to the sequence of levels as stratigraphy. At Qumran, we can distinguish at least three successive occupation levels (which de Vaux called periods) in the sectarian settlement (first century B.C.E. to first century C.E.).

Although it is helpful to visualize the strata of ancient sites as a layer cake, the reality is never that neat and simple. Ancient inhabitants frequently disturbed earlier levels when constructing the foundations of new buildings or when digging pits. In the course of such activities, they cut into or through earlier strata, churning up earlier material, such as potsherds and coins, along with the dirt and stones they dislodged. This means that at multiperiod sites we always find earlier artifacts mixed in with the later material. For this reason, we use the latest artifacts to date the stratum we are excavating and disregard the earlier material (at least for dating purposes).

Imagine that we are standing inside a modern school building in Philadelphia that was built in 1972. When the school was built, a deep pit (trench) was dug into the ground for the foundations. At the time the floor was laid, it sealed the foundation trench and everything in it. If we dig under that floor today, we should find nothing later than 1972 in the fill. However, we would almost certainly find objects dating from before 1972 in that fill, such as old Coke bottles, coins dating to the 1950s and 1960s, and so on. Now suppose that the latest datable object we find under that floor is a penny minted in 1968. This coin would provide what archaeologists call a *terminus post quem* (Lat. "date after which") for the construction of the school. In other words, the coin would tell us that the school was constructed in 1968 or later, but not earlier. Now suppose that the school was destroyed by an earthquake in 1985, which caused the building to collapse, burying everything inside. The objects found on top of the floors would represent those items in use at the moment when the building collapsed. They would also provide us with a *terminus ante quem* (Lat. "date before which") for the construction of the school. That is, if the latest objects found buried in the collapse were books printed in 1985, we would know that the school building must have been constructed on or before that date. One of the most famous examples of such a catastrophic destruction is the eruption of Mount Vesuvius in 79 C.E., which buried Pompeii and Herculaneum in volcanic ash and mud. Walking through the excavated streets of those towns today gives us a glimpse into what they looked like at the moment of their destruction.

During the course of excavation, archaeologists destroy the evidence they dig up: once a shovel of dirt or a stone is removed from the ground it can never be put back in the same way. For this reason, archaeologists record the excavation process using every means possible. Visitors to an excavation might notice that archaeologists dig in squares measuring 5 by 5 or 10 by 10 meters on a side. The squares form a grid and are separated by banks of earth about one meter wide called baulks (or balks). This system enables archaeologists to measure and record the exact location of every excavated object and feature (feature here means something that is constructed, as opposed to an artifact, which is a portable, manmade object). The recording is done by measuring levels (absolute heights within the excavated squares), keeping daily diaries, making drawings and taking photographs, and now with the aid of computers. Ideally, once a final excavation report is published, it should be possible for the reader to reconstruct the site as it looked before everything was dug up.

Archaeologists use various devices to keep track of the point of origin, or provenance, of every excavated artifact and feature by subdividing each square horizontally and vertically. One of the most common subdivisions used in excavations is a *locus* (Lat. "spot" or "place"; pl. *loci*). In archaeology the term locus can be used to designate any excavated feature: an oven, a pit, a room, or any part of a room. It is simply a device to help subdivide the area being excavated, to enable us to later pinpoint the exact spot where an artifact or feature was found. For example, imagine that we begin excavating a square on top of the modern ground surface. We would give the entire square one locus number (L1 = locus number one). About ten centimeters below the ground surface, we notice that the soil is changing in color and composition, from reddish brown to dark brown mixed with lots of stones. At this point, we would measure the absolute height (with the same kind of equipment used by surveyors) and change the locus number (from L1 to L2). Five centimeters below this, we begin to come upon a line of stones cutting diagonally across the square which looks like the top of a wall. We would again measure the absolute height and change the locus number, giving the areas on either side of the wall different locus numbers (L3 on one side and L4 on the other). The pottery and other objects discovered during the course of excavation would be saved and labeled according to their context.

This system of excavating and recording is the standard one used by archaeologists working in Israel today, with minor variations from excavation to excavation. Because this system has evolved over time, not all of the elements were used by earlier generations of archaeologists (just as this methodology will undoubtedly be refined by future archaeologists, especially as new technologies develop). Although de Vaux used locus numbers at Qumran, he used the same locus number to designate a single room from the beginning to the end of the excavation, instead of changing the number as he dug through different levels or distinguished different features in the rooms. Although some scholars have recently criticized de Vaux's excavation techniques, it is important to remember that he was working according to the methods used in his time. Ten years after de Vaux's excavations at Qumran, Yadin excavated at Masada using locus numbers in the same way to designate a single room for the duration of the excavation. At the same time (in the early 1960s), a University of Missouri expedition at the late Roman site of Jalame in Galilee did not use locus numbers at all; instead they used trench numbers. And as at Qumran, we have few section drawings (drawings of the stratigraphy visible in the baulks) from the Masada and Jalame excavations.

How do archaeologists date the remains they dig up?

When we excavate an ancient house, what objects or artifacts can we find that will tell us when it was built, occupied, and destroyed or abandoned? The types of objects that provide an accurate date should fulfill one of two criteria: (1) the object must be a very common find on archaeological excavations; or (2) it must carry its own date. The main methods of dating used by archaeologists specializing in Roman Palestine include: (1) radiocarbon dating (sometimes called carbon 14 or C^{14} dating); (2) coins; (3) inscriptions or other written materials found in excavations; (4) ancient historical sources; and (5) pottery (ceramic) typology.

Before we discuss each of these dating methods, we should note that this list does not include human or animal bones, tools, or architectural styles. Although human and animal bones can provide much useful information (animal bones, for example, can tell us about the ancient environment, and human skeletons can provide information about ancient populations), they cannot be dated unless enough collagen is preserved for the purposes of radiocarbon dating. The skeletons from the cemetery at Qumran do not contain enough collagen to be radiocarbon-dated.

Tools are another matter. Stone tools used by prehistoric populations can be dated according to their type in a manner analogous to the dating of pottery. But once pottery appears in Palestine (ca. 5000 B.C.E.), it replaces stone tools as a preferred method of dating, because pottery has greater chronological resolution and because stone tools become rarer over time. On the other hand, tools made of bronze or iron are not common finds on archaeological excavations because all metals were precious and costly to manufacture in antiquity. Once broken, metal tools were not discarded but were repaired or melted down for reuse. Nearly all of the classical Greek statues of the fifth and fourth centuries B.C.E. were made of bronze, and most disappeared long ago because they were melted down and made into something else. All we have left today are later Roman copies in stone of the original Greek masterpieces and rare examples of bronze originals, most of which have been recovered from ancient shipwrecks. In addition, because metal tools tend to be utilitarian they change very little in shape over time. An ancient iron pick from Cave 11 at Qumran looks just like a modern one. For these reasons metal tools are not useful for dating even when they are found in excavations.

What about architectural styles? Although archaeologists sometimes use distinctive architectural styles (or tomb types) as a means of dating, this can be done accurately only in rare instances. This is because once an architectural style was invented it could be copied or imitated by later generations. Some modern banks and court buildings, for example, are constructed in a revivalist Greco-Roman (Neoclassical) style. However, most of the remains archaeologists dig up are not that distinctive. The construction at Qumran is very simple, consisting mostly of uncut field stones and mudbrick.

Now let us consider the dating methods listed above. Each method has its own advantages and disadvantages.

1. Radiocarbon (Carbon 14) Dating

The Oxford Companion to Archaeology defines radiocarbon dating as "an isotopic or nuclear decay method of inferring age for organic materials."[9] This method works by measuring the amount of carbon 14 that is present in the remains of plant or animal matter. Carbon 14 is a radioactive isotope of carbon 12. All plants and living creatures contain carbon 14 while they are alive, and when they die, they begin to lose the carbon 14 at a steady rate: approximately half of the carbon 14 is lost every 5,730 years (the "half-life" of radiocarbon). Consider a piece of charcoal that archaeologists find in an excavation. By measuring the amount of carbon 14 in it, a lab can determine roughly when the tree from which the charcoal came was chopped

9. Fagan, The Oxford Companion to Archaeology, 586.

down. A type of radiocarbon dating called accelerator mass spectrometry (AMS) can be used for dating smaller samples of organic matter.

Radiocarbon dating has the advantage of being the only "scientific" method listed here, in the sense that it generates a date that is provided by a laboratory. However, it has the disadvantage that every date returned by the lab has a plus/minus range, or margin of statistical error. There is a 67 percent chance that the date provided by the lab falls within the plus/minus range. A date of 4000 plus/minus 100 would mean that our tree was chopped down roughly 4,000 years ago, with a 67 percent chance that it was chopped down within a range of 100 years either way (the accuracy goes up if the range is doubled). Radiocarbon dates are conventionally published in the form of uncalibrated radiocarbon years "Before Present" (BP), with present measured from 1950 C.E., approximately when radiocarbon dating was invented. Conversion of these dates to calendar years requires calibration because of past fluctuations in the level of carbon 14 in the atmosphere; calibration can increase the range of a radiocarbon date.[10]

For these reasons, radiocarbon dating is most useful in cases where there are no other methods of dating, such as prehistoric sites in Europe or Native American sites in the United States. It is less useful at a site like Qumran where we have other, more accurate methods of dating available. On the other hand, radiocarbon dating has been used effectively on some of the scrolls and linens from the caves around Qumran. In this case, radiocarbon dating is useful because these objects do not have a stratigraphic context (they come from caves instead of from a series of dated layers at an archaeological site). Radiocarbon dating confirmed the second century B.C.E. to first century C.E. date that paleographers (specialists in ancient handwriting styles) had already suggested for the scrolls; this date is also consistent with the pottery types found with the scrolls in the caves.

Another disadvantage of radiocarbon dating is that it can be used only on organic materials, which are exactly the kind of materials that are rarely preserved in ancient sites. The arid conditions inside the caves around Qumran preserved the Dead Sea Scrolls, which are made of parchment (animal hide). In contrast, nearly all of the organic materials at Qumran (which would have included wooden furniture, rugs, woven mats and baskets, clothing, leather footwear, and perhaps even scrolls) were consumed by the fire that destroyed the settlement.

10. For an explanation of radiocarbon dating and calibration, see http://c14.arch.ox.ac .uk/embed.php?File=calibration.html. See also the chapter by Martin Abegg in this volume.

Although other laboratory-based methods of dating exist, I do not list them here because they have not been used at Qumran. These include dendrochronology, or tree-ring dating, and potassium-argon dating (which is used to date igneous or volcanic rock).

2. Coins

Coins have the advantage of carrying their own date. However, there are also disadvantages associated with coins. First, coinage was not invented in the Mediterranean world until about 600 B.C.E. This means that coins do not exist at Mediterranean sites that antedate the sixth century (or in other parts of the world such as North America until much later). Second, coins in antiquity often remained in circulation for long periods — up to hundreds of years — after they were minted. Although this is especially true of precious gold and silver coins, it can also be true of lower value bronze coins. For this reason, finding a coin that was minted in 100 C.E. on the floor of a house can be misleading: it is possible that the coin fell onto the floor as much as one or two hundred years later. It is best to use more than one coin when possible or coins plus other methods of dating to obtain an accurate date. Third, because coins were valuable, ancient people were careful not to lose them. This means that it is possible to excavate a level at a site and not find any coins at all. Fourth, since most ancient coins are tiny pieces of bronze, they have often corroded to the point where the date can no longer be read. Although some of the coins that de Vaux found at Qumran were illegible, there were also many identifiable coins, including a hoard of silver sheqels (Tyrian tetradrachmas).

3. Inscriptions or Other Written Materials Found in Excavations

Although this type of object is an archaeological find because it comes from an excavation, it falls into the category of historical materials because it contains a written text. Qumran is an unusual site because of the wealth of written materials, which include the scrolls found in the nearby caves as well as a small number of ostraca, or inscribed potsherds, from the site. The scrolls from Qumran are an exceptional find, preserved due to the arid conditions of the region.

4. Relevant Ancient Historical Sources

These can be helpful for dating when they are available. For example, the Hebrew Bible is often used as a source of information by archaeologists excavating Iron Age sites in Palestine. In the case of Qumran, we are fortunate to have three valuable sources of information: Flavius Josephus, Philo Judaeus, and Pliny the Elder. When de Vaux found that Qumran was destroyed at some point during its existence by an earthquake, he was able to date this event to 31 B.C.E. because Josephus mentions that a strong earthquake affected the Jericho region during that year.

5. Pottery

This is the only type of object in this list that does not carry its own date. Instead, pottery is dated through the construction of typologies. Here it is useful to imagine that we are excavating a multiperiod site with ancient occupation levels (strata) one above the other. In the lowest stratum, we find a certain type of bowl with red-painted decoration. In the next stratum up (the middle level), we find a different type of bowl with rounded walls and a flat base. In the uppermost stratum, we find another type of bowl covered with a black glaze. We can now construct the following relative typology (that is, a relative sequence of types): the bowl with the red-painted decoration is the earliest type; the bowl with the rounded walls and flat base is the middle type (in date); and the bowl with the black glaze is the latest type. We determine the absolute date of these pottery types based on the dated objects found in association with them. For example, if we find coins minted by Augustus together with the bowl with the red-painted decoration, in the same stratum, we can assume that this type of bowl dates to the first century or later. And if in the future we find that same type of bowl at the next site down the road, we will know its date.

Dating pottery in this way is a complex process, for not only do pottery types change over time but they vary among geographical regions. When I was working on my dissertation I found that the types characteristic of Jerusalem and Judea in the fourth to seventh centuries C.E. are completely different from those of the same period in Galilee. In addition, certain types are better chronological indicators — they can be more closely dated than others. The best types for dating purposes are fine wares and oil lamps, which tend to change in form and decoration fairly quickly. Fine wares are the dishes that were used for dining, including table wares such as cups, plates, and bowls. Fine wares and oil lamps are often decorated, although this is not always the case, as at Qumran where the table wares are undecorated. In contrast, utilitarian types such as storage jars and cooking pots tend to be plain and are more difficult to date precisely. We refer to undecorated utilitarian types as coarse wares. Because of their utilitarian nature, such coarse wares display little change in shape over long periods.

Pottery typologies must be constructed for different sites in different geographical regions and for every period and every vessel type. This has to be done on the basis of carefully excavated, multiperiod sites that provide sequences of levels and associated pottery types. Sometimes people wonder how ceramics specialists can tell different types apart. After all, couldn't the same types have been imitated in later periods? In fact, this is not true of pottery. The combination of shapes, clays, firing processes, and decorative techniques yields a unique product. This means that even if a shape was precisely duplicated in a later period (and this rarely happened), the combination of other factors would yield a visibly different product. For example, even a nonspecialist can tell the difference between modern imitations of Greek black-figured vases (such as those offered for sale in tourist shops in Athens) and the originals displayed in museums.

Why do archaeologists go to so much trouble to date pottery? Why not rely on other methods of dating? The reason is simple: pottery is ubiquitous at archaeological sites. In antiquity everyone owned it, whether they were rich or poor. And pottery that is fired in a kiln can be broken but otherwise is virtually indestructible. This means that an archaeologist might excavate a structure in which no organic materials were found for radiocarbon dating, no coins were found, and there were no inscriptions or ancient historical sources to provide information. But if we find nothing else, we know we will find potsherds — and lots of them — at archaeological sites in Palestine. And if we can date the pottery, we can date the levels we are excavating.

Although it is possible to date pottery using scientific techniques such as luminescence dating, these are expensive and have been employed little if at all for the pottery of Roman Palestine. Other techniques such as petrography and neutron activation analysis are more commonly used in Israel to determine the source of the clay used to manufacture pots. Some of the pottery from Qumran has been subjected to these types of source analyses, with varying results.

What are the limitations of archaeology?

Archaeologists can often determine the date and function of the buildings and installations that we dig up, based on the artifacts found in them and on comparisons with other sites. From certain types of archaeological remains, such as burials and cultic installations, we can make inferences about ancient people's belief systems. But there are some kinds of information that archaeology alone cannot provide. For example, the kilns and other remains in the southeast corner of the settlement at Qumran indicate that this was a potters' workshop. But was this pottery produced by the sectarian inhabitants of the settlement, or does this workshop indicate that Qumran was a pottery production center and not a sectarian settlement, as has recently been suggested? My belief that this community manufactured its own pottery because of purity concerns is based on information provided by the scrolls and ancient historical sources, not by archaeological evidence (Fig. 2). In other words, here I use literary information to better understand the archaeological remains.

Archaeology is not an exact science; it involves human behavior, both past and present. Present behavior includes the variable of interpretation. Excavation itself is an act of interpretation, since archaeologists must decide which site to excavate, which part of the site to excavate, and so on. Even when an entire site is excavated (and this occurs rarely, although de Vaux uncovered nearly all of the settlement at Qumran), the remains archaeologists dig up represent only a small part of what originally existed. Rarely do we find preserved such organic materials as wooden furniture, carpets and rugs, ceilings and roofs made of wood or reeds, clothing, or other objects made of organic materials (such as wooden dishes and utensils, mirror cases, jewelry boxes, combs, spindles, wood-frame looms, and woven baskets). And, of course, the original human and animal inhabitants have not survived. Usually, the last or latest levels of occupation at a site (those at the top) are better preserved than earlier levels below. This means that archaeologists reconstruct a picture of the past based on very incomplete information. The incomplete nature of the archaeological remains makes it possible for the same evidence to be interpreted differently, as illustrated by the various interpretations of the settlement at Qumran.

If this is the case, how is it possible to judge which interpretations are valid or reasonable? It is difficult for scholars who are not archaeologists (such as Scroll specialists) and virtually impossible for others to judge the validity of different interpretations, because this requires a certain level of expertise. Nonspecialists would have a difficult time evaluating the pottery

Figure 2. Dishes in the "pantry" (L86) adjacent to the communal dining
room (L77) at Qumran.   (Courtesy of the Ecole Biblique et Archéologique
Française de Jerusalem)

evidence that I have cited in my discussions of Qumran, just as I do not
have the expertise to independently evaluate many of the arguments concerning the scrolls. As a general rule, the interpretation that solves the
most problems or accounts for the greatest percentage of the evidence is
probably the correct one.

I am sometimes asked whether we would interpret Qumran as a sectarian settlement had the Dead Sea Scrolls not been found. I have two answers to this question: (1) No, we would probably not interpret Qumran as
a sectarian settlement without the scrolls, although I doubt we would interpret it as a villa, fort, or anything else, either. I think it would be an
anomalous site, because it has too many features that are unparalleled at
other sites, including the animal bone deposits, the multiplicity of large ritual baths *(miqva'ot),* and the adjacent cemetery (see Fig. 3). (2) More importantly, why would we want to disregard the evidence of the scrolls, as
advocates of the alternative interpretations have attempted to do? Qumran
provides a unique opportunity to use archaeological evidence combined
with information from ancient historical sources and the scrolls to recon-

Figure 3. Miqveh (L48-49) at Qumran. (Courtesy of Jodi Magness)

struct and understand the life of a community. Why would we disregard the scrolls or use only part of the evidence instead of all of it — especially when the scrolls and our ancient sources provide information that complements the archaeology? Furthermore, archaeology establishes the connection between the scrolls in the caves and the settlement at Qumran, since the same types of pottery (including types that are unique to Qumran) are found in the scroll caves and in the settlement. In addition, some of the scroll caves are accessible only from inside the settlement.

Current Debates Surrounding the Archaeology of Qumran

The interpretation of Qumran as a sectarian settlement depends on whether one accepts or rejects the association of the scrolls with the site. Simply put, scholars who accept the connection between the scrolls and the site identify Qumran as a sectarian settlement; this is true regardless of whether these scholars identify the sectarians as Essenes or not. This school of thought is sometimes described as "consensual" or consensus. Scholars who reject the identification of Qumran as a sectarian settlement (the "nonconsensual" or nonconsensus school of thought) must argue that there is no connection between the scrolls and the site. According to this view, the inhabitants of Qumran did not own and use the scrolls or deposit them in the nearby caves.

A pronounced element of postmodernism underlies the nonconsensual school's interpretation of Qumran. This is evident in the prioritizing of the archaeological evidence and the rejection of any connection between the scrolls and the site. As a result, Qumran is ripped from its social-religious-historical context, leaving us with the archaeological remains alone: stones, potsherds, coins, glass, and so on, taken in isolation. Although these remains provide certain types of information (for example, the presence of a large number of miqva'ot suggests a concern with ritual purity), they cannot inform us about the religious beliefs and ideology of the inhabitants of the site (it is only from the scrolls that we learn that the sect was concerned with ritual purity because they conceived of their community as a substitute temple). Without the scrolls, the archaeological remains are ambiguous enough to support any of a variety of possible interpretations of the site.

Denying any connection between Qumran and the scrolls automatically creates ambiguity — a situation in which Qumran can be interpreted in any one of a number of ways and all interpretations are equally valid. This is another reflection of postmodernism, according to which no one interpretation is correct and all interpretations have equal value. I would argue that the exact opposite is the case. Qumran could not have been a sectarian settlement *and* a villa, or a fort, or something else — at least, not all at the same time. Although it is possible to interpret both the literary and archaeological evidence in different ways, only one interpretation is supported by a majority of the evidence, and only one interpretation creates a minimum number of problems. If one rejects the connection between Qumran and the scrolls, one must explain how the scrolls came to be deposited in caves immediately below the settlement at the same time the site was occupied. Some scholars claim that the scrolls were brought from the Jerusalem temple before the Roman destruction in 70 C.E. and deposited in the caves around Qumran. However, much of the literature from Qumran expresses opposition to the (non-Zadokite) priestly establishment in Jerusalem and therefore could hardly have originated there. Many of the works from Qumran reflect a distinctively sectarian outlook, including a different calendar than the one used by other Jews at the time and different interpretations of halakhah.

Similar postmodern tendencies underlie the minimalist-maximalist debate raging over the origins of the Israelites and the nature of the United Monarchy.[11] The minimalists reject any element of historicity in the biblical accounts. This removes the archaeological remains from their historical and religious context, making it possible to argue for different ranges of dates and for different interpretations (for example, that the kingdom of David and Solomon was just a small chiefdom, and that the monumental building remains traditionally associated with them date to a later period).

We have developed a reluctance to be critical even when criticism is constructive or necessary. Ironically, this is one outcome of our multicultural society, which recognizes and celebrates diversity. Although the notion that all opinions matter is fundamental to public discourse in a democratic society, this attitude has negatively impacted the field of Palestinian archaeology in general and Qumran archaeology in particular. Whereas in the realm of public opinion and discourse all views might be considered equally valid and important, the scholarly endeavor requires an ability to determine the relative value and validity of different kinds of evidence and interpretations through a rigorous process of critical evaluation.

Although postmodern trends have helped set the stage for the current controversies surrounding Qumran, not all (or even most) advocates of alternative interpretations are necessarily influenced by a postmodern approach. Furthermore, the fact that postmodernism creates a situation that allows for different interpretations of Qumran does not excuse poor scholarship, sloppy research, or the selective presentation of data. Sensationalism — the desire to create headline-making news — has also fueled the Qumran controversies. Books and articles suggesting that Qumran was not a sectarian settlement, or which describe Vatican and scholarly conspiracies, or claim that Jesus lived at Qumran have been highly publicized, as illustrated by the media hype surrounding the recent announcement that Qumran was a pottery production center.[12]

11. For examples of the different views, see http://www.bibleinterp.com/articles/Contra_Davies.htm and http://www.bibleinterp.com/articles/copenhagen.htm.

12. See M. L. Grossman and C. M. Murphy, eds., "The Dead Sea Scrolls in the Popular Imagination" (1-5) and the accompanying articles.

The Sectarian Settlement at Qumran

The settlement at Qumran appears to have been established around 80 B.C.E. by a group of Jewish sectarians. This sect seems to have formed initially around the mid-second century, when the Zadokites lost control over the priesthood in the Jerusalem temple. Apparently the sect was established by one branch of the Zadokite priesthood, although not all members (or even leaders) were Zadokites. They called themselves by various names including the Yahad and the Sons of Light. Others including Josephus, Philo, and Pliny referred to them as Essenes, a Greek and Latin term. Members of the sect lived in towns and villages around the country, including in Jerusalem, and some practiced desert separatism. Qumran was one such community; we do not know whether there were others.

This was an apocalyptic sect which believed that the end of days and the beginning of a messianic era were imminent. One of the peculiarities of this sect is that they anticipated the arrival of not one but two messiahs. To the usual royal messiah descended from David they added a priestly messiah descended from Aaron, not surprising in light of the priestly orientation of the sect. They believed that the end of days would be preceded by a forty-nine-year long war between them (the Sons of Light) and everyone else (the Sons of Darkness). Another peculiarity of this sect is that they believed in predeterminism. Therefore, the apocalyptic war and its outcome — victory for the Sons of Light — were preordained by God. The Qumran community's apocalypse arrived in 68 C.E., when the settlement was destroyed during the First Jewish Revolt against the Romans. They disappear afterwards from the stage of history.

Because the sect was established by dispossessed Zadokite priests, they did not recognize the current Jerusalem priesthood as legitimate. They believed those priests were impure and unfit to serve. They considered the temple polluted and refused to participate in the sacrifices offered there. Instead they constituted their community as a substitute temple, with each full member living in imitation of the priests serving in the Jerusalem temple. This meant maintaining the highest level of purity required in Judaism, which required avoiding contact with anything or anyone at a lower level of purity and necessitated frequent immersion in miqva'ot. To be admitted as a full member, one had to pass through a series of stages of initiation, attaining with each stage a higher and higher level of purity. The sect universalized a priestly lifestyle to all of its full members. They consumed only pure food and drink and wore white linen garments like the priests in the temple. The sect expected that they would one day regain control of the Jerusalem temple and reinstitute the sacrifices as they saw fit. In the interim, they considered participation in their communal meals to be a substitute for participation in the temple sacrifices.

In de Vaux's time Qumran appeared to be unique because few sites in the Dead Sea region had been excavated. The excavation and publication of many more sites since then — including Herodian Jericho, Ein Boqeq, Ein Gedi, Herodium, Masada, Kallirrhoe, and Machaerus — further highlight the unique nature of Qumran. Only at Qumran do we find such a large number of miqva'ot (and in large sizes) relative to the size of the settlement, and only there do we find animal bone deposits, a large adjacent cemetery, communal dining rooms with adjacent pantries containing hundreds of dishes, numerous workshops, and an unusual ceramic repertoire (including the distinctive cylindrical jars). These features are physical expressions of this community's priestly lifestyle and peculiar halakhah, which involved maintaining the highest possible level of ritual purity. This is why these features are unparalleled at other sites. Rarely does archaeology so clearly reflect a system of religious beliefs and practices.

Dead Sea Scrolls and the Historiography of Ancient Judaism

Hayim Lapin

In 1996, during excavations at the site of Qumran, two ostraca — pieces of pottery with writing on them — were found inscribed with documentary texts.[1] Of these, one (KhQ2) has proven largely uncontentious, if only because so little can be read from it. The other (KhQ1) has garnered a fair amount of critical attention. Its official editors, Frank Moore Cross and Esther Eshel, discovered the text to be of central importance. The text was a conveyance of property, including a house and a slave, to the community (*yaḥad*) on the completion of the donor's trial period. Thus, in one shot were solved some of the central problems of Qumran scholarship: the habitation site at Qumran *was* connected with the caves; the sectarians *did* live out their lives in conformity with the rules in the scrolls, at least to the extent of trial memberships; and members *did* cede property to the common ownership.

Almost immediately, Ada Yardeni challenged, among other things, the reading of the crucial words "when he fulfills (his oath) to the *yaḥad*," seeing it instead as a pedestrian reference to "every other tree." Among the lessons we could draw from this clash of titans (Cross is one of the founders of Hebrew and Aramaic paleography at Qumran, Yardeni among its most important and prolific practitioners), I wish to highlight the problem

1. "Documentary" is shorthand for texts such as deeds, contracts, accounts, or letters, as opposed to "literary" texts (e.g., histories, hymns, rule texts). In the case of the Qumran caves, literary texts make up the vast majority of material recovered. For the ostraca (esp. KhQ1), see F. M. Cross and E. Eshel, "Ostraca from Khirbet Qumran"; "Khirbet Qumran Ostracon," DJD 36; A. Yardeni, "A Draft of a Deed on an Ostracon from Khirbet Qumran."

of what scholars read into the Qumran material and what they claim to be able to read out of it. Cross and Eshel provide what we might call a very expansive reading. In the line with *yaḥad*, for instance, they interpret the first word as a phonetic misspelling of a verb with an assumed object — hence "(his oath)" is in parentheses — while "community" is restored from three broken letters, one of which, they note, does not match the way the scribe wrote the same letter elsewhere in the document. Yardeni's reading is rather more restrictive, less confidently asserting the presence of letters (with far fewer deemed visible at all), and frequently marking alternative readings in the transcription itself.

Yet we cannot call one reading "subjective" and the other "objective," one based on "interpretation," the other on "just the facts." Both Cross and Eshel and Yardeni import — and appropriately so — data from outside the ostracon into their reading of it: their knowledge of paleography, of Hebrew grammar, of the history of the Hebrew language and Semitics, and of the forms and formulae expected in a document of this type. The source of the problem is instead the fragmented and effaced document itself, which requires such investment of scholarly interpretive energies. In interpreting artifacts such as this, it is harder to go wrong if one does not commit to too expansive a reading, but harder too to uncover new information. But with too assertive an interpretation it is easy to go badly wrong, by allowing a reading so brilliant that it simply must be true.

1. What Is Historiography?

It is useful to keep this example in mind as we examine how a historian of ancient Judaism might read the Dead Sea Scrolls. For present purposes I define historiography very generally as *a disciplinary practice using data to produce knowledge about the past*. It is "disciplinary" because professional historians — whether they understand themselves to engage in a kind of social science, a mode of interpretive analysis of texts, or a reconstruction of narratives about the past — are trained in graduate school, and in turn train others, to work with characteristic materials and to ask of those materials characteristic questions (e.g., about chronology, social structure, episodes of war, revolution, or political change). Despite recent blurring of disciplinary boundaries (which find anthropologists and literary scholars doing history, or historians doing ethnography), history remains for the most part an empirical discipline providing localized analyses of phenomena occurring in specific places and times as documented by identifiable sources and eschewing too strong a dependence on abstract explanatory theories.

Historians, especially those working on the modern period, typically favor data collected from particular kinds of sources: written or printed texts rather than objects of material culture, and archival or documentary texts rather than literary. As with the range of topics historians work on, however, the field is thankfully far less rigidly constructed in practice. For historians of premodern periods, preserved documentary sources are rare and archives (in most times and places) rarer still. Consequently, historians of ancient Judaism, and of Mediterranean antiquity more generally, must work with a range of sources, mostly literary texts, but also inscriptions, coins, pottery, other material artifacts, and the evidence of the built or worked environment. Individual historians may gain considerable expertise in, e.g., paleography, numismatics, pottery analysis, agricultural anthropology, demography, and so on, but the more technical the area the more likely it is that the historian (like other specialists on the ancient world, such as archaeologists) will need to rely on analyses provided by others.

In asking historical questions of chosen source material, historians produce knowledge about the past. Social history (itself now quite a venerable area of research) rose to prominence in the mid-twentieth century as an attempt to address a different order of data and to provide a different kind of knowledge from "old fashioned" political or narrative history.[2] The "older" historiography focused primarily on states, wars, and elites (or so it was characterized) and generated knowledge in the form of narratives, detailing the unfolding of events, their causes, and the motivations of principal actors in time. By contrast, social historians aimed to write history "from the ground up," consciously seeking out data about the lives of workers, peasants, and the poor, and often about their clashes with elites (in food riots, factory strikes, etc.). Thus, social history often produced structural rather than narrative results: the payoff was not so much the elucidation of chronology or of the intentions of important individuals, but the identification of the parties (often collective: peasants, rebels, villagers) and their goals within social and economic structure and class, frequently in conflict. In part, the nature of the documentary sources encouraged this approach, but so did the direct or indirect influence on social

2. See C. Conrad, "Social History."

historians of Marx's and Engels's view that underlying social structure and its internal conflicts were the real motors of history.

While historians strive to establish facts about the past ("as it actually happened," *wie es eigentlich gewesen ist,* in the expression of Leopold von Ranke, d. 1886), what they at best succeed in producing is a normative disposition toward a reconstruction of the past as fact. Certain reconstructions become standard parts of the educational curriculum and required reading for graduate students, and they define the way subsequent research projects get carried out. But reconstructions and therefore "knowledge" can be and regularly are overturned. Only a few decades ago the standard reconstruction for the history of the Dead Sea sect was the Essene Hypothesis: scholars knew that the sect was more or less identical with the Essenes as described in Josephus, Philo, and Pliny the Elder. That view continues to be prominent today but competes with a major modification of it (e.g., Florentino García Martínez's "Groningen Hypothesis")[3] and alternative reconstructions that reject the connection with Essenes altogether,[4] in addition to theories that are outliers in current scholarly discussion.[5] Along the same lines, the association of the site of Qumran with the caves where the Dead Sea Scrolls were found has long been challenged by Norman Golb and more recently by stalwarts of the Israeli archaeology establishment.[6]

Historians of ancient Judaism and of modernity share the need to interpret their sources, to convert them, as it were, from source material into "data," and from data into "knowledge." There is, of course, no document or artifact so transparent that it can communicate without interpretation, and the production of knowledge always requires a balance of "reading in" against what we might "read out." The ostracon mentioned above is an extreme case, because scholars must constitute the very source material from which they wish to derive the data. As a consequence, we can read nothing more out of the artifact (e.g., the finances of the yahad), than we have literally already read into it.

---

3. F. García Martínez and A. S. van der Woude, "A 'Groningen' Hypothesis of Qumran Origins and Early History"; García Martínez and J. C. Trebolle Barrera, *The People of the Dead Sea Scrolls*, 77-96.

4. E.g., L. H. Schiffman, "The New Halakhic Letter (4QMMT) and the Origins of the Dead Sea Sect"; A. I. Baumgarten, "Who Cares and Why Does it Matter? Qumran and the Essenes Once Again."

5. E.g., R. H. Eisenman and M. O. Wise, *The Dead Sea Scrolls Uncovered*, 9-15.

6. N. Golb, *Who Wrote the Dead Sea Scrolls?* Y. Magen and Y. Peleg, *The Qumran Excavations 1993-2004;* Y. Hirschfeld, *Qumran in Context.*

The project of constructing the sources has been central to scrolls scholarship from the beginning. Scholars perform this at the elementary level of joining fragments, deciphering letters, filling in lacunae, and assigning dates to manuscripts on the basis of paleography.[7] At a deeper level of construction, scholars may propose hypotheses about the origins and development of the works they study, as well as the textual transmission, redaction, and change evident in the manuscripts of those works.[8]

In this, Qumran scholars are hardly unique. The necessity of reconstruction is shared especially with epigraphers (scholars of inscriptions on stone and other media) and papyrologists (who study ancient texts preserved on papyrus and other writing materials), as well as with other fields. Similarly, in offering hypotheses about the prehistory of their texts to account for their present states, they follow paths long trodden by scholars of Hebrew Bible, New Testament, and classics. For the Qumran scrolls, the sheer number of manuscripts and the fact that scholars rely overwhelmingly on paleography for dating make the research problem especially acute.[9] Nor does the problem permit of a definitive solution: in making arguments about the history of the Dead Sea Scrolls and their writers and preservers we are always in the realm of more or less plausible but ultimately circular reconstructions, rather than of conclusive proof. To reconstruct history requires both a delicacy and a considerable self-awareness. Both should warn us away from overly naïve readings of our sources (harmonizing diverse traditions within the Dead Sea Scrolls with no less diverse accounts of Essenes), but even more from overly strong theories that remove all doubts about the dates of the manuscripts, the identity of the Teacher of Righteousness, or the prehistory of the sect.

2. From the Manuscripts Outward

The two sections that follow examine two areas of the history of the Dead Sea sect. The first focuses on the corpus of manuscripts as a whole and asks what kinds of social-historical questions can be asked about it. The second

7. On the scholarly construction of manuscripts, see Eibert Tigchelaar's contribution in this volume. See also F. M. Cross, "Palaeography and the Dead Sea Scrolls," revisiting a subject for which he wrote the classic essay.

8. On source and redaction criticism, see Charlotte Hempel's chapter in this volume.

9. B. Webster, "Chronological Index of the Texts from the Judaean Desert"; G. Doudna, "Dating the Scrolls on the Basis of Radiocarbon Analysis."

examines some aspects of the question of origins, with a particular focus on the "Essene Hypothesis."

Let us begin our discussion of the manuscripts with what we think we know. Between eight hundred and one thousand manuscripts were discovered in eleven caves near the site of Khirbet Qumran. A substantial number of manuscripts (716 by "official" numbers) have been assigned *ranges* of dates on the basis of paleography. (For example, 1QH^a, the *Hodayot* scroll from Cave 1, is thought to have been written in the period 30-1 B.C.E.) Figure 1 (see p. 114) approximates the distribution of those manuscripts by fifty-year periods. To obtain this data, I began with the summary information in DJD 39 and then divided the number of manuscripts in each paleographic range of dates by the number of years in the range, proportionally assigned the results to fifty-year periods, and totaled the number of manuscripts for each half century.[10] The results are in no way "objective": by definition, they collapse paleographical assessments made over the course of half a century by many scholars of varying expertise and with sometimes conflicting standards (consider that Cross and Eshel dated the hand of the KhQ1 Ostracton to "late Herodian," while Yardeni dated it to "early Herodian," a half century earlier or more). Additionally, any biases in the practice of paleography in general are reproduced in the chart.[11]

A further example of bias — the introduction of nonpaleographic factors into manuscript dating — appears in the dating of the latest manuscripts. Thirty-two manuscripts have been assigned date ranges that end with 68 C.E. — not because of any paleographic endpoint but because that is the year when the Qumran habitation site is thought to have been destroyed by the Romans. For the chart in Fig. 1 this assignment has only minor consequences, but this choice complicates any possible reconstruction of the relationship between the manuscript history and the occupation of the site, which is already far from clear. The chart also incorporates a few

10. For the figures see Webster, "Chronological Index," 371-75, Table 375. Where single year dates were assigned at the border of a fifty-year period (e.g., 50 C.E.) I have divided the manuscripts between the two fifty-year periods. While my total number of mss. matches his (Table 4b, p. 370), I cannot square the subdivision there with the subdivision in Table 5. In cross-referencing Webster's tables I have occasionally reassigned an individual ms. to a different chronological range (see, e.g., 4Q164, moved from "Early Hasmonaean" to "Early Herodian"). Chronological assignments vary greatly (see Webster, 356-62).

11. For the argument that paleography at Qumran works with inherent biases see G. Doudna, "The Legacy of an Error in Archaeological Interpretation."

Figure 1: Qumran Manuscripts by Paleographic Date

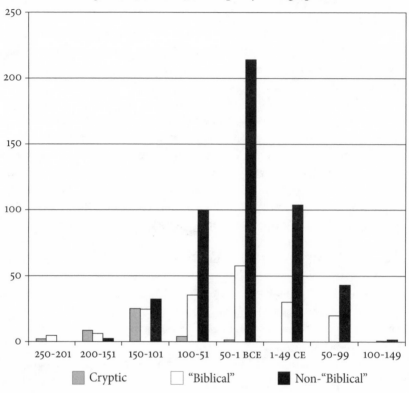

Source: B. Webster, "Chronological Index of the Texts from the Judaean Desert," in *The Texts from the Judaean Desert: Indices and an Introduction to the Discoveries in the Judaean Desert Series* (ed. Emanual Tov; *DJD* XXXIX; Oxford: Oxford University Press, 2002), 351-446 (adapted). N=716 (Cryptic, 41; "Biblical," 178; Non-"Biblical," 497*).

items assigned paleographically to a period that extends into the second century C.E. (one "biblical" and two non-"biblical"). The consensus view holds, probably correctly, that no new manuscripts were added after 68 C.E. Still there was a late- first- and early- second-century occupation at the site (de Vaux's Period III), including coins from the Bar Kokhba revolt (presumably implying occupation by Jews), and second-century manuscripts cannot be entirely excluded. (The second-century deposits associated with Nahal Ḥever, but probably from Wadi Seiyal [Nahal Ṣe'elim], included a Greek manuscript of the Minor Prophets, 8ḤXIIGr, DJD 8.)

Given these limitations, it is nonetheless interesting to note that both the "biblical" and the non-"biblical" manuscripts show a decided peak in the second half of the first century B.C.E. (50-1 B.C.E.). Although the term "Bible," if taken to mean a uniquely authoritative canon, may be an anachronism in this period, there is nevertheless a utility to distinguishing these texts. Whoever produced and/or commissioned and then deposited these manuscripts did so for non-"biblical" texts in larger numbers and at a faster rate of increase than for the texts we now understand as biblical. The difference is already noticeable in the first half of the first century B.C.E., where the number of non-"biblical" manuscripts triples (from 32 mss. to 100; for biblical mss. the increase is "only" 40 percent) from the half-century preceding. Together, the biblical and nonbiblical manuscripts from these two half centuries (100-1 B.C.E.) account for about 57 percent of the entire corpus of paleographically dated manuscripts.

The right side of the graph appears to show a pattern of decline similar to that of growth at the left. However, the production and deposit of manuscripts is widely assumed to have been interrupted by the revolt. It is tempting to speculate that but for the revolt the difference between the first half and the second half of the first century C.E. might have been less severe, and biblical manuscripts in particular might have remained fairly level, or even seen an increase.[12]

Significantly, of the manuscripts checked for individual date ranges, none reflecting the specific sectarian identity of the scrolls community (e.g., the pesher texts, the various rule texts, or *Miqṣat Maʿaśe Ha-Torah*) dates from before 100 B.C.E.[13] By contrast, we do find early manuscripts of, e.g., books of the Bible or *1 Enoch*, which might be described as "legacy"

---

12. This is more strongly suggested if we group the data by twenty-five-year periods, where the period from 1-75 C.E. holds fairly steady. In fact, for the period 26-50 C.E. there are more "biblical" and non-"biblical" mss. than in the 25 years preceding; reduction occurs in the period 51-75, in which 68 C.E. falls. It is unclear how much biases like setting a terminal date of 68 affect this distribution.

13. 4QH[b] (4Q428) and 11QFragment Related to Serekh ha-Yaḥad (11Q29) may push us back to the late second century B.C.E. (see Webster, "Chronological Index," 388). I have checked the "official" date ranges of texts listed in DJD 39 under: Community Rules (1.3.1), Eschatological Rules (1.3.2), MMT (1.3.5), Hodayot and Hodayot-like Texts (1.5.2.1), and the entire range of Eschatological Texts (1.8). See A. Lange and U. Mittmann-Richert, "Annotated List of the Texts from the Judaean Desert Classified by Content and Genre," DJD 39, 131-32, 138, 141-42. For a discussion of how to identify "sectarian" documents, see D. Dimant, "The Qumran Manuscripts: Contents and Significance." For dating, cf. M. O. Wise, "Dating the Teacher of Righteousness and the *Floruit* of His Movement."

documents: important for, but not exclusive to, the group itself. Here a word about the "cryptic" texts is in order. As Steven Pfann has dated them, they almost all fit within the pre-100 B.C.E. period, with a peak in the late second century B.C.E. However, only one manuscript unmistakably belongs with the "sectarian" documents (4Q298), and it is dated by the conventional Hebrew script used for its title to the late first century B.C.E.[14]

3. Toward a Social History of the Scrolls: A Sketch

What might a historian do with all of this? Qumran scholars typically focus either on the historical underpinnings of the foundation myths of the movement and the personalities mentioned in them or on the development of texts and sectarian ideas. In both cases the weight of scholarly discovery is on the time before the founding of the site, in the early Hasmonaean period or earlier. As an alternative, I propose that the present assemblage of *manuscripts,* which may not have begun until the first century B.C.E., be a principal starting point, even if some of the *works* in the manuscripts, perhaps even many, predate that period.

The relationship of the Dead Sea Scrolls to the site of Khirbet Qumran continues to be the subject of intense discussion. In general, I have accepted Jodi Magness's arguments for associating the caves and the settlement largely on the grounds of the distinctiveness of the Qumran pottery assemblage and the connections in pottery between site and caves.[15] The periods of intense manuscript production and the appearance of manuscripts with characteristically "sectarian" documents both coincide with Magness's revised date of initial occupation for the site of Qumran (i.e., beginning about 100 B.C.E.), as well as the chronology of Yizhak Magen and Yuval Peleg, despite their differing interpretations of

---

14. See S. Pfann, DJD 36, 522-23. The benchmarks for chronology are two manuscripts with titles in conventional script (4QMidrash Sefer Moshe [4Q249], mid-second century B.C.E., and 4Q298, late first century B.C.E.). 4Q249 and 4Q317 were radiocarbon-dated. Pfann (523) took the results to imply a date in the early to mid-second century B.C.E.. Subsequent retesting suggests a range extending to the mid-first century B.C.E., with a midpoint toward the end of the second century B.C.E.; Doudna, "Qumran Manuscripts," 470. Using computer-assisted searching, Pfann (516, summary 534-43) argues that it is possible to identify a substantial number of fragments with known texts, most significantly with 1QSa, one of the "sectarian" documents otherwise not attested in manuscript before 100 B.C.E.

15. See J. Magness, *The Archaeology of Qumran and the Dead Sea Scrolls,* and her contribution to this volume.

the remains at the site.[16] The difference in manuscript assemblage between the first century B.C.E. and the first C.E. also corresponds roughly to an archaeological transition dated by Magness to the period after 9/8 B.C.E.[17] By contrast, the documents seem unlikely to have been deposited by refugees or to reflect the library of the Jerusalem temple at the time of the revolt of 66.[18] If such were the case, we would have expected the evidence to reflect ongoing manuscript production and to peak nearer that date.[19]

Qumran scholars within the consensus view that associates the site with the scrolls differ over whether the caves, particularly Cave 4, served as an active library or a depository of documents no longer in use, on analogy with the medieval Cairo Genizah.[20] In either case, the number of manuscripts preserved from the last half century B.C.E. is surprisingly high. By the method used to compile the chart, 272 dated manuscripts belong to this period, or an average of about 5.5 manuscripts a year, of which about 4.3 were non-"biblical." Factoring in the corresponding proportion (38 percent) of manuscripts without paleographical date adds as many as two additional manuscripts yearly. And if the caves represent a depository of "inactive" scrolls — with another "active" corpus of manuscripts in use elsewhere — then the total number produced or acquired by the community would be higher still.

This quantity of manuscripts is striking, for several reasons. Let us grant for the moment that the Qumran community was a closed intentional community of sectarians putting into practice some form of ritual

16. Magness, *The Archaeology of Qumran and the Dead Sea Scrolls,* 63-68; Magen and Peleg, *The Qumran Excavations 1993-2004,* 28-32.

17. See D. Stoekl Ben Ezra, "Old Caves and Young Caves," for the suggestion that "old" caves may have been emergency deposits, which went out of active use after the crisis at the end of the first century B.C.E.

18. Magen and Peleg, *The Qumran Excavations 1993-2004,* 64-65; Golb, *Who Wrote the Dead Sea Scrolls?,* 143-150.

19. Cf. however, the scroll fragments at Masada, arguably brought by "refugees" from Qumran. The fragments are for the most part dated to the late first century B.C.E. but range from the second century B.C.E. to the first C.E. For ms. dates, see S. Talmon, ed., *Masada VI,* 20, 37, 40, 53, 60, 79, 92, 157, 117, 120, 106, 101, 134, 138ff, 136. This would give it the profile of one of the "old" caves as delineated by Stoekl Ben Ezra, "Old Caves and New Caves." Stoekl Ben Ezra (private communication) has suggested that the manuscripts from Masada might be due for reassessment of paleographic dates.

20. Library: Dimant, "The Qumran Manuscripts," 35-36; L. H. Schiffman, *Reclaiming the Dead Sea Scrolls,* 54-57. Depository: E. Tov, "The Nature of the Greek Texts from the Judean Desert," favored by Stoekl Ben Ezra, "Old Caves and New Caves."

and purity regime that corresponded to the documents in the caves. The wealth of legal material makes this a reasonable guess, although differences in legal traditions among texts and among recensions of the same legal texts make any reconstruction of such a regime difficult at best. In any case, the presence of large numbers of manuscripts produced at a rapid rate immediately requires us to consider the intertwined issues of the community's wealth and its connections with the "outside" world.

Producing manuscripts in antiquity was not cheap, and the cumulative cost of the Qumran manuscripts would have been substantial. We have no direct measure of cost, but a rough calculation suggests that a single large manuscript like the *Isaiah Scroll* from Cave 1 (1QIs) would have had a cost equivalent to several weeks of day-labor.[21] It is possible that individual members contributed manuscripts, which implies that they had the resources to acquire them; if manuscripts were obtained collectively, then the community must have been able to draw on a treasury or on members' benefactions. It is possible, also, that members of the community did the writing themselves without remuneration. (If so, we might then have hoped for greater material evidence for scribal activity — at present amounting to three inkwells — among the small finds at Qumran.)[22] Even in that case, papyrus was used as a writing material and was almost certainly imported from Egypt (directly? through merchants in Jerusalem?), which required both funds and trade connections.

A large leather or parchment scroll like the *Isaiah Scroll* would probably have required the hides of several animals.[23] Preparation of animal skins for writing might have been done by members of the community, but nothing indicates that they were prepared on the site (Jean-Baptiste Humbert's interpretation of vats at ʿAin Feshkha as tanning vats can be no more than speculation). Leather preparation is dirty, smelly work,[24] and for the people of the scrolls it was also affected by purity concerns.[25] It might, therefore, be

21. The calculation is made on the basis of *relative* prices in Diocletian's *Edict on Prices* from 301 C.E.; S. Lauffer, ed., *Diokletians Preisedikt*, supplemented, for papyri, with N. Lewis, *Papyrus in Classical Antiquity*, 131-134.

22. See, conveniently, Hirschfeld, *Qumran in Context*, 97, fig. 46. De Vaux had also reconstructed furniture for a "scriptorium," although this is less convincing.

23. For the size of commercially available skins today (almost certainly larger than ancient animals) see, e.g., http://talasonline.com/info/TalasCatalog.pdf, accessed 30 October 2007.

24. Cf. *m. B. Bat.* 2:9; *m. Ketub.* 7:7.

25. 4QMMT B 22-23; unfortunately, too damaged to be certain what is at issue.

work better carried out by others. Even if carried out by members, the community would need a source of sheep or cattle, either in the form of stocks owned by members or the community itself or acquired by other means. (This is true also of the buried animal remains found around the site.)

Similar tendrils of outward-reaching economic connections are implied by some of the Qumran pottery. Magness notes that neutron activation analysis (NAA) showed that cylindrical "scroll" jars from the caves — one of the distinctive markers of the Qumran site — were among items produced from Jerusalem clay.[26] We have to imagine one of several scenarios: residents bringing clay they have mined themselves, purchasing processed clay in Jerusalem, or transporting whole pots. At the same time, there is substantial evidence for some local forms of production, including pottery kilns, a press of some sort,[27] agricultural and other tools,[28] a mill installation,[29] and enough date pits to hypothesize the cultivation and processing of dates.[30]

The complex itself, particularly the water system, shows a substantial degree of sophistication — expertise I would associate with paid artisans rather than volunteer labor. It also required a massive amount of lime for plaster and considerable human effort and fuel. At some phase of its history, the site had one or more arches and several well-formed columns (based on the number of column bases, capitals and drums found in reuse), a paved floor with well-cut paving stones (*perhaps* used in Roman-style *opus sectile*), and other elements of formal Hellenistic and early Roman architecture.[31] Again, this implies skilled artisans and substantial resources. Among the artifacts are lathe-turned limestone vessels — the product of skilled artisanship and possibly brought from elsewhere — and glass, including, surprisingly enough, unformed glass for use in glass-blowing locally.[32] These artifacts and architectural remains thus tell

26. Magness, *The Archaeology of Qumran and the Dead Sea Scrolls,* 74.

27. Hirschfeld, *Qumran in Context,* 138-39.

28. Locus numbers given in J. Magness, *Debating Qumran,* 134, n. 102.

29. J. B. Humbert and A. Chambon, eds., *Fouilles de Khirbet Qumrân et de Aîn Feshkha I,* Photos 295, 296, 300, Locus 100.

30. Magen and Peleg, *The Qumran Excavations 1993-2004,* Preface and passim; H. Eshel and Z. Safrai, "Economic Life," in Schiffman and VanderKam, *Encyclopedia of the Dead Sea Scrolls,* 228-33.

31. Much of this is summarized by locus number in Magness, *The Archaeology of Qumran and the Dead Sea Scrolls,* 69; further detail in A. Chambon, "Catalogue des blocs d'architecture localisés ou erratiques."

32. Summarized in C. M. Murphy, *Wealth in the Dead Sea Scrolls and in the Qumran Community,* 328-29.

us something about the cultural expectations of the inhabitants of the site. If Magness is correct that the columns and other architectural features date to before 31 B.C.E. (and were brought down by an earthquake in that year), the disappearance of that decorative construction in her (and de Vaux's) Period II (beginning 4-1 B.C.E.) may reflect changes in the aesthetic requirements or the economic capacity of the inhabitants at that point.

Whoever lived at Qumran also had access to good quality silver coinage: a hoard of 561 coins, mostly Tyrian tetradrachmas.[33] Whether or not it was set aside for the temple tax (in my opinion, an unnecessary assumption), this is a substantial accumulation of funds. For a sense of scale, consider that a (now notional) Tyrian tetradrachma was equated in the early second century with 4 Roman denarii (cf. *P. Yadin* 47), and a sample of sales of houses or of agricultural land from the Judaean Desert documents yields prices of 112 and 160 denarii (*P. Yadin* 2, 3, 97/98 C.E.) and of 30, 50, and 100 denarii (*P. Mur.* = DJD 2, 30, 22; *P. Yadin* 47, 131-134 C.E.). To get these coins, people had to exchange lower-value coins through a money changer (and pay an exchange fee) or else might have sold products at a sufficiently high volume to warrant payment in silver, which they then selected out and stored. In either case, collectively if not individually, inhabitants had access to substantial sources of wealth and something to exchange for silver.

These sources of wealth may have been the fruit of labor and production at the site, but the finds at Qumran suggest another kind of resource as well. The ostracon found in 1996 (KhQ1), whatever its ambiguities, does appear to be a deed gifting real property (fruit-bearing trees following Yardeni, a house and slave following Cross and Eshel). The deed was executed at Jericho (l. 2), again linking people at the site to activities and property elsewhere. Additional fragmentary documentary texts are associated with Cave 4 at Qumran (4Q342-360), although that identification has been called into question.[34] If the remaining documents do belong to Qumran, however, they reinforce the suggestion that the inhabitants were propertied.

To return to the manuscripts, finally, their volume and the intensity with which they were produced suggest a literate readership. Literacy may be presupposed in the instructions in the *Community Rule* that groups of

---

33. Magness, *Debating Qumran,* 73 n. 47 for references.
34. Yardeni, DJD 27, 298.

ten take turns taking on the role of searching the torah (דורש התורה) con-
tinuously, while the whole group gathers for a third of every night "to read
in the book, and search the law, and to recite blessings together (or: as a
yaḥad)" (1QS VI 6-8).[35] In our era we take literacy for granted. Failure of a
proportion of the population to read is generally viewed as a social problem. In the Hellenistic and Roman worlds (and not uniquely so!) such an
assumption simply does not apply. Nor did literacy correlate smoothly
with wealth or social status.[36] Trained slaves or low-status functionaries,
for instance, might take on the menial tasks of reading and writing, such as
record-keeping or letter-writing for a wealthier householder with little or
no facility with written words. The training to read sophisticated literary
texts, however, is a presumptive marker of elite status.

What does all of this evidence suggest? Our social-historical investigation, provisionally assuming the connection of the site and the caves,
highlights property ownership, literacy, and (at least at one phase) elite
taste. This should not be entirely unexpected: A. Baumgarten has argued
that it is precisely among the not-poor that we should expect the formation
of movements such as that of the Dead Sea Scrolls. At the same time, this
conclusion should not be taken as the end of a research program, but as its
beginning. Other complex evidence remains unexamined (the age and
makeup of the cemetery, for example), and some of our examined evidence must still be put into proper perspective (how do we interpret the
hoard of 561 silver coins? for a single household, it would be impressive; as
the collective purse of a community it would be less so).

In addition, due concern must be given to the limitations of an argument about social location. To a great extent, what we learn reflects the
limitations of our sources: given the patriarchal character of the late Hellenistic and early Roman Levant, the stratification of society, and the distribution of literacy, we should expect to learn from literary sources primarily about literate, propertied males. Nevertheless, social location is a point
of departure, from which the specific concerns of the group, its identity, its
politics, and its origins can be studied. It also offers us points of compari-

---

35. L. H. Schiffman, *The Halakhah at Qumran*, 32-33, 56-60, arguing that forms of
דרשה have the technical implication of "study."

36. See the encyclopedic treatment in C. Hezser, *Jewish Literacy in Roman Palestine*,
although with little direct application to the Dead Sea Scrolls. See also the brilliant discussion of the implications of mass illiteracy for the literature of early Christianity in
K. Hopkins, "Christian Number and Its Implication"; K. Haines-Eitzen, *Guardians of Letters*;
W. V. Harris, *Ancient Literacy*.

son. In what ways, for instance, do Qumran people differ (or not) from their contemporary Judeans, from non-Judeans, or from later Jews with similar wealth and literacy profiles?

4. Reintegrating the Scrolls into the History of Palestine and Judaism

The purpose of beginning with the manuscripts as historical artifacts is that these are easier to locate in place and time (scholarly disputes notwithstanding) than are the putative origins of the group that produced them or the ideologies reflected in them. But this approach does not replace the study of the texts, either as such or in the larger social and religious history of Jews and Palestine. I wish to close this essay with a number of methodological notes about how a history of the Dead Sea sect should be written.

a. The Question of Origins

The first century B.C.E. is of central importance in the foundation of both the Qumran habitation site and the cave deposits. The late second and first centuries are also significant within the scrolls themselves. In the *Nahum Pesher* (4Q269), despite the persistence of coded language (Manasseh, Ephraim, the Wicked Lion), we have what is among the few unambiguously datable events in the life of the sect responsible for the scrolls: an episode in the reign of Alexander Jannaeus (104-76 B.C.E.) in which Demetrius III invaded Palestine on the invitation of Jannaeus's enemies, whom Jannaeus subsequently crucified (Josephus, *Ant.* 13.377-83). The pesher, a characteristic Qumran commentary, dates from no earlier than the mid-first century B.C.E., since it refers to the coming of the Kittim (or Kittiyim), usually code for the Romans, who first actively intervened in Palestinian affairs in 63 B.C.E. Indeed, it is striking that almost[37] the only identifiable political figures mentioned in the Dead Sea Scrolls appear to have flour-

---

37. Exceptions include Antiochus (IV?) in 4Q169 3-4 i 3; seemingly, a list of high priests going back to the Bible and including Hasmonaeans (4Q245), the nonspecific Ptolemy or Ptolemies in 4Q578 2, 3, 4, and Jonathan the brother of Judah the Maccabee (d. 152 B.C.E.) in 4Q523 1-2, 2 (note that Jannaeus, too, is possible, and one should allow for an unknown Jonathan).

ished at the end of the second to the middle of the first century: Demetrius (as mentioned), Alexander Jannaeus (4Q448, possibly 4Q523 1-2, 2), Salome (4Q331 1 ii 27 [and in the same document, possibly a reference to John Hyrcanus I, 1 i 7]; 4Q332 2, 4), Hyrcanus II (4Q332 2, 6), and Aemilius Scaurus, the governor of Syria appointed by Pompey (4Q333 1 4, 8). The latest is likely to be Peitholaus (4Q468e 3, identification uncertain), who, according to Josephus, was active in support of Aristobulus II, the son of Jannaeus, in the 50s C.E. The most curious and unexpected is 4Q448, an unfortunately fragmentary hymn of praise for "King Jonathan" (if we are to judge by titulature, more plausibly Jannaeus than the High Priest Jonathan of 50 years earlier).[38]

Josephus first writes of the Pharisees and Sadducees as factions in Judea in the context of the reigns of John Hyrcanus and Salome (and in the deathbed recommendations of Jannaeus). The episode told of Hyrcanus has the hallmarks of an aetiological legend told from a viewpoint sympathetic to the Pharisees: how it came about that Jannaeus followed the views of the Sadducees. There is, however, nothing in Josephus's narrative up to that point to suggest that the Pharisees or Sadducees would have had influence over a Hasmonaean priest or anyone else.[39] By contrast, Josephus's discussion of Pharisees under Alexandra is a piece of political propaganda of a different kind that construes the Pharisees as a real political force taking advantage of a weak monarch to pursue a religious and political agenda (*Ant.* 13.408-15; *B.J.* 1.110-12). A reconstruction of sect-formation should, I think, take seriously the early first century as the context for sectarian activism, conflict, disappointment, and alienation.

The second-to-first century transition also seems to be significant for another element in the history of piety in Judaea. According to Ronny Reich, purpose-built ritual baths *(miqva'ot)* appear in the archaeological record precisely then, and Reich links this phenomenon chronologically and ideologically to the use of stone vessels and to secondary inhumation in stone ossuaries.[40] At the least, ritual bathing and stone vessels seem to

38. Compare M. B. Abegg, "A Concordance of Proper Nouns in the Non-Biblical Texts from Qumran," DJD 39, 234-35; Wise, "Dating the Teacher of Righteousness," 76-81; G. Vermes, "Historiographical Elements in the Qumran Writings."

39. Josephus inexplicably inserts a notice that there were three schools among the Jews into the history of Jonathan the Hasmonaean: *Ant.* 13.171-73. In his earlier *Jewish War* Josephus had put the corresponding information more plausibly after the deposition of Archelaus in 6 C.E.; *B.J.* 2.129-66.

40. R. Reich, "*Miqwa'ot* (Jewish Ritual Baths) in the Second Temple, Mishnah and

reflect purity concerns, and both are attested at Qumran. This suggests the rise of impurity and its removal in the cultic life for some Judeans outside of the specific requirements of sacrifice and pilgrimage at Jerusalem. *Which* Judeans remains an open question. Does this attest to the spread of priests as property-holders in Judaea, for instance, the increasing consumption needs of a Jerusalem elite, or the appropriation of priestly purity by nonpriests? In any case, what is distinctive at Qumran may be the intensification of religious concerns and practices more broadly attested and, as 4QMMT implies, intensely debated, but also of fairly recent origin.

The origins of the movement reflected in the Dead Sea Scrolls may well go back farther than the late second or first century B.C.E., and the dislocations of the period between 170 and 142 are a reasonable place to look for them. It is also possible that we should allow, as both García Martínez and Gabriele Boccaccini have argued, for an earlier stream of thought out of which the Qumran movement emerged. Scholars have looked for evidence of these in the pesher texts and especially in the opening column of the *Damascus Document,* which depicts an identity that extends backward to a "Teacher of Righteousness" who began to set things right and farther still to the dissolution set in motion by God's giving Israel over to the hands of Nebuchadnezzar (CD 1:3-11).

But a word of caution is in order. Groups create histories for themselves and in doing so can cobble together into a single tradition elements of a more fragmented and disparate past, or in fact invent a past altogether. Rabbinic and Christian writers offer examples from a somewhat later period, but the best contemporary example relates to the translation of the Torah into Greek. The elaborate story in the *Letter to Aristeas* of its translation under the auspices of Ptolemy II is a myth. Yet the event was commemorated by Alexandrian Jews in an annual festival (Philo, *Life of Moses* 2.41-42). So too, with the Qumran sectarians, we must allow for the possibility that the group created an identity for itself by placing itself in relationship to the myth of terrestrial corruption of *1 Enoch* and *Jubilees*. Positing a preexistent stream of Judaism going back a century or more may not be necessary.

Talmud Periods," 151-53; for vessels see Y. Magen, "Jerusalem as a Center of the Stone Vessel Industry during the Second Temple Period," dating their origin to the second half of the first century B.C.E.

b. Qumran and Essenes

A version of the "Essene Hypothesis," i.e., that the Qumran sect is some-how related to the Essenes described by Josephus, Philo, and Pliny, is the most economical way of dealing with the variety of our sources. Again, however, care is in order.[41] All of our sources in Greek or Latin are from the first century c.e. or (in the case of Hippolytus of Rome) later still, and three decades or more separate Philo's account from Josephus's or Pliny's. By Philo's time the settlement at Qumran had been around for a century or more. There is no reason to presuppose precise insider knowledge on the part of these later, and in the case of Philo and Pliny, geographically and culturally distant authors. Each had his own reasons for depicting his ex-otic Essenes as he did.

Moreover, even if each account derives from good firsthand infor-mation based on earlier source material, the variety of legal texts from Qumran still does not provide any firm indication of the practice of a community at any given moment. Although at least one document seems to reflect a registry of people disciplined (4Q477, too confidently pub-lished as "Rebukes Reported by the Overseer"), the penal codes of both the *Damascus Document* and *Community Rule* seem to have been subject to substantial revisions over time. A transition among the people of the Dead Sea Scrolls from eschatological enthusiasm in the first century b.c.e. to a life modulated around a receding or realized eschaton in the first century c.e. might, for instance, make sense of the total absence of eschatology in the later accounts of "Essenes." It is worth noting that by Josephus's own time, Pharisees, who imposed a reign of terror in the period 76-67 b.c.e., were better known for their theological positions about fate or resurrec-tion or their fussiness about purity.

c. Comparanda

How unique were the Dead Sea Scrolls people? I have already suggested that in terms of periodization, sect formation, and characteristic piety, it may be more illuminating to study the Dead Sea Scrolls within the broader context of religious and political change in Palestine. It is also helpful to think about other ways to place the evidence of Qumran into a less close

41. See A. I. Baumgarten, "Who Cares and Why Does It Matter?," 174-90.

circle of historical evidence and argumentation. One mode of approach that may yet bear important results is comparison with other late-Hellenistic and early-Roman voluntary associations or philosophical schools.[42] To object that the Qumran community was not a philosophical school or that the similarity between associations known through epigraphy and Qumran codes does not go much deeper than terminology is, while technically correct, to miss the point. If the emergence of organized sectarianism among well-off, literate Judaeans is a new and relatively unprecedented feature of the late Hellenistic and early Roman periods, we should be looking widely for vernaculars of association and for motifs of idealized association and for ways that self-identified "Israelites" appropriated (or avoided) these in forming their own groups.

One almost entirely unutilized body of material for comparison is a collection of papyri associated with the Epicurean philosopher Philodemus from Herculaneum in Italy. The remains are nearly contemporary with Qumran (Philodemus lived approximately 110-40 B.C.E., was originally from Gadara in Palestine, and resided in Italy from the early first century B.C.E.; the villa was destroyed by Vesuvius in 79 C.E.), similar in size (an estimated one thousand works), and structurally similar (manuscripts go back to the third century, with some multiple copies of the same works). In some way that is hard to specify this library is connected with the flourishing of Epicurean study and association at Herculaneum, much as the Qumran scrolls are related to a group at Qumran. Here, then, is a real-world opportunity for comparing the formation and extension of "school" collections.[43] It is worth noting that one of the arguments offered by Golb for the Qumran scrolls being a Jerusalem library was the apparent absence of autograph copies (although how would we recognize these?). Herculaneum, too, lacks autographs, despite the fact that this is a private collection inescapably associated with Philodemus personally, which includes multiple copies and versions of his own works.

The Dead Sea Scrolls are often studied for their "secrets" and "mysteries," for their exoticism and uniqueness. Obvious considerations of marketing have driven this agenda, as have Qumran scholars' own understanding that they were exposing documents — and with them groups and

---

42. D. Mendels, "Hellenistic Utopia and the Essenes"; M. Weinfeld, *The Organizational Pattern and the Penal Code of the Qumran Sect.*

43. M. Gigante, *Philodemus in Italy;* see the cautious assessment by D. Obbink, "Craft, Cult, and Canon in the Books from Herculaneum."

ideas — that were previously largely unknown. Like the classic works of social history, the approach suggested here has instead emphasized what we can learn from the material, the prosaic, and the everyday. It is only by being able to estimate the scale of the scribal labor encapsulated in the scrolls, for instance, that we may be able to trace the history of their deposit and the economy of their producers or owners. Datable materials (scrolls, pots, coins) offer benchmarks for further analysis. If Khirbet Qumran and the scrolls in the nearby caves are connected, their closely overlapping chronologies suggest that we think seriously about the first century B.C.E. as a crucial period for both, providing a moderately stable basis from which to ask about the "prehistory" of the movement, whether that be Essene or Zadokite or that of an unknown Jewish sect. If we can do this with a real acknowledgment of the limitations of our knowledge, a willingness to have our most cherished facts overturned, and a robust hermeneutic of suspicion to help keep us from reproducing what our texts claim as our sole knowledge about them, we may well make some steps toward reintegrating the Dead Sea Scrolls into the history of Second Temple Palestine and Judaism.

Counterfactual History and the Dead Sea Scrolls

James R. Davila

The history of what did not happen has long been a staple of fiction. Besides movies, such as Frank Capra's 1946 film, *It's a Wonderful Life,* alternate history fiction is a recognized subgenre of science fiction literature.[1] It is intended merely as thought-provoking entertainment, but the concept of alternate history has also been used in more serious contexts. The idea of writing histories of events that did not really happen as a historiographic exercise, rather than as straight fiction, has existed for many years.[2] Two important and more serious recent examples are Geoffrey Hawthorne's book, *Plausible Worlds,* and Niall Ferguson's collection of essays titled *Virtual History.*[3] Beginning with the work of Rob-

1. Two recent retrospective collections of alternate history stories are H. Turtledove with M. H. Greenberg, eds., *The Best Alternate History Stories of the 20th Century;* and G. Dozois and S. Schmidt, eds., *Roads Not Taken: Tales of Alternate History.* Robert B. Schmunk's Uchronia website (http://www.uchronia.net/) compiles bibliographical information on thousands of alternate history stories and novels.

2. As far as I am aware, J. C. Squire edited and published the first collection of alternate history essays: *If It Had Happened Otherwise* (1st ed. 1931). Many similar collections have been published since then.

3. G. Hawthorne, *Plausible Worlds;* N. Ferguson, ed., *Virtual History;* note esp. his introductory essay (1-90). Other important methodological discussions of counterfactual history include P. E. Tetlock and A. Belkin, eds., *Counterfactual Thought Experiments in World Politics,* esp. 1-38; and R. N. Lebow, "What's So Different about a Counterfactual?"

I am grateful to the Arts and Humanities Research Board (now Council), which provided me with research leave funding that made time available for the research for this chapter.

ert Fogel and his contemporaries in the 1950s and 1960s, the use of counterfactual speculations has also been important for the "new economics" or cliometrics.[4] More general terms for the study of the history of what might have happened but did not are "alternate" or "counterfactual" history.

In this short chapter I apply counterfactual history to a problem I have been pursuing in my research for some time. On the one hand, Christians in antiquity adopted and transmitted otherwise lost Jewish quasi-scriptural books pertaining to the Hebrew Bible (the general term for these is "Old Testament pseudepigrapha"), often in translation from Hebrew or Aramaic into Greek, or in secondary and even tertiary translations into other church languages. But on the other hand, Christians also sometimes heavily redacted the pseudepigrapha they transmitted and even authored such works themselves, composing them in and translating them into any number of church languages. All this being the case, what can we know about the origins and transmission of Old Testament pseudepigrapha that have been transmitted only by Christians? What connection, if any, might they have to a Jewish textual tradition?

I have explored these questions at length in a recent monograph using more traditional methods.[5] The problem itself does not directly pertain to the Dead Sea Scrolls, but I use the scrolls here as a tool to attack it from a fresh angle, one that moves from the known to the unknown in an entirely new way. My objectives are, first, to see what we can learn about the transmission of Old Testament pseudepigrapha by studying the process, from the inside so to speak; and, second, to test the limits of the critical tools that scholars currently apply to this problem, to see how well their results hold up when applied to a particularly challenging case whose true details are actually known to us.

This chapter applies an approach that, to my knowledge, has not been used before in the particular formulation I have constructed. It draws first on strands of poststructuralist literary criticism from the second half of the twentieth century in a formulation owing much to Maxine Grossman's "alternative historiography," which she has applied to the *Da-*

---

4. Fogel, *Railroads and American Economic Growth: Essays in Econometric History.* Fogel won the 1993 Nobel Prize in economics (shared with Douglass C. North) for this book and his subsequent work in cliometrics. To my knowledge, the most recent survey of the state of the question for counterfactual history in general is R. Bradley MacKay's dissertation, "Counterfactual Reasoning in Strategy Context," 166-218.

5. J. R. Davila, *The Provenance of the Pseudepigrapha.*

mascus Document and other Qumran texts.[6] These poststructuralist strategies are combined with alternate or counterfactual history. Unlike most — perhaps all — previous attempts at counterfactual history, my approach focuses on a very narrow counterfactual scenario: What if one of the better preserved Hebrew Dead Sea Scrolls had been translated into Greek by a Jewish author, transmitted by Greek-speaking Christians, then translated into Syriac and read by Syriac-speaking Christians? And what if the original Hebrew of this document (and indeed the whole Qumran library) had been entirely lost, so that scholars in the twenty-first century had access to this document only through a single manuscript of the Syriac translation of this work? What could we tell about its origins and about its transmission in Christian circles? And might this, in turn, shed new light on the process of transmission of Old Testament pseudepigrapha and the current scholarly study of it?

My points of departure from our actual history are on a very local and limited scale and involve the imagined transmission of known ancient works by means different from those by which they actually reached us.[7] This counterfactual history of transmission is merely plausible and suits my purposes; it does not arise inevitably from the counterfactual conditions I set up in the following scenario. Its narrow focus allows me to ignore possible knock-on effects the different transmission of these texts might have had on the rest of history, thus sidestepping the problem of the "butterfly effect" (the principle in "chaos theory" that systems which operate by the laws of "classical" [non-quantum] physics are "sensitively dependent on initial conditions" and, unless the initial conditions are known impossibly perfectly, the slightest perturbation rapidly introduces massive and unpredictable changes).[8]

The method is as follows: I trace the counterfactual history of the transmission of a single ancient document from antiquity to the present, offering a "thick description" — a literary-ethnographic analysis of the attending social circumstances — of the process.[9] I have developed two main tools to construct the thick description and to keep it as plausible as possible. The first involves establishing some *basic specifications* for the central elements of the scenario (the basic physical realities and major ele-

---

6. M. L. Grossman, *Reading for History in the Damascus Document.*

7. G. Levi, "On Microhistory."

8. D. Deutsch, *The Fabric of Reality,* 201-3.

9. Cf. C. Geertz, "Thick Description," esp. 10 (note the apt metaphor of reading a manuscript) and 27.

ments of transition). I refer to these specifications as *settings.* The settings I envision for this example consist of (1) the text to be studied, including the specific manuscript that starts the process of transmission; (2) the technique of the translator of the imagined translation of the Hebrew text into Greek; (3) the technique of the translator of the imagined translation of the Greek text into Syriac; and (4) the specific Syriac manuscript in which the text is imagined to be preserved when it comes into the hands of a modern scholar. Each setting is constructed using *templates* — objects or values that actually exist in our world and which therefore anchor the counterfactual scenario in physical reality and impose limiting factors on the speculative element of the scenario.

The first setting involves the choice of the specific Qumran works for which to construct alternate histories. I have chosen the *Hodayot* Scroll (1QH^a) as the template in this case, because it is a Hebrew work in a well-preserved first-century manuscript whose provenance is known. The *Hodayot,* or Qumran hymns, are a collection of sectarian poetic pieces that may have been used either in the sect's liturgy or for private devotional study. The hymns are best preserved in 1QH^a, a single manuscript of twenty-six or more columns dating from around the turn of the era and recovered from Qumran Cave 1.

As the template for the second setting, the translation technique of the Greek translator, I adopt the Greek translation of Ben Sira. Greek Ben Sira is a translation of a Hebrew apocryphal book whose translation technique has been studied in detail: it is idiomatic, free, and inconsistent, and it tends not to translate scriptural allusions in Hebrew with any attention to the Greek translations of those passages in the Septuagint (LXX).[10]

The template for the third setting, the Syriac translation of the Greek, is the Syriac version of the apocryphal book of Judith, which was translated from Greek and has been studied in a reasonable amount of detail. Its technique moves in the direction of the idiomatic, while remaining closer to the literal pole than not, rather like the LXX of the Pentateuch.[11]

The fourth template needed is one for the manuscript in which the Syriac text of the specific work survives. Here I wish to explore a scenario in which the Syriac version of 1QH^a has been preserved in a single Syriac manuscript whose nature will be discussed below.

10. B. G. Wright, *No Small Difference.*
11. J. E. Bejon, "A Study of the Recensional Position, the Style, and the Translation Technique of the Syriac Translation of Judith."

The second tool, *reading with,* is an adaptation of Grossman's "alternative historiography," which involves reading the target text as readers at key points in its history of transmission would have, by reading the text alongside other contemporary texts (in this case the Hebrew Bible, the LXX, the New Testament, and selected noncanonical works). This tool draws on insights from reader-response criticism, intertextuality, and deconstruction.

The Thick Description

I proceed then with a short version of a thick description of this counterfactual transmission of the *Hodayot* Scroll from Qumran Cave 1.

The Jewish Translator

If 1QH^a fell into the hands of a Hebrew- and Greek-speaking Jew in the late first century C.E., I suspect that this reader would have been intrigued by this relic from the mysterious and now defunct, or at least scattered, sectarian group (the Essenes?) and might have sought some basis for regarding it as an authoritative work. The most natural approach for a first-century Jew who wanted to read the work as authoritative would be to read it alongside the Scriptures to try to make sense of it. We do not have the beginning of the manuscript, but we may assume, as with the other sectarian works from Qumran, that no title with substantive information was included. I propose that the reader, having gone through the work carefully once, would find many connections with the book of Isaiah and, upon further study, could well have concluded that this was a lost collection of hymns by the prophet himself.

A number of themes in both Isaiah and the *Hodayot* would point in this direction. Prominent among them would be Isaiah's visionary experiences (cf. Isa 1:1), especially the vision described in chapter 6. In it, he sees the Deity enthroned in the temple, with angelic seraphim in attendance. The *Hodayot* hymnist likewise thanks God for raising him "to an eternal exaltation" (1QH^a 11:20). Isaiah is dismayed because he is "a man of unclean lips" and he lives among "a people of unclean lips," yet he has seen God (Isa 6:5). Likewise, the *Hodayot* hymnist is dismayed by his own corruption and impurity as "one born of woman" (1QH^a 9:21-22; 11:20-22). He describes himself as one of uncircumcised lips (10:7) among people who have "uncircumcision of lip" (10:18). Isaiah is purified by one of the seraphim, who touches his mouth with a hot coal from the altar and who declares his sin to be forgiven (Isa 6:6-7). The *Hodayot* hymnist undertakes to purify himself and calls on God to purify him (1QH^a 8:18-20; 19:30), indeed to purify him sevenfold like silver refined in a furnace (1QH^a 13:16). Having been purified, his spirit is ready to take its station among the holy ones and to psalm God in unity with the angels (1QH^a 11:21-23). By foregrounding these passages in the two works, our reader could make a convincing case (by the standards of first-century exegesis) for the identification of the prophet with the hymnist.

Moreover, Isaiah and the *Hodayot* hymnist share similar enemies. Isaiah complains of "the prophet who teaches a lie" (9:14[EVV 15]) and of drunken priests and prophets who "err in the vision" (28:7), prophets and priests whom God has stupefied (29:10-12). The wicked people silence the seers and prophets and demand that they speak "smooth things" (30:10). The *Hodayot* hymnist also faces the "seekers of smooth things" (1QH^a 10:32). Frequently echoing Isaiah's language, he disputes with opponents who have "made it smooth for them," "beguiling interpreters" who have led others into error (12:7-8) and who are "false interpreters and deceitful visionaries" (12:9-10).

Various clues in the *Hodayot* and the Scriptures might make the idea of a newly revealed book from the prophet Isaiah palatable to an exegete who was inclined so to regard the *Hodayot*. The prophet himself, in a difficult passage, could be regarded as commanding that the "testimony" be bound up and the "Torah" be sealed among his disciples (Isa 8:16), perhaps to be read as a reference to esoteric teachings transmitted outside the canonical book. In 1QH^a 15:20-21, the hymnist asserts that God "set me as a father to the sons of loyalty and like a wet-nurse to men of the sign," perhaps to be taken as a reference to these same disciples. Further support might be found in two scriptural passages outside the book of Isaiah. 2 Chr 26:22 and 32:32 tell us that Isaiah wrote at least two books in addition to the book of Isaiah. Although the *Hodayot* do not fit the description of either of the lost books, their very existence strengthens the possibility that another could have been written.

These literary observations provide a backdrop against which I can frame the assumptions for the next template in our discussion. In this context, I assume that our bilingual, first-century Jewish reader concluded that the Hebrew work that had fallen into his or her hands was an ancient and esoteric book by a prophet, the prophet Isaiah, which had been preserved by a mysterious and now scattered or eradicated Jewish sect. I also assume that this reader translated the book into Greek with a translation technique more or less identical to that found in the Greek Ben Sira, and that the single Hebrew manuscript (our 1QH^a in its pristine form) eventually deteriorated and was lost without ever being copied or translated again. Finally, I assume that the translator made a single addition to the work: a title that read "The Odes of Isaiah" (ΩΔΑΙ ΤΟΥ ΗΣΑΙΟΥ)

The Greek-Speaking Christian Audience

A Greek-speaking Christian reader in the second or third century would read the *Odes of Isaiah* in light of its title and, therefore, in light of the LXX book of Isaiah in the first instance. I am assuming that the translator did not make any special effort to echo the language of the LXX Isaiah in his translation, since the translator of Ben Sira into Greek did not try to correlate his translation of Hebrew allusions to Scripture with their LXX equivalents. Nevertheless, most of the connections between the *Hodayot* and the book of Isaiah would probably be visible when the Greek translations of both were compared.

We may assume that the Greek-speaking Christian reader had access to the Gospels and Pauline Epistles and would have drawn on them for an understanding of the new work. The reader would know that Isaiah prophesied of the coming of Jesus the Messiah (Matt 1:23; 3:3; 4:14; 8:17; 12:17-21; Mark 1:2-3; Luke 3:4-6; 4:17-21; John 1:23; 12:37-41; Acts 8:30-35); spoke of the hypocrisy of his hearers (Matt 15:7-9; Mark 7:6-8; John 12:37-41); and predicted that Israel would reject the Messiah while the Gentiles accepted him, but that a remnant of Israel would be saved in the end (Rom 9:27-33; 10:16-21; 15:12). If one New Testament verse stands out as a key for the early Christian interpreter of Isaiah, it is John 12:41: "Isaiah said these things because he saw his glory and he spoke about him," that is, about Jesus.

In addition, the Greek *Odes of Isaiah* would have contained a passage that a Christian reader would certainly have regarded as a messianic prophecy, one entirely consonant with what could be expected from the pen of the prophet Isaiah. Generally referred to by scholars as the "Self-Glorification Hymn," it appears in very fragmentary form in 1QH^a 26 (frags. 56 ii; 46 ii; 55 ii), but much more of it can be reconstructed by comparison to two other copies of the same version (Recension A) in 4QH^a 7 i and 4Q471^b 1-2, as well as a slightly different version (Recension B) preserved in 4Q491^c 11 i.[12] Recension B (4Q491^c 11 i 8-14a) preserves some additional material belonging to the earlier part of the hymn.[13] In this remarkable hymn a human speaker boasts of ascending to heaven, consorting with divine beings, and perhaps being enthroned there. He has a special relationship with God yet also is despised and bears incomparable evil. Even granting a certain degree of slippage of meaning as the hymn was translated into Greek, the identification of the speaker with Jesus would be irresistible to an early Christian, and such a reader would find it utterly appropriate that the prophet who revealed the Song of the Suffering Servant in Isa 52:13–53:12 should reveal this song of Jesus in another book of hymnic oracles.

The Odes of Isaiah in Syriac

To establish the setting for our third template I assume that sometime in the second or third century a bilingual Syrian Christian came upon a

---

12. E. Eshel, "*4Q471*^{b}: A Self-Glorification Hymn."

13. A reasonable reconstruction of what survives of Recension A would be something along the following lines:

> . . . despised like me, for in the habitation of holiness is everything precious to me. . . . Who bears evil so as to be comparable to me, and who is like me together with the holy ones, and who is equal to me? . . . teaching is not comparable to my teachings. . . . Who is like me among the gods? Who will cut off the words of my mouth, and the flow of my lips who will contain? Who will *advise me* with the tongue and be comparable to my judgments? I am beloved of the King, friend to the holy ones, and there shall not *come in* to me. . . . Who is reckoned as booty by me and who is comparable to me in my *glory?* For as for me, with the gods is my station, and my glory with the sons of the King. I shall not crown myself with fine gold and gold of Ophir is not . . . shall not be reckoned *by me.*

Recension B reads as follows:

> . . . wonderful things. . . . His mighty acts . . . they chant and holy ones rejoice . . . in righteousness. . . . [I]srael. He has established His truth of old and the mysteries of His shrewdness in al[l] . . . and the counsel of the poor for an eternal congregation . . . sound ones of [et]ernity, a throne of power in the congregation of the gods. None of the *kings of old* are enthroned in it and their nobles did no[t] . . . my glory is incomparable and none is *exalted* (or "silent") except me, and none shall come to me, for I am enthroned (or "I dwell") in . . . in heaven and there is not. . . . I am reckoned with the gods and my abode is in the holy council. Not like flesh is [my] desire. . . .

The words that survive from the hymn in 1QH^a are italicized in the translations of both Recension A and Recension B. The presence of the hymn in 1QH^a is not in doubt.

Greek copy of the *Odes of Isaiah,* complete with the Greek title, and translated it into Syriac, using the same translation technique as that of the Syriac translation of Judith. I assume that these Syriac *Odes of Isaiah* survive in a single manuscript, one that actually exists. This template manuscript is London, British Museum, Add. MS 14.538 (hereafter, "Codex Nintriensis"), a vellum codex written in Jacobite (Western) script and dating as late as the thirteenth century, although the leaves of interest may constitute the remains of an earlier, tenth-century codex.[14] Most of the manuscript is taken up with extracts from various church fathers. Folios 149-52, obverse only, contain the badly damaged texts of the *Odes of Solomon* and the *Psalms of Solomon,* numbered consecutively as a total of sixty units (forty-two odes and eighteen psalms). The first part of the *Odes of Solomon* is missing and the surviving text commences with 17:7b. There is no break between the two works and no separate title is given to the *Psalms of Solomon,* although the two collections are distinguished by the fact that each ode ends with the word "Hallelujah," whereas none of the psalms do. If there was a title to the combined text of the two works, it is lost with the beginning of the *Odes of Solomon.*

Let us imagine that the Syriac *Odes of Isaiah* were originally appended as a third section of poetic material in Codex Nintriensis, just after the *Psalms of Solomon.* A rough guess would be that the *Odes of Isaiah* would take two more leaves, which would belong to the earlier manuscript from the tenth century. We can assume that no title was given to it and that the hymns contained in it were numbered consecutively with the earlier poetic units, beginning with sixty-one. It is impossible to know how many individual hymns were preserved in the text. We can isolate perhaps twenty-one or so units by their opening lines, usually "I thank You, Lord," or something similar, but there must have been considerably more whose beginnings are lost due to the fragmentary state of the manuscript. Our reader would have known the number; we do not. Likewise, the editor of the tenth-century manuscript would have known whether the threefold collection of poetry was assigned a title or not. Again, we do not. I propose to assume that our hypothetical reader of this counterfactual version of Codex Nintriensis did not know either, because the beginning of the *Odes*

---

14. W. Wright, *Catalogue of Syriac Manuscripts in the British Museum Acquired since the Year 1838,* 1003-8. Photographs of folios 149a-151a of Codex Nintriensis appear in J. H. Charlesworth, ed., *Papyri and Leather Manuscripts of the Odes of Solomon,* 21-26. On the date of the relevant leaves, see Charlesworth, ed., *The Odes of Solomon,* 7-8.

of Solomon was already damaged and whatever title had been there was lost by the time it was bound into the larger codex. I do not claim that this was in fact the case, but assuming that it allows us to proceed without trying to guess whether a title was there and, if so, what it said.

How, then, would a Syriac-speaking reader of Codex Nintriensis understand the Syriac *Odes of Isaiah* in the context described above? There would be very few clues for making sense of the collection of perhaps a hundred odes, psalms, and hymns. The context of the section might lead the reader to assume that the poems, like most of the other passages, were written by a church father or fathers and that they had theological import. Some themes are shared by all three works. The Messiah is mentioned in the *Odes of Solomon* (e.g., 9:3). His descent into hell appears in 17 and 42; the Virgin Birth in 19; his eschatological victory (viewed retrospectively) in 22; the persecution of him on earth in 28; and his exaltation in 36. The *Psalms of Solomon* look forward to the earthly victory over the nations of a sinless Messiah at the eschaton (17-18; note esp. 17:36). And in the Self-Glorification Hymn, the *Odes of Isaiah* describe the heavenly exaltation of one who can be presumed to be Jesus. The Paradise of God and its proleptic identification with the believer is an important theme in the *Odes of Solomon* (11; 12:1-3; 20:7; 38:17-22) and in the *Odes of Isaiah* (1QH^a 14:13-18; 16:4-26), and it appears in *Pss. Sol.* 14:3-4.

The *Psalms of Solomon* reads much more like a Jewish work than the other two, with its emphasis on Israel and the assaults of the Gentiles on Jerusalem, so one reading strategy would be to understand the threefold collection as a whole by foregrounding these Jewish elements alongside the shared themes and taking the collection as a protevangelistic work by an anonymous Jew or perhaps an Old Testament character (Isaiah might be an obvious guess). A second strategy might be to read the collection as a work by an ancient Christian writer who spoke allegorically of Israel and Jerusalem as the church and of the Gentiles as unbelievers. Many other reading strategies could be imagined, but this gives an idea of some of the possibilities.

The Odes of Isaiah as Read by a Modern Scholar

To set the stage for a reading by a twenty-first-century scholar, I postulate two things. The first is that Codex Nintriensis had been passed down to the present containing the same three poetic works and that the Syriac version of the *Odes of Isaiah* had deteriorated so that the elements of it that were preserved correspond to what survives in our copy of 1QH[a] as far as its original order can be reconstructed. Second, I postulate that a single poetic unit from the *Odes of Isaiah* also survived in Greek. Specifically, I assume that it was extracted with the Greek title ΩΔΗ ΗΣΑΙΟΥ, "Ode of Isaiah," in Papyrus Bodmer XI, a third- or early-fourth-century papyrus that was probably composed by a Sahidic Copt in Thebes. This is a real manuscript that contains a collection of extracts from various early Christian sources (including *Odes of Solomon* 11) plus two biblical psalms.[15] I locate the *Ode of Isaiah* in ninth position, after Psalms 33 and 34 and before the two Epistles of Peter. Moreover, I assume that the *Ode of Isaiah* extracted was the Self-Glorification Hymn discussed above and that the leaf it was copied on had been damaged in transmission such that what survives of its content corresponds roughly to what we can reconstruct today of this hymn from its various witnesses. What, given these conditions, would a modern scholar make of the *Odes of Isaiah*?

First, based on the evidence of the Greek translation of the *Psalms of Solomon*, as well as on the internal evidence of the different transition markers in each of the three collections, it would be clear that three originally distinct groups of poems were collected together as one in Codex Nintriensis, with the middle one being called the *Psalms of Solomon*. Other evidence that need not detain us here would establish that the first section was called the *Odes of Solomon*.[16] The overlaps of the Greek poem with one of the Syriac poems in Codex Nintriensis (= 1QH[a] 26 frag. 7 i) would show that the title of the Syriac work was the *Odes of Isaiah*. The Greek poem would also show that the work existed in Greek form in Egypt by the third or fourth century C.E., although its exact content at that stage could not be known for certain. A careful reading of the whole work would show that there were no compelling indicators that it had been deliberately written as an Isaiah pseudepigraphon: there is no mention of specific events or characters in the life of the prophet. Nevertheless, many details do cohere with the story of Isaiah, including the echoes of his language, the visionary experiences, the opposition to false prophets, and the messianic material.

15. The Greek *Ode of Solomon* has been published by M. Testuz in *Papyrus Bodmer X-XII*, 49-69, with a plate of a page of the manuscript immediately preceding these pages. Charlesworth discusses the manuscript in *The Odes of Solomon*, 9-10, and publishes the leaves containing *Odes Sol.* 11 in *Papyrus and Leather Manuscripts*, 7-12, with some comments on p. 5.

16. See Charlesworth, *The Odes of Solomon*, 1-14.

I should expect that the question of the original language of the work would be difficult and perhaps somewhat controversial. The Syriac translation would show relatively little sign of its Greek origins, and most evidence of an original Hebrew *Vorlage* would be masked either by the Semitic features in Syriac or by the tendency of this particular Syriac translator to smooth out such Hebraisms as survived in the Greek. One might think that the survival of the single poem in Greek might solve the problem, or at least make it easier, but I do not believe that this would necessarily be the case.[17] One would still have to ask whether the Greek or the Syriac was more original and whether either was the original language. The Syriac would show few signs of translation from Greek. The brief surviving sample of the Greek would have been translated from a late form of Hebrew, and would be idiomatic, yet with some Semitisms, and might be argued to have been translated either from a lost Hebrew *Vorlage* (which we know to be correct) or from the surviving Syriac version.

It is difficult to say whether the doubly translated poetry of the Syriac *Odes of Isaiah* could tell our modern scholar more about its date and provenance. Although Bonnie Kittel has given us a thorough analysis of the parallelism and other poetic techniques of the *Hodayot,* there are not many comparable studies of other Semitic poetry of the same period, and none are as comprehensive.[18] The attention of our modern scholar might be drawn to a number of clearly early poetic pieces that invite comparison with the *Odes of Isaiah,* including Ben Sira, the poems in Luke 1, and, once again, the *Odes of Solomon.* The poetic lines of Ben Sira are generally shorter and closer to what we find in biblical poetry. Maurya P. Horgan and Paul J. Kobelski find a number of themes and poetic canons to be shared by the passages in Luke and the *Hodayot,* but many of these features in Luke 1 are not carried over into the Syriac Peshitta of Luke.[19]

The definitive study of the poetic canons — especially the parallelism and meter — of the *Odes of Solomon* remains to be written. We can say, however, that, like our imagined *Odes of Isaiah,* they make frequent but loose use of various forms of parallelism; their poetic lines tend to be rather longer than those in the biblical book of Psalms; and they do not use isosyllabic meter, intricately patterned stanzas, or acrostics, features typi-

---

17. Despite the survival of the eleventh *Ode of Solomon* in Greek in Papyrus Bodmer XI, the original language of the *Odes of Solomon* continues to be debated.

18. B. P. Kittel, *The Hymns of Qumran.*

19. M. P. Horgan and P. J. Kobelski, "The Hodayot (1QH) and New Testament Poetry."

cal of Syriac poetry from the mid-fourth century on.[20] Both works also lack clear indicators of use in a liturgical context. One might be tempted to place them in similar cultural and chronological horizons.

Form criticism would also be important for a modern scholarly evaluation of the *Odes of Isaiah*. Günter Morawe finds the *Hodayot* to consist of two basic genres, the individual "Danklied" or "thanksgiving song" and the "hymnische Bekenntnislied" or "hymnic song of confession," whose genre elements he lays out in detail.[21] In a later study he also compares the genre characteristics of the *Hodayot* to those of the later psalms in the Hebrew Bible and other poetic texts from the Qumran library and Second Temple Judaism.[22] He finds that the genres of the *Hodayot* derived their basic structural elements from the biblical psalms but developed these, both by making some elements more rigid and by expanding the possibilities of the genres in other directions. But there would be difficulties with using these Gattungen as a typological tool for dating, especially seeing that the structures of some early Christian poetic works (including Rev 11:17-18; *Didache* 10:2-3, 4-6; and *Acts of Thomas* 15) are just as close to the *Hodayot* as the earlier Jewish poems. In short, application of our current form-critical understanding to the *Odes of Isaiah* would place them within the general context of late Second Temple Judaism and the first few centuries of Christianity but would not help us to pin down their date or provenance any more precisely.

Our modern scholar would also consider whether positive evidence of either Christian or Jewish authorship could be found in the work. He or she would find nothing that was a certainly Christian signature feature, although the Greek version of the Self-Glorification Hymn could be read as coming from the mouth of Jesus if one were so inclined. But there is also very little that could be regarded as a Jewish signature feature.[23] There is no hint of nationalistic concerns; such mention of Jewish law as we find is very generic; there is no clear interest in the Jewish ritual cult. The most

---

20. E. Werner, "Hebrew and Oriental Christian Metrical Hymns: A Comparison," esp. 397-408; S. P. Brock, "Syriac and Greek Hymnography: Problems of Origin"; A. S. Rodrigues Pereira, *Studies in Aramaic Poetry (c. 100 B.C.E.–c. 600 C.E.)*, chs. 5 and 7.

21. G. Morawe, *Aufbau und Abgrenzung der Loblieder von Qumrân.*

22. G. Morawe, "Vergleich des Aufbaus der Danklieder und hymnischen Bekenntnislieder (1QH) von Qumran mit dem Aufbau der Psalme in Alten Testament und im Spätjudentum."

23. For the term "signature feature," see Davila, *The Provenance of the Pseudepigrapha*, 59-71.

promising indicator is the frequent mention of the covenant. Although it is true that the concept of the covenant with God is centrally important in Judaism and is frequently mentioned in Jewish texts, it was also assimilated by Christianity, which acknowledged the past validity of the covenant with Israel and regarded God's relationship with the church to be a new covenant predicted in the Scriptures. The precise nuance and context of the covenant in the *Odes of Isaiah* could be open to debate and, indeed, to considerable misunderstanding.

The concept of the "covenant" (both the Syriac word and the Greek transliteration) was important for the early Syriac-speaking church. The fourth-century authors Aphrahat and Ephrem the Syrian were members of a group known as the *bene qyama*, the "sons of the covenant" or "covenanters," a celibate class of men and women in the church who lived alone or together in gender-segregated groups.[24] The covenant in the *Odes of Isaiah* is not tied explicitly to a vow of celibacy, but its nature is left quite undefined and, at minimum, one could see how the discomfort in the work toward human birth and the mortal body could be congenial to such a group (e.g., 1QH^a 5:20; 7:25; 17:16; 18:5; 19:3; 20:24-27; 23 top 12-13).

Our modern scholar might then reasonably find a plausible context for the *Odes of Isaiah* in the Syriac-speaking church of the second through fourth centuries. The language, prosody, and forms of the Syriac version would allow for composition in Syriac by Christians in the second or third century. For a collection of Christian poems or liturgical pieces, it would include relatively little explicitly Christian content, although the Self-Glorification Hymn could be read as a christological ode. But one could take the attribution to Isaiah as coming from the Syriac-speaking author, in which case the author might have consciously avoided disrupting the illusory context of the implied author, Isaiah, by more obvious references to Christian matters. Nevertheless, the christological ode and the frequent reference to the importance of the covenant here would betray in part the theological foci of that Syriac-speaking author. The very low density of boundary-maintaining Jewish signature features would provide an ancillary argument from silence in favor of this reconstruction. According to it, the Greek version attested to in the Greek text of the Self-Glorification Hymn would be secondary, translated from the Syriac, and Semitisms in the Greek could be mobilized in support of this possibility. In short, we can excuse our scholar for mistakenly looking to composition by Syriac-

---

24. G. Nedungatt, "The Covenanters of the Early Syriac-Speaking Church."

speaking Christians as the best initial working hypothesis for the origin of the *Odes of Isaiah.*

Conclusion

In this chapter I have outlined a new method that I have applied to a specific Qumran scroll, but which also has the potential for wider applications in the field of ancient historiography. The method involves constructing a counterfactual history of the transmission of a particular object — here, the text of a literary work written on an actual ancient scroll — which history encompasses a limited stretch of time and which ignores any possible impact of the alternate transmission of the text outside its immediate environment. This alternate history is filled in with a "thick description," a literary-ethnographic analysis of the social circumstances attending the history of the object (here a Hebrew Qumran scroll being translated into Greek by a Jewish author, transmitted by Greek-speaking Christians, and then translated into Syriac by a Christian and read by Syriac-speaking Christians). Besides the judicious use of historical analogy, I have used two tools to construct the thick description so as to keep it as plausible as possible. The first is an adaptation of Grossman's "alternative historiography," which involves reading the target text as readers at key points in its history of transmission would have, by reading the text alongside other contemporary texts. The second is the construction of the most critical elements of the alternate history using "templates" from our history, in this case a specific Syriac manuscript, along with translation techniques actually used on specific Old Testament apocrypha. These templates give realistic depth to the counterfactual history of translation and transmission of the Qumran text. This thick description of the alternate transmission of the text is then subjected to historical-critical analysis by a counterfactual twenty-first-century specialist who applies scholarly methods to understand the text.

One may reasonably ask what the immediate payoff is for this intensive exercise in counterfactuality. First, it gives us a new measure of control over previously inaccessible aspects of the problem of Christian transmission of Jewish apocrypha and pseudepigrapha. By following an actual ancient Hebrew document through an analogous counterfactual transmission we can view the process from the inside and both test hypotheses about the process and test the methods scholars use to uncover this process. We see that these methods may not always lead us to the correct conclusion.

But there are more subtle payoffs as well. We have highlighted areas that are not yet thoroughly researched but about which we would like to know more in order to understand the Christian transmission of Jewish works. We need to understand the process of translation of quasi- or nonscriptural works from Greek into secondary church languages. Research into the translation techniques of the Syriac translations of the Greek Old Testament Apocrypha, where we have the original and the translation and can control the process, would give us much welcome information. The origin of the Syriac Apocrypha also constitutes an important but little studied problem. When were they translated? Were the translations done by Jews or Christians? Was the work done book-by-book by different and independent translators or was it done as a single project by a school of translators? The answers to such questions would help us understand the transmission of the Apocrypha and the broader historical context of the transmission of many Old Testament pseudepigrapha.

Another payoff is more general but worth pondering. One aspect of history that separates it from the hard sciences is its unrepeatability and therefore the impossibility of applying the experimental method to historiographic hypotheses and methodologies. Yet counterfactual history, in the form I have developed here, to some degree bridges the gap between history and the sciences by allowing us to construct alternative microhistorical scenarios and explore them, even introducing small variables one at a time to study their effects. Granted, these scenarios are merely imaginative exercises, but by introducing careful controls by way of off-the-shelf templates for important settings, we gain at least some ability to subject historiography to experimental falsification.

The last payoff I see from the counterfactual history has to do with the way we see ourselves as scholars. It is a commonplace of postmodern thought that though historians strive for objectivity, they are always complicit in the history they write, and even at its best it is always in part a reflection of their time and place and who they are. My alternate history looks not only at a different history of a Qumran text, it looks at modern scholars looking at that history. It allows us to enter our own thought processes as historians and philologists and to think them alongside ourselves as outsiders, and, one hopes, to look at them more objectively. This method provides a rare opportunity to watch ourselves as historians and to view our own complicity in the history we construct. This is not, of course, to claim that it allows us to attain objectivity, but only that it brings us a step closer.

The potential usefulness of counterfactual history is not exhausted by this example. It could provide valuable insights into many historical situations that involve the transmission and transformation of texts and artifacts. The basic principles of the method are focusing on the transmission of a single text or artifact during a carefully circumscribed period; providing a thick description of this transmission by means of cautious analogies — physical or intellectual templates that are already well documented and well understood — and reading the text or artifact as an intertext among ancient texts and artifacts contemporary with postulated audiences at key points in its history; and exploring how and how well a modern scholar would understand the transmission were he or she to have only the information we usually have in such situations. The history of, say, ancient sculpture, codicology (the study of manuscripts as cultural artifacts), and the translations of various literatures whose original-language versions are lost (the Pali, Chinese, Tibetan, and Japanese translations of lost Buddhist texts in Sanskrit come to mind) could be illuminated by this approach. I do not doubt that many other applications are possible as well.

Methodological Reflections on Determining Scriptural Status in First Century Judaism

Eugene Ulrich

Often since Socrates' strong denunciation of "the unexamined life," methodological reflection has enhanced not only personal life but also the practices of scientific inquiry. Methodological reflection, both on the setting of the Scriptures within general Judaism during the first centuries B.C.E. and C.E. and on modern scholars' attempts at evaluating the Qumran scriptural evidence, has already produced major advances and holds great promise for further advances. Were earlier generations of scrolls scholars, and are we today, looking, seeing, and interpreting the nature of the Scriptures with correct vision? Or might there be distortions in our vision that it would be good to correct? What can we learn from observing scholarly assessments of the evidence provided by the Qumran discoveries?

The first section of this chapter will consider certain general questions regarding the development of Scripture and what might be called the canonical process. The second section will turn to a discussion of theoretical issues, while the third will treat specific issues with regard to Scripture and particular manuscript evidence.

The Collection of Scriptures

At the time of their discovery, the Dead Sea Scrolls represented a unique body of evidence for the history of scriptural development, both in terms of individual texts (as will be discussed at length below), and in terms of the collection of texts that eventually became the canon of Scripture. Exploration of the dynamics of the process leading to the formation of a biblical canon promises to be a rich field for enhancing our knowledge of the history of Judaism in this crucial period. Meanwhile, a less exciting but methodologically quite important task is to define appropriate terminology and to clarify the various elements that constitute or contribute to the canonical process. Some discussions since the discovery of the scrolls have been confusing and at cross purposes due to the absence of clear definitions and terminology, and thus have hindered scholarly progress. In fact a full volume was collected to try to address the problem.[1] Two areas in particular will benefit from discussion: the web of trajectories for the various books on their road from national literature to canon of sacred Scripture, and the definition of "canon" and related aspects.

From Literature to Scripture

The Bible as transmitted is the end product of a lengthy and complex set of historical trajectories. Each complete literary book of Scripture is regarded as verbally inspired or recorded revelation; it is the textual basis of the Jewish and Christian religions, and its textual content is fixed and unchangeable, with a definitive and exclusive list of contents collected into a single book. But what eventually became the Bible did not have its origins as Scripture.[2] Here there is space for only a brief sketch, but it would be a rewarding project to analyze in detail the transformational shift for each of these five aspects, from an original situation to a final state:

- the gradual shift from being regarded as *literature* to being regarded as authoritative *Scripture,* which probably happened in different ways for each different book or group of books;[3]
- the shift from a collection of *individual sayings* or utterances originally understood to be God's message to the people to an *entire book* understood as divinely inspired;
- the shift in the *status* of texts, from *secondary* to *primary,* after the temple was destroyed in 70, and the religion — whose central focus

1. L. M. McDonald and J. A. Sanders, eds., *The Canon Debate.*

2. We will consider below, e.g., whether Ben Sira was envisioning the sources for his Praise of Famous Men as Scripture or simply as literature.

3. See E. Ulrich, "From Literature to Scripture: The Growth of a Text's Authoritativeness."

had been the temple and its sacrifices and rituals — was forced to change into one whose unifying focus for the dispersed communities was now the transportable texts;[4]

- the shift from a centuries-old process of dynamically *growing and pluriform* textual forms to a static situation of a *stable and unchangeable* text for each book;
- the shift from a long-developing *undefined collection* of separate scrolls to *a single book* with a front and back cover which *included* those texts that were consciously chosen for inclusion *and excluded* all others.

Thus, the Bible had its origins in numerous disparate units, many of which were oral, and only some of which were viewed as repeating God's inspired message. Each of the books developed organically along its own particular trajectory as part of the nation's literature, but the sacrificial rituals of the temple were the primary focus of the religion. The organic and pluriform character of the texts was the norm until the process of textual growth was abruptly halted by the results of the two revolts. Finally, it was only late in the process that debates arose about which books should be included or excluded and that conscious decisions were made which eventuated in the canon.

There is also need for exploration in a related direction. Just as there was a web of historical trajectories for the different books as they were transformed from national literature to Scripture, so too are there trajectories from earlier to later editions of the scriptural books and subsequently from scriptural books to rewritten scriptural compositions. George Brooke describes the issue well:

> What emerges from a consideration of the scriptural and rewritten scriptural compositions in this overall manner is that there is no neat separation of the two classes of works. It is certainly not the case that the emerging authoritative collection contained no rewritten works

---

4. 1 Maccabees mentions Scripture only a few times; but note an earlier occurrence of a shift of rising importance of text after loss of temple, when Judas and his warriors "opened the book of the law to inquire" (1 Macc 3:48) after they were excluded from the temple. Moreover, when 1 Macc 4:41-58 recounts the cleansing and rededication of the sanctuary, it is the altar of burnt offering that is first to be mentioned (4:44, 47); while there is extended discussion of the furnishings of the sanctuary, sacrifices, and celebration, note that texts are mentioned only in a subordinate clause ("as the law directs" 4:53) in reference to the *sacrifice* on the new altar.

[e.g., Deuteronomy or Chronicles]. The categorization into canonical and non-canonical does not serve our purposes suitably. Rather, it seems as if there is a sliding scale of affinity or dependence and that function needs to be considered in a qualified way too. This sliding scale approach prevents us from applying the anachronistic labels of scriptural or non-scriptural too quickly to manuscript evidence which is so obviously replete with variety, pluralism, multiple editions of books and a range of secondary compositions.[5]

Canon and Related Concepts

The second area for which clarification will prove helpful is the definition of "canon" and related concepts. The term "canon" is a long-established theological *terminus technicus* with a precise meaning: it is the official, exclusive list of books accepted by the community as authoritative, because inspired, Scripture. Though the term can mean both "rule" and "list," the phrase "canon of Scripture" is predominantly used to denote the list. It was the end result of a lengthy "canonical process" of valuing, sifting, and debating that finally resulted in reflective judgments to include the essential books and to exclude those judged not so. Ancient discussions apparently involved only books, and not the specific textual form of a book. Canon as such is a static concept, the result of a retrospective conclusion that the state of affairs that has been guiding the community has now come to be seen and judged as permanent.[6] Talk of an "open canon" is self-contradictory, as is "a square with uneven sides and angles" (see "canonical process" below).

A number of aspects that are closely associated with the concept of canon often get intermingled and confuse discussions, and so it helps to differentiate them and use each properly:

- An *authoritative* work is a writing which a group, secular or religious, recognizes and accepts as determinative for its conduct and as of a higher order than can be overridden by the power or will of the group or any member. A constitution or law code would be an example.

---

5. G. J. Brooke, "The Rewritten Law, Prophets and Psalms: Issues for Understanding the Text of the Bible," esp. 36. See also S. White Crawford, *Rewriting Scripture in Second Temple Times.*

6. For fuller discussion see E. Ulrich, "The Notion and Definition of Canon."

- A book of *Scripture* is a sacred authoritative work believed to have God as its ultimate author, which the community, as a group and individually, recognizes and accepts as determinative for its belief and practice for all time and in all geographical areas.
- The *textual form* of most books of Scripture (including content, wording, and orthography) was pluriform in antiquity. A book may have been widely and definitively considered Scripture, but it could circulate in several textual forms and may have been still developing. It is the book, and not the textual form of the book, that is canonical.
- The *canonical process* is the journey of the many disparate works of literature within the ongoing community, from the early stages when they began to be considered as somehow authoritative for the broader community, through the collection and endorsement process, to the final judgment concerning their inspired character as the unified and defined collection of Scripture — i.e., until the judgment of recognition that constituted the canon. If the focus is on a book or the collection of books while a historical, developmental trajectory is envisioned or is still in process, then the proper term is "process toward canon" or "canonical process."
- *A collection of authoritative Scriptures* was certainly in existence and taken to be fundamental to the Jewish religion from sometime in the first half of the Second Temple period. But it is necessary to keep in mind Bruce Metzger's distinction between "a collection of authoritative books" and "an authoritative collection of books."[7] One can designate the growing collection of authoritative books as "canonical" (adjective) in the first sense of rule, but there is not yet a canon (noun) in the second sense of an authoritative list.
- The *Bible*, in the singular, denotes a textual form of the collection of canonical books. Whereas the canon is the normative list of the books, the Bible is the text of that fixed collection of books, conceived of as a single anthology, and usually presented as such. In a sense, the term may seem anachronistic until the format of the collection of scriptural books was the codex (third century C.E.?). "The Scriptures" may be an open collection, but the "Bible" would seem to indicate an already closed collection.[8]

---

7. B. M. Metzger, *The Canon of the New Testament*, 283.
8. Ulrich, "The Notion and Definition of Canon," 29-30.

A further area related to canon that could profit from close analysis is the precise time when a third subcollection (the Ketubim) of the Scriptures came to be recognized. We have space here for brief consideration of three examples. First, the Qumran evidence, though not conclusive, strongly suggests that the collection was still bipartite up to the end of the first century C.E.: we find in the scrolls a heavy emphasis on the Torah and the (Latter) Prophets, including *Jubilees* and *1 Enoch,* but virtually no attention to the Former Prophets and Writings.[9]

Second, was Ben Sira, in his Encomium on Israel's Famous Men (44–50), drawing on what he considered "Scripture," or did he view his sources simply as his people's proud literature? Regarding structure, his praise apparently begins with Enoch and ends with the high priest Simon. Regarding genre, he explicitly lists those types of ancestors he will praise: rulers, heroes, counselors, prophetic oracles, wise leaders, instructors, musical composers, wealthy estate owners; "all these were honored in their generations and were the pride of their times" (44:7). Does he not appear to be envisioning a list of national heroes recorded in their literature, rather than scriptural saints recorded in the Scriptures?

Third, how should the evidence in the Prologue to Ben Sira and in 4QMMT be interpreted? What was the intended object of the Grandson in his triple, but nonetheless persistently vague, expression in the Prologue to Ben Sira: a bipartite or a tripartite canon? Is there any validity in the claim that 4QMMT attests a third subcategory beyond "the Law and the Prophets"?[10] The most compelling conclusion to these questions is provided by James VanderKam, who states clearly, and to my mind correctly: "As nearly as we can tell, there was no *canon* of Scripture in Second Temple Judaism. That is, before 70 C.E. no authoritative body of which we know drew up a list of books that alone were regarded as supremely authoritative, a list from which none could be subtracted and to which none could be added."[11]

9. For the evidence and assessment see E. Ulrich, "Qumran and the Canon of the Old Testament."

10. Discussed in E. Ulrich, "The Non-attestation of a Tripartite Canon in 4QMMT," esp. 212-14; and "Qumran and the Canon," 71.

11. J. C. VanderKam, "Questions of Canon Viewed through the Dead Sea Scrolls," esp. 91.

Theoretical Issues

If, at the time of their discovery, the Dead Sea Scrolls represented a unique challenge for scholars of scriptural development, it is true also that scholars fell back on familiar categories to make sense of this new material. But when we encounter something radically new, in whole or even in part, that goes beyond our acquired knowledge, we are at risk of failing to interpret it correctly or adequately. Since the texts and the collection of Scriptures evidenced by the scrolls are distinctly different from the biblical text and canon of the twentieth and twenty-first centuries, it is possible that our interpretation and explanation of them could be less than adequate. A primary concern here is one of perspective, or coign of vantage. Where should our standing point be, and where should we aim our focus, when setting out to think and speak about the scriptural scrolls? We might rely on modern concepts, categories, and terms. Or we might use the concepts, categories, and terms that would have been appropriate in the "first centuries," at the close of the Second Temple period.[12] If, instead of viewing them from the present, we immerse ourselves in the first centuries, observing and discussing the scriptural manuscripts according to the understanding the people had then and the reality they knew, we may achieve a clearer, more accurate understanding.

Epistemologically, we come to achieve new knowledge through a process of experience, understanding, and judgment. Through experience or sense perception we take in new data and then begin the work of understanding, conceptualizing, interpreting. The conceptualization or interpretation takes place according to the categories we already know, categories well established and confirmed by our past experience of their repeated usefulness for absorbing and correctly classifying knowledge. When the data are complex, alternate interpretations are possible, and then it is the task of judgment to decide which of the interpretations is in fact the correct one, the one that best explains the data.

Pedagogically, that is the first step. But should it be our final, definitive step? Examination of this process exposes a possible pitfall to attaining a proper understanding of the new evidence. If our present categories are

---

12. The term "the first centuries" here denotes the first centuries B.C.E. and C.E., the time period on which this study is focused. The bulk of our manuscript scriptural evidence comes from these two centuries, and they are crucial for understanding the emergence of Christianity and rabbinic Judaism.

not adequate or not sufficiently refined for accurate interpretation of the new evidence, we may adopt a judgment regarding the evidence that, though perhaps partly accurate, may also be partly misleading. Thus, articulations of that judgment and future decisions could reinforce the misleading viewpoint.

Accordingly, one can discern two models for conceptualizing the biblical text and two methodologies according to which people proceed to understand the evidence for the biblical text. One model or methodology, often unexamined, is to start by presupposing that we know what the content, wording, and orthography of the biblical text are — we have known then all along, we know them well from the Masoretic Text (MT). The MT, which provides the textual basis for the canonical Hebrew Bible as we understand it today, has had an amazingly stable existence since about the early second century C.E., and much of it is demonstrably based on a form of text that goes back to the second century B.C.E. When we discover new data that appear to be biblical or biblically related, we know how to understand those data because we know what the biblical text is supposed to look like. Our categories and well-learned criteria are determined by our present knowledge, and data from antiquity are interpreted according to these categories.

A second model or methodology, in contrast, acknowledges that conclusions should follow upon data and upon an adequate understanding of the data. We should operate according to the empirical principle that we must start our intellectual construct from the data, not from preconceived notions of what historical reality must have been like. Every source of evidence we have for the nature of the biblical text in the Second Temple period — the Qumran scrolls, the Samaritan Pentateuch (SP), the Septuagint (LXX), the New Testament, and Josephus — demonstrates that the content, wording, and orthography of the biblical text were pluriform and dynamically growing, with variant literary editions for many of the biblical books. According to the second model, the data are first understood on their own terms, in their historical context. If that picture clashes with our modern picture, one honestly asks whether our modern picture ought not be revised.

According to the first model, if a text does not look similar enough to the traditional MT, or even the MT-SP-LXX, then it is classified as "nonbiblical," or "parabiblical," or "reworked Bible." But according to the second model, as we will see below, that same text could be classified as "biblical," if it fits the profile of what the biblical text was really like in antiquity. Once seen in this new light, it can help us better understand the history of the biblical text.

An illustration may help. When the *Great Isaiah Scroll* (1QIsaᵃ) was first discovered, it was labeled a "vulgar" or even "worthless" manuscript.[13] It did not conform to the "biblical" text some scholars knew — the MT. They had their categories well learned and their criteria well formed, and they knew what a biblical manuscript should look like; 1QIsaᵃ did not make the grade. A number of other, analogous judgments were made, many of which have since been revised in the light of ongoing investigation.

Thus, a paradigm shift is needed, one element of which is the adoption of an ancient, in contrast to a modern, perspective.

The Scriptures

A significant element in this paradigm shift is the revision of our view of the MT in comparison with other witnesses to the biblical text. The common, sometimes unreflective, view of the text of the Hebrew Bible is that it is basically a "purified" Masoretic Text. That is, the single "standard text" form that the rabbis and the Masoretes handed on, the traditional *Textus Receptus*, once the obvious errors are removed, is considered to present the "original text," or the closest one can come to it. Accordingly, most Bible translations translate "the MT except where there is a problem," at which point they look to the SP, the LXX, the versions, or emendation. But the Qumran scrolls show that the textual form of the MT was not and is not the central text of the Hebrew Bible, but is simply one of several forms that existed in antiquity. As early as 1988 both Emanuel Tov and I had challenged the centrality of the MT. Tov correctly stated that the Qumran texts have "taught us no longer to posit MT at the center of our textual thinking";[14] and I discussed a series of variant editions of biblical books, several Qumran scrolls, and LXX readings which "prove to be superior in general to the MT" and which thus demonstrate "the decentralization of the MT as *the* text of the Hebrew Bible."[15] Beginning from these observations, we must reassess how we approach the text of the Hebrew Bible.[16]

13. H. M. Orlinsky, "Studies in the St. Mark's Isaiah Scroll, IV," esp. 340.
14. E. Tov, "Hebrew Biblical Manuscripts from the Judaean Desert: Their Contribution to Textual Criticism," esp. 7.
15. E. Ulrich, "Double Literary Editions of Biblical Narratives and Reflections on Determining the Form to Be Translated," esp. 46-47; and "The Biblical Scrolls from Qumran Cave 4," esp. 223 (emphasis in original).
16. *The Oxford Hebrew Bible,* currently in preparation, is the first effort since the dis-

The common mentality of privileging the MT is usually formed from the very beginning of a reader's interest in the Bible. The translation a casual reader picks up is generally based on the MT. If further interest spurs that reader to pursue knowledge of the original language, the introductory Hebrew textbook will present the details of Tiberian Hebrew, the form solidified in the medieval period by the Masoretes. When one advances to reading the text, one purchases a *Biblia Hebraica Stuttgartensia (BHS)*, which is a transcription of Codex Leningradensis. Advanced problems get solved by Wilhelm Gesenius, who explains MT anomalies mainly within the Tiberian system. To be fair, since this is the only Hebrew text tradition that was transmitted after the second century C.E., it is difficult to do otherwise, and prior to the scrolls it was virtually impossible to do so. But we should now be aware of the situation and attempt to broaden our patterns.

Biblical versus Parabiblical Distribution in DJD

Another area where modern terminology does not adequately address the situation in the first centuries is along the border between what are labeled "biblical" and "nonbiblical" scrolls. Understandably, before a full picture of the nature of the biblical text in antiquity was achieved, the early editors of the DJD series classified the scrolls according to modern classifications and divided the "biblical" scrolls from the "nonbiblical" scrolls according to the contents of the MT. For the continuation of the series Tov and I decided to follow the established practice, classifying mechanically according to these same modern formal categories. Thus, those manuscripts that correspond to books of the traditional Hebrew Bible, and only those, would be classified as "biblical." That practice does, however, involve the double anomaly that some books that were very likely considered Scripture at Qumran (such as 4Q["Reworked"] Pentateuch, *1 Enoch,* and *Jubilees*) are classified as "nonbiblical," while many of the Ketubim, which were evidently not yet considered Scripture, are classified as "biblical." In a recent article, VanderKam correctly notes more broadly that "what are identified as 'biblical' manuscripts are often treated separately by scrolls scholars, with some focusing all or almost all of their scholarly labors on them. It seems to me

---

covery of the scrolls to produce a critically established text; for a description of the project plus individual samples, see R. Hendel, "The Oxford Hebrew Bible: Prologue to a New Critical Edition."

that this segregation of texts is not a valid procedure in that it does not reflect what comes to expression in the ancient works found at Qumran."[17]

A "Standard Text" in the First Centuries?

Another problem concerning the perception of the MT is the view that the text tradition that it represents was the "standard text" in the first centuries. By "standard text" people usually envision some form of the "original text" minimally marred by human copyists' errors, or the "correct" texts preserved by the priests in the Jerusalem temple, somehow transferred to the Pharisees or rabbis, or some combination of the two.[18] The Qumran manuscripts that show no evidence of being "sectarian," but are representative of the Jewish Scriptures generally in that period, bountifully demonstrate not only that textual pluriformity was the common state of the biblical text but also that there was no expectation of conformity to a standard text. The SP, the LXX, the quotations in the New Testament, and the biblical texts used by Josephus all resoundingly confirm this widely accepted state of pluriformity. To be sure, scribes attempted to copy their source texts as accurately as possible, including (as also seen in the MT) accurately copying errors already solidified in the text. But the source texts they were copying were already widely different from each other. The MT of each book was more or less accurately copied from *some* text that existed in the Second Temple period, but the specific text form for many books was only one of the equally valued forms in which the text of that book existed in antiquity.

Despite suggestions to the contrary, the future still awaits demonstration that the texts preserved in the medieval MT transmit the texts guarded by the priests in the Jerusalem temple as opposed to other popular or "vulgar" texts that were less well preserved by less well qualified people. Nor has a line of succession — from temple priests to Pharisees to rabbis — been convincingly shown. If any group had temple texts that they preserved and

---

17. VanderKam, "Questions of Canon," 95.

18. But the developmental composition of the biblical books shows that "the original text" is a naïve and unattainable concept, often based on an unnuanced view of an *Urtext*. Moreover, to my knowledge, no one has demonstrated how we could know either the textual nature of the priests' manuscripts in the Jerusalem temple, or how the Pharisees/rabbis, usually considered a lay group, would have received them in contrast to the (probably priestly) LXX translators and the Qumran leaders who were presumably very strict priests.

copied, the Qumran group would seem to be the most likely candidate. Their early members are widely believed to have been priests in the temple who separated themselves because they believed the temple had been defiled. There does not seem to be any evidence that the Pharisees were conscious that their texts differed from other less valuable textual forms. Nor did they have the religious authority — acknowledged by other Jewish parties — to claim that their texts were standard and others were not.[19] The specific texts for each book in the rabbinic collection as reflected in the MT are, as far as we can tell, not selected or chosen but chance or coincidental.[20] The poor state of the text, for example, of Samuel and Hosea, would seem to preclude conscious textual preference and selection; and the criteria for the choices of the MT versus the Hebrew *Vorlage* of the LXX could not have been the same for all books (cf., e.g., Jeremiah and Daniel). It is difficult to prove that there was a centralized and dominant group within Judaism prior to the revolts that possessed the detailed attention and concern for a "standard text," or indeed the power to establish one.[21]

It is possible, although undocumented, that some individuals may have been conscious of differences between variant editions of particular books and may have chosen one deliberately instead of another. But scrolls not in use were usually rolled up; and if there was more than one scroll of a book, it seems more in line with the evidence that a reader would have picked up one of the available rolled-up scrolls marked "במדבר" without knowing and, apparently from the Qumran evidence, without caring which text form of Numbers was inscribed inside. If there were an awareness of different editions and a conscious choice between them, the articulation of the choice is less likely to have been in terms of "pre-Samaritan versus proto-MT" and more likely "the newer, fuller edition versus the earlier, shorter edition."

Classification of Qumran Scriptural Scrolls

The set of categories used most commonly today for describing scriptural scrolls from Qumran proposes five classifications: "Proto-Masoretic texts,"

---

19. L. H. Schiffman, *From Text to Tradition,* 98 and 112.

20. See E. Ulrich, "The Qumran Biblical Scrolls — The Scriptures of Late Second Temple Judaism," esp. 72.

21. See the quotation from VanderKam, above.

"Pre-Samaritan texts," "texts close to the Septuagint," "texts written in the Qumran Practice," and "Non-Aligned texts."[22] This system has the distinct pedagogical advantage, especially for students or nonspecialists, of helping one understand and classify the textual situation of the new scrolls quickly. Thus, VanderKam in an article on the canon uses these classifications as a *starting point,* saying that they "give one extremely well informed scholar's overview of the situation."[23] But I suggest that one must quickly go further and redescribe the situation in terms appropriate to a first-centuries mentality for proper focus. VanderKam apparently agrees, since he also points out that "there are some problems with these categories,"[24] and indeed some manuscripts actually must be assigned to more than one category according to those criteria.

Significant problems appear in our use of these categories. People at that time would not have used or even had conceptually available textual categories such as "Masoretic or Proto-Masoretic Text," "Samaritan" or "Pre-Samaritan." The category of Masoretic, or Proto-Masoretic Text, or even Proto-Rabbinic, seems anachronistic, as does "Pre-Samaritan." The term "Samaritan" would be used of the religion or of a person, but it would be used of a text only when describing the theologically changed texts with a Mount Gerizim perspective. The category "texts close to the Septuagint" raises the anomalous situation that most manuscripts (including the MT texts!) of Genesis or Leviticus could be so classified, since there is minimal difference between the LXX and the MT for those books.

An additional complication is that the textual character of the MT changes from book to book, and so the criteria for labeling any text "Proto-MT" change, depending on whether, for example, the text is Numbers or Jeremiah or Daniel. A further problem is that the MT and the LXX are not text types; the text of each of the books is simply the only manuscript (for MT) or one of the only manuscripts (for LXX) preserved. They are, in varying degrees, simply more or less accurate *copies* of whichever edition they happen to attest; they do not present their edition in pure form nor do they constitute proper standards against which other manuscripts should be compared.

Regarding the fourth category, I have suggested elsewhere that "the

22. E. Tov, *Textual Criticism of the Hebrew Bible,* 114.

23. VanderKam, "Questions of Canon," 94.

24. VanderKam, "Questions of Canon," 94. Some problems that he mentions are that "not all of [the categories] are of the same kind" (spelling system vs. textual nature) and that sometimes a manuscript "agrees with both the MT and the Samaritan Pentateuch."

Qumran Practice" is probably not unique to Qumran but is representative of the scribal practice generally in the latter half of the Second Temple period in Palestine.[25] E. Kutscher, who wrote an exhaustive monograph on the linguistic character of the *Great Isaiah Scroll*,[26] also stated that "we may assume that many of those points in which the Scroll [1QIsa[a]] differs linguistically from the Masoretic Isaiah represent characteristics of the literary Hebrew of the last centuries of the first millennium B.C.E."[27] The scribal practice visible in the scrolls is not one single, moderately clear system as opposed to a different system in the MT. Rather, there is a spectrum of features which appear to be natural developments of the morphology and the expanding orthography of late Biblical Hebrew, as can also be seen in the Targums. The features appear somewhat arbitrarily and erratically in the Qumran manuscripts, which at some points use the spelling familiar from the Tiberian-MT practice(s), and at other points (often in the same verse) use the "Qumran practice." The features also sometimes appear in distinctly non-Qumran places: on Hasmonaean coins, in the Nash Papyrus from Egypt, and in an Aramaic inscription from Hatra. Perhaps most interestingly, many of these features show up in the MT itself. A few examples may be listed:[28]

כול: cf. לכול Jer 33:8; כולם Jer 31:34

לוא: cf. לוא Isa 16:14; Jer 7:28; Nash Papyrus

כיא: cf. נקיא Joel 4:19; Jonah 1:14

המה-: cf. מהמה Jer 10:2

קטלתה: cf. וראיתה Num 27:13; וצויתה Num 27:19

כה-: cf. ידכה Exod 13:16

אקטולה: cf. אשקוטה Isa 18:4.

For the final category, in light of the lack of a "standard text" in the late Second Temple period, as discussed above, the category "Non-Aligned texts" ought not to be viewed as an operative category in this period. Rather, it seems increasingly clear that the text of each book developed

---

25. E. Ulrich, "Multiple Literary Editions," 110-13.

26. E. Y. Kutscher, *The Language and Linguistic Background of the Isaiah Scroll* (*1QIsa[a]*).

27. E. Y. Kutscher, *A History of the Hebrew Language*, 95.

28. For the distinctive features of "the Qumran practice," see E. Tov, "The Orthography and Language of the Hebrew Scrolls Found at Qumran and the Origin of These Scrolls"; *Textual Criticism of the Hebrew Bible*, 107-10; and *Scribal Practices and Approaches Reflected in the Texts Found in the Judean Desert*.

through successive revised literary editions, whereby an earlier form of the book was intentionally revised to produce a newer revised edition. Thus, I have alternatively proposed that the text types for each book be classified according to the successive editions for which we have evidence, e.g.:

Edition[29]	Exodus	Numbers	Joshua	Jeremiah	Daniel	Psalms
n + 1	OG-Exod 35–40	MT-Num	4QJosh[a], Josephus	4QJer[b,d], OG	MT-Dan	MT-Pss
n + 2	MT-Exod	4QNum[b]	[SamPent, OL][30]	4QJer[a,c], MT	OG-Dan	11QPs[a]
n + 3	4QpaleoExod[m]		OG-Josh			
n + 4	SamPent-Exod		MT-Josh			
n + 5	4QPent-Exod					

The biblical books each developed through a number *("n")* of "new and expanded editions" prior to the earliest surviving manuscripts. For the Exodus example above, the earliest preserved edition *("n + 1")* is that in the OG for chapters 35–40. The MT has a revised edition *("n + 2")* of those chapters. 4QpaleoExod[m] displays a yet expanded edition *("n + 3")* beyond the MT edition, etc. The *"n + 1"* symbols may appear less elegant than "proto-MT," etc., but since the successive editions form the primary lines for charting the history of the text of the individual books, the system, once understood, arguably describes the shape(s) of the biblical texts in the first centuries accurately, more so than the previous categories. For an extended period of time, the earlier edition would have coexisted alongside the newer edition, and both would have been used, probably with little awareness of the differences in the editions. Thus, terms and classifications such as "earlier or shorter edition" of Jeremiah versus "secondary, expanded edition" of Jeremiah seem preferable. We should appreciate the pedagogical usefulness of medieval and modern concepts, categories, and

29. E. Ulrich, "The Dead Sea Scrolls and the Biblical Text," esp. 85. The *"n + 1"* type of designation for successive editions of a text assumes that there have been a number *("n")* of editions during the composition of the text which constitute its growth leading up to the first extant witness *("n + 1")* to a given book. The last line, *"n + 5* 4QPent-Exod," was not yet in the 1998 article but is added here in light of the revised classification of 4QPentateuch (see below).

30. The SP has בהר גריזים and the OL has *Garzin* at Deut 27:4, where Moses gives the corresponding command which is executed in Joshua by the building of the first altar at Gilgal (4QJosh[a], Josephus), Mount Gerizim (SP, OL), or Mount Ebal (MT).

terms as a starting point, but I suggest as the necessary next stage the adoption of concepts, categories, and terms that would have been appropriate to the first centuries.

4QPentateuch and 11QPsalms[a]

There are many more topics than can be treated here which deserve reexamination in light of the more richly detailed understanding of the biblical text in antiquity afforded by the scrolls. A carefully thought-out discussion of the *Urtext* is one such topic. Another is the "biblical" or "nonbiblical" status of various manuscripts, in view of the shift in scholarly awareness as seen especially regarding 4QPentateuch (*olim* 4QReworked Pentateuch) and 11QPsalms[a].[31]

Already in 1993 I suggested that 4QRP should be reconsidered as possibly a variant form of the Pentateuch, since the characteristics listed for describing the texts as "reworked" were becoming increasingly recognized as typical characteristics of the biblical text in the Second Temple period.[32] In a 1997 conference in Jerusalem, Michael Segal argued persuasively for the same position.[33] And in 2007 the same conclusion was reached by Emanuel Tov,[34] one of the two editors of 4QRP.[35]

When James Sanders edited 11QPsalms[a] and treated it as a biblical Psalms manuscript in 1965,[36] many leading scholars disagreed, arguing that it was a postbiblical, liturgical manuscript.[37] But also in 1993 the char-

---

31. For 4QRP see E. Tov and S. White, "364-367. 4QReworked Pentateuch[b-e]," DJD 13, 187-351. A fifth manuscript, 4Q158, has been connected with 4QRP[b-e], but it remains debated whether these five manuscripts are all copies of one work or simply similar expansions of the Pentateuch.

32. E. Ulrich, "The Bible in the Making: The Scriptures at Qumran," esp. 92 n. 51; repr. 32.

33. His lecture was presented in 1997 and published in 2000: M. Segal, "4QReworked Pentateuch or 4QPentateuch?"

34. Tov now agrees that 4QRP is "to be reclassified as a biblical text, '4QPentateuch,'" and needs "to be studied as Hebrew Scripture." I am grateful to Professor Tov for an advance copy of his article.

35. See now S. White Crawford, *Rewriting Scripture in Second Temple Times.*

36. For 11QPsalms[a] see J. A. Sanders, DJD IV.

37. S. Talmon, "Pisqah Be'emṣa' Pasuq and 11QPs[a]"; M. H. Goshen-Gottstein, "The Psalms Scroll (11QPs[a]): A Problem of Canon and Text"; and P. W. Skehan, "A Liturgical Complex in 11QPs[a]," plus "Qumran and Old Testament Criticism," esp. 168-69.

acteristics just mentioned above, along with other correctives (such as the use of the Palaeo-Hebrew script for the divine name in other square script manuscripts), suggested that the arguments against the biblical nature of 11QPs[a] could no longer be seen as determinative.[38] In 1997 Peter Flint presented the evidence more comprehensively.[39] Thus, fresh analysis of a wide variety of manuscripts may produce advances in understanding many texts.

Conclusion

Methodological reflection on the three areas discussed above promises to yield continuingly greater precision in our understanding of the Scriptures in this period so crucial for the emergence of both Christianity and rabbinic Judaism. First, careful analysis of methodological procedure in itself is always warranted in scientific endeavors. It is important that we reflect on how it is that we have come to know what we know, and on whether there might be flaws in our perception. We should be aware that our store of knowledge and our ways of thinking are largely derived from the preceding generation; as grateful as we are for that, we should always ask whether current advances require revision of our ways of thinking.

Second, methodological rigor should be applied to assessments and discussion of both individual texts and the process toward the canon and beyond. Just as clarifying advances have been made on texts such as 4QPentateuch and 11QPs[a] and have vindicated the trustworthiness of the SP and the LXX, other texts undoubtedly hold analogous promise.

Finally, the process leading toward the canon and beyond remains mostly unexplored terrain, but it holds rich promise of shedding important light on the scriptural process and socio-political history throughout the Second Temple period and continuing through the early Christian and rabbinic centuries.

38. See Ulrich, "The Bible in the Making," 30, and more fully, "Multiple Literary Editions," 115-20.

39. P. W. Flint, *The Dead Sea Psalms Scrolls and the Book of Psalms*, esp. 202-27.

Sources and Redaction in the Dead Sea Scrolls: The Growth of Ancient Texts

Charlotte Hempel

Introduction

One of the most fascinating insights provided by the scrolls is the way they allow us a firsthand glance at how ancient texts grew. By looking at the original manuscripts, sometimes corrected by other scribes, sometimes available in radically different witnesses to a single composition, we can almost watch ancient texts grow and evolve before our eyes. The question of how ancient texts developed over time is of great interest to Hebrew Bible scholars; the important difference for Qumran studies is that we have actual ancient manuscripts to check the theory in crucial places.[1] What I hope to do in this chapter is to look at ways in which readers and interpreters of the scrolls can feed off biblical criticism and ways in which the disciplines are unique. I will use as my conversation partner the methodological observations of John Barton on source and redaction criticism of the Hebrew Bible.[2] Barton's observation on the current phase of Hebrew Bible scholarship with particular reference to the Pentateuch might just as well

---

1. For a similar point see S. Metso, *The Textual Development of the Qumran Community Rule*, 5.
2. See J. Barton, "Redaction Criticism: Old Testament"; "Source Criticism: Old Testament."

I would like to thank Max Grossman for her vision, leadership, and enthusiasm during the project that culminates in this book. I also wish to thank Michael Stone for his incisive comments on a draft of this chapter.

refer to Qumran: "OT studies seem in this as in many other ways to have arrived at a pluralistic phase, with no one theory holding the field."[3]

We may compare this to the sentiment expressed by Albert Baumgarten some years ago with reference to the scrolls: "For the moment, however, the contribution of newly available Dead Sea Scroll sources [his chief concern being with the *Community Rule*] has been to generate much more confusion than clarity."[4]

In what follows I will offer some reflections on the methodological bridges that may be built between the source and redaction critical study of the Hebrew Bible and the source and redaction critical study of the scrolls.

Qumran and Methodology: "On the Job Training"

In Qumran studies, methodologies have evolved gradually as more and more evidence became available in a more or less haphazard order. The extraordinary circumstances of the discovery of the scrolls are arguably an immense bonus as well as a significant challenge. They are a bonus because we have texts that were found *in situ,* in the very place where their ancient owners left them. Many of these ancient manuscripts go back to a time not very far removed from the date of their composition, though very few if any are autographs.[5] The context of the discovery also posed a considerable challenge because it suggested initially that the material was more coherent and unified than it turned out to be on closer inspection.

One revealing perspective gained from studying the manuscripts is their testimony to some very complex literary developments and interrelationships between texts. A number of these developments are particularly clearly attested, especially in the case of the *Community Rule,* where we are fortunate to have several copies of the same composition with significant differences.[6] In what follows I will draw most of my examples from this text.

The first generation of scholars faced the vast tasks of identifying and deciphering an immense number of fragments as well as allocating

---

3. Barton, "Source Criticism," 163.

4. A. I. Baumgarten, "The Zadokite Priests at Qumran: A Reconsideration," esp. 155f.

5. On the difficulty of positively identifying autographs in the scrolls, see E. Tov, *Scribal Practices and Approaches Reflected in the Texts Found in the Judean Desert,* 28-29.

6. For an overview with further references, see M. A. Knibb, "Rule of the Community."

them to particular compositions. Inevitably one was looking for a provisional classification system that could be refined over time. One obvious approach was to separate biblical from nonbiblical material and then previously known nonbiblical material from entirely new texts. Many of the previously unknown texts became associated with the community that resided at the nearby settlement. It was further supposed that this group was responsible for the depositing and at times also the copying and/or composing of some of the texts.

Qumran studies started off, rather naturally, with the assumption that, given the antiquity of the manuscripts, we need not expect the same level of complex literary growth that is frequently argued for with reference to the composition of biblical texts. The antiquity of the manuscripts was not the only factor that contributed to a relaxing of methodological defenses. We also have texts describing the life of a particular community, its organization and history, as well as references to key individuals such as a teacher of righteousness.[7] The image of a tightly-knit desert community led by the charismatic teacher had a powerful influence on the ways that many of the texts were read for a time, and it seemed natural to many to assume that this teacher wrote many of the most important texts himself. While some have tended to think of the teacher as the single author of a number of texts, others argued that key texts are composite and advocated the view that the teacher was responsible for some of their component parts. The learned hunch that the *Rule of the Community,* for instance, is a composite document[8] has now been dramatically confirmed by the Cave 4 manuscripts, which reveal a number of significant variants. The twelve manuscripts of the *Community Rule* from Caves 1, 4, and 5 effectively leave us with at least three different traditions of what the text of the *Rule* looked like.[9]

This short overview already demonstrates some ways in which scholarly approaches to the scrolls differ fundamentally. There are those who are sensitive to unevenness and differences between and within texts — the

7. For the term, see Joel 2:23; cf. Hos 10:12. The passage in Joel is often rendered "early rain for righteousness." The same Hebrew noun can mean either teacher or early rain. On this figure, see Knibb, "Teacher of Righteousness"; and T. H. Lim, *Pesharim,* 74-78.

8. See esp. J. Murphy-O'Connor, "La genèse littéraire de la *Règle de la Communauté.*" For a convenient summary of his conclusions in English cf. his "Community, Rule of the (1QS)."

9. Cf. P. S. Alexander and G. Vermes, DJD 26, 9-12; and Metso, *Textual Development,* esp. 147.

"splitters." Such approaches are in their infancy or early youth as far as the Qumran texts are concerned, and there have as yet not been the excessive flights of fancy, as are known from some corners of biblical studies, for instance. Then there are others who have a profound dislike of cutting up a perfectly good text — the "clumpers." The interesting thing is that the ancient copies of the *Community Rule* have added some spice to this debate. Here we have hard and fast manuscript evidence that the kind of thing splitters love actually happened in antiquity. In what follows we are able to begin our analysis of the scrolls with the ancient manuscripts. We will look at the splits and cracks in the different manuscripts themselves before considering whether there are further cracks hidden under the surface.

Scribes at Work

George Brooke has recently written a stimulating paper, "The Qumran Scrolls and the Demise of the Distinction between Higher and Lower Criticism," where he reflects on ways in which the study of the scrolls has made the once popular distinction between higher and lower criticism redundant.[10] Barton sums up the way the term "higher criticism" was once employed: "This term indicated that questions of a higher order were being asked — questions about the origins of the material, not just about the accuracy of its transmission by scribes."[11]

Brooke's paper deals mainly with the evidence of the scriptural manuscripts.[12] However, what he has to say is of great relevance to the nonscriptural texts as well. Almost contemporaneously with Brooke's paper, Emanuel Tov published an important article, "The Writing of Early Scrolls: Implications for the Literary Analysis of Hebrew Scripture."[13] In this article Tov was able to draw on his authoritative knowledge of the scribal practices reflected in the Dead Sea Scrolls in order to argue that the technical aspects of scrolls production left only limited scope for major reworking.[14] He concludes that changes were made in the scrolls through the production of new copies that differed in minor and sometimes major

10. G. J. Brooke, "The Qumran Scrolls and the Demise of the Distinction Between Higher and Lower Criticism."

11. Barton, "Source Criticism," 164.

12. The designation "biblical" is somewhat anachronistic for this period.

13. *DSD* 13 (2006): 339-47.

14. See his monumental study, *Scribal Practices and Approaches*.

ways from the old. Both Brooke and Tov have put the question of the creative role of scribes at the forefront of our minds. This is an area also debated previously by Shemaryahu Talmon, who coined the phrase "insufficiently controlled copying" with reference to the scrolls, and Geza Vermes, who speaks of "scribal creative freedom."[15]

This raises the important question of what it means to speak of an author in antiquity. Here the scrolls are important witnesses. A number of scholars have observed that the distinction between scribe and author is blurry for the scriptural scrolls. Thus Talmon notes with reference to the Hebrew Bible manuscripts, "at that stage of the development of biblical literature, and also before it, authors and copyists were not clearly separable classes of literary practitioners."[16]

It will become apparent in what follows that the manuscripts of the *Community Rule* provide scholars with one of the most fertile pieces of evidence for the gradual growth and fluid transmission of an ancient text. We will notice significant changes from one manuscript to another but also, on a smaller scale, within a single manuscript.

The Community Rule Manuscripts

Qumran revealed twelve at times quite different manuscripts of this work, which were composed, copied, and revised over the greater part of two hundred years (ca. 125 B.C.E.–50 C.E.) with little concern for the elimination of manuscripts that differed from one another, let alone from a perceived "norm." I have argued recently that this relaxed attitude towards a variety of text forms is reminiscent of the scriptural scrolls at Qumran.[17] A concern for the most authoritative text, scriptural or otherwise, seems to occupy the minds of modern scholars rather more than the ancient communities behind the Qumran library.

In the remainder of this chapter I would like to take the reader on a ride that starts at the lower end of the critical scale and moves up, taking us through the quagmire of Qumran and methodology while addressing dif-

15. S. Talmon, "The Textual Study of the Bible — A New Outlook," esp. 380; and G. Vermes, *The Dead Sea Scrolls Forty Years On*, 14. Further Tov, *Scribal Practices and Approaches*, 7-8, 24-28; and J. Van Seters, *The Edited Bible*, 346.

16. Talmon, "The Textual Study of the Bible," 336. See also E. Tov, *The Textual Criticism of the Hebrew Bible*, 188-90.

17. C. Hempel, "Vielgestaltigkeit und Verbindlichkeit: Serekh ha-Yachad in Qumran."

ferent examples from the corpus, most of them from the *Community Rule* manuscripts, along the way. The first stage in our encounter with the scrolls is the deciphering and transcription of the manuscripts and the ordering of fragments into a composition. Reconstruction of gaps in the texts also figures — at times too prominently — in the repertoire of the Qumranologist. These issues are expertly dealt with in the contribution to this volume by Eibert Tigchelaar. The stages that follow will include attention to marginal scribal markings, scribal corrections, differences and similarities in multiple copies of the same composition, shared material in different compositions, and, finally, unevenness in a text in the absence of manuscript evidence.

Marginal Scribal Markings in the Community Rule

Increasingly a focus of scholarly attention, scribal markings in the margins of scrolls texts can be closely related to the literary growth of texts. Sterling work has been done on these textual features by the late Odil Hannes Steck, with regard to the *Great Isaiah Scroll,* and by Emanuel Tov.[18] The latter coined the term "paratextual elements" to refer to such features;[19] in the Netherlands this approach has been termed *delimitation criticism.*[20] Important examples of delimitation critical evidence can be found in the margins of the Cave 1 manuscript of the *Community Rule* (1QS), at three important junctures:[21]

> 1QS 5:1 *paleo-Hebrew* waw[22]
> 1QS 8:1 *paleo-Hebrew* zayin *combined with an unknown character*[23]

18. Cf. O. H. Steck, *Die Erste Jesajarolle von Qumran (1QIsaᵃ);* and Tov, *Scribal Practices and Approaches.*

19. Cf. Tov, *Textual Criticism of the Hebrew Bible,* 49-51.

20. Cf. M. C. A. Korpel and J. M. Oesch, *Delimitation Criticism: A New Tool in Biblical Scholarship.*

21. The identification of the markings goes back to Tov. See the excellent overview in C. Murphy, *Wealth in the Dead Sea Scrolls and in the Qumran Community,* 110-15, in a section devoted to the "Scribal Structure" of 1QS; and Tov, *Scribal Practices and Approaches,* 178-213, esp. 206-8.

22. See Tov, *Scribal Practices and Approaches,* 361, fig. 5.5.

23. See Tov, *Scribal Practices and Approaches,* 363, fig. 11, where the position of the sign is given as the bottom margin of 1QS 7.

1QS 9:3 *paleo-Hebrew* zayin *combined with* samekh *and a* para-graphos.[24]

The scribal mark at 1QS 5:1 coincides with other factors that indicate that 1QS 5 is an important new beginning in the text, or even the very beginning (as is the case for 4QS^d).[25] The coincidence of the scribal mark with an important juncture in the literary growth of the text should alert our attention to scribal marks in other places. In the two other instances it is difficult to be sure what the mark signifies. It may be no more than an indication that a particular passage is important, and this may, ultimately, also be the reason for the mark in 1QS 5:1.[26]

Apart from these major scribal markings in the margin, 1QS contains a great many *paragraphos* signs at more frequent intervals; cf., for instance, 1QS 5:13, 25; 6:8, 24; 8:4, 20; 9:5, 12, 19.[27] According to Tov, "some, and perhaps all, were inserted in the manuscripts by later scribes and users."[28] In one case at least, the *paragraphos* coincides with another important piece of evidence. One manuscript of the *Rule* from Cave 4 (4QS^e) lacks almost a whole column of material that appears in 1QS 8:15–9:11. The interesting thing is that the point at which both manuscripts come together again is marked with a *paragraphos* sign in the 1QS manuscript (cf. 1QS 9:12). Scholars disagree on whether the shorter text of 4QS^e is best explained as an abbreviation or whether we should consider 1QS's longer text as a secondary expansion.[29] In any case, it is difficult to escape the impression that "paratextual elements," to use Tov's term, are at times indicators of places where the text evolved. Whether or not these correspondences are the result of deliberate efforts on the part of a scribe, or a later user of the scroll[30] intent on drawing attention to a new beginning, is a different matter. Ob-

24. See Tov, *Scribal Practices and Approaches*, 363, fig. 11.2a.

25. On the physical features that indicate that 4QS^d began with the equivalent of 1QS 5 and never contained the material found in 1QS 1–4, see Alexander and Vermes, DJD 26, 85 and Pl. X; and Metso, *Textual Development*, 37.

26. Cf., E. Tov, "Scribal Practices," esp. 828. Further, *Scribal Practices and Approaches*, 207, 211.

27. For a complete list, see Tov, *Scribal Practices and Approaches*, 181.

28. *Scribal Practices and Approaches*, 145.

29. Cf. Metso, *Textual Development*, 71-73; and P. S. Alexander, "The Redaction-History of *Serekh ha-Yaḥad*: A Proposal."

30. See Tov, *Scribal Practices and Approaches*, 145, noting the possibility of *paragraphos* signs and other marginal marks going back to later users rather than the original or a subsequent scribe.

servations such as these indicate again that the apparently dichotomous technical side of copying and the compositional side can be mutually illuminating when it comes to studying the ancient Qumran manuscripts.

Scribal Corrections

The next step in the process takes us to scribal corrections. The most important example of this kind of activity is the work of scribes A and B in 1QS 7-8. It has long been recognized that two different scribes were at work in 1QS 7-8.[31] Scholars have discussed the possibility that scribe B, who supplemented and corrected the work of scribe A, may have used a different manuscript from the one used by scribe A, a revisor-exemplar.[32] One scholar argued that scribe B may have been using 4QS[e] or a manuscript close to it.[33] Sarianna Metso's examination of the corrections and supplementations by scribe B in the light of the Cave 4 evidence has found that the work of scribe B occasionally agrees with a reading in a Cave 4 manuscript, but not consistently with the same one. It appears unlikely, therefore, that scribe B employed one of the manuscripts known to us to aid his work. Whatever the exact procedure of scribe B may have been in any given instance, his or her activity provides important further evidence for the growth of this ancient text.

Another fascinating case involves the changing form of a recurring formula that has for a long time been important in the literary analysis of the *Community Rule.* 1QS 8-9 repeatedly employs the formula "When these exist in Israel," and Edmund Sutcliffe and Jerome Murphy-O'Connor convincingly argued that the material associated with a soon-to-be-founded community probably forms part of the earliest layers of this document.[34] The formula appears in 1QS 8:4, 12; 9:3 and in some corresponding material in 4QS[d] and 4QS[e].[35] What is of interest is that a shorter, and prob-

31. Cf. Metso, *Textual Development,* 95-105 and further literature referred to there. Further, Tov, *Scribal Practices and Approaches,* 222-30.

32. Cf. M. Martin, *The Scribal Character of the Dead Sea Scrolls,* 464-66.

33. Cf. E. Puèch, "Remarques sur l'écriture de 1QS VII-VIII," esp. 43. See also Tov, *Textual Criticism of the Hebrew Bible,* 213.

34. Cf. E. F. Sutcliffe, "The First Fifteen Members of the Qumran Community"; and J. Murphy-O'Connor, "La genèse littéraire." See also C. Hempel, "Emerging Communal Life and Ideology in the S Tradition."

35. See the helpful table in Alexander and Vermes, DJD 26, 113; the inclusion of a reference to the *yaḥad* for 1QS 9:3 is in error.

ably more original, form of the formula[36] is found alongside a more elaborate one, and that these variations are found in the texts of both scribe A and scribe B, as well as in multiple S manuscripts.

Short formula:	Longer formulae:
"When these exist in Israel"	"When these exist as a community in Israel
1QS 8:4 Scribe A	according to these rules"
4QS^e 2:13[37]	1QS 8:12 Scribe B
1QS 8:12 Scribe A	4QS^d 7:4[39]
4QS^d 6:6[38]	
	"When these exist in Israel according to all these rules"
	1QS 9:3 Scribe A

Again, the precise history of this formula is unclear, although Alexander and Vermes's explanation that the shorter version is the more original appears convincing, but it is significant that we can note the evolution of this formula both within a single manuscript (1QS) and across manuscripts.

Several Manuscripts of the Same Composition: Telling Differences and Equally Telling Similarities

We have already touched upon the significance of different readings of a particular passage in multiple manuscripts of the *Community Rule*. A considerable number of texts from the corpus of the scrolls, both scriptural and nonscriptural, are attested in multiple copies.[40] The number of copies of a particular composition provides scholars with important pointers as to the significance of a text and the level of interest in it in antiquity. Devorah Dimant has offered a seminal article in which she outlines the

---

36. As convincingly proposed by Alexander and Vermes, DJD 26, 113.

37. Cf. Alexander and Vermes, DJD 26, 139-44 and Pl. XV. It is clear that 4QS^e did not include the words "according to these rules." It is more difficult to be certain whether or not the words "as a community" *(leyaḥad)* were part of the lacuna.

38. Cf. Alexander and Vermes, DJD 26, 105-9 and Pl. XI.

39. Cf. Alexander and Vermes, DJD 26, 109-14 and Pl. XII.

40. See the table listing "Major Overlaps of Qumran Compositions," in Tov, *Scribal Practices and Approaches,* 26.

spread of various documents across the different caves.[41] Copies of the *Community Rule* were found in at least two, maybe as many as four, of the eleven caves.[42] The attestation of a text in various copies also allows us to estimate the period of time over which a particular work continued to be copied; as we have seen, in the case of the *Community Rule* we are dealing with a period of almost two hundred years.

Whereas some texts that are attested in significant numbers display very few significant variants of content from manuscript to manuscript, others contain some highly revealing variants. The ten ancient manuscripts of the *Damascus Document,* for instance, correspond rather closely to each other in their scope and readings.[43] By contrast, the variants in the Cave 1 and Cave 4 manuscripts of the *War Scroll* have for a long time been seen as indicating two different stages in the growth of this composition.[44] Access to the full surviving evidence of the *Community Rule* manuscripts from Cave 4 has revealed an extraordinary amount of variation in the growth of this text. Because of the wealth of evidence preserved in the S manuscripts for an evolving ancient textual tradition, the significance of these manuscripts reaches far beyond the confines of their particular background.

The presence of major variants of content between different copies of the work is beyond dispute. What they do not tell us, alas, is the direction in which the developments occurred: from short to long or *vice versa,* from simple to complex and so forth. Let us have a closer look at the major differences between the manuscripts of the *Rule* and the ways in which they have been interpreted by scholars.

1. None of the Cave 4 manuscripts contain parts of the two annexes to the *Community Rule* (1QSa [Rule of the Congregation] and 1QSb [Rule of Blessings]) found appended to this text in the Cave 1 copy.

41. See D. Dimant, "The Qumran Manuscripts: Contents and Significance."

42. The provenance of 1QS from Cave 1 and 4QS^{a-j} from Cave 4 is generally accepted. The identification of further copies of the Rule from Cave 5 and 11 is less certain; cf. J. T. Milik, DJD 3, 180-81. Alexander and Vermes do not regard 5Q11 as a copy of S (cf. DJD 26, 1-4, 24) whereas others do (cf. Knibb, "Rule of the Community," 793; and Metso, *Textual Development,* 65-66). Finally a text related to S has been identified in Cave 11; cf. F. García Martínez. E. J. C. Tigchelaar and A. S. van der Woude, DJD 23, 433-34.

43. Cf. J. M. Baumgarten, DJD 18; and C. Hempel, *The Damascus Texts.* Remarkably this impression of stability across the D manuscript spectrum even extends to the relatively consistent number of lines per column in different 4QD manuscripts (range: 20-24 lines) in contrast to the S manuscripts (range: 10-27 lines); cf. Tov, *Scribal Practices and Approaches,* 97-99.

44. Cf. J. Duhaime, *The War Texts: 1QM and Related Manuscripts.*

2. 4QS^b is the only Cave 4 manuscript to include material covering all parts of 1QS from the early columns 1QS 1–4, via the central section 1QS 5–9, to the closing hymn in 1QS 10–11. However, 4QS^b differs significantly from 1QS in the material found in the central section of 1QS, especially 1QS 5. Here 4QS^b has a text that displays many similarities to 4QS^d.

3. 4QS^d did not include the material preserved in 1QS 1–4 but begins with the equivalent of 1QS 5 with major differences from 1QS's text. In particular 4QS^d begins in 4QS^d 1:1 with a different heading, which constitutes the title of this manuscript, and names a different group ("the many") as the major authority in the community in contrast to the leading group familiar from 1QS 5 (i.e., "the sons of Zadok and the multitude of the people of the community").

4. 4QS^e lacks the equivalent of 1QS 8:15–9:11 and closes with a calendrical text (4QOtot) instead of a closing hymn.

These major differences between the manuscripts of the *Rule* leave little doubt that the text of this document evolved in complex ways. It is more difficult to determine the exact route this evolving process took. A number of scholars have argued that the shorter version of the *Rule* attested in 4QS^d is the more original despite the fact that the copy of 4QS^d (dating from ca. 50-1 B.C.E.) is not as old as the manuscript 1QS (dating from ca. 100-75 B.C.E.).[45] Philip Alexander, by contrast, argued that the earlier date of the 1QS manuscript strongly suggests that its text is the earlier one, which was subsequently shortened.[46] Similarly, a number of scholars propose that the shorter text of 4QS^e (lacking the equivalent of 1QS 8:15–9:11) is the result of an *omission*, whereas Metso suggests, by contrast, that the longer 1QS text includes an *expansion*.[47] Thus, whereas the primary evidence tells a story of textual growth and change, scholars have traced the developments behind this evidence in radically different ways.

Let us look at one of the most talked about examples, namely the differences between 1QS 5 and 4QS^b/4QS^d.[48] The key passages in translation read as follows:

45. For a concise outline of the issues and the debate as well as bibliographical details, see Knibb, "Rule of the Community."

46. Alexander, "The Redaction-History of *Serekh ha-Yaḥad*," a view accepted by Tov, *Scribal Practices and Approaches*, 27.

47. See note 29 above.

48. For the Hebrew text of 1QS, see E. Qimron, "Rule of the Community [1QS],"

1QS 5	4QS^b and 4QS^d (composite text)
₁*And this is the rule for the people of the community*	b₁/d₁*Midrash for the Maskil over (or: concerning) the people of the law*
who eagerly volunteer to turn back from all evil and to hold fast to all that He has commanded	who eagerly volunteer to turn back from all evil and to hold fast to all b₂that He has commanded.
as His wish.	
They shall keep separate from the congregation of ₂the people of injustice to form a community with regard to law and wealth. They shall be accountable to	d₂They shall keep separate from the congregation of the people of injustice to form a community with regard to la[w] and wealth. They shall be accountable b₃to
the sons of Zadok, the priests who keep the covenant, and to the multitude of the people of ₃the community who hold fast to the covenant. On their authority decisions shall be taken	*the many*
regarding any matter pertaining to law, wealth . . .	regarding any matter d₃pertaining to law and wealth . . .

The obvious focal points of the debate have tended to be differences between manuscripts, with disagreement and discussion often centered on the question of which manuscript has preserved the earlier stage in the growth of the text. I have highlighted the remarkable differences between 1QS 5 and 4QS$^{b/d}$ in italics in the table above. In a recent article I emphasized the importance of overlap between manuscripts.[49] Struck by the way in which remarkable overlap occurs even in the very same passages that differ radically at other points, I suggested that the earliest form of the text is to be found in the shared material. Such shared textual traditions are likely to go back to a time before the differences that now catch our attention had emerged. This is best illustrated by looking at the same text again, but this time with the overlap highlighted rather than the differences:

PTSDSSP 1:6ff.; for the 4QS manuscripts, see Alexander and Vermes, DJD 26. English translations are my own.

49. C. Hempel, "The Literary Development of the *S* Tradition — A New Paradigm."

1QS 5	4QS^b and 4QS^d (composite text)
₁And this is the rule for the people of the community	ᵦ₁/ᵈ₁Midrash for the Maskil over (or: concerning) the people of the law
who eagerly volunteer to turn back from all evil and to hold fast to all that He has commanded	*who eagerly volunteer to turn back from all evil and to hold fast to all* ᵦ₂*that He has commanded.*
as His wish.	
They shall keep separate from the congregation of ₂*the people of injustice to form a community with regard to law and wealth. They shall be accountable to*	ᵈ₂*They shall keep separate from the congregation of the people of injustice to form a community with regard to la[w] and wealth. They shall be accountable* ᵦ₃*to*
the sons of Zadok, the priests who keep the covenant, and to the multitude of the people of ₃the community who hold fast to the covenant. On their authority decisions shall be taken	the many
regarding any matter pertaining to law, wealth . . .	*regarding any matter* ᵈ₃*pertaining to law and wealth . . .*

The best hypothesis on how these texts evolved seems to me one that accounts for both differences and overlaps between the manuscripts. In a nutshell, I have suggested that the common ground, the overlap between the manuscripts — rather than the earlier of two variants — constitutes the earliest layer.

In sum, being in the possession of multiple copies of ancient manuscripts allows us to see the texts evolve in front of our eyes. This may occur not only in one and the same manuscript, where the original or a subsequent scribe might add some words, but also in the differences and overlaps between manuscripts of the same document.

Shared Material in Different Compositions

Just as important as the variant readings and overlaps in manuscripts of the same composition are tantalizing connections of various kinds between compositions. Metso aptly refers to this phenomenon as "intertextual" evidence.[50] One of the most obvious examples is the complex relationship of the *Community Rule,* the *Damascus Document,* and 4QMiscellaneous Rules (4Q265). Each document appears to have incorporated the same single block of text, and differences between documents are often no more significant than differences between the various manuscripts of the *Community Rule.* The best-attested example is found in the penal code traditions, present in all three texts.[51] The following passage taken from the penal code may serve to illustrate this point.

1QS 7:10b-12a//4QS[e/g]	4QD[a] 10 ii 5b-9a[52]	4Q265 4 i 12-ii 2[53]
Whoever lies down and sleeps during a meeting of the many:	[Whoever lies do]wn [and] sleeps during [a mee]t[ing of the many	[Whoever lies down and slee]ps during a meeting of the man[y
thirty days.	*shall be excluded] for thirty days [and] punished for ten days.*	*shall be punished thir[ty days*
And the same applies to the person	[And the same applies to the person	[And if he]
who leaves during a meeting of the many without consent . . .	*who lea]ves*	*drops off* [when they sit down to read from] *the book up to three times . . .*
	[with]out the consent of the ma[n]y . . . and [with]out [cause]	

This small excerpt from the penal code shows some intriguing overlaps and differences. The interrelationships among the three compositions are as close as the kinds of textual relationships we witnessed between different copies of the *Rule of the Community.* Again, it seems feasible that the common ground shared by the three texts points to the earliest stage in the growth of this material: an offence of falling asleep during a meeting of the many, to be punished by a penalty of thirty days. Just as a number of textual traditions have been incorporated into more than one book of the Hebrew Bible (e.g., the Ten Commandments), so here too we find originally

---

50. Cf. S. Metso, "Methodological Problems in Reconstructing History from Rule Texts Found at Qumran," esp. 330. See also E. Tigchelaar, "Annotated List of Overlaps and Parallels in the Non-biblical Texts from Qumran and Masada," DJD 39, esp. 319-20.

51. Cf. J. M. Baumgarten, "The Cave 4 Versions of the Qumran Penal Code"; C. Hempel, "The Penal Code Reconsidered"; and S. Metso, "Methodological Problems," 317-22.

52. See Baumgarten, DJD 18, 74-75.

53. See J. Baumgarten et al., DJD 35, 64-67.

independent blocks of material incorporated and adapted into different contexts.

In the Absence of Hard Manuscript Evidence

Scholars of ancient texts are frequently forced to draw conclusions about the composite or unified nature of a text in the absence of clear-cut manuscript evidence. On reading a text closely scholars come across unevenness which may suggest that some parts of a document contain source material that found its way into the final form of the text but was probably not composed by the same author as other parts of the document. In the case of the *Community Rule,* detailed work of this kind was undertaken by Jerome Murphy-O'Connor and Jean Pouilly.[54] Long before the evidence from Cave 4 was fully available, Murphy-O'Connor and Pouilly proposed a literary development of the *Community Rule* from Cave 1 (1QS) in four stages:

Stage 1: 1QS 8:1-10a, 12b-16a, and 9:3-10:8a

A manifesto written before the community had emerged (cf. 1QS 8:4-5 "When these exist in Israel, the council of the community shall be established"). It lays down the program for a new community and is characterized by idealism.

Stage 2: 1QS 8:10b-12a; 8:16b–9:2

After the community had existed for a period of time a certain amount of discipline became necessary. This pragmatic need led to the composition of some penal material.

Stage 3: 1QS 5:1-13a and 6:8b–7:25

The community has grown much larger, as suggested by elaborate rules dealing with the admission process and meetings as well as a detailed penal code.

---

54. Cf. Murphy O'Connor, "La genèse littéraire"; and J. Pouilly, *La Règle de la Communauté de Qumrân.*

Stage 4: 1QS 1:1–4:26; 5:13b–6:8a; 10:9–11:22

Various kinds of material were added with the purpose of inspiring enthusiasm in the members who by now lacked proper commitment.

Thus, Murphy-O'Connor proposed a literary development of the text around an early core in 1QS 8-9 and perceived the material in 1QS 1-4 and most of 1QS 10-11 as later. He arrived at these conclusions on the basis of a careful reading of the text of 1QS, paying particular attention to the content and flavor of each section.

In most other branches of ancient history scholarly debates on the rights and wrongs of Murphy-O'Connor's proposal would be confined to the theoretical realm. In the case of the scrolls we are sometimes in the fortunate position to check insights based on close, intuitive, and intelligent readings against ancient primary sources. This is certainly the case here. Whereas Murphy-O'Connor had only very limited knowledge of the Cave 4 manuscript readings, their full publication allows us to assess not only his particular reconstruction of the growth of 1QS but, more generally, our own scholarly methods. By no means are all of Murphy-O'Connor's conclusions borne out by the Cave 4 manuscripts. However, it does seem remarkable that the general direction of his thinking is supported by them. Thus, both the early columns of 1QS (1QS 1-4) and the final columns (1QS 9-10) are lacking in some of the Cave 4 manuscripts (4QS[d] and 4QS[e] respectively).

Outside of the *Community Rule,* I have tried to suggest distinct stages in the growth of the Laws of the *Damascus Document*[55] (others have proposed a similarly developmental path for this document's Admonition).[56] Specifically, I argued that it is possible to distinguish communal rules dealing with a particular organized community from more widely applicable Jewish legal traditions. In that study I worked with the following criteria:

1. *Frame of Reference:* I paid close attention to whether a text refers to a particular community or whether it is, at least theoretically, of general application, displaying a national, all-Israel perspective.
2. *Terminology:* I noted that some texts make use of distinctive terms (such as "overseer" or "the many") that are absent elsewhere.

---

55. Cf. C. Hempel, *The Laws of the Damascus Document.* For a summary of scholarship, see also Hempel, *The Damascus Texts,* esp. 4-53.

56. See esp. J. Murphy-O'Connor, "An Essene Missionary Document? CD II,14–VI,1"; and P. R. Davies, *The Damascus Covenant: An Interpretation of the "Damascus Document."*

3. *Form:* This criterion was particularly fruitful in distinguishing general halakhic material from communal rules, because the halakhah is frequently presented under headings "Concerning X" followed by a series of prohibitions of the form "No one shall do X" sometimes also including an explicit reference to Scripture.[57]

4. *Polemical Stance:* While the legal part of the *Damascus Document* largely lacks a polemical edge and is couched in a neutral, matter-of-fact style, I drew attention to a small number of passages that stand out from the bulk of the collection because of their polemical tone. Thus, CD 16:2-3, for example, speaks polemically of "the blindness of Israel."[58]

In the discussion thus far we have approached the scrolls — and our principal text, the *Rule* manuscripts — from a variety of angles in the hope of shedding light on their literary growth. We began by looking very closely at the manuscripts for any signs of new beginnings, changes and overlaps. The antiquity of the manuscripts allows us a close experience of the growth of these texts that biblical scholars can only dream of. Where direct evidence of development is lacking, however, the methodological challenges facing interpreters of the scrolls are very similar to those tackled by biblical scholars.

If we leave the particular texts behind and try to reflect on the methodological leaps involved, I think we can constructively draw on biblical criticism. In the terminology used by John Barton in his entry "Source Criticism" in the *Anchor Bible Dictionary,* after "breaking up the text" on the basis of reasonable criteria, we might arrange the pieces "into a few piles, each marked by a very strong family resemblance."[59] We might envisage, for instance, one pile with penal code material attested in the *Community Rule,* the *Damascus Document,* and 4QMiscellaneous Rules. On another pile we might have halakha as attested in the Laws of the *Damascus Document,* 4QMMT, and 4QOrdinances[a], for instance.

Another area where we might be able to draw on biblical criticism is redaction criticism. Some scholars have read the scrolls as a unified corpus from which we may derive "a theology of Qumran" as envisaged by Helmer Ringgren,[60] or in generic groupings (e.g., exegetical texts or wisdom texts).

57. See Hempel, *The Laws of the Damascus Document,* 25-72.
58. Hempel, *The Laws of the Damascus Document,* 18.
59. Barton, "Source Criticism," 163-64.
60. See H. Ringgren, *The Faith of Qumran.*

It seems worthwhile to investigate the possibility that rather than thinking of the wholesale production of sectarian works we might allow for redactional processes that have left their marks on more than one text at a time.[61] The role of the redactor or editor in Hebrew Bible scholarship has recently been subjected to a critical analysis by John Van Seters, who argues that the work of redactors in the Hebrew Bible has been vastly exaggerated. He goes so far as to speak of "the myth of the 'redactor' and redaction criticism."[62] Van Seters refers to the evidence of the Dead Sea Scrolls, but when he does so it is largely with reference to the scriptural manuscripts. Whether or not we like the terminology "redactor," "redactional," or "editing" with reference to ancient Hebrew literature, it is quite clear from the *Rule* texts that these kinds of processes indeed went on.[63]

A question that seems worth pondering is whether the scrolls, in their final form, reflect indications of a dominant voice or distinctive conceptual pattern, comparable to the Deuteronomistic redaction in the Hebrew Bible. Should we look for traces of the voice of the Yachadist or Yachadist school? One of the observations that came out of my close study of the Laws of the *Damascus Document* was the variation in degree of redactional work or updating attested in different components of the Laws. Thus, the stratum I labelled "halakhah" displayed a more faithful transmission than that of the communal legislation.[64] In other words, the level of updating of material depends on how "alive" the material is, how much it is subject to change. This can also be related to how much it matters to those who are using it. If a company changes its name, the new owners will update the publicity fairly promptly and paint a new sign over the shop. They might leave as it is the sign reading "Storeroom" or, indeed, "Ladies."[65]

I mentioned earlier that in some cases it was possible to prove that a scholar's source and redaction critical work was pointing in the right di-

---

61. The argument made for a Zadokite redaction both in 1QS and in 1QSa may be a case in point; see C. Hempel, "The Earthly Essene Nucleus of 1QSa."

62. *The Edited Bible*, 335.

63. Van Seters acknowledges that ancient works are made up of different literary components; see, e.g., *The Edited Bible*, 22, 281, 389. The issue he raises seems to be predominantly one of terminology. See now the judicious review by H. G. M. Williamson in *JJS* 58 (2007): 333-34.

64. See Hempel, *The Laws of the Damascus Document*, 188.

65. For a similar assessment with reference to the Hebrew Bible see Barton, "Redaction Criticism," 657.

rection. This boosts the strength of the method and vouches for the skills of attentive modern readers. It does not mean, on the other hand, that the manuscripts as we have them in snapshot tell the whole story. Given that some manuscripts testify to complex literary developments, such processes may also have taken place in some texts where there is no manuscript evidence.[66]

Conclusion

As far as the source and redaction critical study of the scrolls is concerned, the methodological way forward is to start fairly and squarely with the manuscripts themselves and to derive as much evidence as possible from them about the kinds of developments they attest. What we can learn from the study of the Hebrew Bible, it seems to me, is that different compositions can share a number of important, sometimes very close, relationships. It seems fruitful to me to assess the relationship between texts on the level of their final form as well as on the level of sources or component parts.

In biblical studies, diachronic readings of the kind favored in this paper are rather out of vogue. Large areas of contemporary biblical scholarship are much more interested in the final form of the texts. There seems to me an important difference, however, between abandoning the well-trodden — and in some cases overused — track of source and redaction criticism in the case of the Hebrew Bible and not even making a decent effort at exploring the diachronic relationships in the case of the scrolls.

Recent years have seen renewed interest in the identity and role of scribes in the Second Temple period; cf. Christine Schams's important study and the *magnum opus* by Tov to name but two recent examples.[67] This is an area where the scrolls have a lot to offer. Vermes perceives the importance of this when he writes in the third edition of *The Dead Sea Scrolls: Qumran in Perspective*, "If one had to single out the most revolutionary novelty furnished by Qumran, the choice of its contribution to our

66. This is rightly stressed also by Metso, "Methodological Problems," 330, where she observes, "Methodologically, we should keep the option open that complex developments were likely to have been in place even in those parts of the Qumran library for which physical evidence attesting to these developments is no longer preserved."

67. Cf. e.g. C. Schams, *Jewish Scribes in the Second Temple Period;* and Tov, *Scribal Practices and Approaches.*

understanding of the genesis of Jewish literary compositions would surely be justified."[68]

This begs the question of where we draw the line between *reproducing* a composition and being part of *producing* an evolving text. Vermes's choice of terminology "redactor-copyists" places a great deal of emphasis on the copying aspect of the job description. Many of the details of how these things worked in practice are probably going to remain a mystery. However, Brooke is surely right that the evidence of the Qumran texts of the Hebrew Bible, and we might add also the nonbiblical texts, does away with the notion of scribes as "technical copyists."[69] Our manuscript evidence — particularly that of the *Community Rule* — points, in fact, in the direction of a complex evolution of texts. Source and redaction criticism provide the tools to investigate the growth spurts and adjustments of textual development in all its complexities. In most cases the conclusions depend solely on the quality of the arguments and the insights of the interpreter, with little chance of proof or consensus. But with the manuscripts of the Dead Sea Scrolls, especially those of the *Community Rule,* we are in the privileged position to be able to trace their textual evolution firsthand.

68. P. 23.
69. Brooke, "Demise of the Distinction," 30; see also 37-38.

Sociological Models for Understanding the Scribal Practices in the Biblical Dead Sea Scrolls

Steve Delamarter

The Dead Sea Scrolls are not just texts; they are artifacts. When we understand them merely as texts we impose blinders on ourselves. These blinders filter out entire categories of information and prevent us from seeing rich domains of human activity that lie behind the scrolls. Emanuel Tov's 2004 publication of *Scribal Practices and Approaches Reflected in the Texts Found in the Judean Desert* has opened the way for a much deeper exploration of an area of study that has, quite literally, been overlooked. In our haste to read the text on the parchment, we have tended to look past the evidence of the scribal practices that can be found over, under, around, and through the text before us. In this study I would like to provide a few glimpses of the sort of knowledge that can be obtained from the Dead Sea Scrolls through attention to scribal practices.

Test Case: The Paleo-Hebrew Biblical Texts from Qumran

Dozens of biblical and nonbiblical manuscripts from Qumran have the divine name written in paleo-Hebrew characters. But, among the 204 biblical scrolls from Qumran, twelve are written entirely in paleo-Hebrew characters.[1] Scholars quickly determined that the paleo-Hebrew manuscripts were not older than the others. These manuscripts were written in the same era as the other Hebrew texts, which were written in the Herodian script, the

---

1. Tov, *Scribal Practices and Approaches*, 238-48, and the literature cited there.

standard script of the day. Thus, it seemed clear that the paleo-Hebrew manuscripts represent an intentional use of an archaic script. Naturally, the question arises, "for what purpose?"

Attempts to answer this question have proceeded along standard lines. Scholars begin by detailing rabbinic texts regarding the handling of the divine name (*y. Meg.* 1.71d and parallels in *b. Šeb.* 35b, and in *Sop.* 4.1-8) and the use of the paleo-Hebrew script (*m. Yad.* 4.5 and *b. Sanh.* 21b) and conclude that the Qumran texts "closely reflect the spirit of the practices" (or some similar wording) mentioned in the rabbinic literature.[2] Based on this type of argument, Tov, for instance, concludes that the use of paleo-Hebrew for the divine name by the Qumran community reflected the same purpose as the thinking expressed in the rabbinic texts, namely, to avoid erasing the tetragrammaton.[3] However, when scholars ponder the purpose behind writing a biblical text entirely in paleo-Hebrew characters, their explanations are very tentative indeed.[4] This seems to be due in part to the fact that the rabbinic literature rejects the practice and, thus, provides no rationale for it.

While these types of arguments have provided some suggestive answers, in my opinion they have never been able to transcend what, by everyone's admission, they are: anachronistic historical arguments. No one would suggest that a legitimate historical argument can be traced backwards. Yet, because of the limitations of the evidence, this area of investigation is replete with arguments of this sort. Even the terminology that has become standard in this area is technically anachronistic. The texts at Qumran are not *proto*-Masoretic, nor are they *proto*-Samaritan; that is, they do not reflect earlier developments of something that came later. The very term "earlier development" is itself an anachronism. The Masoretic Text and masoretic scribal practice are *reminiscent* of something that was already going on in some of the texts preserved at Qumran. Likewise, the Samaritan text and scribal practice is a *later development* of something that was already going on in some of the texts preserved at Qumran. The worst

---

2. Tov, *Scribal Practices and Approaches,* 245.

3. Tov, *Scribal Practices and Approaches,* 245. This conclusion is bolstered by the example of 11QPsᵃ, "in which twenty-eight words were erased . . . while the Tetragrammaton, written in paleo-Hebrew characters, was not erased," but "in two instances the Tetragrammaton was marked with cancellation dots."

4. See, e.g., E. Tov, "The Socio-Religious Background of the Paleo-Hebrew Biblical Texts Found at Qumran"; "Scribal Practices Reflected in the Paleo-Hebrew Texts from the Judean Desert," and the literature there.

thing about the use of these anachronistic terms is that they divert attention away from the true object of our inquiry — the situation in late Second Temple times. The practice of writing a text entirely in an archaic
script was not an anticipation of some social institution or ideological
practice in later times; it is an expression of the already-fully-developed
sociology and ideology of some group at work in the last centuries before
the Common Era.

One of the theses of this chapter is that we may be much better
served in this area of investigation if we develop explicitly sociological
models and arguments for understanding scribal practices at Qumran.
These must take the place of the anachronistic historical models and arguments that we have developed to this point.[5]

A similar critique can be made about the theories of textual affiliation that have dominated much of the study of the biblical Dead Sea
Scrolls, first with Frank Moore Cross's theory of local texts,[6] and more recently with Emanuel Tov's four categories (three of which have to do with
textual affiliation).[7] These theories of textual affiliation attempt to align
the texts of the various biblical Dead Sea Scrolls with the major families of
texts known to us, including the Septuagint text, the Masoretic Text, and
the Samaritan text. Whereas biblical scholars tend to view a manuscript of

---

5. When it comes to the application of sociological theory to the study of the community at Qumran, I have found the work of Shemaryahu Talmon to be most instructive. Of
Talmon's significant scholarly output, I have focused particularly on "The Transmission History of the Text of the Hebrew Bible in the Light of Biblical Manuscripts from Qumran and
Other Sites in the Judean Desert"; "Anti-Lunar-Calendar Polemics in Covenanters' Writings"; "Calendar Controversy in Ancient Judaism: The Case of the 'Community of the Renewed Covenant'"; "The Essential 'Community of the Renewed Covenant': How Should
Qumran Studies Proceed?"; "The Community of the Renewed Covenant: Between Judaism
and Christianity"; "The Internal Diversification of Judaism in the Early Second Temple Period"; "Between the Bible and the Mishnah: Qumran from Within"; "Oral Tradition and
Written Transmission, or the Heard and the Seen Word in Judaism of the Second Temple Period"; "The Emergence of Jewish Sectarianism in the Early Second Temple Period"; "Waiting
for the Messiah: The Spiritual Universe of the Qumran Covenanters"; "Types of Messianic
Expectation at the Turn of the Era"; "The Old Testament Text"; "The New Covenanters of
Qumran"; "The Calendar Reckoning of the Sect from the Judean Desert."

6. *The Ancient Library of Qumran and Modern Biblical Studies*, 140-45; 2nd ed.; 188-
94; "The Evolution of a Theory of Local Texts." See also G. Howard, "Frank Cross and
Recensional Criticism."

7. *Textual Criticism of the Hebrew Bible;* "Further Evidence for the Existence of a
Qumran Scribal School"; and "The Biblical Texts from the Judaean Desert: An Overview
and Analysis of All the Published Texts."

a biblical book mainly as a mine for textual readings, sociologically-trained codicologists view a manuscript as a cultural artifact that witnesses in a host of ways to the complex social matrix that produced it in the first place. While textual affiliation is one aspect of what was going on in the production of the scrolls, it was not the only or even the most dominant element, at least for many of the manuscripts. For reasons I will explain below, the sociological perspective suggests that it would be much more telling to look for evidence of schools of scribal practice than to focus exclusively on textual affiliation.

Indeed, Tov's recent work on scribal practices begins to move in this direction, but in the end it provides a compelling explanation for only one set of the scrolls, those he has identified as having been produced by the Qumran Scribal Practice (QSP). By his count, only a quarter of the biblical manuscripts from Qumran were produced by this practice. Obviously this raises questions about the other 75 percent. Where were they produced and by whom? What is needed is a more robust model for interpreting the data on scribal practices that are in evidence in the scrolls. This is what I shall attempt to provide in this chapter.

Sociological Models for Understanding Scribal Practices

Historical arguments assume a series of cause-and-effect links in an unbroken chain across time, in which developments can be traced from one state of affairs to another. By their nature, they can only "explain" events or states that can be shown to be connected either synchronically or diachronically. By this mode of interpretation, it would be very difficult to establish any link between scribal practice in Qumran in the late Second Temple period and scribal practice in, say, modern Ethiopia. Sociological arguments, on the other hand, are based on documented patterns of human behavior. Developed first through the study of living social systems, these sociological models can then be transported, as it were, to times and places quite unconnected in history, but which seem to evidence many of the same patterns of behavior. Obviously, then, one enormous advantage that sociological models have over historical ones is that they are not limited to what one can prove by establishing the cause-and-effect links between events or states across time. But the corresponding disadvantage is that one has to show that the illumination of the latter by the former is not merely a figment of the imagination of the researcher.

What counts for evidence in a historical argument is the close documentation of the links between states and times. Sociological models work in a different way. They offer a ready-made matrix of possible meanings in the light of which the fragmentary artifact from antiquity is illuminated. The model "works" when the artifact "comes to life" with the explanatory power offered by the sociological model. To put it another way, the model offers a possible explanation of the life behind the artifact. Thus, "proving" a sociological argument can be much more difficult than "proving" a historical argument. In fact, a sociological argument probably cannot be proven in the same sense that historical arguments can be. For this reason, it is quite accurate to see historical arguments and sociological arguments as complementary. We take the historical information (archaeological and textual) as far as we can, and then we see if sociological models can take us any farther.

What I offer here, then, is a set of sociological models for understanding scribal practice. These have been worked out in a series of papers and articles,[8] in a sabbatical year in which I went to Israel and Ethiopia to interview scribes about their work,[9] and in the cataloging and digitization of Ethiopian manuscripts in England and North America.[10]

---

8. Presentation of this work has included nearly twenty scholarly talks in a wide variety of contexts, including meetings of the West Coast Dead Sea Scrolls Work Group (annually, 2003-2006); regional and national meetings of the Society of Biblical Literature (2002, 2003, 2005, 2006, and 2007); and international SBL meetings in Cambridge, England, and Groningen, the Netherlands (2003, 2004). I have also presented my findings at the Institute of Ethiopian Studies in Addis Ababa (2004), in the 2004 Fall Faculty Lecture at George Fox University, and in an invited faculty lecture at Trinity Western University and at a conference sponsored by that institution (2006).

9. I spent early February through early May of 2004 in Israel, Egypt, and Ethiopia, studying the scribal practices of several Christian and Jewish groups and the sociology of scribal communities. These studies were carried out in Israel at the Tantur Ecumenical Institute for Theological Research, the Ecole Biblique, and Hebrew University, and in Ethiopia at the Institute of Ethiopian Studies, followed by field interviews with scribes in Addis Ababa, Axum, Debre Damo, Iste, Gelawdawos, Zege, and Kebran Island (in Lake Tana).

10. I have made presentations about the Ethiopian Manuscript Imaging Project in various regional and annual meetings of the Society of Biblical Literature, and the International Conference of Ethiopian Studies in Trondheim, Norway, 2-6 July 2007. See "The SGD Digital Collection: Previously Unknown and Uncatalogued Ethiopian Manuscripts in North America," *SBL Forum*, February 2007 (http://www.sbl-site.org/Article.aspx?ArticleId-622); and "More Ethiopian Manuscripts in North America," *SBL Forum*, October 2007 (http://www.sbl-site.org/Article.aspx?ArticleId=736).

The Social Location and Roles of Scribes

Encoding the right meanings in the right way into a manuscript of a sacred text is neither left to chance nor performed casually in religious communities: the job is assigned to specialists, those we call scribes. In Ethiopia and throughout history and across cultures, biblical scribes are themselves almost always priests or other communal authority figures, embedded in families with such authority.[11] As such they are leaders in the religious community and participate in the social functions of leaders. Arguably, the two main roles of religious leaders are the propagation of the community's master story and the differentiation of the group from other groups, whether from other religious groups or from the general culture. And here is the main point: The role of scribes is best understood not simply as copyists, but as community leaders whose scribal work constitutes a deep participation in the leadership tasks of the community. Since this is so, manuscripts of sacred texts are ultimately not just carriers of the sacred text, but elaborate expressions of community identity and differentiation.

The Social Matrix of Manuscript, Scribe, and Community

From this first premise follows a second model, this one providing a theoretical framework for explaining the scribal practices in evidence in manuscripts of sacred texts. It involves a matrix of relationships that interlink at least five things: uniform elements among manuscripts, scribal practices, the originating and sustaining forces behind the practices, social institutions, and community ideology.

When we see *identical features* in manuscripts that were produced by multiple hands, across several centuries and a wide geographic dispersion, it is customary and logical to speak of *scribal practices*. But the idea of a scribal practice is, actually, a theoretical framework accounting for the identical features. With just a little reflection, we can begin to see that a theory of scribal practice is just the tip of a much larger necessary iceberg.

Each scribal practice has an originating force behind it and sometimes more than one. And these forces are of diverse kinds. Some forces are functional, relating to the practical technologies available to scribes;

---

11. Only rarely in history were sacred texts produced by book-making artisans whose identity derived first and foremost from membership in their guild as bookmakers.

others are aesthetic, in the sense that they appeal to a widely accepted standard of what is pleasing or good; still others are artistic, reflecting an individual creativity or competence. Other forces may be economic, historical, theological, or ideological. For instance, a codex needs a binding. This is a functional issue. But the fact that Ethiopian codices all employ what is known as Coptic chain stitching to accomplish the binding reflects not only a functional need but also a historical connection with the Coptic church. Likewise, older Ethiopian codices (from before the seventeenth century) tend to be square in their proportions of height to width. However, they become more and more rectangular across time, apparently witnessing to an increased influence from European book culture.[12] Here we see an aesthetic decision influenced by historical and social processes. The existence of various economic niches (common, sumptuous, ecclesial, royal, etc.) drive several aspects of book and scroll production, including covering, linen lining, margin width, script size, illuminations, mode of correction of errors, and selection and grade of materials. Many more examples could be given; suffice it to say here that each and every scribal practice is held in place by a force or a set of forces, which either sustain them against change across time or permit changes across time, for a variety of reasons. And, in every case, there is a story.

Where scribal practices are in evidence across time and geography, it can only be because there were *social institutions* in place, which trained up scribes and ensured that their work conformed to the standards set by the community. These institutions require such huge expenditures of community effort and resources that we must ultimately look to the *identity and ideology of the community* as the engine that drives the entire operation.

Every religious community has its master story. It begins with a canonical story, but it does not end there. In almost every case, the story is understood to culminate in the text's arrival at the doorstep of that community, in its own language, and offering to that community a special identity and role in the work of God in the world. The fascinating phenomenon here is that, with each succeeding generation, groups invest more and more meaning into their texts, not only as carriers of their master story but also as carriers of a host of additional expressions of community identity, in physical characteristics of the text as a material object. This is particularly clear when we see how much energy religious commu-

---

12. I documented this in one small part of my 2006 national SBL paper on "Scribal Practices in Ethiopian Psalters as Expressions of Identity and Differentiation."

nities invest in differentiating themselves from the general culture around them, on the one hand, and from other religious communities on the other. Eventually their sacred texts carry emblems that express their individuation and differentiation from other groups. It would take more time than we have here to unpack this statement, but it is very clear to a codicologist that manuscripts of sacred texts are most proximately expressions of the community's master story and self-understanding and only secondarily witnesses to the canonical story.

In sum, we see that the concerns of the community extend well beyond the textual affiliation of the canonical text; ultimately they are concerned about the correct canonical content, surrounded by the correct paracanonical content, put on the page in the correct format, by means of a correct process — with the overriding goal of producing a copy of the sacred text that conforms to the acceptable norms of the community that will use it. Understanding and explaining the uniformities of manuscripts is accomplished not simply by cataloguing the scribal practices of a religious community. To accomplish true explanation one must trace the interconnections between the scribal practice, the originating and sustaining forces that hold the practice in place, and the social institutions that identify, train up, and hold scribes accountable. Though some scribal practices may start out as more loaded than others in terms of community identity and differentiation, eventually it is the *entire collection of practices* that comes to exemplify the sacred text of a community. No one set of details may be all that important — in fact, some domains make multiple options available — but in the end, every detail is important because they all form part of an integral whole. With surprising ease, any semi-informed member of the community can tell, from several feet away, whether a manuscript is an acceptable representation of the sacred text of that community or not. And much of that can be judged before the first word is read, on the basis of paratextual information that began, at its origin, by merely addressing mundane issues.

Domains of Meaning Encoded in Sacred Texts

A third model has to do with the domains in a manuscript in which meaning is encoded. Communities of faith embed meaning in their sacred manuscripts in a host of ways, but these can be categorized in three domains. The domain of the canonical text is the first and, as we shall see, a number of crucial decisions must be made with reference to the canonical text. These include, but are not limited to, the content of the text (i.e., what counts as canonical),[13] the language of the text, and the textual affiliation of the text. Community decisions about textual affiliation are often bolstered by claims of inspiration of the particular form of the canonical material — either in the mode of its production or in the means of its preservation. The Septuagint, the Syriac, the Vulgate, the Masoretic Text, the Douay-Rheims, the Samaritan Pentateuch, Old Church Slavonic, the Textus Receptus, the King James Version, and Ge'ez Bibles are merely some of the editions of the canon that have been touted as divinely inspired by one group or another. Communities of faith can take stands on any number of these issues — canon, language, and textual affiliation — in the production of their copies of the sacred text.

The second domain in which communities of faith embed meaning in a manuscript comprises what we might call the paracanonical material. Here we are not referring to the extent of a community's canon, but to the inclusion of front matter, back matter, charts, tables, marginal matter, footnotes, chapter headings and summaries, illuminations, and illustrations. We call this material paracanonical because it is included very intentionally by the community and often it is *this material* that sends the clearest signals to the members of the community that this is, indeed, one of their authorized manuscripts of the sacred text. The paracanonical material in the manuscript is intended to accompany the canonical material and create for the reader the correct interpretational context in which to understand the canonical material properly, i.e., according to the views of the community. This is graphically illustrated, for example, in a copy of a rabbinic Bible, or a glossed Latin Bible, or the latest edition of *Biblia Hebraica*. Biblical textual critics are not unfamiliar with the existence of paracanonical material in biblical manuscripts, but we tend to look right past it. We judge it to mean nothing to our program of textual criticism.

The third domain in which communities of faith embed meaning in a manuscript of a sacred text is what is called the paratextual domain. By this we refer to those characteristics of a book having to do with scribal practice and book production: the use of the correct writing materials,

13. Thus, there are a host of different canons, from the shortest belonging to the early Syriac Orthodox church which rejected the General Epistles and Revelation and used Tatian's Diatessaron instead of the four Gospels, to the longest belonging to the Ethiopian Orthodox church with eighty-eight books, including, besides all the Apocrypha, a number of works we know from the Pseudepigrapha.

correctly prepared,[14] the type of script,[15] the script size (particularly in relation to other marginal and interlinear materials), the page layout, the relative sizes of margins, the manner of making columns, the manner of making lines, the manner of designating sections within the text, the use of colored ink for special purposes, acceptable forms of scribal intervention for the correction of errors, the method of binding the codex and other codicological decisions, the format (e.g., whether scroll or codex), the length of the book, and the relative uniformity of content, from page to page and manuscript to manuscript. In many of these cases, the scribal practice and form of book production begin merely as matters of convention, with little or no deep meaning attached to them. However, in almost every case it can be shown that communities of faith come to render certain scribal practices and codicological aspects as significant, or invested with special meaning.

Our general point relating to these three domains is that communities of faith encode meaning into their sacred texts on levels that go well beyond the one in which modern textual criticism is most interested, that of textual variants and affiliations. As we can see, textual affiliation is merely one among several dozen other venues in which communities of faith embed meaning.

Language as an Expression of Community Identity

Choice of language is one of the most fundamental social mechanisms for expressing the identity of a group and simultaneously differentiating it from others. The pattern of religious communities across time suggests that the religious use of language often has as much to do with community identity and ideology as with simple linguistics, if not more. The Ethiopian Orthodox community employs a Ge'ez text in both its liturgy and its literature, but this is not because it makes it easier for people to understand the content of the faith. Ge'ez has not been the living mother tongue of any group in Ethiopia for centuries. The same is true of other liturgical and canonical languages, from the Armenian Orthodox community through the

14. Beginning with the types of animals whose skins are permitted for use and including preparation of parchment according to particular steps and processes, dyeing of parchment (where relevant), and so on.

15. These might include a script currently in general use, an archaizing script, or a contemporary script set aside for exclusive use for the biblical text, among other possibilities.

Syrian Orthodox, Russian Orthodox, and Greek Orthodox communities, and on to Roman Catholic communities (through the Second Vatican Council), most Jewish religious communities, and some conservative Protestant circles in America, in their use of "King James English." This phenomenon is ubiquitous among religious communities. What, then, is the function of language in these religious communities?

Though the choice of language of a sacred text may begin historically with the practical consideration of rendering the sacred text understandable within a group, eventually communities come to believe that the canonical content *must* be conveyed in that language and *that language alone*. And as we mentioned above, this conviction is bolstered by stories about the unique inspiration of their translation. Whenever this happens, the result is a sacred text fixed in a form of the language that is eventually left behind by the natural developments of the living language (parallels might be made here to the Hebrew biblical text within Jewish tradition and to the Arabic Qur'an within Islam). In such situations, language begins to take on a new set of functions, which serve as means of social differentiation. This unique function of language in religious communities creates a fabulously efficient sociological mechanism that separates outsiders from "normal insiders" (the ordinary members of the community) and "deep insiders" (priests and other such persons) from regular insiders. There is a clear correlation between mastery of the sacred language of a community and influence in the community. Thus, the opportunity to master the sacred language of a community was usually restricted, in the first place to males over females, and then to the males of connected families over males of families on the fringes of the community.

What is true about this general characteristic of language in religious communities — the tendency to fix and freeze one language as the only legitimate language of revelation — is also true of several, more specific, characteristics of language. For instance, many groups have designated a certain ancient script or font as the only proper form of the sacred text. This is not to say that all groups make this decision. But any group can, and many have. One need only reflect on the use of a Gothic script for certain German and King James Bibles. These types of decisions appear to begin as ordinary and functional, but they ultimately become expressions of group identity and differentiation. Once this happens, these issues are never any longer merely functional.

Implications for the Study of the Scrolls

What might happen when we bring these sociological models to bear on the study of the biblical scrolls from the deserts of Judea?

General Sensibilities

The very first "payoff" is a set of general sensibilities about manuscripts of sacred texts. First, if a manuscript is part of a manuscript tradition (i.e., evidencing uniform elements in scribal hands coming from multiple geographic sites and across time), then it came into being and served its community as part of the social matrices described above. There is no such thing as a "dis-en-communitied" manuscript.

Second, to know a manuscript tradition is not only to know the scribal practices that characterize that tradition, but it is to understand which practices are merely functional and which are specially freighted as symbols of group identity and differentiation. Every group has a distinctive recipe of scribal practices and meanings attached to those scribal practices. Within this recipe are core ingredients, about which the group requires strict adherence, and other practices about which variation is permitted. This is one of the reasons that it is easily possible for different groups to employ the same scribal practice and yet weight and freight it differently.

Third, this means that we should not expect the scrolls written in the Qumran scribal practice to operate by the same scribal rules as those produced in circles committed to a form of text that would ultimately be adopted as the Masoretic Text, nor to those produced in circles that wrote their texts entirely in a paleo-Hebrew script.

Fourth, all of this suggests quite strongly that the collection of manuscripts discovered at Qumran cannot possibly have been produced by a single community. To even begin to think this possible involves conceiving of a group unlike any group we know of in history that would commit itself to multiple, elaborate systems of scribal practice. Just on the face of it, it is significantly more probable that the various groups of manuscripts (other than the QSP manuscripts) were produced by different communities in different places and only secondarily brought to Qumran by persons who joined the community.

Fifth, having come to understand that communities invest identity and differentiation in a manuscript in a host of ways, we should be immediately wary of describing a manuscript tradition in terms of one single scribal characteristic, especially textual affiliation, unless it can be shown that this scribal characteristic was one of the central commitments of the community that produced the manuscripts and was characteristic of their identity.

To elaborate on this last point a bit, I find it very unlikely that the terms "proto-Samaritan" or "proto-Septuagint" describe anything characteristic of an identifiable sociological entity that existed in Second Temple times. In the latter case it certainly makes more sense to speak of Hellenistic Jewish manuscripts. But any reference to the Septuagint will be anachronistic on the one hand and inaccurate on the other, since the Greek manuscripts' "attitude" toward the Hebrew text seems to be one of their central characteristics and the manuscripts reflect among themselves divergent attitudes toward the need for conformity to the Hebrew text that was already being standardized. In the former case, it is already clear that the so-called "proto-Samaritan" texts were not produced by any group of proto-Samaritans, but only that a text form that they represent either already had been taken up by the Samaritan community or would be taken up by them at a later time. This correlation is, as far as we know, a completely accidental one — although I would put forward the idea that this text form may have suggested itself for selection by the Samaritan community precisely because it was not already a characteristic feature of the sacred texts of some other group (or even precisely because it was different from the text form chosen by another group). For the reasons I described above, the term proto-Masoretic is a misnomer, since it points away from any group in the Second Temple era and toward a group that came into being centuries later. I have the same suspicions about the usefulness of "paleo-Hebrew manuscripts" as a practical term, since it merely describes an external scribal characteristic without any argument that this characteristic is a central one that defines a group of manuscripts.

Having made these criticisms, I want to say a brief word about what qualifications a good label should have. I hasten to acknowledge that the labels currently in use have no doubt arisen more as working titles than as final decisions about the essence of manuscript groups. But for me, the starting point in this discussion goes back to one of my earlier claims, that there is no such thing as a dis-en-communitied manuscript. The most useful labels with respect to a manuscript will point ultimately to the group that produced the manuscript and, if possible, will capture something of the central commitments that seemed to be important to or characteristic of the group and its manuscripts. I think this will be true even if we cannot correlate it to a known historical group, whether Pharisees, Sadducees, or another.

Finally, as a general sensibility we should expect to find the manuscripts of a group coming from and expressing the social niches that the group occupies. This is true in very much the same way genre and setting are understood to be two inextricably-linked expressions within one social fabric.

Specific Proposals

And now we return to the question of the manuscripts discovered at Qumran and written in paleo-Hebrew.

Clearly the scribal practice of writing entirely in paleo-Hebrew presents an easy way to distinguish these twelve texts from the other Qumran manuscripts. Further, I suspect that this feature is, indeed, a feature that characterizes in some important way the social niche, ideological commitments, and identity of the group that produced them. However, to gain clarity about this, it is critical to set forth the full recipe of scribal practices that characterizes this group of manuscripts. Tov carefully sets these forth in chapter 7b of his *Scribal Practices and Approaches*.[16] First, we might note the scribal practices that are shared in common with the other texts, those written in square Hebrew script:

- Writing in scrolls, consisting of sheets of leather, and in columns.
- Most texts ruled horizontally (indicating lines) and vertically (indicating the beginnings and usually also the ends of columns).
- Written text suspended from horizontal lines.
- Sense units separated from one another by open and closed sections.
- A special layout of the text in poetical units pertaining to texts written in square characters as well as to 4QpaleoDeut^r (Deut 32) and probably 4QpaleoJob^c.
- Words separated from one another, albeit in different ways.
- Biblical texts belonging to both the Masoretic family and the so-called pre-Samaritan group found written in both scripts.

16. See esp. 254-56.

While the analysis has to begin somewhere, and Tov is unusually careful to present the data in as thorough a manner as possible, we must question, right at the outset, the ultimate usefulness of comparisons between groups of manuscripts based on the narrow criteria of one category of scribal practice. When we do so, we end up making comparisons between things that appear on a surface level to have something to do with one another (a decision about script) but in actuality may have very little to do with one another. While the use of the paleo-Hebrew script seems to be a reflection of something fundamental to group identity in the paleo-Hebrew manuscripts, the selection of square script is essentially a functional decision for the groups that produced the other manuscripts. This becomes clear as we analyze the manuscripts written in square script. They subdivide into at least two different groups: those evidencing a central commitment to a particular textual affiliation (the so-called proto-Masoretic text) and others, including the ones written at Qumran according to Tov's Qumran Scribal Practice (QSP), which do not evidence this commitment to a proto-Masoretic textual affiliation. In the former case, textual affiliation appears to be perhaps the distinguishing characteristic of the scribal practice for the group that produced them; in the latter cases, it is not. We will thus likely find their distinguishing characteristics in some other scribal domain or domains.

Among the list of scribal practices unique to the paleo-Hebrew biblical manuscripts, most of the rest appear to be, in my opinion, functional decisions. But there are at least two other scribal practices that distinguish this group of manuscripts from others and that could, perhaps, help us to refine our understanding of the social niche within which these manuscripts were prepared and used. The first is the near-total lack of any intervention by scribes to correct errors in the text. The second is the visual layout of the text on the parchment. Tov notes: "As a result of the splitting of words between two lines in the paleo-Hebrew texts almost straight left margins could be obtained."[17] These two characteristics produce a similar outcome: a clean and uncluttered visual appearance to the manuscripts.

It seems to me that when our sociological models about communities and their manuscripts of sacred texts are brought to bear on this group, the following profile emerges: This is a group for whom the use of Hebrew language and its physical appearance function as key indicators of group identity and differentiation. The use of Hebrew already sets this group

17. Tov, *Scribal Practices and Approaches*, 256.

apart as deep insiders, along with the other groups that used Hebrew texts. But the additional device of using paleo-Hebrew script adds a further sociological mechanism, to distinguish some deep insiders from others. Thus, this group is made up of deep, deep insiders for whom the use of Hebrew in the ancient script laid out cleanly on a page without extraneous marks serves as a visual emblem, perhaps blending symbols of antiquity and nationalism. This suggests to me some sort of a ceremonial use, not necessarily exclusive to a vaunted setting like the temple, but anywhere that the group or members of the group might parade their text as an expression of group identity. This could happen in group settings, but it could also serve the same purpose sitting on a table and open for passersby to see.

A second central characteristic of these manuscripts might be their purported Mosaic authorship. If the data made it certain that the group that produced these manuscripts was committed only to texts supposed to be written by Moses, this would certainly contribute to the profile of the community, indicating some special status (perhaps canonicity) to only these works. The only biblical texts written in paleo-Hebrew are from the Pentateuch and from Job — all supposed to be written by Moses. Stating the evidence in this manner makes it clear that we have an argument from silence, and since our number of data points is as small as it is, we will never be completely certain about whether this was another distinguishing characteristic of the group that produced these manuscripts. However, the evidence we have is at least consistent with such a theory, even if it offers no definite proof.

I would certainly not be the first scholar to suggest a connection between the paleo-Hebrew manuscripts from Qumran and the Sadducees.[18] The profile I have described above seems to fit that group best, though we all hasten to admit how little we really know for sure about Sadducees and Pharisees in the Second Temple period. And though I am not the first to suggest the origin and use of these manuscripts within Sadducean circles, it seems to me that the use of these sociological models about scribes, scribal practices, and group ideology has enabled us to come at the question in ways that have not been available to us before.

---

18. Tov, *Scribal Practices and Approaches,* ch. 6b; others before him have come to the same conclusion.

Rhetorical Criticism and the Dead Sea Scrolls

Carol A. Newsom

> *Rhetoric is a mode of altering reality, not by the direct application of energy to objects, but by the creation of discourse. . . . The rhetor alters reality by bringing into existence a discourse of such a character that the audience, in thought and action, is so engaged that it becomes [a] mediator of change.*

> Lloyd Bitzer, "The Rhetorical Situation"

As the opening quotation from Lloyd Bitzer suggests, rhetoric is the study of how to do things with words.[1] In its broadest perspective almost all speech has a rhetorical element in it, in that it attempts to have some effect on reality. We are daily bombarded with the words (and images) of advertising, which attempt to get us to consume various products by persuading us that we will become sexy, popular, healthy, or whatever if we buy the item in question. A teenager's use of a particular type of slang may be an attempt to persuade others — and perhaps himself as well — that he is "cool." Even the stop sign with its uncluttered single imperative can be seen as the use of discourse to change the behavior of drivers. Some texts, of course, are quite overt about their intent to persuade; others hide that role. But rhetorical analysis can be applied to any text, oral or written. It is simply a matter of asking what a text is attempting to do, how

---

1. Although that phrase was made famous by J. L. Austin's study of speech acts, it is perhaps even more apt as a characterization of the rhetorical dimensions of language.

it is attempting to affect social reality, and what techniques it uses to effect the desired persuasion.

Rhetorical Criticism as a Method

To what extent is rhetorical criticism a "method"? While it is a disciplined and self-conscious way of asking questions about a text and its effects, rhetorical criticism certainly cannot be laid out as a series of steps to be followed in each case by every critic. Rhetorician Edwin Black's comments are apt.

> Methods, then, admit of varying degrees of personality. And criticism, on the whole, is near the indeterminate, contingent, personal end of the methodological scale. In consequence of this placement, it is neither possible nor desirable for criticism to be fixed into a system, for critical techniques to be objectified, for critics to be interchangeable for purposes of replication, or for rhetorical criticism to serve as the handmaiden of quasi-scientific theory.[2]

Even though rhetorical criticism does not take place as a rigid procedure, one can identify a number of general questions that should be in the rhetorical critic's "tool kit." First, what is the genre of the text in question? Genres serve as contracts between writers and readers, laying out common expectations for what the text in question is intended to do and what means it is likely to use. Thus the rhetorical techniques employed will differ depending on the genre of the text in question. Second, how does the text frame the issue with which it is concerned? Just as a photographer frames a scene, including some things and excluding others, so does the author of a text. The issue may be examined in "close up" or from a broad perspective. What is not said may be as important in persuasive speech as what is said. Third, what are the primary terms of value, what Kenneth Burke termed "vocabularies of motive"?[3] Most texts contain a repertoire of positive and negative terms which the text wishes the reader to share and by which the text construes its particular perspective on the social world. Fourth, how does the text identify its author and its audience and the rela-

2. E. Black, *Rhetorical Criticism: A Study in Method*, x-xi.
3. K. Burke, *On Symbols and Society*, 158-76.

tionship between them? Sometimes these matters may be explicit, but often they are implied through the tone or style of the text. As James Boyd White put it, every text constructs a character for both author and reader.[4] The reader is invited to recognize him or herself in that character or to become more like that character. Rhetorical persuasion may thus be not simply about changing one's ideas or emotions but even one's very identity or sense of self. Fifth, what is the relationship between rational argument and explanation on the one hand and metaphors and other tropes? Where parties share many of the same assumptions, explicit arguments may be the preferred form of persuasion; but where worldviews are divergent, evocative metaphors, narratives, and other such tropes may predominate. Metaphors in general are often of importance, as they may present condensed forms of the cognitive structure of the act of persuasion. Formal features of the text (e.g., repetition, use of contrast pairs, crescendo effects) may also echo or model aspects of the argument and so add to the persuasive effect. The list of possible questions to be explored in an act of rhetorical criticism could be extended indefinitely, but these should be sufficient to suggest the general nature of the analysis.

Rhetorical Criticism and the Dead Sea Scrolls: Prospects and Problems

Rhetorical criticism is as yet a little used method in Qumran studies. This near absence of rhetorical criticism is both surprising and unfortunate. Although virtually any text lends itself to rhetorical criticism, the literature of a sectarian community has particular affinities for this type of analysis. Burke even observed that rhetoric "considers the ways in which individuals are at odds with one another, or become identified with groups more or less at odds with one another,"[5] certainly an apt description of the way sects position themselves and make their appeal. As a sectarian organization that drew extensively upon adult converts for its membership, the Qumran community was deeply involved in using language to effect persuasion. To join the community required a decision to separate oneself from previously held identities, perspectives, and beliefs and to embrace new ones defined by the community. This new world of meaning was not

4. J. B. White, *When Words Lose Their Meaning*, 14-18.
5. K. Burke, *A Rhetoric of Motives*, 22.

totally novel, of course, but was constructed in relation to the central religious and cultural symbols of the broader Jewish community. Thus the community's texts are often engaged in explicit and implicit struggle with other ways of understanding the meaning and significance of these symbols. Since the sectarian movement existed in the midst of a variety of other ways of being Jewish, the plausibility of the community's own structures, practices, beliefs, and dispositions required continuing acts of self-persuasion by members. These were enacted through formal instruction and examination, rituals, liturgies, biblical interpretations, and a variety of other formal and informal speech practices, as well as nonverbal forms of symbolic communication.

Applying rhetorical criticism to the sectarian texts from the Dead Sea Scrolls offers both serious challenges and great rewards. Perhaps the most obvious challenge is that we do not know precisely how the various texts from Qumran were used and by whom. Thus important aspects of the rhetorical situation are simply unknown. But the problem may not be as serious as it first appears. Scholars can make educated guesses about the likely purposes and contexts of use for particular texts, even if the specific details remain elusive. Furthermore, it may be misleading to think of the rhetorical situation as some necessarily objective state of affairs to which a speech or a text is a response. On the contrary, it may be the speech itself that creates the rhetorical situation.[6] Speakers, for example, may have reasons for using the language of crisis to create a sense of urgency on the part of the audience whether or not an objective crisis exists. Thus, just as one distinguishes between the actual author of a text and the implied author constructed by the text, so one might think in terms of an implied rhetorical situation called into being by the text.

The texts found at Qumran, even the specifically sectarian ones, may come from different periods within the community's life and in many cases have been reworked numerous times to meet changing needs. Thus the very model of *an* author addressing *an* audience in a *particular* context is too simplistic. It is important to remember that one does not have access to any particular author's psychological intentions in a text. What is being analyzed is the force of the language itself. Indeed, even to speak of *the* community is somewhat misleading, since the people who occupied the site of Qumran and who were responsible for the preservation of the scrolls appear to have been only one part of a much larger and more com-

6. R. Vatz, "The Myth of the Rhetorical Situation."

plex religious movement. Scholars have not yet been able to determine with certainty how the communities referred to in the texts related to one another. Nevertheless, so long as one is aware of the limitations of the evidence, there is a great deal that one can learn about the general nature of the persuasion that various texts undertake.

Case Study I: The Rule Texts

One of the novel genres discovered in the sectarian literature of Qumran is the *serekh* or "rule." Texts of this type include the *Damascus Document,* the *Community Rule,* and the *Rule of the Congregation.*[7] These texts appear to be composite documents that describe the way of life in the community. Although scholars have debated the possible functions of these rules, there is a general consensus that they were associated in some fashion with instruction in the ethos, beliefs, and practices of the community. Perhaps they were to be read and studied by the *maskîl,* the figure Philip Alexander calls "the spiritual mentor" of the community,[8] or perhaps they were used more directly in instruction of new members, even being memorized by initiates, as James Charlesworth suggests.[9] In either case, one of the important purposes of the texts is to serve in the formation of the sectarian. Significantly, both the *Damascus Document* and the *Community Rule* begin with an explicitly motivational section before turning to the more detailed information about the sectarian community. In these motivational sections one can see examples of a rhetorical appeal designed to consolidate the member's commitment to the life of the community. Despite the similar function, however, the rhetoric in these two texts is quite different.

The Damascus Document

The *Damascus Document* exists in multiple fragmentary copies from Caves 4, 5, and 6, as well as in two partial but relatively well preserved medieval copies found in the Cairo Genizah (manuscripts A and B).[10] This rule con-

7. Although the *War Scroll* also uses the term *serekh,* it refers to the order for the conduct of the eschatological war and so will not be considered here.

8. P. S. Alexander, "Rules," *EDSS,* 2:800.

9. J. H. Charlesworth, et al., *Rule of the Community and Related Documents,* 1.

10. For a convenient introduction, see C. Hempel, *The Damascus Texts.*

sists of a long hortatory section, usually termed the Admonition, followed by a collection of laws. The basic structure thus suggests that the Admonition served to provide the motivation and self-understanding that would make the reader/listener receptive to the laws that follow. Indeed, as one looks at the Admonition itself, it moves from more general exhortation at the beginning to incorporate discussion of particular legal positions held by the sectarian community in the latter parts. Although the very beginning of the Admonition is preserved only in very fragmentary fashion in 4QDᵃ, the section with which the Cairo Genizah manuscript A begins gives a good sense of the general rhetorical strategies of the Admonition.

The Admonition is quite explicit about giving its audience an identity, as it addresses them directly. "And now listen, all you who know righteousness and who understand the works of God" (CD 1:1-2). Any contemporary reader would recognize the style of the address: the speaker takes up the position of a wisdom teacher addressing his students (cf. Prov 5:1-2; Ps 78:1-4; Sir 3:1; *1 En.* 91:3). Later the Admonition will make reference to important teachers in Israel's history (CD 1:11; 4:8; 6:2-3, 7, 11), so that the speaker implicitly claims to stand in continuity with an ancient authoritative tradition of instruction. In contrast to the typical wisdom custom of referring to students as "my sons," however, the speaker explicitly attributes ethical and religious understanding to his audience. They are neither unformed nor uninformed. This rhetorical positioning is significant. It lessens the distance between the speaker and the audience and it sets up an implicit contrast between themselves, as those who possess this vital knowledge, and others who do not. Thus the sectarian interest in drawing a line between insiders and outsiders is already established through the characterization of the speaker and his audience.

As the speaker turns to the content of his message, he also invokes language that the audience would recognize as like that of the prophets: "For he [God] has a dispute with all flesh and will execute judgment against all who spurn him" (CD 1:2). Thus the speaker adds to his own authorization. But in contrast to much prophetic rhetoric that often directed its indictments against the people who were themselves portrayed as guilty (cf. Micah 6), here the audience has been characterized as those who *do not* spurn God. What the speaker will tell them will be directed not toward getting them to change their identity but to reinforce their existing identification with the good and their sense of separation from and opposition to the evil. The polarizing language also strategically simplifies reality. While many people might have considered the choices that Jews must make about the interpretation of God's will and law to be complex and subject to much debate, the rhetoric of this address allows for no such ambiguity. There are two options: right and wrong. And the speaker and his audience belong to those who have it right.

Since the speaker's task is not to change the minds of his audience so much as to confirm them in their identity, he proceeds by reciting to them several versions of their own history (CD 1:1–2:1; 2:2–4:6; 5:15–6:11). He seeks to give them a sense of how they have emerged out of a much longer story about Israel, and indeed, about the history of the world. That this is not a previously unknown story is evident from the fact that it is narrated in a very allusive fashion. Scholars have difficulty in identifying all of the references with certainty, because often very little information is given. But those who are members of the community would have had little difficulty in making the connections. This is a story that they already know well, and the recitation of it serves not to give new information but to reinforce their solidarity with this vision of their place in the world. Despite the allusive style, the major elements of the story are intelligible to the biblically literate reader.

The first recounting of the history runs from CD 1:3 to 2:1. It is framed, as the introductory lines indicate, as the story of God's judgment against those who scorn him. Thus the focus is primarily on the villains. No story has an absolute beginning, of course, and it is rhetorically important where a speaker chooses to begin. This speaker frames the story by reference to the Babylonian destruction of Judah and the Jerusalem temple, more or less as it had been interpreted in the Deuteronomistic tradition. "For when, in their unfaithfulness, they abandoned him, he hid his face from Israel and from his sanctuary and gave them over to the sword" (CD 1:3-4). Later references to Nebuchadnezzar confirm the reference. The traumatic event of the Babylonian destruction of the temple was a central experience in early Jewish self-understanding, and so makes an effective rhetorical point of reference.

But is the destruction of the temple for the people's unfaithfulness not the end of the story rather than the beginning? Here the speaker makes use of another traditional prophetic motif, the notion of a remnant saved from the destruction (CD 1:4-5; cf. Jer 31:7; Mic 2:12; Zeph 3:13). Thus an ending makes way for the story of an unexpected beginning, one that takes place at divine initiative. Just as stories do not have objective beginnings, neither must they deal with time in a uniform fashion. The speaker skips over what is not relevant to the story he is shaping and selects for emphasis what is vital. So here, some 390 years is passed over to get to the next relevant event, God's visiting the remnant, now referred to as "the shoot of the planting," to cause them to grow. Here one approaches the more recent history of the audience, perhaps a generation or so before the speaker's present.

The allusive style makes it uncertain exactly when this part of the history takes place (if the 390 years are symbolic rather than literal), though the original audience would have recognized the events immediately. The time that the speaker refers to is in critical ways presented as analogous to the judgment on Judah at the time of Nebuchadnezzar, since this period, too, is referred to as "a time of wrath" (CD 1:5). Most likely, it is an allusion to the time of the crisis in Jerusalem that led up to the persecution by Antiochus IV Epiphanes (ca. 175-165 B.C.E.). By establishing this analogy, the speaker rhetorically prepares the audience for a similar development in the plot — danger and destruction followed by a divine nurture of a chosen remnant. But as the story comes closer to the present, the events are more detailed and complex. Instead of being simply the passive recipient of God's salvation, the community at this point in its history is described as "like blind persons" for some twenty years (CD 1:9-10). The critical act in their salvation thus is God's decision to "raise up for them a Teacher of Righteousness, in order to direct them in the way of his heart" (CD 1:11). The story of their salvation in turn is the story of right teaching. The speaker's own teaching is a conduit for the knowledge imparted by the Teacher of Righteousness. Moreover, the audience has been addressed from the beginning of this section as "you who know righteousness."

Just as the beginning of the section established a contrast between the audience and their opposites, "those who spurn" God, so here their identity is framed by the contrast with "the congregation of traitors" (CD 1:12). Significantly, the speaker spends far more time describing the congregation of traitors than those to whom he is speaking. Their awful fate in fact forms the climactic conclusion to this section and illustrates what happens to those who spurn God. "The wrath of God was kindled against their congregation, to destroy all their multitude, for their deeds were unclean before him" (1:21–2:1). Presumably these are also events that the ancient audience could have readily identified and which would have served as confirmation that what the speaker said was true. But it is not finally the audience's ability to correlate the speaker's interpretation with events that is the lynchpin of the act of persuasion. More significant is the speaker's ability to relate the events of the recent past to scriptural prophecies: "This is the time concerning which it was written . . . ," continuing with a citation of Hos 4:16, "like a straying heifer, so has Israel strayed." While the correlations that the speaker makes may seem arbitrary to a modern reader, within scripturally oriented sectarian communities the ability to correlate events of the present with scriptural predictions by means of an allegorical hermeneutics is a powerfully persuasive tool. That the speaker uses it at the climax of the first movement of his speech is certainly intentional. Although he will repeat and expand his arguments in the following sections of the Admonition, the speaker has already accomplished his purpose of reinforcing the community's identity by locating them within a meaningful history, distinguishing them sharply from outsiders who are very negatively characterized, and situating their choice as literally one between life and death.

The Community Rule

Like the *Damascus Document,* the *Community Rule* is also a text for the *maskil* or instructor in his work in the formation of members. It is in many ways quite different from the *Damascus Document,* however. Possibly, the *Damascus Document* reflects life in the sectarian communities that existed in the towns and villages of Judah, while the *Community Rule* pertains to the more rigorous form of sectarian life practiced at the site of Qumran itself; but it is not possible to be certain. Even more than the *Damascus Document,* the *Community Rule* appears to have been assembled from a variety of preexisting materials. It also exists in more than one edition, some longer or shorter, some having different materials at the beginning or end of the document.[11] Nevertheless, there are clear indications of intentional rhetorical shaping, most clearly in the placement of motivational material before discussions of sectarian theology and procedure. One of the shorter versions (4QS^b = 1QS 5-9) began with a motivational section presented as a series of infinitives and a treatment of a ritual of entry into the community (the solemn oath), followed by sections dealing with the procedures of life within the community. In the expanded version represented by 1QS, four columns of material were added at the beginning, but replicating the same rhetorical shape — first a motivational paragraph cast in infinitives (1:1-17), then a description of a ritual of entry (the covenant ceremony, 1:18-3:12). Afterwards comes a theological teaching (3:13-4:26). Although this

11. For the most thorough discussion see S. Metso, *The Textual Development of the Qumran Community Rule.*

additional material gives the document something of a reduplicated structure, the basic rhetorical movement from motivation to instruction is preserved and even emphasized.

1QS shows additional evidence of rhetorical shaping in the materials chosen for the conclusion. After the body of diverse procedural and regulatory materials, the document concludes with two sections pertaining to the *maskil* himself, instructions for the *maskil* (9:12-26) and a hymn of the *maskil,* couched in the first person singular (10:1–11:22). Since the *maskil* embodied the highest values of the community, it makes sense that the materials pertaining to him are placed at the end. He represents the epitome of what the disciplines and teaching of the community were designed to produce. That these materials are very intentionally placed here is indicated by the fact that there are strong verbal echoes between the introductory materials in cols. 1-2 and the materials pertaining to the *maskil* in 9:12–11:22. The shift from third person instruction to first person confessional speech in the concluding hymn provides a powerful representation of just the sort of "I" that the sectarians aspired to become through their training. Thus the rhetorical shape of 1QS as a whole shows a clear progression analogous to the life of the sectarian: from motivation to admission, to instruction, to life together, and finally to the ideal figure embodied in the leadership of the *maskil.*

It is frustrating not to know how 1QS was actually used, since much of the rhetorical effect of a text depends on how a reader or hearer engages it. Recent studies, however, have emphasized the widespread practice in antiquity of memorizing texts that served as a kind of educational curriculum, a practice referred to as "writing on the tablets of the heart."[12] Given these practices, it seems likely that the *Community Rule* would have been memorized, at least by the *maskil* himself, if not also by the members he taught. Thus the rhetoric of the document would be internalized and become part of the self-understanding of the sectarian.

Although one might expect that the motivational rhetoric of the *Community Rule* would follow the same pattern as that of the *Damascus Document,* it is quite different in its tone and strategy. Whether these differences reflect different times and social settings in the history of the movement's development, and hence different audiences, or simply the different tastes of different instructors is difficult to say. Whereas the plu-

---

12. D. M. Carr, *Writing on the Tablet of the Heart: Origins of Scripture and Literature,* 124-34.

ral imperatives of the *Damascus Document* and the recitation of a mutually known history give a highly personal quality to its opening motivational rhetoric, the *Community Rule* begins with a highly formalized and quite impersonal form of speech. The first several lines are couched in infinitives, forms of speech that give no information about the speaker or the addressee. Infinitives rather shift the focus to purpose: "in order to do x," or "for doing y." Thus rather than conferring identity by means of reminding people of who they are and the place they occupy in a history of God's judgment and salvation, the *Community Rule's* infinitives do two things. They identify the purposes of the teaching and they consequently indicate the desires that motivate those who seek this teaching: you are what you desire. It is difficult to render the style of the Hebrew adequately in English. Translators often add a phrase to smooth out the translation, e.g., "(The Instructor shall teach them) to seek God . . . (he shall teach them) to do what is good and upright." But the sequence of infinitives is actually an allusion to the way the book of Proverbs opens, "The proverbs of Solomon son of David, king of Israel: For learning about wisdom and instruction, for understanding words of insight, for gaining instruction in wise dealing, righteousness, justice, and equity; to teach shrewdness to the simple, knowledge and prudence to the young" (Prov 1:1-4 NRSV). This allusion implicitly likens the discipline of life in the community to the discipline of learning wisdom. Although using a rhetorical strategy and verbal style different from the *Damascus Document,* the *Community Rule* also presents itself as a wisdom teaching and the *maskil* as a wisdom teacher.

But what is it exactly that the *Community Rule* presents as the desires of those who seek its wisdom? The first few lines are framed in value terms that would express the desires of any good Jew of the Second Temple period: "To seek God with [a whole heart and soul] in order to do what is good and right before him as he commanded by the hand of Moses and by the hand of all his servants the prophets; and to love all that he has chosen and to hate all that he has rejected, in order to keep far from evil and to cling to all good works; and to do truth and righteousness and justice in the land, and not to walk any longer in the stubbornness of a guilty heart and promiscuous eyes, to do all manner of evil" (1QS 1.1-7). This is Deuteronomistic-style rhetoric, widely used in religious literature of the period. If one understands the sectarian community to have drawn many of its members from adult seekers, then the rhetoric of the opening lines addresses the person not from the beginning as an "insider" of the sect but in terms of the values he shares with virtually all Jews. The purpose of the teaching of the *Community Rule,* however, will be to transform the outsider into an insider, as it teaches him that the only way in which he can actually fulfill those desires is through the special knowledge and disciplines available within the sectarian community.

Thus, as the motivational introduction continues, it recasts, and one might say reinterprets, those words of common value in terms of specifically sectarian vocabulary and concepts. "And to bring in all those who volunteer freely to do the statutes of God in the covenant of grace, to be united in the council of God, in order to walk before him in perfection [according to] all that he has revealed with respect to the times appointed for them, and to love all the children of light, each man according to his lot in the council of God, and to hate all the children of darkness, each man according to his guilt in the vengeance of God" (1QS 1.7-11). Whereas the initial lines had used the unmarked vocabulary common to all Jews, here the "covenant" is understood in relation to the sectarian "council of God"; walking in perfection can only be done in light of "all that he has revealed." The predestinarian worldview of the sect is reflected in the phrase "the times appointed for them." And the general reference to loving what God has chosen and hating what he has rejected is recast in sectarian terms as the "children of light" and "children of darkness." While everyone may have the same religious desires to serve God, only those who are "brought into" the sectarian community will be able to fulfill them.

What one sees reflected in this motivational introduction is an index of the highly competitive religious marketplace that was late Second Temple Judaism. As Kenneth Burke observed about rhetoric in general, it is concerned with "the ways in which the symbols of appeal are stolen back and forth by rival camps."[13] Many teachers and movements competed to represent themselves as the true or correct way, and the rhetoric of the opening of the *Community Rule* situates itself within that horizon of rival teachings.

Case Study II: The Hodayot (Thanksgiving Hymns)

The Admonition section in the *Damascus Document* refers to an important period in the formation of the community when, after twenty years of

---

13. K. Burke, "Synthetic Freedom," *New Republic* 89 (20 January 1937) 364. Quoted in R. L. Heath, *Realism and Relativism,* 212.

blindly groping for direction, God sent them a "Teacher of Righteousness" who guided them in the right way. It may well have been through his leadership that a somewhat disorganized religious movement crystallized into a sect with a strong sense of identity and purpose. For reasons that are not clear, the sectarian documents do not give the personal names of their leaders, so scholars have not been able to identify this important religious leader, other than to ascertain that he was a priest, perhaps even the high priest who served from 159 to 152 B.C.E.[14] Both the *Damascus Document* and the Qumran *pesharim* indicate that he was engaged in controversies with an opponent referred to as "the scoffer" (CD 1:14) and "the liar" (1QpHab 2:1-3; 5:9-12; 4QpPs^a 1:26–2:1) and was harassed and persecuted by a figure called the "wicked priest," probably Jonathan the Hasmonean (1QpHab 11:4-8). While it is not possible to ascertain whether or not the Teacher was the author of any of the Qumran sectarian literature, as has sometimes been suggested, several of the *Thanksgiving Hymns* are presented in the voice of a persecuted leader. Most scholars assume either that these hymns are actually the composition of the Teacher of Righteousness himself or that they were composed by members of the community in order to represent his life and experience. It is also possible that they were the hymns of various leaders.[15] For present purposes, however, let us assume that these *Hodayot* were heard by the Qumran community as compositions of the Teacher.

As hymns or thanksgiving prayers, the compositions are formally addressed to God: they begin with the words, "I thank you, O Lord." But thanksgiving prayers were traditionally not private expressions but intended to be recited in a communal context. They may have been addressed to God explicitly, but they were intended also to have an effect on the community who overheard them. And it is this rhetorical dimension that is of particular interest here. Unfortunately, we do not know precisely in what setting the *Thanksgiving Hymns* were used and who recited them. One plausible suggestion, based on an analogy with the practices of the Therapeutae, is that they were publicly recited after communal meals.[16] However, it is also possible that, on analogy with the biblical Psalms, they were memorized as part of the educational curriculum of the sect.

14. M. A. Knibb, "Teacher of Righteousness."

15. See the discussion in C. A. Newsom, *The Self as Symbolic Space*, 287-300.

16. B. Reicke, "Remarques sur l'histoire de la form (Formgeschichte) des textes de Qumran."

The rhetoric of the prayer tradition that is developed in the *Thanksgiving Hymns* has several important features that are relevant to the effectiveness of these compositions in the sectarian context. First, the prayers are framed in the first person singular, as the confession to God of the speaker's innermost thoughts and feelings. Thus, if these prayers were believed to represent the words of the Teacher himself, then no matter how much time had passed since the death of the Teacher, every time they were recited, they would make his voice and his leadership once again present to the community. Second, in prayer only one voice speaks. The one who prays may quote the words of others, his friends or his foes, but he alone controls what is said and how matters are presented. Finally, the tradition of prayer out of which the *Hodayot* developed is one that elaborately displays the speaker's subjectivity: his humiliation and triumphs, his hopes and fears, and even the sensations of his body. It is an extraordinarily personal and intimate rhetoric. Even though the *Hodayot* of the Teacher take up many issues of conflict and community disaffection, the rhetoric of the *Hodayot* shifts the focus from whatever the content of the conflict was about and instead places it on the suffering but courageous persona of the Teacher. Thus the hymns invite the listener (both God and the human audience) to feel compassion for and to accept the Teacher who presents himself within them.

Analyzing one such prayer may help to illustrate how effective this rhetoric could be. In 1QH 13:24–15:5[17] the speaker alternates descriptions of the antagonism of his opponents and the effect of their opposition on the speaker with expressions of divine assistance. In the first movement of the prayer (13:22-26) the Teacher draws on traditional language to identify himself as the "orphan" and "the poor one," terms that signaled rectitude and piety, as well as vulnerability. Then he describes the conflict, using traditional images from psalms of complaint. He is "a cause of controversy and quarrels with my neighbors, and an object of jealousy and anger to those who enter into covenant with me," and so on. Echoing traditional psalmic language, these are not objective descriptions but phrases that position the speaker as one who is innocent and has been wronged. Only toward the end of the passage is the specific, sectarian context of the dispute suggested: "with the secret you had hidden in me they have gone around as slanderers to the children of destruction." To betray esoteric knowledge to

---

17. Column and line numbers follow those in F. García Martínez and E. J. C. Tigchelaar, *The Dead Sea Scrolls Study Edition*, 1:146-203.

those outside the restricted group is hardly the type of misfortune that a traditional psalm of complaint or thanksgiving would address. Here the speaker is using traditional forms of speech to colonize the new moral territory of sectarian ethics. Since the actual betrayers are unlikely to be part of the audience, the speaker's words can be understood as a sort of "spin control," an interpretation of a possibly ambiguous event that the speaker casts as rank betrayal. But despite the wicked efforts of the betrayers, God has supported the speaker: "But in order to [show your gre]atness through me, and on account of their guilt, you have hidden the spring of understanding and the foundation of truth" (13:25-26). In point of fact, who was entitled to disclose what to whom (and even what counted as "disclosure") may have been disputed issues. But the language of the psalm dispels all ambiguity — what happened was a victimization of the speaker. The speaker is vindicated, his opponents are judged, and their efforts are shown to have been in vain.

If one looks at the whole text, however, it is not simply interested in demonstrating divine judgment but also in taking the hearer back again and again to a focus on the conflict itself and in particular on the effect of the conflict on the speaker (13:26-32; 13:35–14:6). The nasty quality of the opponents is captured through the imagery of snakes with darting tongues and poisonous venom. But it is the description of the distraught emotional state of the speaker that truly forms the central focus of this part of the prayer. Thus the composition solicits sympathy for the speaker.

As the prayer turns to a description of divine assistance, the attention turns away from the speaker himself. Surprising as it would be to someone who was familiar only with biblical psalmody, the relief offered to the speaker appears to have to do with God's provision of a community that boldly confronts its members about moral shortcomings. "[But you, O my God,] you opened my ears with the ins[tru]ction of those who reprove justly." Gradually, the focus moves from the speaker's own reception of instruction to the instruction of the community and the benefits it provides: "You refine them in order to purify from guilt [and from s]in all their deeds by means of your truth. And in your kindness you judge them with overflowing compassion and abundant forgiveness, teaching them according to your command." Even though the speaker casts these events in wholly positive terms, the aspects of community life to which he refers would have had the potential to create social friction and disaffection (even the *Community Rule* recognizes that the practice of mutual reproof can lead to social friction and has to be controlled carefully; see 1QS 5:25–

6:1). Although it would be difficult to draw the lines of connection too specifically, one might suggest that this hodayah is a response, in general terms at least, to the system of moral evaluation, mutual critique, and status hierarchy that the social structure of the community created and which could well have provided the environment in which "refractory murmurers" might have been a recurring problem. Thus the author seems to be acknowledging that even as the very practices of the community may produce dissatisfaction in some members, they are nevertheless the very source of what supports the speaker. But the appeal is bolstered by the further description of the benefits that will accrue to all who stand with the speaker — communion with the angels and a collective role as both the world tree and a spring of light in which all the guilty will be burned up (1QH 14:12-19).

Yet once more the speaker describes the scenario of conflict and relief (14:19-36). Again, the cause of distress is described as defection: "they, who had attached themselves to my witness, have let themselves be persuaded by [. . .]"). The speaker's distress is presented under the image of a sailor caught in a raging storm, while deliverance comes in the image of a secure and fortified city, apparently an image of the covenanted community that the leader directs. In some ways it may seem curious that the community — which apparently has been the source of the "refractory murmurers" — is represented as sure and reliable and that the leader, who is clearly a figure to be reckoned with, prefers to represent himself as deeply vulnerable, rescued from death and dissolution by the strength he receives from this community of God's truth. But perhaps this staging of images is highly strategic. In situations where the loyalty of a group is in doubt, there may be an advantage to putting before them images of their proper role and crediting them with fulfilling their function, even if their past performance has been a bit shaky.

If this is indeed the rhetorical strategy of the composition, then it ends in a provocative fashion, for the final preserved lines of the composition apparently follow yet another description of faithless defection. Rather than concluding with a confident assertion of God's deliverance of the speaker, they end instead with language of the speaker's distress. Thus the prayer seems to end with an implicit plea. Four times the audience has been told that God has always aided the speaker in his distress. In the final two cases this aid has been described as manifested through the faithful life of the community itself. By leaving the final act of deliverance unstated, the text implicitly calls upon the community to recognize its support of the speaker as the needed act of divine deliverance. Whether the rhetoric was successful, we cannot know. It is clear, however, that much thought and art went into the shaping of these *Hodayot* of the Teacher and that they were attempts to affect the reality of a situation through speech.

As these examples have attempted to demonstrate, language was a vital instrument in the creation and maintenance of the sectarian community. Carefully crafted speech aided in transforming outsiders into insiders, gave a sense of identity and purpose to members, and was a means of addressing and transforming conflicts. Rhetorical criticism opens up the mechanisms by which language was put to these uses. As a method of analysis, rhetorical criticism is an important complement not only to literary criticism but also to social scientific approaches, ritual studies, and theological analysis of the texts of the Dead Sea Scrolls.

Of Calendars, Community Rules, and Common Knowledge: Understanding 4QS^e-4QOtot, with Help from Ritual Studies

Robert Kugler

An Explanatory Prologue

It is important that I begin this essay in a volume on interdisciplinary approaches to the Dead Sea Scrolls with a confession. When the editor asked me to contribute to the volume, my assignment was to address how ritual studies might aid our understanding of the scrolls. But in a gathering of the contributors in November 2006 the editor noted that attention to calendrical issues at Qumran from any one of the authors would also be most welcome.[1] Her comment prompted me to look more closely at one calendrical text in particular that had seized my imagination, 4QOtot (4Q319). It is but one of the many texts from Qumran that betray the community's fascination with calculating and schematically organizing the passage of all time — past, present, and future. Before long I was absorbed in the interpretive issues associated with 4QOtot, and ritual studies was but a glimmer on the horizon of my research agenda. But as the following chapter proves, ritual studies reentered the picture soon enough, and it did so to provide the key to solving the mystery presented by 4QOtot. That is to say, the exercise itself demonstrated the wisdom of the editor's impulse in assembling the essays in this volume: there is much help to be had from

---

1. Thanks are due to Prof. Grossman for organizing a meeting of the contributors on the day prior to the beginning of the 2006 SBL Annual Meeting in Philadelphia. The occasion reflected the best lights of the scholarly life: Prof. Grossman afforded the volume's contributors a chance to share ideas, critique each other's work, and engage in face-to-face intellectual exchange.

other disciplines in our effort to understand the scrolls and their authors and keepers. The endeavor also suggests something of how we might position ourselves relative to the resources other disciplines offer. I elaborate these latter insights in concluding comments. For now, let me narrate the research story that produced the insights in the first place.

The Trouble With 4QOtot: Introducing the Issue

The people of the scrolls, ordinarily believed to have been the Essenes mentioned by Josephus, Philo, and Pliny,[2] considered themselves to be God's elect among the people of Israel. As such, they claimed to be privy to the ways and knowledge of God that were concealed from the rest of Israel. Among the things they considered themselves privileged to apprehend was the calculation of time from its beginning to its eschatological conclusion. They used a variety of means to measure the passage of time, including priestly rota *(mishmarot)*, the year of release *(shemitah)*, festival schedules, Jubilee Year cycles, and the sun and the moon; they even used these in combination, to create especially elaborate accounts of time's passing. Of course, reconciling these vastly different measures of time to provide a comprehensive account of the past, present, and future was a complex endeavor, one that produced the wealth of "calendrical" texts found at Qumran.[3]

One special problem that faced the Qumran community was how to make practicable the various calendars entailed by such measures: for instance, without the intercalation of an additional one-and-a-quarter days each year, using the priestly *mishmarot* to measure the passage of time would eventually result in observing festivals out of season. This is where the text that interests us enters the picture. 4QOtot, named for its repeated use of the term *ot* ("sign"), is evidence that the Essenes did develop a system of intercalation to ensure the practicality of their idealized schematizations of time; as we see in greater detail below, most agree that the *otot* ("signs") signal aspects of intercalation that made a 364-day calendar useful. The trouble with treating 4QOtot as a manual for actual prac-

2. For the most convenient assemblage of the pertinent primary texts with appropriately modest secondary contributions, see G. Vermes and M. D. Goodman, eds., *The Essenes According to the Classical Sources.*

3. For a full and convenient discussion of the various kinds of calendrical texts, see J. C. VanderKam, *Calendars in the Dead Sea Scrolls.*

tice, though, is that it appears in a *late* manuscript of an *early* and *out-moded* recension of the group's *Community Rule,* a handbook of thought and practice for Essenes living in community. In other words, the one apparently practicable calendar the group produced survives in a manuscript of their community handbook that, by the time it was inscribed, had already been superseded by later versions. Thus the "trouble with 4QOtot" prompts the question this essay seeks to answer: How could a calendar designed for actual use be of use when it survives in a manuscript of a text that had gone out of use?

The Trouble With 4QOtot: Elaborating the Issue

J. T. Milik, the first editor responsible for 4QOtot, knew it to be from the same scroll as an early recension of the *Community Rule,* 4QS^e, but because of its calendrical character and 4QS^e's parallels with 1QS 7:8–8:15 + 9:12-24, he deemed the two to be different works.[4] Subsequent study of the scroll has proved, however, that 4QS^e and 4QOtot are a single work: the physical evidence indicates that they were not separated by any lacuna. Moreover, in spite of Milik's early judgment, the placement of a calendrical text in 4QS^e where the hymn appears in 1QS is thematically unsurprising: the hymn that concludes 1QS begins with a passage extolling God's control over the astral measures of time and declaring the speaker's commitment to praise God at the turnings of the days, seasons, and years (10:1–11:22; see esp. 10:1-8).[5]

As for the scope of the original work, its fragmentary state makes it difficult to be certain, but the most reliable reconstruction of the scroll suggests that there could have been enough original manuscript surface to ac-

4. J. T. Milik, with the collaboration of M. Black, ed., *The Books of Enoch: Aramaic Fragments of Qumrân Cave 4.* Note that Milik numbered 4QS^e (4Q259) and 4QOtot (4Q319) as 4Q260 and 4Q260B, respectively. For the *editio princeps* of 4QOtot, see J. Ben-Dov, "319. 4QOtot," DJD 21, 195-244; for the *editio princeps* of 4QS^e, see P. S. Alexander and G. Vermes, "259. 4QSerekh ha-Yahad^e," DJD 26, 129-52.

5. The case for rejoining 4QS^e and 4QOtot as a single work on a single scroll as a matter of physical reconstruction was made by S. Metso, "The Primary Results of the Reconstruction of 4QS^e"; *The Textual Development of the Qumran Community Rule,* 50; and U. Glessmer, *Die ideale Kultordnung,* 174-84; Glessmer and Metso are followed by Ben-Dov, DJD 21, 199; and Alexander and Vermes, DJD 26, 131-32, 150-52. The thematic coherence of 4QOtot with 1QS 10:1-8 is now widely recognized; see, e.g., the comments in VanderKam, *Calendars in the Dead Sea Scrolls,* 81.

commodate the equivalent of 1QS 5:1–7:7.[6] As a whole, then, 4QSᵉ-4QOtot may have embraced general instructions for the community (= 1QS 5:1-20; all lost), specific rules for various members of the community and a penal code (= 1QS 5:21–7:25; only 7:8-25 fragmentarily preserved in 4QSᵉ 1:4-15; 2:3-9a), guidelines for the council of the community (= 1QS 8:1-15; fragmentarily preserved in 4QSᵉ 2:9b–3:6a), instructions for the *Maskil* (= 1QS 9:12-25; fragmentarily preserved in 4QSᵉ 3:6b–4:5), and the *Otot* text where the Hymn of 1QS 10:1–11:22 would have appeared (= 4QOtot).[7]

The contents of 4QOtot are only partially certain. Of around one hundred fragments, only frgs. 1-8 and 23 can be assembled together to make up clearly identifiable portions of four columns of text (roughly 4QOtot 4:10–6:18). Fragments 1, 2, and 3g comprise 4:9-19; frgs. 2, 3, 4, 5, 9, and 23 comprise 5:1-19; frgs. 5, 6, 7 i, and 8 comprise 6:1-19; and frg. 7 ii comprises 7:1-8.[8] Luckily, most of this more-or-less contiguous text provides "a unique correlation of three discrete time-reckoning devices: the standard Qumran six-year *mishmarot* cycle, the seven-year *shemitah* cycle, and the forty-nine-year jubilee cycle."[9] To be complete, such a correlation

6. Metso, *Textual Development*, 51.

7. Metso, *Textual Development*, 48-51. There is some debate as to whether 1QS 9:26, the lead-in to the hymn in 1QS 10-11, was present in 4QSᵉ-4QOtot, and the loss of columnar material makes it impossible to be certain (Metso, *Textual Development*, 50; Ben-Dov, DJD 21, 200-201; Alexander and Vermes, DJD 26, 51-52). On the basis of the traces of ברוך in 4QOtot 4:9, the line that followed 1QS 9:25 in 4QSᵉ 4:8, Ben-Dov plausibly suggests that this may also have belonged "to the following calendrical portion, serving as a doxology of praise to YHWH, who created the luminaries and maintains them as everlasting signs," just as a blessing formula opens the "creational astronomical list" in 11QPsᵃ 26:13; DJD 21, 216.

8. Ben-Dov, DJD 21, 214-22.

9. Ben-Dov, DJD 21, 201. Ben-Dov labels the remainder of the preserved columnar material, 6:19 and 7:1-8, a roster of the "Leaders of the Quarters," and perhaps the beginning of a roster of the "Leaders of the Months," like those known from 4QMishamarot F and G; DJD 21, 222; cf. 4Q328-329 in S. Talmon, DJD 21, 139-46. In the remaining fragments of 4QOtot, Ben Dov sees hints of a "festival calendar of the six year cycle on frgs. 12, 13 and possibly frg. 77," and yet another "different *mishmarot* composition"; DJD 21, 213. Our lack of certainty regarding the nature of this remaining material is troublesome; see, e.g., U. Glessmer, "Investigation of the Otot-text (4Q319) and Questions about Methodology," esp. 438; "Calendars in the Qumran Scrolls," esp. 263, but to take Ben-Dov's tack and dub 4QOtot, in spite of its clear coherence with 4QSᵉ, merely "a compendium of calendrical information" (DJD 21, 201) is to downplay too much the undeniable internal coherence of the *Otot* section. That coherence, along with the clear interest of the fragmentary remains of the rest of 4Q319 in priestly courses, speaks more strongly than not of some larger unity for the work as a whole.

requires a 294-year period (49 × 6 = 294), such as the one covered by this portion of text. The most outstanding characteristic of the text, though, is what won it its moniker:[10] it reports the occurrence of אותות, "signs," in each Jubilee it records, and it either introduces or concludes each Jubilee with a summary of the number of "signs" that occur in the Jubilee, indicating as well which ones occurred in the year of release, the שמטה (Deut 15:1, 2, 9; 31:10). Opinion as to the meaning of אות varies: conjectures include Jonathan Ben-Dov's "observable heavenly phenomena" and Uwe Glessmer's time spans "which regularly re-synchronize the beginnings of years and lunations."[11] That said, the term's function and that of the roster as a whole are universally understood to be intercalary in some way. A quotation from James VanderKam, used approvingly by Ben-Dov as well, is worth repeating here.[12]

> It is likely that the signs of 4Q319 have something to do with a system of intercalation that would bring the 364-day system into harmony with the true solar year. Whether that system is the more complicated sort that Glessmer suggests or a simpler one reconciling the schematic lunar and solar calendars every three years [thus Ben-Dov], the text

---

10. Two other peculiarities merit note as well: the reckoning begins with creation, but only on the fourth day, when the heavenly luminaries necessary for reckoning time were created (4:10-11), and the Jubilees are numbered beginning with the second and continuing to the seventh (cf. 4:16-17; 6:17). The former characteristic is unsurprising, but the latter one has generally befuddled commentators. The idea that it was the result of some scribal error has been rejected, and all agree that the scribe intended the "omission" of the first Jubilee. Ben-Dov, DJD 21, 208, represents well the laconic puzzlement that characterizes scholarly responses to this oddity: "For some reason, the first jubilee of creation is seemingly not designated הראשון but rather השני, 'the second'. This seems to imply a previously unknown concept of primordial time. Unfortunately, insufficient information is known to account for this surprising feature of time-reckoning and creation theology in Second Temple Judaism."

11. For the first view, see Ben-Dov, DJD 21, 209-10, who sees the *Otot* roster as "technically speaking, a manual for the maintenance of the lunar calendar" by the addition every three years of a lunar month; for the second, see Glessmer, "Calendars in the Qumran Scrolls," 263-68 (and his earlier discussions cited there), who sees in the *Otot* register a formula that aligns a 364-day year with a solar year of 365.25 days.

12. VanderKam, *Calendars in the Dead Sea Scrolls,* 84; for further discussions of 4QOtot in general and the meaning of the term "signs" in the work, see esp. U. Glessmer, "Der 364-Tage-Kalender und die Sabbatstruktur seiner Schaltungen in ihrer Bedeutung für den Kult"; M. Albani, "Die lunaren Zyklen im 364-Tage-Festkalender von 4QMischmerot/ 4QS^e"; *Astronomie und Schöpfungsglaube,* 283-96; F. García Martínez, "Calendarios en Qumran (I)."

does point to some intercalary system and thus to an interest on the part of the author(s) in making the calendar practicable over a very long period.

The authorial interest that VanderKam refers to was surely best served by what seems to have been the likely use of 4QS^e-4QOtot: like other manuscripts of the *Community Rule,* it served as a publicly read "constitutional" document for the gathering of covenanters at Qumran.[13]

That 4QS^e-4QOtot represents a version of the *Community Rule* different from the form evident in 1QS is obvious, as is its variance vis-à-vis the other Cave 4 manuscripts of the same work.[14] There is wide agreement that 1QS reflects the latest recension of the *Community Rule* found at Qumran, and that this recension existed already by 100 B.C.E., the paleographic date of 1QS. By contrast, the recension evident in 4QS^e-4QOtot predates 1QS and its recension, yet the *manuscript itself* dates to 50-25 B.C.E., well after the 1QS recension had achieved ascendancy.[15] From these facts we may conclude that the community continued to produce copies of the early 4QS^e-4QOtot recension of the *Community Rule* long after it had been superseded by the later recension evident in 1QS.

The preceding summary of the state of the question regarding 4QS^e-4QOtot demonstrates clearly the "trouble with 4QOtot": if its calendar is meant to address the necessity of intercalation, how did it fulfill that purpose while ensconced in a version of the *Community Rule* that had been surpassed by later recensions? How did 4QOtot create the communal awareness of its temporal tinkering that would be necessary to make its solution to intercalation useful to the community? It is with this question that we meet the limits of traditional methods and resources of scrolls scholarship and are bidden to seek help from ritual studies.

13. Indeed, some of the characteristics of a manuscript that suggest preparation with oral presentation in mind are present in 4QS^e-4QOtot: the orthography is full, virtually all letters that can take a final form do so when they appear in final positions, and *vacats* are, with one exception, placed appropriately to facilitate oral presentation (Alexander and Vermes, DJD 26, 133; the exception is in 4QS^e 3:6, where 1QS leaves a full-line *vacat* and indents the new line to begin the instructions for the *Maskil* in 9:12).

14. See above all, Metso, *Textual Development,* 48-54, 143-49; Alexander and Vermes, DJD 26, 1-25, 134.

15. This is the judgment of Frank Moore Cross in J. H. Charlesworth, et al., eds., *Rule of the Community and Related Documents,* 57; it overturns the earlier judgment of Milik, *The Books of Enoch,* 61, that the text should be dated to the second half of the second century B.C.E.

Ritual Studies on Common Knowledge and Coordinated Action

That ritual studies might prove helpful in this regard should not be surprising: after all, ritual is, among other things, public action that creates common knowledge, which in turn licenses and even compels beliefs and practices. Oddly, though, the way in which ritual studies helps *is* surprising. Until very recently scholars devoted themselves almost exclusively to establishing grand theories of ritual and its relationship to the origins and functions of religion, society, and/or culture.[16] A turn toward a narrower-gauge, rational-functional understanding of ritual came with the help of a political economist and game theorist who was chiefly concerned to explain why groups occasionally take coordinated actions that are not at first obviously in their own best interests. Michael Suk-Young Chwe shows in *Rational Ritual: Culture, Coordination, and Common Knowledge* (2001) that taking such coordinated actions is, in fact, a rational choice licensed by common knowledge that is engendered through public ritual.

Chwe observes that the necessity of common knowledge for coordinated action is revealed famously in the rabbit hunter's dilemma posed by Jean-Jacques Rousseau in *Discourse on Inequality* (1755). The subsistence hunter knows that abandoning the solo rabbit hunt to cooperate with other hunters to bring down large game is to his and his neighbors' long-term advantage, but that such a change in strategy is a rational choice only if virtually all of the hunters know and join in the plan from the start. Likewise, other solo subsistence hunters are encouraged to join a stag hunt only if they too know the advantage of group hunting and that the other hunters in the forest share that knowledge. In other words, for the new hunting strategy to work, each hunter needs to know that other hunters know what he knows, and that they know that he knows what they know, and so on. Only when such extended common knowledge is ensured will

---

16. For a careful survey of the details behind this three-dimensional summary of ritual studies, see C. Bell, *Ritual: Perspectives and Dimensions*, 1-92; for greater depth of analysis of the specific schools of thought and approaches to ritual studies, see the essays on "Classical Topics Revisited" in J. Kreinrath, J. Snoek, and M. Stausberg, eds., *Theorizing Rituals: Classical Topics, Theoretical Approaches, Concepts*, 101-261. For my earlier attempt to bring ritual studies to bear in study of the Dead Sea Scrolls, see R. Kugler, "Making All Experience Religious: The Hegemony of Ritual at Qumran," in which I relied heavily on the categories of ritual Bell provided in her book, *Ritual Theory, Ritual Practice*. For a different approach to using ritual studies in work on the scrolls, see S. Weitzman, "Revisiting Myth and Ritual in Early Judaism."

solo hunters understand the *need* to abandon their uncoordinated, individual actions in favor of coordinated, group action.

The solution to the hunters' dilemma is surprisingly counter-
intuitive. One might imagine that "strong-link encounters" — one-on-
one, word-of-mouth encounters between hunters in the forest — would
most readily create the common knowledge necessary to engender the
coordinated action of a stag hunt. But the opposite is true: such one-on-
one exchanges may be "strong-link encounters," but they do not ensure
the extended common knowledge that makes what might have been an ir-
rational choice suddenly rational. By contrast, "weak-link encounters" —
group assemblies — do provide the necessary assurance of extended common knowledge. The solo rabbit hunters' real solution is to forego word-
of-mouth as a means of sharing the plan in favor of a group meeting in
the forest where all participants share simultaneously the knowledge of
the stag-hunting plan and know through their meeting together that they
all share that same knowledge: not only do they see the *advantage* in co-
operating, but by virtue of sharing that knowledge, they individually *need*
to join the hunt, lest they lose out. Chwe points out that if we treat the
meeting in the forest as a ritual, "the purpose of a ritual is to form the
common knowledge necessary for solving a coordination problem."[17] By
making certain that one party knows what the other party knows, and
that the other party knows that the first party knows what the other party
knows, and so on — by creating unequivocally *common* knowledge — coordinated action is made possible and even necessary for the individuals
involved.

Chwe's theory provides a solid framework for understanding how religious rituals function. Consider, for instance, the rite of believer's baptism practiced among some Christian groups. They understand baptism to
authorize its recipient to believe that in exchange for a confession of faith
in Jesus as Lord and a vow to resist further sin, the ultimate consequence of
sin — that is, death — will be replaced with a promise of eternal life. Inas-
much as the rite of baptism in such circles is enacted publicly among fellow
believers through a "weak-link encounter," the knowledge that the ritual
conveys is not limited to the baptismal candidate. By witnessing the rite,
the candidate's neighbors in faith share in the knowledge of baptism's effect; by seeing her neighbors witnessing the rite, she knows that they know
these things; by seeing her observe them as they observe her, the candi-

17. Chwe, *Rational Ritual*, 25-26.

date's neighbors know that she knows that they know the consequences of the rite of baptism; and so on.

This extended network of common knowledge ensures the group's coordinated renunciation of behaviors deemed by the group to be sinful, even when avoiding such behaviors (e.g., dancing, sexual intercourse before marriage, or drinking alcohol) might make individual group members appear unusual in their day-to-day surroundings. Indeed, group members have not only been *authorized* by the ritual experience to violate social norms for the sake of their religious beliefs; they are *compelled* to do so by the host of compatriots whom they know to know what they know, and so on.

Using the Theory of Rational Ritual to Understand How 4QOtot Worked

Returning now to the question of *how* 4QOtot engendered the common knowledge necessary to prompt the Qumran group's coordinated implementation of a 364-day calendar, we find that Chwe's theory of rational ritual proves to be very useful. If we understand the general consensus that *Community Rule* texts were recited in the community's regular assemblies at the Qumran site in light of Chwe's hypothesis, then the function of 4QS^e-4QOtot in making adherence to the group's unusual 364-day calendar a rational choice becomes clear. Public recitation of general and specific guidelines for group members' behavior, supplemented by a penal code for failure to meet those obligations, surely created the expanded common knowledge that authorized and commanded coordinated action in keeping with the terms of 4QS^e-4QOtot. These terms included reckoning time from creation through a 294-year period to make a 364-day year practicable. Sharing that approach to reckoning time in the "weak-link encounter" of the group assembly made it possible to keep such a calendar — at odds with the calendar of other Judaisms of the day — not only at Qumran, but in daily life apart from like-minded group members. Because group members knew the proper pattern for reckoning time, *and* that their confrères not only knew the pattern as well, but also knew that they knew, and so on, they were empowered, even required, to keep the 364-day calendar that 4QOtot made practicable in all phases of their life.

But of course, an obvious problem remains: 4QS^e-4QOtot was superseded by the recension known from 1QS, a recension that does not include the calendrical section in 4QOtot. Thus it is highly unlikely that 4QS^e-4QOtot was still being read aloud in the public assembly, seemingly canceling its capacity to engender the expanded common knowledge of the practicable 364-day calendar that was necessary for the calendar's implementation by the group's coordinated action. Here, again, Chwe's insights are useful, but only when we extend them beyond his own work.

One of the most charming examples Chwe cites to demonstrate the explanatory power of his hypothesis is the story of Listerine's marketing as a mouthwash.[18] In the first decades of the twentieth century Lambert Pharmacal (now part of Pfizer Pharmaceutical) sought to increase the market for its hospital antiseptic, Listerine. A company employee suggested that the solution be sold as a mouthwash because he had found it useful in eliminating bad breath. However, bad breath, dubbed "halitosis" by the advertisers at Lambert Pharmacal, was not at the time considered a particular social ill that required remediation. Thus the company undertook an advertising campaign that placed "story ads" in widely-read American weeklies and monthlies (including *Harper's Magazine, The Saturday Evening Post, Woman's Home Companion, Ladies' Home Journal*) meant to persuade readers that bad breath was a social sin and the cause of myriad social ills. In the most famous ad of the campaign, advertisers borrowed the theme of the Fred W. Leigh and Charles Collins 1917 song, "Why Am I Always a Bridesmaid?" to tell the socio-drama of Edna. Edna is depicted pictorially as a distressed, late twenties single woman who laments that she is "often a bridesmaid, but never a bride." The narrator explains that Edna unknowingly suffers from a tragic social disease no one has the courage to tell her about: halitosis, better known as bad breath. If only Edna knew, continues the socio-drama, she would use Listerine to extinguish her bad breath and finally attract the man of her dreams.[19]

The genius of the ad campaign was its use of an American ritual of the day as its vehicle for distribution: the nearly universal consumption of magazine weeklies and monthlies as a basic form of entertainment. The makers of Listerine could be certain that millions of Americans would read their advertisements nearly in concert and as a result not only know that Listerine could save them from a theretofore unacknowledged social

18 Chwe, *Rational Ritual,* 38-41; for the full account of the advertising campaign's genesis and efflorescence, see V. Vinikas, *Soft Soap, Hard Sell: American Hygiene in an Age of Advertisement.*

19. *Ladies' Home Journal,* March 1924.

gaffe, but also that their relatives, neighbors, friends, coworkers, present and future business contacts, potential employers, and so on, knew the same thing, *and* knew that they knew! On these terms, no one could afford to be without Listerine as a guardian against halitosis. It is hardly surprising that Lambert Pharmacal's profits from Listerine rose from around $100,000 in 1921 to over $4 million in 1927. The campaign is a classic in advertising and outstanding proof of Chwe's theory of the relationships among ritual, common knowledge, and coordinated action.

What Chwe does not take into account is the further history of the Listerine advertising campaign; as it turns out, that history points to an answer to our question regarding the continuing influence of the 4QS^e-4QOtot recension of the *Community Rule* long after it had become obsolete as a text used for oral presentation. By the early 1930s the makers of Listerine had displaced Edna and her tale of woe in favor of a different kind of socio-dramatic advertisement. An advertisement from 1931 features a newspaper story cutout with the headline, "Sentence Society Pair to Halitosis Island for 60 days." Below the headline is a *faux* newspaper article, complete with a New York dateline, and accounts of how the couple had been seized while at a "fashionable dinner party at the John J. Smith's home in the upper fifties," on a complainant's anonymous tip, and subsequently convicted of bad breath and sentenced in "Judge Jenkins' court" to two months on Halitosis Island. Above the headline is a portrait of the dejected prisoner couple being taken by their jailers across a storm-tossed sea to a bleak and barren island. The advertisement itself is nearly an afterthought placed below the *faux* newspaper article, and it doesn't actually mention Listerine until it has argued at length that such a newspaper article as the one it accompanies is a distinct possibility within a decade's time, especially since halitosis had become such a well-known and despised social sin.[20]

This "later recension" of the earliest Listerine ads featuring Edna is instructive for what it assumes its audience to know and appreciate already: bad breath is not an acceptable bodily odor, and Listerine is its remedy. Because those facts had already been established as common knowledge by nearly a decade's worth of advertising, they did not bear explicit repetition. It was enough to assume them and let mere echoes of them suffice, echoes evident in language like "Halitosis Island," and in the image of the society couple in the rowboat, downcast and distressed as Edna and countless other ad-world halitosis sufferers had been before them.

20. *Woman's Home Companion,* September 1931.

The same pattern of assuming and merely echoing established common knowledge may help explain why the calendrical details of 4QS^e-4QOtot needed no further repetition to be effective in the covenanters' imagination and in their daily, weekly, monthly, and yearly practices, at Qumran and among their noncovenanter peers. By its own long period of recitation in public assemblies, the time-reckoning knowledge that the calendrical details of 4QOtot communicated had become common knowledge in its most complete sense: every covenanter knew *without being told explicitly* how to reckon a 364-day year, and every covenanter knew that every other covenanter knew this same skill, and that its use was required by the community's ethos, an ethos reinforced by a penalty for those who violated it. Thus later recensions of the *Community Rule* could suffice with echoes of the details — poetic images, as it were — of the calendrical arcana in 4QOtot. Indeed, precisely where 4QOtot appears in 4QS^e-4QOtot, 1QS offers instead a poem that merely echoes the calendrical details of 4QOtot, vowing praise for the Creator according to various measures of time.

> [With pray]er shall he bless Him at the times ordained of God:
> when light begins its dominion — each time it returns — and when,
>   as ordained, it is regathered into its dwelling place;
> when night begins its watches — as He opens His storehouse and
>   spreads darkness over the earth — and when it cycles back,
>   withdrawing before the light;
> when the luminaries show forth from their holy habitation, and when
>   they are regathered into their glorious abode;
> when the times appointed for new moons arrive, and when, as their
>   periods require, each gives way to the next.
> Such renewal is a special day for the Holy of Holies; indeed, it is a
>   sign that He is unlocking eternal loving-kindness each time
>   these cycles begin as ordained, and so it shall be for every era
>   yet to come.
> On the first of each month in its season, and on holy days laid down
>   for a memorial, in their seasons by a prayer shall I bless Him —
>   a statute forever engraved.
> When each new year begins and when its seasons turn, fulfilling the
>   law of their decree, each day as set forth, day after day: harvest
>   giving way to summer, planting to the shoots of spring, seasons,
>   years, and weeks of years.

> When weeks of years begin, Jubilee by Jubilee, while I live, on my
> tongue shall the statute be engraved — with praise its fruit,
> even the gift of my lips.
>
> > (1QS 9:26b–10:8; transl. Wise, Abegg, and Cook)

That the authors of the 1QS recension of the *Community Rule* would adopt such an allusive rhetorical strategy to remind recipients of the 4QOtot calendar is unsurprising: the Dead Sea Scrolls are rife with instances of this compositional strategy, and in the oral-aural culture of the day it was a staple of rhetorical practice.[21]

Still, the reason for continued copying of 4QS^e-4QOtot remains unclear. If echoing the *Otot* passage sufficed, why bother to preserve it? Most probably it survived as the written record of the detailed calendrical reckoning that made a 364-day year possible over time. Even if the authors of 1QS could count on most auditors to know the details of 4QOtot, there would always be some who did not, either by reason of belated conversion to the group or failing memory. And in any case, in so scribal a culture as the one we encounter at Qumran the specific rubrics for making the covenanters' calendar practicable could surely have never been allowed to perish completely from the written record.

A Reflective Epilogue

So much, then, for "the problem with 4QOtot." What remains is to fulfill my promise that I would address more fully the implications of this study for interdisciplinary approaches to the scrolls. First, it is important to remember that ritual studies was not the beginning point of this exercise, and only came to bear when traditional methods no longer sufficed as a means to address the challenge of explaining 4QOtot's function. That is to say, it was the *nature of the evidence* that provoked the turn to another discipline for help. Second, as I began to explore the resources ritual studies offers I learned the importance of appreciating the variant approaches within unfamiliar disciplines: the standard *theoretical* approach to ritual studies proved

---

21. For bibliog. on and discussion of the oral-literate culture at Qumran and in Greco-Roman antiquity in general, as well as examples of the "echoing" strategy in the scrolls, see R. Kugler, "Hearing 4Q225: A Case Study in Reconstructing the Religious Imagination of the Qumran Community."

useless for answering the question of 4QOtot's function, but the recently developed functionalist approach of Chwe — himself an outsider to ritual studies — provided just what was needed to address the matter. That is to say, the *nature of the questions* we ask of our evidence should determine our choice of approaches within a discipline that we use. Finally, I would note that ritual studies was not the only new discipline that came to bear in my research; though only in passing, the study of oral-aural cultures also played a role in explaining the function of 4QOtot. That is to say, we do well to remain open to the use of multiple disciplines in combination with one another to answer the *questions* we ask of the *evidence*.

To some readers these may seem paltry insights, little more than expressions of common sense. Yet a profound lack of common sense is often thought to plague the academy-wide turn toward interdisciplinarity, and that accusation becomes for some observers reason enough to reject the enterprise altogether; thus one can be glad on this occasion for having been charged with mere common sense. Likewise, some might suggest that these insights counsel a certain eclecticism that undercuts any possibility of programmatic approaches to interdisciplinarity, and for that charge I would be particularly grateful; for if there is one real danger in the turn toward interdisciplinarity that genuinely threatens its chances of success in advancing intellectual discourse, it is the tendency among some to make a program of interdisciplinary scholarship into a dogmatic commitment to one discipline to the exclusion of others that may be of help. Clearly, such a move is contrary to the impulse that moves us in the direction of new disciplines, the drive to always see the evidence we investigate and pose the questions we ask in ever new and revealing ways.

Women and Men in the Rule of the Congregation: A Feminist Critical Assessment

Maxine L. Grossman

For the earliest generation of Dead Sea Scrolls scholars, the argument that the scrolls represented the library of an ancient Essene community had certain significant implications: that the authors of the scrolls were celibate men (as Philo, Pliny, and Josephus assert), that some small number of them might indeed marry, but only for the purpose of procreation (this from Josephus), and that a population of celibate Essenes could be found in the vicinity of Qumran, while marrying Essenes were to be found elsewhere in the land, where they lived together in "camps" (this from a harmonistic reading of Pliny, Philo, Josephus, and the scrolls).[1]

The fact that scrolls scholars today might nuance or even flatly contradict many of these originating assumptions is the product of several distinct developments. The publication of new texts (including the vast fragmentary array of material from Cave 4) has, without question, transformed the field. So too has the work of later scholarship, which by definition reconsiders earlier claims.[2] But a third key element in our reconsider-

---

1. Josephus, Philo, and Pliny the Elder provide our primary sources for the Essenes. For texts, translations, and key bibliography, see Geza Vermes and Martin D. Goodman, eds., *The Essenes According to the Classical Sources* (Sheffield: JSOT Press, 1989). The premise of a division between marrying and celibate scrolls sectarians is based on a reading of the *Community Rule* (1QS) and the *Damascus Document* (CD), in light of Josephus's treatment of marrying and celibate Essenes (see esp. *War* 2.160-61) and the reference to families and children in CD 7:6-10 (parallel, 19:2-5). Cecilia Wassen rethinks this entire picture in *Women in the Damascus Document* (Leiden, Boston: Brill, 2005), 122-29.

2. Eileen Schuller was the first to work extensively on a reconsideration of the scrolls

ation of Qumran has to do with the intellectual frame that is brought to bear on the larger interpretation of the evidence. The first generation of scholars, by and large, tended to share the androcentric perspective assumed in both the scrolls and our ancient secondary evidence. They assumed, that is, that these texts were written by men and for men, and that the normative or (so to speak) "neutral" actor at their center was generically male. This masculinist bias colored their work and at times limited the range of perspective that they were able to bring to the evidence.

More recently, scrolls scholarship has seen a shift in perspective, with the observation that none of the scrolls refers explicitly to celibacy (although choices and behavior around marriage can be of significant concern). This has contributed to the argument that perhaps a majority of sectarians were of the marrying sort, even if celibacy fit into the picture for some sectarians. At the same time, more direct attention has been paid to the treatment of women in the scrolls and the possible roles that women might have played in communities associated with them.[3]

In interpreting ancient sources, scholars necessarily rely on some present-day expectations and assumptions. In part, scholarly assumptions are products of prior academic knowledge; the texts and material evidence that are already familiar provide the backdrop against which new evidence is, comparatively, configured. But in part they are products of a scholar's own social perspective, which brings present-day experience to bear on an understanding of ancient parallels. When both the modern scholarly realm and the world of the ancient sources assume an androcentric perspective, the two can reinforce one another and generate a historical picture that is biased in a single direction and fails to make full sense of the evidence at hand.

Feminist critical scholarship works as a corrective to such problematic convergences, by explicitly pointing out the basic assumptions of our

---

in terms of their treatment of women and gender; see, for example, Schuller, "Women in the Dead Sea Scrolls," in *The Dead Sea Scrolls after Fifty Years: A Comprehensive Assessment* (ed. P. W. Flint and J. C. VanderKam; vol. 2; Boston: Brill, 1999), 117-44.

3. See, e.g., Sidnie White Crawford, "Not According to Rule: Women, the Dead Sea Scrolls and Qumran," in *Emanuel: Studies in Hebrew Bible, Septuagint, and Dead Sea Scrolls in Honor of Emanuel Tov* (ed. S. M. Paul et al.; Boston: Brill, 2003), 127-50; Wassen, *Women in the Damascus Document*, 5-9. For a view of married life as normative among the sectarians, see Lawrence H. Schiffman, "Women in the Scrolls," in *Reclaiming the Dead Sea Scrolls: The History of Judaism, the Background of Christianity, the Lost Library of Qumran* (Philadelphia: Jewish Publication Society, 1994), 127-43; M. L. Grossman, "Reading for Gender in the Damascus Document"; and Wassen, *Women in the Damascus Document*.

androcentric evidence: that men are the usual authors of texts and are their intended audiences, that masculinity is the neutral social category, and that women — when they appear in texts or public settings at all — are to be understood as exceptions to the more general rule. By pushing us to look for new sources of evidence and to interpret familiar androcentric texts "against the grain," such scholarship allows us to identify ancient actors who were otherwise lost to history and to think more clearly about the ways that they were imagined, if not also how they actually lived. These approaches also encourage us to think in terms of particularities and to recognize that constructions of gender — the dynamics implicit in what it means to be a man or a woman, or to be "masculine" or "feminine" more generally — are always implicated in complex power dynamics and are everywhere the product of specific social norms and cultural values. Although some feminist projects appeal to universals in their treatment of gender, the dominant approach in contemporary gender studies is grounded in the recognition of cultural difference. To study gender in this way, then, is to recognize that we should not expect to find familiar gender norms in the evidence from other times and places, but that we should instead be willing to query both the evidence and our own assumptions in the process of trying to understand gender in its historical perspective.[4]

A "Test Case" from Qumran

A good test case for examining the potential impact of gender studies on our understanding of the texts and world of the Dead Sea Scrolls can be found in the *Rule of the Congregation,* or so-called *Messianic Rule* (1QSa). Several factors make this text particularly useful for our present endeavor. First, this is one of only a handful of texts that directly address the gendered roles of women and men in the sectarian community they envision. It is among our earliest published scroll texts, and it has generated a significant scholarly response, including discussions on precisely the issue of how we should treat the text's presentation of men's and women's roles. In addition, we can now read this text against important "late breaking"

4. For a wide-ranging introduction to the field of feminist criticism, see C. R. McCann and S.-K. Kim, eds., *Feminist Theory Reader.* A classic of feminist historiography is J. W. Scott, *Gender and the Politics of History.* For an introduction to the feminist critical study of the period and setting under discussion here, see R. S. Kraemer, *Her Share of the Blessings;* and Kraemer, ed., *Women's Religions in the Greco-Roman World.*

comparative evidence: fragmentary manuscripts of another rule document, whose publication in the 1990s included parallels to key passages in 1QSa. Among these fragmentary manuscripts — which include eight copies of the *Damascus Document* (4Q266-73) — we find passages that encourage a rethinking of earlier scholarly interpretations of 1QSa.[5] They thus provide a nice context in which to evaluate the assumptions, missteps, and successes of former scholarly readings of that text.

Our only full witness for the *Rule of the Congregation* was originally part of a manuscript better known for containing our most complete witness of the *Community Rule* (1QS).[6] Although sometimes labeled an appendix of that text, the *Rule of the Congregation* differs from 1QS in significant ways.[7] It imagines a sectarian group made up of husbands, wives, and children (roles that do not appear in 1QS) and pays attention to the "native Israelite" (האזרח בישראל, 1QSa 1:6) — one born into the sectarian group — rather than the adult "volunteers" (הנדבים, 1QS 1:7) who are addressed in 1QS. Its sectarian terminology, meanwhile, also overlaps with that of the *Damascus Document* in ways that add to the complexity of the picture. The most sophisticated readings of this text have suggested that it is the product of a series of literary redactions, possibly reflecting a process of sectarian development over a period of time.[8] It has been argued, too, that the text may be unconnected to any real sectarian group and might represent an anthology of mixed traditions or perhaps an imagined account of an end-times congregation.

Whatever its connections to an actual sectarian group, the *Rule of*

---

5. A number of other texts from Cave 4 might also be brought to bear on this discussion. Two texts that were published relatively early in the scholarly process are 4Q184, the so-called "Wiles of the Wicked Woman" text, and 4Q502, which has been described variously as a marriage ceremony, a Golden Age ritual, and a New Year's celebration. The more recent publication of 4QInstruction provides us with a text that speaks, in part, to a female audience. See Schuller, "Women in the Dead Sea Scrolls," 134-39. Texts, translations, and bibliog. can be found in F. García Martínez and E. J. C. Tigchelaar, *The Dead Sea Scrolls Study Edition*.

6. Stephen Pfann has argued for the additional presence of early manuscripts of the *Rule of the Congregation* among the texts written in cryptic script. See Pfann, "4Q249a-z and 4Q250a-j," DJD 36, 516-74; see also the evaluation of Pfann's argument in M. O. Wise, "Dating the Teacher of Righteousness and the *Floruit* of His Movement," 62 n. 26.

7. The initial discussion of these issues appears in D. Barthélemy and J. T. Milik, "28a. Règle de la Congrégation (1QSa)," DJD 1, 108. Unless otherwise noted, the text for 1QSa in this chapter is taken from Barthélemy and Milik, DJD 1, 108-18. For a comprehensive introduction to the text, see L. H. Schiffman, *The Eschatological Community of the Dead Sea Scrolls*.

8. E.g., C. Hempel, "The Earthly Essene Nucleus of 1QSa."

the Congregation offers important insights into an imagined formulation of sectarian practices. The text opens with a description of the group's formal gatherings, which resonates with scriptural accounts by explicitly including not only men but also children and women (מטף עד נשים).[9] A second section outlines the sectarian life cycle, from childhood and early education through marriage and a sectarian's adult responsibilities, which include participation in collective judgment and leadership. The text segues from there to limits on participation (in connection with physical or mental disability), before continuing with descriptions of collective processionals, various sorts of meetings, and ultimately a messianic banquet.

Of particular interest for us here is the sequence of life-cycle stages that appears in 1QSa 1:6-16.[10] This passage is, not surprisingly, framed in androcentric terms. It opens with a reference to "all the hosts of the congregation" (כול צבאות העדה, 1:6), a term that has military resonances but perhaps more importantly brings scriptural language to bear on the "native Israelites" associated with it.[11] The text then quickly shifts to a masculine singular formation, referring to the education of the sectarian "from his youth" in the "Book of Hagi" (1:6-7). Education is developmental; according to his age (כפי יומיו, 1:7), the young sectarian is taught the precepts of the covenant and the judgments associated with it. From age ten to age twenty, apparently, the sectarian is counted among the children,[12] and

9. 1QSa 1.4. See Barthélemy and Milik, DJD 1, 112, for scriptural resonances including Deut 31:1-12; see Schiffman, *Eschatological Community,* for connections to Deut 29; see also Schiffman, *Reclaiming the Dead Sea Scrolls,* 133. The final פ in this phrase is written here in medial form.

10. An extensive introduction to this section can be found in Schiffman, "The Eschatological Community and the Stages of Sectarian Life." For attention to textual problems in the discussion that follows, see Barthélemy and Milik, DJD 1. Note also the translational choices of J. H. Charlesworth and L. T. Stuckenbruck, "Rule of the Congregation (1QSa)," PTSDSSP 1:108-17; and F. García Martínez and E. J. C. Tigchelaar, "1Q28a (1QSa) 1QRule of the Congregation," in *The Dead Sea Scrolls Study Edition,* 1:98-103.

11. Barthélemy and Milik, DJD 1, 112, downplay the military sense of this term, while it is treated as a significant aspect of the sect's eschatological worldview in H. N. Richardson, "Some Notes on 1QSa," 110 n. 19.

12. Although this seems to be the best interpretation, the text here is ambiguous. See Richardson, "Some Notes on 1QSa," 120; Schiffman, *Eschatological Community,* 15-16. The reference to a ten-year period ranked among "the children" could refer to the period from birth to age ten or from age ten to age twenty. A scribal error (the word טף is initially written as טב and then corrected) further complicates the picture. For readings along these lines, see Charlesworth and Stuckenbruck, "Rule of the Congregation," 110-11; and García Martínez

at age twenty he enters the ranks of adult membership in the "holy congregation," counted within the lot of his family.

At the age of twenty, the sectarian is also deemed mature enough for marriage. He is expected to refrain from "drawing near to a woman to know her by lying with her sexually" (לוא [יקרב] אל אשה לדעתה למשכבי זכר, 1:9-10) until that age, when he (or perhaps she, depending on how we read a broken suffix in the manuscript) is deemed to have reached the age of reason ("knowing good and evil").[13] The text then follows, famously, with the assertion that "she shall be received to give witness against him (תקבל להעיד עליו) (about) the ordinances of the law (משפטות התורא) and to take a [p]lace (ולהת[י]צב) in the hearing of judgments (משפטים במשמע),"[14] before proceeding with accounts of the tasks that a sectarian can undertake at age twenty-five (performing the service of the congregation) and age thirty (serving as a judge and as a leader of subgroups in the congregation).[15]

Early interpretations of this text were particularly concerned with the surprising reference to women as witnesses — a concept that was otherwise largely unattested in ancient Jewish literature.[16] It is interesting to note, then, that a feminist critical assessment of 1QSa not only allows us to make sense of this passage but also contributes a number of other clarifications that a masculinist reading might miss. We will begin with a detailed discussion of this witnessing passage before turning to some more general comments on how a feminist critical reading offers new insights into this text and others from among the Qumran corpus.

and Tigchelaar, "1QRule of the Congregation," 100-101; a different solution is reached in Barthélemy and Milik, DJD 1, 112-13.

13. The text is damaged. The majority of scholars read בדעתו [טוב] ורע at 1:9-10, but the original publication marks the final waw with an overdot (indicating an uncertain reading), and the reading בדעתה, "upon *her* knowing" is also possible.

14. 1QSa 1:11. Both the מ of משפטות and the ת of ולהת[י]צב are marked as uncertain in the transcription of Barthélemy and Milik, DJD 1, 109. Translations of this passage range widely. See, e.g., Barthélemy and Milik, DJD 1, 112; Richardson, "Some Notes on 1QSa," 111; J. M. Baumgarten, "On the Testimony of Women in 1QSa," 268; Schiffman, *Eschatological Community*, 18-19; Charlesworth and Stuckenbruck, "Rule of the Congregation," 112-13; García Martínez and Tigchelaar, "1QRule of the Congregation," 100-1.

15. 1QSa 1:12-16.

16. Baumgarten points readers to m. Soṭah 6.2, for evidence that women could testify in cases where only a single witness was required. See Baumgarten, "On the Testimony of Women," 267 n. 3. On women's testimony in rabbinic literature, see J. Hauptman, "Testimony," in *Rereading the Rabbis*, 196-220. I thank Susan Marks for this reference. See also Wassen, *Women in the Damascus Document*, 87-88, 181-82. For a history of scholarship related to this passage, see D. Rothstein, "Women's Testimony at Qumran."

Women Witnesses and Scholarly Interpreters

Dominique Barthélemy and J. T. Milik, the original editors of this text, understand 1QSa 1:11 as a straightforward reference to a wife's testimony with regard to her husband's observance of "the Commandments of the Law." Without additional comment, they note two verbal parallels on the subject of bearing witness, both from the *Damascus Document*.[17] They observe, further, that the "hearing of judgments" in this context refers to passive participation in an audience setting, akin to the women described in 1 Cor 14:34-35, and not to "hearing" in the more technical sense of serving as a judge.[18] They translate the verb התיצב here with the reading "taking one's place," although at two other points in the text they argue that context requires a "strong" translation of this term, along the lines of "taking authority" within the congregation.[19] The editors also make an explicit effort to explain the presence of women as witnesses in the text, by reference to its historical and social context: "In this time when Hellenism exercised its attraction upon the Palestinian population, the woman, naturally more fervent and traditionalist, was charged with observing the fidelity of her husband and if necessary denouncing him to the authorities."[20]

H. Neil Richardson, writing two years later, shares the view that this text refers to women's testimony with respect to their husbands' behavior but refrains from framing his argument in terms of social norms about gender. Rather, he argues for methodological caution, warning against readings that privilege outside evidence, such as Philo and Josephus's claims that the Essenes were "suspicious of women," or rabbinic assertions that women could not serve as witnesses. Instead Richardson argues that such evidence must be treated as "secondary sources to be read and understood in the light of the Qumran documents, not vice versa."[21] He also warns against using the later standards of rabbinic Judaism as the basis for interpreting the communal norms of the scrolls, noting that "there is in fact no biblical injunction against women giving testimony in court." Lastly, he argues for reading the text as it is written, rather than treating the reference to women's witnessing

---

17. CD 9:22, 19:30; see Barthélemy and Milik, DJD 1, 113.

18. In support of this claim they note the reference to the presence of angels in the midst of the congregation (1QSa 2:8-9). They also note a point of terminology: משמע דברים is a scriptural expression for a judge's "hearing" of testimony; see Barthélemy and Milik, DJD 1, 114.

19. Barthélemy and Milik, DJD 1, 114-15.

20. Barthélemy and Milik, DJD 1, 113; translation is my own.

21. Richardson, "Some Notes on 1QSa," 119.

as some sort of scribal error. As he puts it, "To emend the text of the Qumran documents to make them conform either to Josephus or rabbinic sources seems to this writer to be an erroneous methodology."[22]

In an essay responding to these publications, Joseph Baumgarten argues emphatically against the legal claims of both and the gender assumptions of the first:

> On what grounds Barthélemy extols so generously the traditionalism of the Jewish women of the Hellenistic period is not clear. Certainly the women of the biblical period do not appear to have been markedly immune to the inroads of idolatry and heathen practice. Furthermore, this regulation would not only constitute a kind of converse to the biblical ordinance concerning the jealous husband, but it would give to the wife general competence as a witness and jurist.[23]

In place of this reading, Baumgarten argues for an emendation of the text, to read "*he* shall be received to testify (יקבל להעיד) in accordance with the laws of the Torah (על פי משפטות התורא) and to take his place in hearing the judgments" (1:11).

Baumgarten provides a series of reasons for his decision to emend the text. The first might be called literary: a reading of this passage as a reference to a wife's behavior is interruptive of the larger flow of the text; the shift of focus to the wife is out of place in the midst of a discussion of the life-cycle stages of a male sectarian. A second argument concerns legal logic: it makes no sense to assume that a woman's right to testify should be based on her husband's age, rather some other standard of credibility. "Would an adolescent girl marrying a man of twenty become eligible 'to take her place in proclaiming the ordinances'?"[24] A third point might be considered an argument based on historical misogyny. Given the identification of this movement with the marrying Essenes (a point assumed by both of the previous publications), and given the outlook of those Essenes (who married only for purposes of reproduction), Baumgarten asks, "Are we to assume that this group would give to women the dominant function of participating in the judicial proceedings of the community and acting as

---

22. Richardson, "Some Notes on 1QSa," 119. Although published in this form before Baumgarten's "On the Testimony of Women," Richardson's article reads like a response to it or to an earlier formulation of its argument.

23. Baumgarten, "On the Testimony of Women," 266.

24. Baumgarten, "On the Testimony of Women," 267.

witnesses against their husbands?" He follows with an argument based on parallel sources: even if women could testify, the rabbis do not permit people to testify against members of their own family. A final argument is based not on historical misogyny as such but on its social implications: at relevant points in history (he mentions the rabbis but also Athenian and Roman law, as well as the Pauline church) women were not permitted to witness in public. "That the semi-monastic Essenes, of all groups, should have deviated from this pattern is highly unlikely," he concludes.[25]

Interestingly, beyond noting that the fragmentary condition of the text makes his "slight emendation" possible, Baumgarten does not go into an extensive discussion of the material reasons for his emendation, which looks at first glance surprisingly arbitrary. Both תקבל and עליו are absolutely clear in the photographs of the manuscript; unlike most emendations, the initial source of difficulty does not lie in a visible scribal error or oversight. Nevertheless, there are textual supports to argue that the scribe miswrote these words. In at least two other passages the text breaks off in midsentence (the editors explain this in terms of the scribe's having left off in the middle of quoting an earlier source; Richardson argues that the breaks may reflect lacunae in the original text being copied).[26] Errors related to spelling are found in the text as well, including one that is ironically relevant to our discussion (1QSa 1:27 has אלה הנשים, "these are the women" of renown, but this passage is universally translated "these are the men" [אלה האנשים], based both on grammatical framing and on the text's evident tendency to drop alephs in spelling).[27] The expression על פי ("in accordance with") is also common in this text and is not inappropriate to the context in which it has been inserted.

Baumgarten's emendation does a beautiful job with the textual material at hand. It is a clever re-reading of the passage and one that has had significant influence in the field.[28] What is problematic about it is not that

---

25. Baumgarten, "On the Testimony of Women," 267-68.

26. See Barthélemy and Milik, DJD 1, 114; Richardson, "Some Notes on 1QSa," 111 n. 27. Barthélemy and Milik point to a possible third midsentence break, at 1:8 (p. 113), but here an infelicity in the text is just as easily explained by a scribal error of near-homonymy (writing טב in place of טפ).

27. On the dropping of א in texts from Qumran, see Barthélemy and Milik, DJD 1, 111 n. 1.1; Richardson, "Some Notes on 1QSa," 109 n. 13. Martin Abegg explores this phenomenon in his contribution to this volume.

28. It is noted in Charlesworth and Stuckenbruck, "Rule of the Congregation," 113 n. 23; and is chosen explicitly in Schiffman, *Eschatological Community*, 19.

it is in any explicit way wrong, but that it is textually unnecessary. There is nothing in the passage as such to require the change, and in fact even in the 1950s there were textual arguments to support positions at least as strong as those taken by Richardson or Barthélemy and Milik. But as far as Baumgarten was concerned, there *was* a problem in the text, and it could not make sense in its existing manuscript witness.[29]

Feminist Critical Witnesses: Old Evidence Made New

One of the most striking contributions of feminist scholarship is its ability to make sense of "confusing" or "anomalous" data, through a process of re-thinking the basic cultural frames through which that evidence has been interpreted. Carol Christ, in a classic response to phenomenologist Mircea Eliade, and Bernadette Brooten, in a similarly foundational discussion of the methodological issues connected with the history of early Christian women, demonstrate that a shift of perspective can transform our understanding of familiar evidence and help us to rethink prior explanations, showing how the anomalous pieces might have fit in all along.[30] Recent work in the field of Qumran studies has pursued precisely these scholarly challenges. Eileen Schuller and now Sidnie White Crawford have presented state-of-the-field discussions that consider the participation and possible agency of women among communities associated with the scrolls.[31] Cecilia Wassen has brought an explicitly feminist agenda to her reading of the *Damascus Document*.[32] And Philip Davies and Joan Taylor have offered similarly explicit methodological discussions on the *Rule of the Congregation* itself.[33] These

---

29. Baumgarten is also editor of the 4QD material. In his *editio princeps* of those texts, he reconsiders his translation of 1QSa 1.11 and suggests a new translation, based on the view that the wife "must promise (תקבל) to admonish (להעיד) her husband about the laws (משפטות התורא) concerning sexual intercourse, with which she is to familiarize herself by learning them (במשמע משפטים) and fulfilling them (ובמלוא בו)." This translation expands the possibilities for women's behavior, but does not go so far as to suggest a public role for them. See J. M. Baumgarten, DJD 18, 165.

30. See C. P. Christ, "Mircea Eliade and the Feminist Paradigm Shift"; B. Brooten, "Early Christian Women and Their Cultural Context"; see also Crawford, "Not According to Rule," for applications of Brooten's argument in the context of scrolls studies.

31. See Schuller, "Women in the Dead Sea Scrolls," and Crawford, "Not According to Rule."

32. See Wassen, *Women in the Damascus Document*.

33. See P. R. Davies and J. E. Taylor, "On the Testimony of Women in 1QSa."

scholars have demonstrated that familiar evidence can conceal surprising information, if we re-read it in the right light. With their work in mind, let us ask what we might do with the evidence that scholars like Barthélemy and Milik, Richardson, and Baumgarten already had on hand. How can early observations with regard to 1QSa be reconsidered in light of feminist critical perspectives, to create a more coherent context in which to understand their legal conundrum?

The first point worth mentioning — in the interest of "unpacking" before beginning the task of reconstructing — is a reminder with respect to cultural norms and assumptions. At various points in their approach to the material, each of our first-generation scholars showed that he was working with implicit assumptions about gender in antiquity: Barthélemy and Milik imagine the Hellenistic woman (or perhaps even Hellenistic Woman, writ large) in the image of the late-nineteenth- and early-twentieth-century "domestic angel," whose "natural" piety was expected to influence the actions of her husband; Baumgarten, drawing upon biblical and rabbinic witnesses, in response emphasizes stereotypes of women as idolatrous. Richardson, who is so careful to work from the facts alone (and who consequently is most open to letting the evidence fall where it may), still manages in his close, careful reading of the text to reproduce its androcentric perspective rather consistently. The point here, I should reiterate, is certainly not to remove all cultural expectations and somehow achieve a culturally-neutral perspective with regard to gender. Rather, in the course of challenging other people's assumptions about gender, we should try to be clear enough about our own that we minimize our unintentional imposition of them on the evidence.[34]

We might begin this daunting task by considering two short footnotes from Barthélemy and Milik's publication of the *Rule*, which mention the use of language connected with the bearing of witness in two passages in the *Damascus Document*.[35] One of the passages (CD 19:30) reflects a

---

34. This is a perennial problem and one that is best handled with a combination of sensitivity to nuance, constant vigilance, and modesty with respect to one's own expectations. In this light, see Davies and Taylor, "On the Testimony of Women in 1QSa," esp. 225 n. 8. Their critique of other scholars' methodological assumptions is at times blistering, which makes for uncomfortable reading when they (almost inevitably) show evidence for their own unconsidered assumptions (here, their discussion of age of marriage asserts that women "were married generally at puberty," a generalization that is not necessarily borne out by the ancient Jewish evidence).

35. Barthélemy and Milik, DJD, 1, 113.

generalized reference to the sectarians as witnesses to the sins of Israel, but the other (CD 9:22) is found in the context of an extended practical discussion of rules for witnesses (CD 9:16–10:4). The first rule in this longer discussion is especially relevant for us: in the case of a capital crime with only a single witness, the witness is expected to make a report to the Overseer, who is to keep a written record of the transgression. In the event of a second accusation of the same crime on some future occasion, the transgressor's fate is sealed (9:16-20). In cases whose punishment involves restriction from the "pure food" (הטהרה), also, the testimony of a single witness is enough to bring about punishment. The text makes clear that witnesses must be "trustworthy" (נאמנים), and that they must be fully-vested members of the group who are not in a state of punishment themselves. Although there is no reference here to women as witnesses, there is enough of interest in this passage — the multistage process available to prosecutions of capital crimes, the role of the Overseer as recorder of witness testimony — to suggest that testimony might be precisely the sort of context in which we should expect to find innovations among the Qumran scrolls.

Barthélemy and Milik also make interesting use of the term "taking one's place" (התיצב). At two points separate from our passage, as noted above, they argue in footnotes for a "strong" translation of the term, to refer to a position of formal congregational authority (1:16; 1:20). But with respect to this passage they make no such claim. Of course words can have different meanings in different contexts, but in this case the editors seem not to have noticed the semantic distinctions that they have assumed. A strong reading of our own might argue that התיצב must be taken here, too, to refer to an official, recognized position, in this case for the women who served as witnesses. A more limited but still alternative reading suggests an alteration of the semantic domain of התיצב in the text, to reflect a more flexible range of possibility in the community it imagines. This might incorporate both formally-authorized positions of congregational leadership and also less explicit but still recognized positions of public status.[36]

Baumgarten, too, provides food for thought in his reading of this provocative passage. Especially useful from a feminist critical perspective is his observation about the interruptive nature of the reference to women as wit-

---

36. This argument is easy to envision in light of the evidence that will be discussed in the final section of this paper, but whether a feminist critical approach could be so fully prescient without such evidence at hand is a real question. It is also methodologically useful to note the limits that I have put on the possibilities here. Another feminist scholar might choose to argue, e.g., that the text in fact supports the presence of women as judges in the community.

nesses. He expresses concern that the reference to women is out of place in the text, in that it breaks up a more structured discussion of the male sectarian's life, which is laid out in five- and ten-year periods. The reference to women, in contrast, makes no mention of their age, but simply asserts their authority to testify based on their marital status. Baumgarten has made an important observation here, and it is one that can be addressed on several different levels. Davies and Taylor take up the most direct challenge, by offering an explanation for the literary disjuncture that Baumgarten has identified. "Once the man is eligible to marry, he becomes liable to testimony from his wife against himself," they argue. "The point at issue, then, is not the eligibility of the woman to give testimony but the *liability of the man,* once married (at whatever age, twenty or beyond) to testimony from her."[37]

We can also address this observation on a more theoretical level, by returning to one of the basic assumptions of feminist critical discourse, an understanding of androcentric texts. From the perspective of an androcentric text, the normative (even "neutral") actor is male, and women are an exception to that norm. Generic references to "men," consequently, and even to "a man" in the singular, can serve to reflect either explicitly gendered assumptions (of actual masculinity) or more general assumptions (in which case "men" serves as shorthand for "people" of whatever gender). If women in an androcentric context are incorporated into the normative male collective except on those occasions when they transgress that norm (by bearing children, for example, or by menstruating), then what we find in this text is exactly what we should expect to find: sequential references to "men" with only occasional and apparently inexplicable excurses into discussions of women.

Note that my argument does not privilege any particular makeup for a group connected with the text (which its original readers might have imagined as comprising men alone, men and their adjunct women, or even men and women in full partnership). Rather, it serves as a reminder that the masculine language of an androcentric text necessarily conceals more complex ranges of possibility with respect to social situations than its language initially reveals.[38] The absence of women in the wording should not lead us to assume their absence from the world imagined in the text.

---

37. Davies and Taylor, "On the Testimony of Women in 1QSa," 226-27.

38. On the vexed question of membership in a community associated with this text, see esp. Schuller, "Women in the Dead Sea Scrolls," 129-31; Davies and Taylor, "On the Testimony of Women in 1QSa," 226-27; Schiffman, *Eschatological Community,* 16-19.

Baumgarten also raises the concern that women historically did not testify in public and that an Essene community would be an unlikely place to find such a feminist innovation. My response here echoes that of Richardson: although the classical sources present the Essenes in misogynist terms, we are not required to interpret our text from their vantage point. Attention to the text itself, especially with an eye to the parallel text of CD discussed above, might suggest any of several possibilities: that this passage could refer to a woman's private testimony before the Overseer; that public testimony might be understood as remaining within the confines of the congregation and therefore appear acceptable to its gender mores; or even that the text does not assume that women should be silent and hidden, even though it often incorporates them invisibly in its androcentric group descriptions.

Building upon Baumgarten's arguments but with an eye to agendas of his own, Lawrence Schiffman has argued that "It would be attractive for our argument to be able to claim that women even testified in the sectarian legal system. However, then we would have a text allowing women to testify about one and only one thing: the conduct of their husbands."[39] He considers this interpretation implausible, but in fact, it seems to provide precisely the context in which this text should be considered, as our more recently published evidence serves to demonstrate. Let us turn now to a reconsideration of the picture in light of that evidence.

Feminist Critical Readings: New Evidence, New Interpretations

The fragmentary manuscript witnesses of the *Damascus Document* that were discovered in Qumran's Cave 4 (4Q266-73) represent the closest corroborating information we have yet found for the social dynamics imagined in the *Rule of the Congregation*.[40] Of particular interest are the legal passages found in these manuscripts that are not paralleled in our two more-complete medieval witnesses of the *Damascus Document* (CD mss. A and B). Not only do

39. Schiffman, *Reclaiming the Dead Sea Scrolls*, 135. Davies and Taylor quote this passage, and the line that follows "Imagine what marriages this would have made!" in the opening section of "On the Testimony of Women in 1QSa," 223, and it becomes a touchstone for them in their larger methodological critique of the field.

40. For texts, translations, and extensive notes and commentary, see Baumgarten, DJD 18. Extensive discussions of these passages can be found in Wassen, *Women in the Damascus Document*, 72-89. See also Schuller, "Women in the Dead Sea Scrolls," 123-31; Grossman, "Reading for Gender," esp. 218-20, 229-30.

these passages provide a context and rationale for the presence of women as witnesses in communities associated with the texts; they also provide us with a context for thinking about androcentrism, misogyny, women's agency, and other key issues that a feminist critical approach goes far to unpack.

A striking set of passages in the Cave 4 *Damascus* material deals explicitly with issues of marriage and sexuality. Women who have been sexually active (either while unmarried or in a state of widowhood) are deemed unfit for marriage to a covenanter, according to these texts, while women whose reputations are questionable are to be investigated by "trustworthy women," who then presumably report back on their findings.[41] Men, too, may be punished for sexual sins including "fornication" (זנות) with their wives.[42] These passages offer a striking setting in which to imagine women as witnesses, and they go far to respond to Schiffman's incredulous observation on the subject. Indeed, women might be understood here *precisely* as witnesses against their husbands, although in only a limited set of contexts for which they alone might be presumed to have witnessed a transgression. In addition, as witnesses to other women's sexual behavior, they might be seen to display an interesting sort of agency. Their status as "trustworthy" hearkens back to our earlier discussions of witnessing in the *Damascus Document*, which incorporate the explicit assertion that "trustworthy" witnesses must be members in good standing of the group and not in a state of punishment themselves. If we choose to read these two texts as mutually informing, we are left with the impression that women must indeed have had a "place" in the communities (real or imagined) associated with them. How high or low such a status might be remains an ambiguous point, much as we saw in our earlier rendering of the semantic domain of "taking one's place."

A further point from the Cave 4 *Damascus* material might clarify the picture, while providing a cautionary tale for the enthusiastic feminist critical reader. While the *Rule of the Congregation* contains two references to "fathers of the congregation" (1QSa 1:16; 2:16), the Cave 4 *Damascus* material includes references to both "the fathers" and "the mothers."[43] This

---

41. See 4Q269 9 4-8; 4Q270 5 17-21; 4Q271 3 10-15, in Baumgarten, DJD 18, 132, 154-55, 175-77. A father is also required to reveal any relevant blemish (מום) of his daughter's and to be sure to match her to an appropriate groom (although the text does not specify what this means). See 4Q269 9 1-3; 4Q270 5 14-17; 4Q271 3 7-10, in Baumgarten, DJD 18, as above; see also Schuller, "Women in the Dead Sea Scrolls," 127-28, and the bibliog. found there.

42. See 4Q267 9 vi 4-5; 4Q270 7 i 12-13; in Baumgarten, DJD 18, 110-11, 162-66.

43. See 4Q270 7 i 13-15, in Baumgarten, DJD 18, 162-66. See also Wassen, *Women in the Damascus Document*, 184-89, 197.

striking passage is extremely exciting from a feminist critical perspective: it shows a clear and unquestionable case of women and men in shared public roles in a group associated with the scrolls. It builds on our evidence for women witnesses and makes room, in fact, for even more formal public roles for women, if our text can be seen to assume the presence of invisible "mothers" in its own references to "fathers" in the congregation. However, as the *Damascus* text immediately explains, "mothers" and "fathers" are not parallel in all ways. Those who murmur against the fathers are to leave the Damascus covenant group and return no more; those who murmur against the mothers suffer punishment for a period of ten days.[44] The ironic one-two punch of this text brings us back to a pointed reminder for feminist critical readers: although ancient texts may provide evidence for more inclusive social groups and more agency for women than an androcentric reading would initially allow, we must permit that evidence to be exactly as masculinist (and at times misogynist) as it makes the effort to be.

These two examples open the door, however, for a much larger discussion of women's status, participation, agency, and cooptation as imagined in the *Rule of the Congregation*. The nonspecific language around children's education is one obvious point on which girls' and women's participation might be assessed (not only to ask "whether," but also "of what sort" and "to what end": what must a woman know in order to be "trustworthy" to the patriarchy, and what sort of identity does she develop in the process?).[45] Young adults' oath-taking deserves similar attention in precisely this light, as it may provide a means of addressing what is now a stalemate in the field. While some scholars would argue for the possibility that young women would take the oath of the congregation and become full members in their own right,[46] others would see them as absolute adjuncts of their husbands and fathers.[47] General attitudes toward issues of

---

44. Again, see 4Q270 7 i 13-15, in Baumgarten, DJD 18, 162-66.

45. See Wassen, *Women in the Damascus Document,* 105, 164-67.

46. See Wassen, *Women in the Damascus Document,* 90-93, 131-43; Schuller, "Women in the Dead Sea Scrolls," 129-30. Schuller also suggests that the initial referent of the text (a congregation of men, women, and children) be assumed until such time as the text explicitly redirects; see Schuller, "Women in the Dead Sea Scrolls," 131-32. Davies and Taylor, "On the Testimony of Women in 1QSa," 227-28, take issue with this argument.

47. Schiffman asserts that women would not take the oath of the covenant but would be members of it, by virtue of their relationships to their husbands and fathers. See Schiffman, *Eschatological Community,* 17-18.

purity and the mere presence of women also provide food for thought: Schuller notes, for example, that the infirmities that cause a person to be left out of the congregation in this text do not include the infirmity of being female;[48] in addition the text's reference to a three-day purification, resonating with Sinai, speaks only in general terms about the need for purity, rather than incorporating scriptural language of avoiding "going near to a woman."[49]

The challenges implicit in a feminist critical reading are no different from those facing other historical or literary readings of the Dead Sea Scrolls. Confronted with evidence from a very different time and place, we must try to make sense of its scriptural references, its cultural claims, and its social norms and assumptions. What a feminist critical reading can do for us, however, is to position us at odds to the evidence in usefully productive ways. To the extent that we can read "against the grain" of the evidence without standing in our own light — by being aware of our own assumptions and commitments, even as we attempt to make sense of evidence that confounds or offends those sensibilities — we are sure to find such readings intellectually productive and, indeed, potentially transformative of any ongoing scholarly paradigm.

48. As opposed to the claims of the *War Scroll* (1QM), which forbid women and young boys from being present on the battlefield. See Schuller, "Women in the Dead Sea Scrolls," 133-34, Wassen, *Women in the Damascus Document*, 144-56.

49. 1QSa 1.26; see Wassen, *Women in the Damascus Document*, 143. Barthélemy and Milik, DJD 1, 116, let this pass without comment, although they make reference to Exod 19:14-15 and Esd 10:8-9.

Social-Scientific Approaches
to the Dead Sea Scrolls

Jutta Jokiranta

The study of the formation and transmission of the Qumran texts has not always been deeply rooted in an understanding of the social phenomena contextualizing them. Consequently, the study of the "sectarian texts" has sometimes presumed a too straightforward relationship between the texts' image of reality and the history of the movement associated with them. An understanding of the Qumran texts must aim at producing relevant information on their "text world" as well as their "social world," understanding the two together, rather than in conflict with each other. Here the social sciences have a lot to offer, whether they are used as heuristic tools, a reflective mirror, or an interpretative model.

The topic of this chapter is social-scientific approaches to the Dead Sea Scrolls, and what they can help us to know about these texts and especially about the groups associated with them. Within scrolls scholarship, the sociological question that has attracted the most attention is the investigation of sectarianism, especially in the larger context of the Jewish sectarianism of the Second Temple period. Key points of concern include the need to sort out a workable definition of "sect" and the problem of contextualizing sects in their larger social worlds, as well as the methodological issues that complicate the process of identifying sectarian texts

Parts of this article are included in J. Jokiranta, *Identity on a Continuum: Constructing and Expressing Sectarian Social Identity in Qumran* Serakhim *and* Pesharim, forthcoming. I want to thank Maxine Grossman for inviting me to contribute to the present volume and for her valuable ideas in the preparation of this chapter.

and moving from textual evidence to speculations on social realities. Beyond our discussion of sectarianism, this chapter will also introduce and explore a social identity approach to the study of the scrolls.

The Place of Ideology in Identifying Sectarianism and the Sociology of Sectarianism

Sociologists and scrolls scholars alike have struggled with the question of how to define a sect or sectarian movement and how to interpret their definitions for our understanding of the Dead Sea Scrolls. Early approaches paid particular attention to the ideology of sectarian texts. However, as Philip Davies has argued, "It is wrong, in my view, to define a sect simply in terms of its beliefs, unless we can show how and why these beliefs necessitated the formulation of a sect and that these reasons are not only contingent but also necessary."[1] This coheres well with how Max Weber understood sects: sectarian *tendencies* precede the emergence of actual groups.[2] The search for such tendencies might contribute to an understanding of issues around which actual sects might arise, but they should not be understood as evidence for sectarian movements as such.

Albert Baumgarten has drawn attention to the developmental aspects of sectarianism: sects arise in response to the realities of their social setting, and actual sectarian groups can be distinguished from the antecedents and forerunners that preceded them. For example, forerunners of the ancient Jewish sects can be found in the apocalyptic views and halakhic interpretations of *1 Enoch* and *Jubilees*.[3] Vague antecedents extend even further back in time, to the reforms of Ezra-Nehemiah, such as his dissolution of marriages to Gentile women. But the full flourishing of Jewish sectarianism, according to Baumgarten, as witnessed by the Pharisees, Sadducees, Essenes, and the Dead Sea Scrolls group (he consistently distinguishes between these last two) comes after and is a product of their differing reactions to Hellenism, the successful revolt against Antiochus IV Epiphanes, and the rise of the Hasmonean state. With politi-

---

1. P. R. Davies, "Sects from Texts," 72.

2. See D. J. Chalcraft, *Sectarianism in Early Judaism:* "The Development of Weber's Sociology of Sects," 26-51 (32-46); and "Towards a Weberian Sociology of the Qumran Sects," 74-105 (76-78).

3. A. I. Baumgarten, *The Flourishing of Jewish Sects in the Maccabean Era,* 23-28.

cal independence and a new dynasty of high priests came the impetus for various groups to promote their own agendas, whether successfully or not.

For Weber, the *mode of membership* was the core defining criterion of sectarianism. According to David Chalcraft, this understanding persists in Weber's work: "A sect's membership is constituted by volunteers . . . who have proved themselves worthy."[4] Weber's definition cannot be taken out of his basic research question and interest: he sought to analyze the impact that Protestant ascetic sects had for the rise of Western economic and cultural rationalism. From his perspective, sects cultivated the development of individual personalities, *virtuosos,* in ways that had impact not only on their lives, and the lives of the sect members, but also on the *wider* society. In his analysis, sects were able to transform everyday conduct into a more rational direction; this was the central theme in his *Protestant Ethic and Spirit of Capitalism.* He thereby identified the replacement of otherworldly Catholic monastic asceticism with the innerworldly asceticism of Protestant sects.

In a more contemporary period, sociologist Bryan Wilson has been a pioneer in the study of new religious movements and millenarianism, and he has set the research agenda for the past decades in the sociology of religion throughout the world. He stressed *protest/deviance/tension with respect to the larger world* as a general characteristic of sects.[5] He also formulated a list of sectarian attributes, which some biblical scholars have come to treat as a checklist for identifying sectarian movements.[6]

A further methodological concern in using sociology of sectarianism is the appropriate perspective for an interpreter to take. An *etic* perspective, which takes an outsider's point of view, must be accommodated by an *emic* understanding, one that considers social roles, worldviews, and group relations in antiquity from an insider's perspective. In turn, knowl-

4. Chalcraft, *Sectarianism in Early Judaism,* 74.

5. E.g., B. R. Wilson, *Magic and the Millennium,* 11-30; *Religion in Sociological Perspective,* 89-115; *The Social Dimensions of Sectarianism,* 46-48, 66-68.

6. As Wilson described it, a sect is a voluntary association, with membership based on merit; it is exclusive, perceives itself as uniquely elect, and claims to have a monopoly on truth; sectarians aspire to personal perfection, while the sect emphasizes lay participation or a priesthood of all believers; members are expected to be spontaneous in expressing their commitment and hostile towards outside society. Recently, J. H. Charlesworth, "John the Baptizer and the Dead Sea Scrolls," 30-31, uses three of these attributes (sect is exclusive, claims a monopoly, and is antisacerdotal), but notes that only the first two apply to Qumran, and adds a further criterion of his own (schism). Such treatment of sectarian attributes is not very helpful if not expanded and further explained.

edge of the *emic* needs an *etic* point of view in order to be understood in our time, since models with abstractions, variables, or analytical concepts structure our observations and help to formulate hypotheses of the data. Both are necessary, but the two need to be distinguished in order to be utilized with proper care.[7]

Baumgarten's definition of a "sect" as "a voluntary association of protest, which utilizes boundary marking mechanisms — the social means of differentiating between insiders and outsiders — to distinguish between its own members and those otherwise normally regarded as belonging to the same national or religious entity" is an *etic* definition that relies on Weber and Ernst Troeltsch, as well as Rodney Stark, William Sims Bainbridge, and Mary Douglas.[8] On the other hand, Baumgarten aligns himself with Josephus's presentation of *haireseis* — an *emic* perspective — when he regards both the Pharisees and the Sadducees as forms of sectarianism. He then uses Wilson's responses to distinguish between these sects. The Dead Sea Scrolls sect was, in Baumgarten's analysis, a *greedy institution* or an *introversionist* sect, "demanding total loyalty and absorbing all of its member's identity" and primarily concerned with its own transformation.[9] The Pharisees and the Sadducees, in contrast, were *reformist* sects: eager to transform the larger society.[10] This interpretation has been criticized for its conflation of different kinds of social movements and for a too straightforward adoption of Josephus's remarks as evidence of Jewish sectarianism.[11] Not all minority groups had a sectarian stance in their environment.

Tension is certainly a defining point for our understanding of sectarianism, but the treatment of tension necessarily requires attention to its *relational* aspects. A sect is not a sect in itself but rather *in relation to* some-

---

7. Cf. E. Regev, *Sectarianism in Qumran: A Cross-Cultural Perspective*, in this regard. On the one hand, Regev offers an "explanatory rather than descriptive study based on the application of certain models and methods of social sciences, in an attempt to understand the evidence of ancient social and religious history" (17). On the other hand, he states: "What I am trying to do is to focus on the inside story of the Qumran sects and their equivalents. My attempt is to explain their way of life using their own words and ideas, rather than by social formalism and functionalism" (22).

8. Baumgarten, *The Flourishing of Jewish Sects*, 6-7.

9. Baumgarten, *The Flourishing of Jewish Sects*, 12.

10. Baumgarten, *The Flourishing of Jewish Sects*, 11-15. However, for using Wilson's typology in the study of Second Temple Jewish movements and early Christian groups, and for the problems in using Wilson's "reformist response" in this sense, see J. Jokiranta, "Learning from Sectarian Responses."

11. R. A. Horsley, "The Dead Sea Scrolls and the Historical Jesus," 40-41.

thing else.[12] Rather than considering sectarianism in terms of the absence or presence of particular defining traits, I would argue for recognizing variations of degree. The sociological scholarship of Stark and Bainbridge provides tools for just such an approach.[13]

Tension can be heuristically measured by three elements, according to Stark and Bainbridge. The first is *difference:* the behavior and practices of the members are different from the average population, or from the standards of the powerful members of the society; sectarians thus follow deviant norms. The second is *antagonism* towards other religious groups or society, usually expressed in particularistic beliefs denying the legitimacy of other competing groups and resulting in being rejected by them — this is the ideological element. The third is *separation,* restriction of social relations mainly to in-group members. Group norms, activities, or simply devotion to the group may restrict the social relations of the members so that contacts and relations to outsiders are reduced. The three elements are in close interplay and any one of them adds to tension usually by strengthening one or both of the other elements as well.

From here it will be useful to turn to the application of these ideas in the analysis of our textual evidence. What makes a text "sectarian"? And how should we best proceed from sectarian *texts* to an understanding of *sects?*

Sectarian Texts and Drawing Sects from Texts

Early scholarship on the scrolls considered the texts in the Qumran corpus to be a unity and therefore "sectarian" in the most general sense that they were the ideological property of the "Qumran sect." Unfortunately, the choice of the term "sectarian" — by which scholars generally meant nothing more specific than "related to a small group or community" — had the immediate implication of suggesting sectarianism in the larger sociological sense discussed above. This has had significant implications for later

12. Wilson's work included analysis of Protestant Christian movements, especially in the nineteenth century; third world movements in colonial settings; and new religious movements in Western societies in the twentieth century. To appreciate his work it is necessary to acknowledge the diverse settings of these sects and the dynamic developments that Wilson saw in the sects in their respective environments.

13. R. Stark and W. S. Bainbridge, *The Future of Religion: Secularization, Revival, and Cult Formation,* esp. 48-67.

interpretation. The recognition of diverse provenances for the texts complicated the picture and led to attempts to distinguish among the scrolls, recognizing some as belonging to a particular group or groups and others as more generally Jewish or "nonsectarian," but again without significant attention to the sociological definitions that underscore the discussion.

Recent scholarship has attempted to address this problem by asking what, in fact, makes a text sectarian. One systematic project considered terminology and ideology as criteria for categorizing the scrolls.[14] Terms such as *yaḥad, serekh* ("rule"), *rabbim, maskil* ("wisdom teacher"), *mevaqqer*, Righteous Teacher, and Wicked Priest, and ideas such as strict dualism and predestination in this context served as indicators of a "sectarian" outlook within a text. From this perspective, the *absence* of any sectarian terminology or ideology would indicate the *"nonsectarian"* character of a text.

An alternative to this approach points out that texts that lack sectarian terminology could yet be authored by a sectarian group. Within ancient Judaism, the literature that Carol Newsom has designated "sectually explicit" might include any whose rhetorics call upon "readers to understand themselves as set apart within the larger religious community of Israel and as preserving the true values of Israel against the failures of the larger community."[15] This might be achieved in a variety of ways, including polemical rhetoric, accounts of the community's history, or constitutional liturgies.

I have suggested that even this is not enough to mark explicit sectarianism in a *sociological* sense.[16] Following Stark and Bainbridge's definition of a sect, we would need to study the relationship of the community's ideology, practices, and social relations *in comparison with* the other ideologies, practices, and social relations of the relevant time periods in order to determine the actual deviance with respect to the society, or at least to come close to it.[17] This would leave us only very few documents from which we could analyze these issues, most notably, the rule documents *(serakhim)*. Together with Cecilia Wassen, I have analyzed and compared the sectarianism in the *Damascus Document* tradition (D) and the tradition of the *Com-*

14. D. Dimant, "The Qumran Manuscripts: Contents and Significance."

15. C. A. Newsom, "'Sectually Explicit' Literature from Qumran."

16. J. Jokiranta, "'Sectarianism' of the Qumran 'Sect': Sociological Notes," *RevQ* 78 (2001): 223-39.

17. Similarly, Newsom would now distinguish between social exclusivism and ideological exclusivism; the latter is not unique to Qumran. See "Response to 'Religious Exclusivism.'"

munity Rule (S) from this perspective.[18] We found that the sectarian stance of the D communities is almost as pronounced as that of S.

Davies, on the other hand, argues that we cannot study sects as social entities directly but instead need what he calls *socio-textual research*.[19] First, texts need to be studied in all their compositional stages and literary layers. Second, texts must be analyzed ideologically: when the ideology of one document is compared to the ideology in other documents or in other sections or layers of the same document, distinct ideological systems may be revealed. Texts like D and S, for example, incorporate ideas about Israel, temple, Torah, and messiah that vary somewhat. Davies concludes from this that they describe different *Judaisms* — and sects.[20]

In contrast to this, it can be safer to speak about differences in *discourses* rather than differences in actual social movements. This protects us from the potentially inaccurate tendency to associate each sectarian text, however defined, with a single sectarian group, instead of recognizing that the texts might reflect development and diversity. The move from texts to sects can put us in danger of creating movements out of nothing, or imagining wrong kinds of movements, or more or fewer movements than were actually present historically.

I would argue, nevertheless, that there is sufficient evidence in the rule texts to speak about a *long-term sectarian movement*. Both D and S belong to this movement. A similar worldview is expressed in the scriptural interpretations known as pesharim, but the forms of the communities they represent are not clear. Their scriptural and stereotypical language is not sufficient evidence for their sectarianism. The fact that the pesharim mention some names of organizational bodies and contain sobriquets of individuals and groups gives the impression that they do reflect an *organized* community. However, the exact stage and form of movement is not explicit in the pesharim, nor do we know if the various groups would have preferred D over S, or vice versa, and if the various groups would have felt comfortable in using *all* of the pesharim or only some of them, or none of

18. C. Wassen and J. Jokiranta, "Groups in Tension: Sectarianism in the Damascus Document and the Community Rule."

19. Davies, "Sects from Texts," 69-82.

20. Davies admits that external evidence would be necessary to demonstrate that such ideological constructs were in fact historical entities; yet he tends to see the necessary evidence of *separation* (or rather exclusion of the covenanters by the temple authorities) in texts like 4QMMT. Cf. the discussion on "Judaisms" from the social identity perspective by R. Hakola, "Social Identities and Group Phenomena in Second Temple Judaism."

them. In order to avoid a picture of the movement that is too monolithic, these questions must not be ignored. It is, nevertheless, justified, in my view, to see the pesharim and the serakhim as related rather than isolated from each other. The pesharim arose in the wide movement which is reflected in the serakhim.

If we are willing to make this sort of link between the serakhim and the pesharim, then we may more safely use the three elements of tension to explore sectarianism in the latter texts. For example, in the 4QPsalms Pesher[a], antagonism is evident in the depiction of the fate of the "wicked." All those who follow the wrong leader ("the Liar"), who do not turn from their iniquity, and who persecute the righteous will be annihilated like smoke (3:8; cf. 2:5b-9a), will die because of covenantal curses (famine, sword, plague, 2:1; 3:4; and the hand of foreigners, 2:20). The expectation of future resolution in this pesher demonstrates particularistic beliefs and the claim to unique legitimacy: a division is seen to exist between clearly definable groups. That this division is not just found in the imagination or visions of the pesherist is suggested by the organizational terminology ("council of the *yaḥad*," "men of his council," "congregation of his chosen"), which links the work to the serakhim. Difference and separation (as defined above, page 250), on the other hand, are more difficult to identify in this pesher.

The assumptions we make concerning the exact forms and developments within a movement associated with these texts require not only close textual and historical study but also social-scientific evaluation. For example, can separation be maintained without physical withdrawal? Do scholars assume a development from more hierarchical forms to more democratic ones or vice versa, and on what basis? What is the role of charismatic leadership in such a movement (if any)? Is there a move from household-based discourse to one of almost total silence concerning biological families, and, if so, why? What are the cultural conditions for different types of sectarian forms? No model or theory offers ready-made answers to these questions, but models and theories can provide testable hypotheses, comparable data from other religious movements, and critical questions for commonly-held suppositions. One theoretical viewpoint into the study of small groups is provided by a social identity approach, to which we will now turn.

Social Identity Approach

In contrast with the sociology of sectarianism, which seeks to understand human behavior as part of a social environment and to understand the special role that religiosity has in this environment, the social identity approach is a *social psychological* theory, which gives more precise character-izations of human behavior since it extends to the psychological level. The social identity theory (SIT) was first formulated by Henri Tajfel and his colleagues at Bristol University in the late 1970s and was elaborated in the 1970s and 1980s, especially by Tajfel's student and follower, John C. Turner, who created the self-categorization theory (SCT) as an extension of the so-cial identity theory. These two theories and their later specifications are here called the social identity approach.

Social identity is defined as "that part of an individual's self concept which derives from his knowledge of his membership of a social group (or groups) together with the value and emotional significance attached to that membership."[21] In short, social identity is one's "self-conception as a group member."[22] Theoretically, it is helpful to distinguish those situations in which a person acts as a member of a group from situations in which he or she acts according to his or her self-concept as an individual; personal identity is defined by those factors that distinguish one from other individ-uals (e.g., unique position in a biological family, special skills and experi-ences, interests). However, the two, personal and social identities, form a complex mixture.

The social identity theory seeks to understand the ways in which groups distinguish themselves in order to form a positive social identity. As the so-called minimal group experiments have showed, merely assign-ing people to different groups, without any previous acquaintance or any common characteristics, caused people to favor their "in-group" col-leagues and view the "out-group" in a biased way.[23] Social identity within a group is not static but needs to be constantly re-created. Because of the in-terplay between personal and social identities and because a person may have several competing social identities, group members may have a dif-ferent idea of what it means to belong to the in-group. This also varies over

21. H. Tajfel, ed., *Differentiation between Social Groups,* 63.

22. D. Abrams and M. A. Hogg, eds., *Social Identity Theory,* 2.

23. J. C. Turner, "Henri Tajfel: An Introduction," 15. See also Turner's response to the critique about the "minimal group paradigm" in Turner and R. Y. Bourhis, "Social Identity, Interdependence and the Social Group."

the course of time, depending on group development and its context. Achieving an agreement about the fundamental contents of in-group identity is an ongoing process.[24] The social identity approach helps us to conceptualize and theorize an individual member's identity in relation to the collective identity of the group, to seek in the texts ways in which the members constructed a positive view of themselves, and to appreciate the struggle visible in the texts to maintain group cohesion.

A Social Identity Approach Applied to the Study of the Pesharim

Scholars usually identify fifteen texts from among the Dead Sea Scrolls as "continuous" pesharim, meaning that they quote prophetical texts in a more or less continuous manner and use the term פשר in the formulas introducing their interpretations.[25] Three qualifications for the study of the pesharim are in order. First, whereas earlier research elevated the pesharim to a central form of biblical interpretation, even *the* model for exegesis at Qumran, recent developments have balanced the position by seeing multiple forms of exegesis within the Qumran corpus, as well as large quantities of halakhic, sapiental, and other material. Biblical interpretation is seen not only in terms of exegesis but also what we regard as eisegesis.[26] *Actualizing* intent is to be found not only in the pesharim and in the New Testament, but also within the Hebrew Bible and other Jewish writings.[27] Thus, pesharim are to be placed on the continuum of biblical interpretation rather than at the top.[28]

Second, the common view has been that the value of the prophetical texts *per se* is downplayed by the pesherists; the contents and settings of the original text are insignificant for the atomizing and actualizing pesher interpretation.[29] Pesher is the only meaning of Scripture. However, Shani

24. See Susan Condor, "Social Identity and Time."

25. See T. H. Lim, *Pesharim*, 1-6. For the somewhat artificial character of the categories "continuous" and "thematic" pesharim, see M. J. Bernstein, "Introductory Formulas for Citation and Re-citation of Biblical Verses in the Qumran Pesharim."

26. See M. J. Bernstein, "Pentateuchal Interpretation at Qumran," 1:129.

27. "Pesher-exegesis" has been seen in Isa 9:13-14 and in Ben Sira 50:27-28; see M. Kister, "A Common Heritage: Biblical Interpretation at Qumran and Its Implications," 103-4.

28. Lim, *Pesharim*, 52.

29. S. L. Berrin, *The Pesher Nahum Scroll from Qumran*, 12-15, mentions Otto Betz

Berrin rightly presents reservations against this view. The Qumran interpreters were likely to have perceived the biblical texts as carrying
multivalent meanings. Berrin concludes that pesher "superseded, but did
not invalidate, the earlier historical significance" of the prophetic texts.[30]
The theological message of the base text as a whole and the pesher interpretations are in dialogue with each other, and attention to the plot of the
biblical text — even though this is quoted in extracts in the pesher and is
understood in one particular way — does characterize the work of the
pesherist.

Third, the various pesharim are diverse in both content and form.
Speaking of the group of pesharim may give the wrong impression of a
uniform collection of scriptural interpretation. Each text deserves its individual treatment. In what follows, we will consider the *Psalms Pesher*
(4QpPs[a], 4Q171) as an example of identity construction taking place in the
sectarian movement.

Psalm 37 of 4QPsalms Pesher[a]

In order to appreciate the *Psalms Pesher* as a whole, it is first necessary to
understand its base text, Psalm 37.[31] Commentators have seen this wisdom
psalm as stressing a close relationship between the righteous and God
("Armenfrömmigkeit").[32] It is fundamental for a person to be "righteous,"
not rich or powerful.[33] Protection and salvation result from subordinating
one's life to the rule of Yahweh.

The Psalm knows the old "Tun-Ergehen-Zusammenhang": deeds

---

and F. F. Bruce as early representatives of this view; see Betz, *Offenbarung und Schriftforschung in der Qumransekte,* 75; Bruce, *Biblical Exegesis in the Qumran Texts,* 10-11. It is often held that the pesherists regarded the biblical texts as a "code" to be solved. A related but
slightly different question is the attitude of the pesher authors towards preserving or modifying the scriptural text form; see T. H. Lim, "Eschatological Orientation and the Alteration
of Scripture in the Habakkuk Pesher"; *Holy Scripture in the Qumran Commentaries and Pauline Letters,* 69-120.

30. Berrin, *The Pesher Nahum Scroll from Qumran,* 15-18.

31. Besides Psalm 37, the beginning of Psalm 45 and its pesher is preserved at the end
of the manuscript.

32. F.-L. Hossfeld and E. Zenger, *Die Psalmen I,* 229. C. Levin, "Das Gebetbuch der
Gerechten," detects a development in the Psalter: the "poor" come to be regarded as a party
within Israel.

33. H.-J. Kraus, *Psalms 1-59,* 406.

and their consequences are closely related. However, the wicked are not accused of specific law-breaking acts — except in their treatment of the "righteous" (37:7, 12, 14, 21, 32, 33, 35, 40). It is this *relationship* between the righteous and the wicked that defines the categories here, in addition to their relationship to Yahweh: the wicked are primarily shown to be wicked in their relationship to the righteous. They perform self-destructive violence, and their end comes inevitably — burning grass and fading smoke illustrate this law of life. The righteous (the poor), on the other hand, will enjoy the riches of the land — the land is the foundation of life and the pledge of Yahweh's blessing.[34]

The Psalm is practical and instructional: it does not dwell on theoretical questions about why God lets the wicked prosper. The wisdom teaching of the Psalm resembles that of the friends of Job.[35] It gives practical and fairly traditional advice not to become angry over the sinners since they will be destroyed. The elderly teacher shares his experiences with the wisdom student. The suffering of the righteous is relegated to the background — or even denied — in the Psalm; only the end counts. The contribution of the Psalm is its memorable and encouraging (alphabetical) poetry that the righteous may find comforting in many situations.[36]

Continuity and Discontinuity between the Psalm and the Pesher

The relationship between the righteous and the wicked is the feature that clearly shows continuity between the Psalm and the *Psalms Pesher*. The opponents in the *Pesher* are called the "liar" and the "wicked priest," but it is not their erroneous teaching or actions in general that are deemed wrong, but their actions against the righteous. As the text reports: they did not listen to the "interpreter of knowledge" (1:26-27), they plotted against those who obeyed the law (2:13-16a; 2:16b-21; 4:7-10a), and they oppressed God's holy people (3:7-8a). The Psalm suited the pesherist's needs as it portrayed the *wicked persecuting the righteous*. Similarly, the *Pesher* also emphasizes future resolution (2:11; 3:1; cf. Deut. 7:9). The land is reserved for the righteous only (2:5b-12; 3:8b-13).

34. Kraus, *Psalms 1–59*, 406-8.
35. H. Gunkel, *Die Psalmen*, 156. Cf. e.g. Ps 37:3-4 and Job 22:21-30; Ps 37:10 and Job 20:4-11.
36. Psalm 37 "actually provides no solution of the problem but rather a testimony to the deliverance," Kraus, *Psalms 1–59*, 408.

The greatest reinterpretation occurs with regard to the hortatory element of the Psalm. The pesherist carefully followed the distinctions between the righteous and the wicked of Psalm 37 but did not much care about changes in first person or second person forms or plural/singular variation and thus ignored the *form* of exhortation. Of special interest concerning this tendency is the interpretation of verses 37:8-9, in which the psalmist exhorts the reader/listener to refrain from anger at the evildoers. The interpretation is revealing for our understanding of social identity construction.

הרף מאף ועזוב חמה ואל תחר אך להרע כיא מרעים יכרתו
פשרו על כול השבים לתורה אשר לוא ימאנו לשוב מרעתם
כיא כול הממרים לשוב מעונם יכרתו וקואי יהוה המה ירשו
ארץ פשרו המה עדת בחירו עושי רצונו

Refrain from anger, and forsake wrath. Do not fret — it leads only to evil. For the wicked shall be cut off. (Ps 37:8-9a) Interpreted, this concerns all those who return to the Law, who do not refuse to turn away from their evil. For all those who are stubborn in turning away from their iniquity shall be cut off. *But those who wait for the Lord shall inherit the land.* (Ps 37:9b) Interpreted: these are the congregation of his elect, those who do his will (4QpPsᵃ 2:1b-5a).

Several terms in the interpretation echo Deuteronomistic theology (Deuteronomy, Psalm 78, Jeremiah) about the people drawing the judgment of God upon themselves with their sins and with their refusal to repent.[37] The infinitive להרע in the quotation of Ps 37:8 is used in Jeremiah to refer to the disaster of exile, the punishment by God: "I am beginning to bring disaster on the city" (Jer 25:29; also 31:28).[38] The intertextual links suggest that, in the context of the *Pesher,* the infinitive receives the sense of "disaster," rather than the meaning "sin." This is supported by the fact that, after quoting 37:8, the pesherist continues to quote 37:9b: "For the wicked shall be cut off." Furthermore, the participle ממרים, "those who are stubborn/rebellious," is dominant in Deuteronomy and Deuteronomistic history: being rebellious provokes God's anger (Deut 9:7, 23, 24). The closest paral-

37. E.g., for מאן, cf. Ps 78:10; ימאנו לשוב, cf. Jer 8:5; שוב מרעתם, cf. Jer 23:14; 44:5.
38. Similarly, the noun רעה "evil, disaster" is frequent in Jeremiah: God is going to bring disaster upon those who refused to hear his words (Jer 11:10-11). Cf. also Dan 9:13-14.

lel to the expression שוב מעונם is found in Dan 9:13, which again speaks of the disaster that has come upon the people.

How does the pesherist understand the nouns אף and חמה in the quotation? Wisdom tradition is familiar with the exhortation not to become angry at one's enemy.[39] The pesherist gives up the form of exhortation, suggesting that the covenanters have said "no" to their "evil inclination."[40] However, from the point of view of an individual member and identification with the group, this act was a continuous process. In the penal code of S, the rule about stubborn speech follows right after the first offense, lying about property. 1QS 6:25b-27a reads:

> And one who answers his fellow with stubbornness (lit., with a stiff neck), speaks with impatience (בקוצר אפים),[41] disregarding the principle of his associate by defying the authority of his fellow who is registered ahead of him, [or tak]es the law into his own hands, shall be punished for on[e] year [and excluded.]

A similar case is described for speech against a priest (1QS 7:2b-3a):

> But if against one of the priests who are registered in the book he speaks in anger (בחמה), he shall be punished for one year and be excluded (to be) by himself from the purity of the rabbim.

Such stubbornness is elsewhere also described with the possibility of returning (1QS 7:18b-19a//4QD[e] 7 1:[8-9a]):

> The man whose spirit turns aside from the principle of the *yaḥad*, betraying the truth and walking in the stubbornness of his heart, if he turns (אם ישוב), he shall be punished for two years. . . .

Interpreted in the light of these passages of the *Serekh,* it is clear that the *Psalms Pesher* acknowledges the need to address also the individual member: turning to the law is a constant act, in which the member has to subordinate himself to the counsel and reproof of the community. Even

---

39. E.g., Prov 22:24-25; 24:1-2, 17-20; 29:8; Sir 1:22.

40. Rabbinic teaching speaks about "the Evil Inclination" against which people must fight; see E. E. Urbach, *The Sages, Their Concepts and Beliefs,* 471-75.

41. The opposite of ארך אפים, "slow to anger," Prov 14:29.

the verbal forms used in the pesher, participles and an imperfect, support this reading; it is not an act made in the past and completed. The members are called to leave their anger, control their temper, and commit themselves to the counsel of the community (cf. 4QpPs^a 2:15). If they do not, they will be excluded or, in the most severe cases, expelled. By using the expressions "who returns," "who does not refuse to turn," and "who is not stubborn in turning," the *Pesher* admits, in an indirect way, that the members of the community can violate the Law.[42]

The nearest parallel to the expression "turning away from their iniquity" is found in Dan 9:13. In this chapter, Daniel openly confesses the sins of his people and prays that God will turn his anger away from his city (9:16). In the background is the question of why the righteous receive the "great calamity" together with the wicked. Daniel's answer is that the responsibility and the punishment are collective. This line of thought can also play a role in the *Pesher*. The anger that needs to be avoided, according to the *Pesher*, is not an inner motion, a personal sin that a righteous person may experience when seeing the wicked prosper. It is rather the unwillingness to put the social identity as a group member to the fore, a collective matter. The noun אף is frequently used in the Hebrew Bible with the verb שוב as a stereotypical formula "that God would turn away from his (burning) anger."[43] The quotation of Ps 37:8 and the pesher appear together as a statement: those who turn to God's law make God turn away his anger for them, and thus they escape doom.

An explicit petition to God to turn his anger and wrath away occurs in 4QWords of the Luminaries: "May your anger and wrath turn away from us" (4Q504 1-2 6:11). These prayers are public prayers and display a biblical, postexilic mood: God's wrath is seen as a deserved punishment for the sins of the fathers and the people.[44] Yet, the prayer bases the plea for help not only on God's mercy and his remembering the covenant, but on the fact that the community praying this prayer has perceived the punishment as a justified one and has suffered in distress: "We have not rejected

42. M. J. Bernstein, "Pesher Psalms," sees those who refuse to turn away from their evil (the opposite of those in 2:3-4) as "backsliding members of the sect."

43. Deut 13:17; Isa 5:25; Jer 23:20; Ps 78:38.

44. B. Nitzan, *Qumran Prayer and Religious Poetry*, 329-32, compares the tone in 4Q504 ("prayer recited in the circles of the sect on weekdays and festivals") to the tone in the individual poetry of 1QH; the public prayers do not distinguish between one kind of Jew and another, whereas the individual poetry has a particularistic view of the sect as the holy remnant.

your trials, and our soul has not despised your punishments to the point of breaking your covenant, in spite of all the anguish of our soul" (4Q504 1-2 6:6-7).

This similar sense of salvation through affliction is present in the *Psalms Pesher*. The righteous accept the time of distress.[45] The *Pesher*, however, lacks the tone of a prayer, and the axis Israel/nations has changed into the axis righteous in Israel/wicked in Israel. Nevertheless, the use of the nouns "anger" and "wrath" as epithets of God in the Hebrew Bible allows the quotation of 37:8 to be read not only in the sense "the righteous must control their anger" but in the sense "the righteous will avoid God's punishment."[46] Similarly, the "evil" of the pesher is not only a personal fall, but eventually a collective disaster and punishment outside the group.

Conclusion

Despite the different disciplines underlying sociology of sectarianism and the social identity approach, there are several links between them. Both deal with the distinctiveness of one group of people from other groups of people. Both pay attention to the point of view of the in-group or sect (especially in terms of how out-groups or others are perceived), although sociology of sectarianism often focuses more on an "objective" state of affairs and the portrait of a sect in comparison with other institutions and society more generally. Both strands of research also include the perspective of the individual: sociology of sectarianism asks, for example, what makes the individual join a sect and how membership in a sect affects his or her personal life. The social identity approach studies the individual's social identity once s/he identifies him/herself as part of a particular group. The call for a positive self-image as a motivating factor for human action is seen in

45. For the expressions "period of humiliation" and the "congregation of the poor," see J. Jokiranta, "Social Identity Approach," 98-108.

46. An interesting point of comparison where the "Anger" and "Wrath" of Ps 37:8 are personified is to be found in *b. Ned.* 32a, referring to the biblical story of Exod 4:24-26; see I. Epstein, ed., *The Babylonian Talmud: Seder Nashim,* 94-95. "Anger" and "Wrath" of Psalm 37 are seen as external threats to a person, angels of doom sent by God. In a similar way, "anger" and "wrath" in the *Psalms Pesher* may signify the doom that the wicked have drawn upon themselves. The righteous are called not so much to control their emotions, but to forsake the desire to turn away from the community's judgment and instruction.

both approaches.[47] Both also deal with schism and conflict: what causes tension within groups and how groups split.

Sociology of sectarianism helps us to grasp the central aspects of sectarian small groups, while recognizing their diversity, since groups that stand in tension with their socio-cultural environment are not similar in every aspect. The three elements of tension discussed by Stark and Bainbridge (antagonism, difference, and separation) provide a useful way to analyze degrees of tension, making space for sectarian ideology without reducing sectarianism to a set of deviant beliefs.[48] Wilson's typology of sectarian responses is found helpful by many for differentiating between different kinds of sects. His studies also pay attention to the cultural conditions that permit distinct sectarian types to emerge and develop.[49] Weber's notions of sectarianism can reveal how sects cultivate individuals as *virtuosos* and how sects affect the larger society. Comparative studies of modern sects present data that cannot be dismissed when sectarian group dynamics are discussed. Different strands of research within sociology of sectarianism have assisted scholars in analyzing the Qumran movement reflected in the "sectarian" texts in terms of its relationship to and impact on the wider society and other groups, as well as the potential in all Qumran texts to create sectarian ideas and behavior.

The social identity approach, for its part, reminds us that a group is made up of individuals who identify with their group to varying degrees. Group behavior is possible because individuals have a social identity: they see themselves as group members rather than primarily as individual human beings. We took the 4QPsalms Pesher[a] as an example of identity construction in the sectarian movement. What we could have missed, without these social-scientific ways of thinking, is the fact that, although the *Pesher* includes a sectarian ideology, the assumption that its authors and users had a *sectarian* identity comes through the association of the text with the serakhim and their sectarian stance. Read from this perspective, many fea-

---

47. For a rational choice theory of religion, see, e.g., R. Stark and W. S. Bainbridge, *A Theory of Religion*, 196.

48. Cf. the common assumption within Jewish life that divergent beliefs are well tolerated but "touch the law and the sect will split." But not all laws have the same impact: the manner in which to slaughter fish might be considered minor in comparison to the question of the exact date on which to celebrate a particular festival.

49. One important observation is that revolutionist sects are usually short-lived whereas introversionist sects can persist longer; see Jokiranta, "Learning from Sectarian Responses."

tures in the *Pesher* allow an interpretation in terms of sectarianism — difference, antagonism, and separation. It is a text that attempted to preserve this tension and thus create sectarianism. Furthermore, the authors and readers of the *Pesher* not only applied the Scripture as a proof-text — quoting Scripture to prove their views — but they also defined their relationship to that Scripture, highlighting certain aspects of it and hiding others, and thus modified their social identity as a group of people in the desired direction. The social identity perspective was useful here — especially when combined with an intertextual study of the Hebrew Bible and other Dead Sea Scrolls — to show how this particular reading and interpretation of Psalm 37 contributed to the social identity construction in the movement. This included maintaining the image of the righteous in conflict with the wicked (in line with the base text) but also moving forward from the base text by understanding distress as a collective matter and as proof of the elect status of the group.

Social-scientifically oriented inquiries into the Qumran texts have increased during the last years. This chapter presents only a few examples of fruitful social-scientific theories — and many more are already in use. Terminology of "sects" is common, but the sociology of sectarianism has much more to offer than these basic concepts. A social identity approach has strong potential to illuminate the relationship between personal and social identities in small groups, strategies for constructing positive social identity, and social identity formation as regards to group development.

The Dead Sea Scrolls, the Essenes, and the Study of Religious Belief: Determinism and Freedom of Choice

Jonathan Klawans

An important transformation is taking place in the study of the Dead Sea Scrolls in American universities, and readers of this volume may well be part of it. At one time in the United States, the study of the scrolls would most likely take place (if at all) within theological seminaries (mostly Christian, some Jewish) or university departments devoted to ancient Near Eastern (i.e., "Semitic" or "Oriental") languages. Currently, such study is just as likely — if not even more likely — to be taking place in departments of religion, where the context is no longer philology or theology, but the study of religion broadly conceived, including ages past and present, locales eastern and western, and traditions living and dead.[1]

This academic disciplinary transformation is potentially of great significance for the study of the scrolls and will likely bring both advantages and challenges to the guild. One benefit is broader exposure for the study of the scrolls, reaching students without a prior commitment to the study of Judaism, Christianity, or the Hebrew language. Beside greater numbers (and at most American universities, raw enrollment numbers do matter to some extent), the classroom can be enhanced by this diversity of backgrounds and interests. Students of religious studies may ask questions that haven't already been asked, or suggest comparisons that have yet to be noticed, based on knowledge of Buddhism, Hinduism, Islam, or the religions of Africa. To be sure, there are drawbacks too. The chances that students

---

1. For a sampling of what the field seeks to cover, see L. S. Cunningham and J. Kelsay, *The Sacred Quest: An Invitation to the Study of Religion*.

taking university courses on the scrolls can read any Hebrew at all may well have decreased over the years.

Ironically, one important facet of Dead Sea Scrolls scholarship has fallen through the cracks during this time of transformation: thorough, systematic, and methodologically sound analyses of the religion of the Dead Sea sectarians. Plenty has been written on various aspects of religion at Qumran. Religious practices have received much attention, especially since the publication of the *Temple Scroll* and 4QMMT. But it is rather surprising that so few books have sought to address, in a systematic way, the religious beliefs of the sect. Helmer Ringgren's *The Faith of Qumran*[2] — which first appeared in 1963 — remains, surprisingly, unsurpassed, even as it is also hopelessly outdated by the wealth of material made known since its publication. More recent works have tried to move us beyond Ringgren.[3] But these works are neither thorough nor sufficiently (or consistently) rooted in the discipline of religious studies. As a result, the field has hardly moved past Ringgren at all. Fortunately, students and scholars of the scrolls at home in departments of religion may discover tools and experiences to help address the present need.

Needless to say, a thorough analysis of sectarian religion is well beyond the scope of this essay. We will focus here on questions pertaining to the relationship between the belief in predestination, as expressed in 1QS and related literature, and the determinism attributed to the Essenes by Josephus. I select this topic for two reasons. First, the topic is of undeniable importance for the field: the Essene Hypothesis (in its various forms) rests in part on the ability to identify the theology of the Dead Sea Scrolls with that of the Essenes as described by the Jewish historian. Second, the topic is one that stands to benefit from a reevaluation in light of lessons learned from religious studies as a discipline. In the first section that follows (part 1), we will briefly review the evidence from Josephus, Qumran, and a few other ancient Jewish sources concerning beliefs about determinism and free will. As we review this material, we will begin to encounter the interpretive problems that have dogged scholarship for some time: Is Josephus accurate? Did the sectarians really hold to a strict belief in predeterminism? Having raised these questions, I then hope to illustrate two ways that the field of religious studies provides tools to help solve these interpretive prob-

---

2. Expanded ed., 1995.

3. Important recent contributions include J. J. Collins and R. A. Kugler, eds., *Religion in the Dead Sea Scrolls;* and the various articles included in *EDSS.*

lems. The first lesson (part 2) can be described as "experiential," drawn not so much from research produced by the discipline of religious studies as from the experience of teaching courses within a religious studies department. The second lesson (part 3) is more substantial in nature, and concerns the ways in which we can learn about the problem of free will versus determinism from the tools and products of the discipline.

1. Determinism and Free Will in Ancient Jewish Theology

We do well to begin with Josephus's brief schematizations of ancient Jewish theology (*B.J.* 2.119-66; *Ant.* 13.171-73; 18.11-25). On a number of occasions in his works Josephus compares and contrasts the three major sects (Gk. *haireseis*) of ancient Judaism: Pharisees, Sadducees, and Essenes. The latter, he states, "declares that fate (Gk. *heimarmenē*) is the mistress of all things, and that nothing befalls people unless it be in accordance with her decree" (*Ant.* 13.172).[4] By contrast, the Sadducees "do away with fate, holding that there is no such thing" (13.173), while the Pharisees hold a middle position, believing that "certain events are the work of fate, but not all; as to other events it depends on ourselves whether they shall take place or not" (13.172). Josephus elsewhere nuances this typology, noting that the doctrine of the Essenes "is wont to leave everything in the hands of God" (18.18). In addition to denying fate, the Sadducees "remove God beyond, not merely the commission, but the very sight, of evil. They maintain that a person has the free choice of good or evil, and that it rests with each person's will whether to follow the one or the other" (*B.J.* 2.164-65).[5]

As we have already intimated, scholars have frequently identified Josephus's description of the Essenes with the theology expressed in sectarian literature from Qumran:[6]

> From the God of knowledge comes all that is and shall be. Before ever they existed, he established their whole design, and when, as ordained for them, they come into being, it is in accord with his glorious design

---

4. Translations of Josephus follow, with slight modifications, the LCL edition, trans. H. St. J. Thackeray et al.

5. For further discussion of these accounts, see S. Mason, *Flavius Josephus on the Pharisees*, 120-77, 196-212, 281-308, 384-98.

6. Translations of scrolls here and below follow, with slight modifications, G. Vermes, *The Complete Dead Sea Scrolls in English*.

that they accomplish their task without change. The laws of all things are in his hand, and he provides them with all their needs. He has created man to govern the world, and has appointed for him two spirits in which to walk until the time of his visitation: the spirits of truth and injustice. Those born of truth spring from a fountain of light, but those born of injustice spring from a source of darkness. (1QS 3:15-19)

> But in the mysteries of his understanding, and in his glorious wisdom, God has ordained an end for injustice, and at the time of the visitation he will destroy it for ever. Then truth, which has wallowed in the ways of wickedness during the dominion of injustice until the appointed time of judgment, shall arise in the world forever. (4:18-20)

Similar sentiments are expressed elsewhere in the Qumran corpus, most notably in the *Damascus Document* (e.g., CD 2:3-10), the *War Scroll* (esp. 1QM 1:1-9), and the *Thanksgiving Hymns* (e.g., 1QH^a 7:12-14; 9:7-20).[7]

Of course, we cannot accurately speak of a simple identity between the theology of Josephus's Essenes and that of the Dead Sea sectarians. Josephus's discussion of fate is unmistakably colored by Hellenistic philosophic concerns. Josephus also says nothing about the dualism expressed in 1QS: if his Essenes believed in powers of darkness, Josephus declined to say. Yet a striking similarity remains: Josephus describes the Essenes as believing in the predetermination of all events, to the exclusion of human freedom. The Dead Sea sectarians, it appears, emphasized God's omniscience and power to such a degree that all proceeds according to a divine plan, which has been put in place long ago. If this isn't a belief in fate, then what is?

Further confirmation of this picture can be found in the Wisdom of Ben Sira, a work commonly believed to have been composed in Jerusalem, early in the second century B.C.E. The book builds on the wisdom tradition of ancient Israel but represents a remarkable synthesis of previous biblical traditions and themes.[8] What is important for our concerns can be found in the following passage (15:11-17).[9]

---

7. For a brief survey, see A. Lange, "Wisdom and Predestination in the Dead Sea Scrolls"; on the *Thanksgiving Hymns,* see E. H. Merrill, *Qumran and Predestination,* 16-23.

8. On the wisdom tradition in general, see J. L. Crenshaw, *Old Testament Wisdom.*

9. Translation of Sirach here and below follows P. W. Skehan and A. A. Di Lella, *The Wisdom of Ben Sira.*

(11) Say not, "It was God's doing that I fell away";
　　for what he hates, he does not do.

(12) Say not, "It was he who led me astray";
　　for he has no need of the sinful.

(13) Abominable wickedness the Lord hates;
　　he does not let it befall those who fear him.

(14) It was he, from the first, when he created humankind,
　　who made them subject to their own free choice.

(15) If you choose, you can keep his commandment;
　　fidelity is the doing of his will.

(16) There are poured out before you fire and water;
　　to whichever you choose you can stretch forth your hands.

(17) Before each person are life and death;
　　whichever he chooses will be given him.

What we find in this passage is the clear combination of three related, but separable, ideas: the freedom of choice (esp. vv. 14-17), the denial that anyone could be destined to do evil (vv. 11-12; cf. 15:20), and God's absolute opposition to evil (v. 13; cf. 15:20). The combination of ideas is strikingly similar to Josephus's assertion that the Sadducees "do away with fate altogether, and remove God beyond not merely the commission, but the very sight of evil. They maintain that man has the free choice of good and evil" (*B.J.* 2.164-65).

The passage is important for our concerns for a number of reasons. First, it confirms that there were Jews in the second century B.C.E. who articulated a theology in line with what Josephus attributes to the Sadducees at a later period. This lends some (albeit indirect) credence to the effort to identify the beliefs of Josephus's Essenes with other known literature from ancient Judaism, such as the Qumran scrolls. The second aspect of the passage that is important for our concerns is its polemical tone ("Do not say...."). Sirach not only confirms that some Jews denied fate in their assertion of free choice; the book confirms that these issues were up for debate. Digging just a bit deeper we find that there are striking similarities between Josephus's Essenes and Ben Sira's opponents: both believed that sinners were destined to sin. Moreover, this text helps us understand why Jews like Ben Sira opposed this sort of determinism: when they deny human beings the freedom of choice — and the moral responsibility that comes along with it — Ben Sira believes his opponents implicate God in the commission of evil. Ben Sira, however, separates God from evil by asserting that evil comes about as a result of human choice. God's punishment of the wicked is therefore both deserved and just. Indeed, it is no accident that the very next chapter of the book (Sir 16:1-23) contains an elaborate discussion of the punishment of the wicked, along with an assertion of divine justice. It is also no accident — and probably for the very same reasons — that Josephus's Sadducees also separate God from the sight of evil. But for the Dead Sea sectarians — and apparently for Ben Sira's opponents as well — God's omnipotence and omniscience trump the concern to separate God from evil, and therefore predetermined wickedness indeed persists, by "the mysteries of his understanding" (1QS 4:18).

But can we so easily identify the theology of the sectarian documents with Josephus's Essenes or Ben Sira's unnamed opponents? Indeed, scholars commonly recognize that alongside the scrolls passages discussed above, other passages appear to step away from predeterminism. The *Community Rule* itself, for instance, insists that those who join the community must repent and decide to do so of their own volition (e.g., 1QS 5:8, 10, 14, 22), while the wicked follow their own stubborn hearts (e.g., 2:25-26). E. P. Sanders noted decades ago that such passages indicate "how far the sectarians were from denying [humanity's] freedom of choice."[10] Eugene Merrill, after surveying references to voluntary repentance in the *Thanksgiving Hymns*, similarly concludes that the sectarians "found it possible to hold for the need for individual voluntary response to Divine promptings within the framework of a rigid predestinarianism."[11] More recently, Eileen Schuller has pointed out that the predeterminism of the sect did not prevent the group from praying for forgiveness from sin (e.g., 1QH^a 19:29-31; cf. 8:29-30) and for victory in the final battle against evil (1QM 15:5).[12] Yet why would the sons of light have to pray for atonement? And wouldn't their victory already be predetermined? Finally, in the *Thanksgiving Hymns*, we find a number of passages that speak of the miserable and sinful state of the speaker (e.g., 1QH^a 11:23-24):

> (23) . . . And yet I, a shape (24) of clay,
>   what am I?
> Kneaded with water
>   What is my worth and my might?

---

10. E. P. Sanders, *Paul and Palestinian Judaism*, 263.

11. Merrill, *Qumran and Predestination*, 45, cf. 16, 58.

12. E. Schuller, "Petitionary Prayer and the Religion of Qumran," esp. 39-43. See also A. P. Jassen, "Religion in the Dead Sea Scrolls," esp. 11.

But why would one destined to be a son of light recite such self-deprecating prayers (cf. also 4:17-25; 9:21-23; 15:1-6, 20:20-24, etc.)?

Indeed, Schuller concludes her essay with the suggestion that the Dead Sea sectarians may never have become thoroughly deterministic.[13] Jean Duhaime points in a similar direction when he suggests that the sectarians' approach to the issue may have been "compatibilist" — where "compatibilism" refers to the balance between fate and free will more commonly associated with Josephus's descriptions of the Pharisees (cf. Josephus, *B.J.* 2.162-63; *Ant.* 13.172; 18.13).[14] Others too have settled on the fact that the sect's theology must have been to some extent unsystematic and possibly inconsistent,[15] a conclusion that is really not so far from the view that compares the Qumran sectarians with Josephus's Pharisees.

Approaching the same issue from another direction, scholars have wondered about the relationship between Sirach 15 (quoted above) and Sir 33:7-12:

> (7) Why is one day more important than another,
>   when the same sun lights up every day of the year?
> (8) By the Lord's knowledge they are kept distinct;
>   among them he designates seasons and feasts.
> (9) Some he exalts and sanctifies,
>   and others he lists as ordinary days.
> (10) So, too, all people are of clay,
>   for from earth humankind was formed;
> (11) Yet in the fullness of his understanding the Lord makes people unlike:
>   in different paths he has them walk.
> (12) Some he blesses and makes great,

13. Schuller, "Petitionary Prayer," 45.

14. J. Duhaime, "Determinism." "Compatibilism" is a term borrowed from philosophy, and it refers to the varied efforts to maintain that determinism and free will are not contradictory, but compatible. For a brief survey addressed to the general reader, see T. Pink, *Free Will*, 18-19, 43-72, 109-10. While the term can usefully be applied to the Pharisaic position as described by Josephus, it is equally important to bear in mind that the contours of the philosophical debate are much wider than the debate within Jewish theology. Philosophy need not necessarily concern itself with an omniscient God (which would lead toward a modicum of determinism) or a just God (leading toward a modicum of free choice, as we will see below). For a fuller treatment see J. Klawuns, "Josephus on Fate."

15. So, e.g., Merrill, *Qumran and Predestination*, 16, 45, 58; Ringgren, *The Faith of Qumran*, 109-11, and Sanders, *Paul and Palestinian Judaism*, 265.

some he sanctifies and draws to himself.
Others he curses and brings low,
    and expels them from their place.

At first reading, the passage has a deterministic sound to it (cf. also 42:24). According to some interpreters, this passage can even be compared to the Treatise of the Two Spirits from the *Community Rule*.[16] The appearance, therefore, of an ostensibly deterministic passage such as this within the same work as another emphasizing free choice (15:11-20) leads some interpreters to see in Ben Sira a precursor to the fusion of fate and free will seen in Josephus's description of the Pharisees as well as in some passages of rabbinic literature (e.g., *m.* 'Abot 3.15).[17]

And now we have come to a serious impasse. If we follow one line of thought (Martin Hengel, Moshe Tzvi Segal, and David Winston), then the juxtaposition of the material from Sirach 15 and 33 leads to the conclusion that Ben Sira was a compatibilist, just like Josephus's Pharisees and the even later rabbis. If we follow another line of thought (Duhaime, Ringgren, Sanders, and Schuller) then we can with some justification compare the theology of the Dead Sea sect with Josephus's Pharisees too! Were all ancient Jews compatibilists?[18] This indeed seems to be the direction in which a number of scholars are moving. But this solution to the seeming contradictions among the sources only leads to further problems: If the *Community Rule* is not deterministic, then what might a deterministic ancient Jewish document look like? If the theologies of both Sirach and 1QS are to be compared with the compatibilism of the Pharisees and later rabbinic Judaism, then are we not left with an undifferentiated hodgepodge of ancient Jewish compatibilism? If all ancient Jews were compatibilists, then what on earth was Josephus talking about when he stated repeatedly that Jews argued about such matters? And whom was Ben Sira arguing with?

16. P. Winter, "Ben Sira and the Teaching of 'Two Ways.'"
17. See, e.g., M. Hengel, *Judaism and Hellenism,* 1:141; M. T. Segal, *Sefer Ben Sira ha-Shalem,* 29; and D. Winston, *The Wisdom of Solomon,* 49-50.
18. See Winston, *The Wisdom of Solomon,* 46-58, who compares Qumran, Sirach, and rabbinic literature to the compatibilist position of the Hellenistic Stoic philosophers.

2. Reconsidering Josephus from the Experience of Religious Studies

Anyone who has struggled to teach an introductory course in religious studies can sympathize with Josephus's predicament. How is one to provide the necessary explanations, while keeping the presentation brief and even entertaining? This is not to minimize the impact or extent of Josephus's biases, but rather to contextualize them in a different way. It is well known that Josephus's accounts are hellenized, though it remains unclear if his use of Greek philosophical terms extends from sources the historian consulted (or plagiarized), from the efforts of his assistants, or from his own desire to present Judaism in a light favorable to his Greek-reading audience.[19] While the first two of these possibilities are (or ought to be) distant from the concerns of modern scholars, the last of these brings us closer to the common experience of religious studies instructors who — for better or for worse — frequently confront students holding common misconceptions or even exhibiting general hostility. Instructors may therefore find themselves defending one religious tradition or another. At times, this pedagogic defense can serve to counter significant misunderstandings. But some have argued that these apologies too frequently align with the instructors' own religious, political, or academic convictions and interests.[20] Either way, modern introductory religious studies textbooks may overlook or underplay the less attractive aspects of given religious traditions and highlight the positive ones. Josephus may have been similarly motivated in his description of the Essenes.

In addition to the issue of apology, two other aspects of Josephus's description of the Essenes can be clarified when we compare them to the presentations that might take place in a modern religious studies classroom. One issue that comes up in practically any religious studies course — and is addressed head-on in the better introductory textbooks — is the inherent conflict between perspectives of practitioners of a religious tradition and those of the scholars who study it. In the field, this is known as the insider/outsider problem.[21] The problem — in its starkest form — is this: outsiders

19. See Mason, *Flavius Josephus,* for a thorough analysis of Josephus's interests in these passages.
20. See T. Fitzgerald, *The Ideology of Religious Studies;* and R. T. McCutcheon, *Manufacturing Religion.*
21. For a thorough review of this problem, see R. T. McCutcheon, ed., *The Insider/Outsider Problem in the Study of Religion.*

accuse insiders of taking a subjective, nostalgic view toward their own religious commitments. Insiders accuse outsiders of being ill-informed and biased against the tradition in question. The significance of the question for the field of religious studies can be seen in the fact that Russell McCutcheon's anthological treatment extends beyond four hundred pages. Leaving aside the important questions concerning whether insider or outsider views have greater validity, we can state here, minimally, that insider and outsider perspectives tend to be *different* — otherwise, there would be no problem. Josephus, of course, claims to have lived as an Essene for a short time (*Vita* 10-12). The problems of this account need not detain us, because the mere fact that Josephus did not remain an Essene is sufficient to label him an outsider by the time he wrote his works. If outsider accounts and insider accounts tend to differ in any case, then we have yet another possible context for understanding discrepancies between Josephus's Essenes and the sectarian literature from Qumran. The simple fact that Josephus is an outsider describing the Essenes is enough for us to have expected, even in advance of the discovery of the Dead Sea Scrolls, that there would be some differences between what he says and what members of the group would say. Be it a result of misunderstanding, a lack of sympathy, or even a glazy nostalgia, the outsider's description is unlikely to match internal accounts of the group in question. The validity of the Essene hypothesis ought not therefore rest on an *exact* correspondence between Josephus's Essenes and the sectarian Qumran scrolls.

The final issue to be considered here is that of pedagogical simplification. Jonathan Z. Smith called attention to the various levels of deception that are frequently involved in typical introductory courses in religious studies.[22] From our frequently unacknowledged use of heavily-edited primary source texts to the simplification of complex doctrinal issues, the material presented in "Religion 101" may be much less true than we like to admit. Of course, others in the field may be more tolerant of pedagogical simplification than Smith. But once the point is raised, the truth can be confronted: simplification often involves falsification. Should religious studies instructors be more open about this issue? The relevance of this issue for our concern is, of course, that Josephus too can be understood as engaging in pedagogical simplification in his artful, memorable — and overly abbreviated — typology of the ancient Jewish sects.

Reflecting on the experience of teaching religious studies courses

22. J. Z. Smith, "'Narratives into Problems.'"

can help us evaluate Josephus's typology. We should take it not as gospel truth, and not as the account of an insider. We should never have expected Josephus's description to match perfectly with an insider account. We can productively compare it to the kind of overly-simplified account of complex phenomena that we find in practically any (and probably every) introductory religious studies textbook. The simplified description can introduce us to the data; it can guide our interpretation, but it cannot govern our understanding of it.

3. Religious Studies Approaches to Monotheistic Determinism

We are now ready to reconsider the relationship between the theologies of the Dead Sea sectarians and Josephus's Essenes in light of more substantial contributions from the discipline of religious studies. The discipline can help us by (1) providing informed definitions of key terms, (2) facilitating comparison with similar ideas in other religious traditions, and (3) offering interpretive insights regarding particular religious beliefs.

Let us begin by offering some clearer definitions of the terms we have been using. Josephus speaks of "fate" (Gk. *heimarmenē*), which can be defined broadly as the belief that things are bought about, of necessity, by set causes or impersonal powers.[23] It is unlikely that ancient Jews who otherwise believed in God granted the existence of a separate or impersonal power — Fate — governing events. Thus when speaking of Jewish theologies, most prefer to use the terms "predeterminism" or "predestination." The former can be taken as referring to the belief that all events have been mapped out ahead of time, denying human beings the freedom of choice — precisely what Josephus seems to have in mind.[24] Predestination is generally understood as a specific, theistic, form of determinism, one that is particularly focused on the destinies of individual human beings. Predestination asserts that God has long ago decided that salvation will be extended to some, but not to others.[25] While the terms can mean vastly different things in disparate religious or philosophical contexts, the differences dissipate somewhat in religions such as Judaism, Christianity,

23. For general discussion and definitions, see K. W. Bolle, "Fate." For Hellenistic definitions, see G. F. Moore, "Fate and Free Will in the Jewish Philosophies According to Josephus." For philosophic definitions, see Pink, *Free Will*.
24. See I. Marcoulesco, "Free Will and Determinism."
25. See D. D. Wallace, Jr., "Free Will and Predestination."

and Islam, which put a premium on questions concerning individual salvation and assert the existence of a single omniscient and omnipotent God. Both "predeterminism" and "predestination" lead toward the denial of free choice, and both assert God's absolute foreknowledge of and control over future events. In what follows, we will eschew the term "fate" (except when speaking of Josephus); the other terms will be used largely interchangeably, while keeping in mind the nuances noted above.

Our next step is to establish a clear difference between predestination and divine election. As we have just indicated, predestination will be understood here as the belief that all has been determined ahead of time, including especially who will be sinful and who will be righteous. Divine election, by contrast, refers to the idea that a certain group or nation has been singled out from among others for both revelation and responsibility. For Jews, of course, divine election refers to the belief that the covenants established with Abraham and Moses are to be passed down from generation to generation, with the accidents of birth deciding who is born into the covenant and who is not. Divine election, however, is not tantamount to predestination; this distinction is at the root of the confusions surrounding Sirach 33 (quoted above). That chapter — with its discussion of sacred and profane days, as compared to holy and sinful people — has been understood by some interpreters as an assertion of predestination.[26] This would then mean that Ben Sira's theology was either compatibilist or contradictory, as Sirach 15 (also quoted above) is rather clear in its assertion of free will.

The resolution of this difficulty is to be found in a careful re-reading of Sirach 33, which demonstrates that predestination is far from the sage's mind here. The juxtaposition of holy and profane days (vv. 7-9) with holy and cursed people (vv. 10-12) is not meant to suggest that God has determined in advance the actions of individual sinners. The juxtaposition, rather, serves to explain the nature of divine election: just as the Sabbath is holy among days, so too the Jewish people are holy among peoples.[27]

There is of course a deterministic element to the idea of divine election; people cannot choose to be born as Jews or Gentiles (though through conversion or apostasy people can possibly change their status). But whatever the element of determinism here, this passage hardly articulates ideas

---

26. See above notes 16 and 17.

27. For this understanding of Sirach, see Skehan and Di Lella, *The Wisdom of Ben Sira*, 395-401.

that *any* ancient Jews with some remaining fidelity to the covenants of Abraham and Moses would have found surprising or objectionable. Surely, practically all committed Jews — Sadducees and other fate-deniers included — believed that God had chosen Abraham and established a covenant that separated the Jewish people from the other nations. Nothing we find in Sirach 33 prevents reaching the conclusion that the sage was a firm believer in free will, just as Sirach 15 tells us. If Sirach 33 is predeterministic, then all ancient Jews become predeterminists. Indeed, this description may not be inherently incorrect, as it depends, after all, on how we define the terms. But if we define predeterminism in such a way that it becomes essentially synonymous with divine election, we gain nothing, and we lose the ability to draw the contrast between the book of Genesis and 1QS. In order to have analytic value, our definitions must be precise enough to allow for the contrasts between even Sirach 33 and 1QS, and between divine election (which practically all Jews believed) and predeterminism (which was likely the belief of the Dead Sea sect and Josephus's Essenes).

But we have also learned something by recognizing that an element of predestination can be found in the notion of divine election. Indeed, this is not the only ancient Jewish idea that contains within itself a small measure of determinism. The notion of prophecy, for instance, assumes an element of divine foreknowledge, at least as far as the predicted events are concerned (Isa 48:3-5):

> (3) The former things I declared long ago,
>> they went out from my mouth and I made them known;
>> then suddenly I did them and they came to pass. . . .
> (5) I declared them to you from long ago,
>> before they came to pass I announced them to you.

Indeed, even the most bare-bones Jewish eschatology — the simplest assertion that at the end of days the righteous will be rewarded and the wicked will be vanquished (e.g., Amos 9:9-15) — also assumes a modest degree of predeterminism. This element of predeterminism is not limited to biblical prophecy. A number of well-known biblical tales also assume that things proceed as they were destined to be. Joseph tells his brothers that the wicked act of selling him into slavery was part of a divine plan (Gen 45:5-8; 50:19-21). In the Exodus story, God hardens Pharaoh's heart (Exod 9:12; 10:1, 20, 27; 11:10; cf. 14:17), suggesting that the decisions of the wicked ruler are determined by God's will. Sayings of ancient Israel's wise sages also lead in this direction: "the human mind plans the way, but the Lord directs his steps" (Prov 16:9); "The lot is cast into the lap, but the decision is the Lord's alone" (16:33).

This is not to say, however, that the Hebrew Bible presents an unambiguous doctrine of predeterminism. In the immortal words of Shakespeare, "Even the devil can cite Scripture for his purpose" (Antonio in *Merchant of Venice,* I.iii.98). For every story like Joseph, there is one like Jonah, in which characters apparently choose to flout God's will. For every seemingly fixed prediction there are also calls for repentance, in the hopes of averting God's decree (e.g., Amos 5:14-15; Jonah 3:6-10). For every hardening of Pharaoh's heart, there is an assertion that Pharaoh hardened his own heart instead (Exod 7:13, 22; 8:15, 19, 32; 9:7, 34). For every proverbial assertion that God is behind the roll of the dice, there are other statements asserting that God detests evil and has nothing to do with it (e.g., Prov 6:16-19; 15:29).

The problem here is a natural one, and it extends from challenges inherent in the nature of monotheism. If we move in the direction of absolute free will, God's omniscience becomes limited (because his knowledge of future human choices is curtailed), his omnipotence is weakened (because he no longer controls human choice), and the inherent truth of prophecy is eliminated (because all is contingent on human decisions). If we move in the direction of absolute predestination, God becomes implicated in evil (by ordaining that some will sin) and can even be accused of being unjust (by punishing those he ordains to be evil).

Ancient Jewish theology is not alone in this respect. The conflict between fate and free will has dogged Christianity too throughout the ages. We cannot trace the history of this dispute here, though it is worth mentioning two well-known and widely available classics: Augustine's *City of God* and John Calvin's *Institutes of the Christian Religion.* To illustrate the issues at stake — and also the ways in which monotheism places limits on the extremes of the dispute — we will consider two rather clear, classic American treatments of the topic, both addressed not to scholars or theologians, but to the general educated (and Christian) public at large: William James's essay, "The Dilemma of Determinism," and Loraine Boettner's *The Reformed Doctrine of Predestination.*[28]

---

28. W. James, *The Will to Believe,* 145-83; L. Boettner, *The Reformed Doctrine of Predestination.*

William James (1842-1910) is a name that should be familiar to students of religion by virtue of his enduring classic, *The Varieties of Religious Experience*. His psychological and philosophical works may be familiar to students of those disciplines as well. In his day, he was a giant in all three fields as they were emerging then in the United States and Europe. In his "Dilemma of Determinism," we find a passionate defense of free will, based on both rational and moral grounds. How can all be predetermined when a thinking person struggles even to decide which road to take home on a given evening? And what kind of God would create a world in which acts of horror such as senseless murder are predetermined? For James, the reality of human freedom is dictated by these arguments.[29] He comes down so firmly on the side of human freedom that he dismisses out of hand the compromise positions he refers to as "soft determinism," or "free-will determinism," which are roughly equivalent to the compatibilism addressed above.[30] Indeed, an essential aspect of James's religiosity — expressed in the 1896 essay "The Will to Believe" — is rooted in the idea that the religious person can (and in his mind should) *choose* to believe.[31]

Yet in line with (a very liberal) Christianity, James affirms a belief in divine justice. The righteous can look forward to rewards in the afterworld and even some form of earthly eschatology. James therefore concludes his essay on determinism by leaving a small place for God's providence, foreknowledge, and ultimate control. He presents an analogy of a chess game between a master and a novice. Without knowing which moves the novice will make, the true master maintains, nonetheless, complete control of the game, modifying his own plan to bring about his victory. As far as the world is concerned, therefore, James states:[32]

> The creator's plan of the universe would thus be left blank as to many of its actual details, but all possibilities would be marked down. The realization of some would be left absolutely to chance. . . . Other possibilities would be *contingently* determined; that is their decision would have to wait till it was seen how the matters of absolute chance fell out. But the rest of the plan, including its final upshot, would be rigorously determined once for all. So the creator himself would not need to

29. James, *The Will to Believe*, 155-64.
30. James, *The Will to Believe*, 149; cf. Marcoulesco, "Free Will," 419.
31. James, *The Will to Believe*, 1-31.
32. James, *The Will to Believe*, 182.

know *all* the details of actuality until they came. . . . Of one thing, however, he might be certain: and that is that his world was safe, and that no matter how much it might zig-zag, he could surely bring it home at last.

So we find that even a most passionate defense of free agency allows for a modicum of predestination, if it is also to maintain a belief in an all-powerful God who will manifest his will on earth at some point in the future.[33]

And what of those who emphasize predestination — can we find, similarly, a measure of free will there? From the time of the Protestant Reformation, the staunchest defenders of predestination have been the Calvinists, represented in America in early days by the Puritans and today by, among others (and with differences), the Presbyterians and the Amish. Loraine Boettner's *The Reformed Doctrine of Predestination* can be taken as a rather conservative exposition of the Calvinist position, as it begins with a pointed polemic against those who downplay predestination by trying to find some degree of balance with free will.[34] Boettner then very clearly outlines the ingredients of the doctrine of predestination: divine sovereignty, omniscience, foreknowledge, and providence, which all come together to make predestination the inevitable outcome of pure monotheism.[35] In good Protestant fashion, each element of the belief is rooted in Scripture. God's sovereignty is seen, once again, in the Joseph story and in the phenomenon of prophecy. The denial of foreknowledge, according to Boettner, "reduces the prophecies of Scripture to shrewd guesses at best."[36] That God controls even chance events is seen in the Jonah story, where the lots fall on him (Jonah 1:7).[37] That God controls the acts of the wicked can be seen not only in the Joseph story, but in the necessary, predicted — but nonetheless evil — crucifixion of Jesus.[38]

But how then is divine justice maintained if all is foreordained, even the acts of the wicked? Here we find some striking parallels between the Calvinist doctrine and the theology of the Qumran sectarians. First, it is intriguing that in both systems we find a strong emphasis on what Calvinists

---

33. Libertarian philosophers also recognize limits to human freedom; see Pink, *Free Will*, 86-87, 104-15.

34. Boettner, *The Reformed Doctrine of Predestination*, 1-9.

35. Boettner, *The Reformed Doctrine of Predestination*, 13-53.

36. Boettner, *The Reformed Doctrine of Predestination*, 42.

37. Boettner, *The Reformed Doctrine of Predestination*, 31-32.

38. Boettner, *The Reformed Doctrine of Predestination*, 24, 37-38.

call "miserable humanity," which can be strikingly similar in effect to the self-deprecating stance expressed in some of the *Thanksgiving Hymns*.[39] The relevance of this notion for predestination is this: if one starts with the position that all human beings are inherently sinful by nature, then God is no longer implicated in evil by allowing or even predestining some people to sin. It is only by virtue of his mercy — or, as Christians call it, his grace — that anyone at all is destined to be righteous and thereby saved. The Calvinists and the Qumran sectarians both argue further that the reasons for all this remain, in part, mysterious. Although God allows and predestines evil, Calvinists would continue to deny that God is directly implicated in evil.[40] Evil people act in sinful ways completely of their own accord — though under the influence, perhaps, of Satan.[41] Yet they do so only in precisely the ways that God foreknew and ordained, and all this is a mystery beyond human understanding.[42] The sectarians similarly deny that God is directly complicit in evil: according to their literature, evil is blamed not on God, but on the powers of darkness that God tolerates in the present day, "in the mysteries of his understanding" (1QS 4:18).

And one final similarity remains: both systems allow for the smallest measure of free will. The Dead Sea sect, as we have seen above, speaks frequently of conversion and repentance — intimations that they believed that people for their own part had decisions to make, even though God had predetermined who would be righteous or sinful. Calvinists too allow for a modicum of free agency: human beings — sinful by their nature — freely choose which way to follow. But the results of these free decisions are not beyond God's control or profound foreknowledge.[43] It goes without saying — but is helpful to remember — that Calvinists, Puritans, and Presbyterians all accepted converts to their cause and prayed for repen-

---

39. See selections from 1QH quoted above — esp. 9:21-23, which juxtaposes the two issues; compare Boettner, *The Reformed Doctrine of Predestination*, 61-82. See also Calvin, *Institutes*, II.1.1-11; III.23.3. For an accessible and reliable English edition, see John Calvin, *Institutes of the Christian Religion*, ed. J. T. McNeill, trans. Ford Lewis Battles (Philadelphia: Westminster, 1960).

40. Boettner, *The Reformed Doctrine of Predestination*, 228-53 (cf. Calvin, *Institutes*, I.17.5; I.18.1-4; II.3.5; III.23.1-9).

41. Boettner, *The Reformed Doctrine of Predestination*, 232-33, 243 (cf. Calvin, *Institutes*, II.4.1-5).

42. Boettner, *The Reformed Doctrine of Predestination*, 228 (cf. Calvin, *Institutes*, I.16.9; II.2.18-22; III.21.1; III.24.14).

43. Boettner, *The Reformed Doctrine of Predestination*, 208-27 (cf. Calvin, *Institutes*, III.21.5).

tance from sin. One cannot point to the perceived reality of human decisions and assume those who claim to be determinists are either exaggerating or incorrect about their own beliefs.

It is also helpful to recall here an observation of Max Weber (1864-1920), who along with Émile Durkheim (1858-1917) was a founding father of the historical and sociological study of religion. Those who reject ideas of predestination often do so out of the concern that such a belief would lead to fatalism or resignation: if my fate is sealed, why should I even bother trying to be righteous? Yet to the contrary, the belief in predeterminism often has precisely the opposite effect, compelling believers to try harder, to repent of sins, and to change their ways, all in order to prove that they are of God's elect.[44] So predeterminism explicitly allows for a modicum of free choice, as even Calvinists admit. It also often works as a significant motivator — influencing the choices that believers make — as Weber has shown.

Although Calvinism and Qumran sectarian theology do not match up in all respects, the comparison has been illuminating. In both cases, God's unbounded knowledge is contrasted with human ignorance, with the result that aspects of the divine plan — despite revelation — remain a mystery. In both cases we also find that divine omnipotence is coupled with a notion of inherent human sinfulness, with the result that redemption for the chosen few comes primarily — indeed exclusively — from divine mercy. Moreover, in both cases, God is not deemed directly culpable for the evil predestined to occur. The sectarians remove God from evil by asserting the time-bound existence of the powers of Belial. Beside the allowance for Satan, Calvinists also remove God from evil by asserting that God's absolute predestination does not preclude the free agency of sinners — even though their free decisions are preordained and foreknown. This particular piece of the puzzle is not as thoroughly spelled out in the scrolls. But the sectarians too believed that people for their own part had decisions to make, even if God ordained long ago whether they were allotted to light or darkness. This does not mean, however, that these groups were compatibilists. After all, if neither Calvinists nor the Dead Sea sectarians were predeterministic, then which monotheists ever were? What we have learned, rather, is that theological determinism isn't as extreme as its philosophical counterpart. Monotheism by its nature puts limits on the extremes of the disputes about fate and free will.

---

44. M. Weber, *The Protestant Ethic and the Spirit of Capitalism*, 98-128; cf. Weber, *The Sociology of Religion*, 143-44.

Conclusions

What have we learned about the conflict between fate and free will? What have we learned about ancient Jewish theology? And how has religious studies aided us in understanding the Dead Sea Scrolls? The first thing we have learned is that the conflict between determinism and free will was a real one. Josephus should be taken at his word when he says these issues were disputed among ancient Jews, as this claim is backed up by the polemical nature of Sirach 15 as well as the unmistakable differences between Sirach and 1QS. Moreover, the comparison with later Christianity supports this case too: disputes about fate and free will played out similarly in subsequent Christian history, as we have seen.

But even as we confirm the basic historical reality of the disputes that Josephus describes, we must also conclude that Josephus has hardly presented these disputes in their true complexity. Rather, Josephus has exaggerated the case at each margin. It is highly unlikely that the Sadducees denied that any event could be brought about by fate. Surely the Sadducees believed in divine election (just as we find also in Sirach 33), and surely they believed that biblical prophets had successfully predicted some events, as any believing reader of the Tanakh would be forced to grant. At the other end of the spectrum, surely the Essenes and Dead Sea sectarians allowed for a modicum of free agency. The group(s) accepted converts, prayed for repentance, and struggled against sin in their own daily lives. So Josephus's typology is like that overly-simplified introductory religious studies textbook. We can use it as a guideline, but we must recognize its limitations.

Still we must avoid the tendency to move back from Josephus's typology and describe most ancient Jewish literature as compatibilist. If we do this, we've simply erased all distinctions and overlooked the evidence that tells us that these disputes were real. We must similarly resist the tendency to dismiss Sirach or the sectarian scrolls as internally inconsistent. To say that the biblical tradition, on which both Sirach and the Dead Sea sect rely, is contradictory is to say very little, because of course the Hebrew Bible is an expansive anthology of composite works, edited and redacted over a great length of time. To assert, however, that either the Qumran sectarian literature or Sirach is contradictory is to avoid the task at hand. These texts exhibit the effort to work out consistent theologies. It remains our responsibility to struggle with these documents long enough to see if we can make sense of them.

When we do so, we find that despite the exaggerations, Josephus provides a helpful guide into these disputes. At one side stand the Sadducees (and Ben Sira). They emphasize freedom of choice to whatever degree their monotheism will allow. Without denying divine election, prophecy, or eschatology, they assert that responsibility for evil rests entirely on those who freely choose to act in evil ways. God does not destine anyone to be sinful, and God is thereby removed from responsibility for evil. On the other side stand Josephus's Essenes and their ostensible compatriots, the Qumran sectarians. While allowing for the reality of human decision — including over such weighty matters as repentance and conversion — they place a great emphasis on divine omniscience and omnipotence, to the extent that all is predetermined, even the decisions that human beings will (and should) freely make. For the Dead Sea sectarians, moreover, God is further removed from evil by the mysterious and temporary permission given to the powers of darkness to lead the wicked astray.

In understanding all of this, we were aided not only by careful definitions and some patient re-reading, but also by comparative material easily accessible to students and teachers of religious studies. The ancient Jewish debates share much with later Christian ones, and examining both together highlights the restrictions that monotheistic theologies operate under when considering (or striking a balance between) determinism and freedom of choice. Does God know in advance what people will choose to do? Has God given over part of his powers to dark forces that compel weaker people to sin? Or is God entirely uninvolved in human sin? Is his foreknowledge therefore at least somewhat reduced? Just as these were real disputes for later Christians, so too were these real disputes among ancient Jews, and we will do well to examine carefully all of the Dead Sea Scrolls — and indeed, all ancient Jewish literature — with these questions in mind.

Bibliography

From *Discoveries in the Judaean Desert*

Discoveries in the Judaean Desert (Oxford: Clarendon, 1955-).

DJD 1   Dominique Barthélemy and J. T. Milik, eds. *Qumran Cave 1.* Oxford: Clarendon, 1955.

DJD 2, 2A   Pierre Benoit, J. T. Milik, and Roland de Vaux, eds. *Les grottes de Murabba'ât.* 2 vols. Oxford: Clarendon, 1961.

DJD 3   Maurice Baillet, J. T. Milik, and Roland de Vaux, O.P., eds. *Les "Petites Grottes" de Qumrân. Exploration de la falaise. Les grottes 2Q, 3Q, 5Q, 6Q, 7Q à 10Q. Le rouleau de cuivre.* Oxford: Clarendon, 1962.

DJD 4   James A. Sanders, ed. *The Psalms Scroll of Qumrân Cave 11 (11QPsᵃ).* Oxford: Clarendon, 1965.

DJD 5   John M. Allegro, ed., with the collaboration of Arnold A. Anderson. *Qumrân Cave 4:1 (4Q158-186).* Oxford: Clarendon, 1968.

DJD 7   Maurice Baillet, ed. *Qumrân Grotte 4:III (4Q482-4Q520).* Oxford: Clarendon, 1982.

DJD 9   Patrick W. Skehan, Eugene Ulrich, and Judith E. Sanderson, eds. *Qumran Cave 4:IV, Paleo-Hebrew and Greek Biblical Manuscripts.* Oxford: Clarendon, 1992.

DJD 13   Harold Attridge et al., eds., in consultation with James C. VanderKam. *Qumran Cave 4:VIII, Parabiblical Texts, Part 1.* Oxford: Clarendon, 1994.

DJD 18   Joseph M. Baumgarten, ed. *Qumran Cave 4:XIII, The Damascus Document (4Q266-273).* Oxford: Clarendon, 1996.

DJD 21   Shemaryahu Talmon, Jonathan Ben-Dov, and Uwe Glessmer, eds. *Qumran Cave 4:XVI, Calendrical Texts.* Oxford: Clarendon, 2001.

DJD 23   Florentino García Martínez, Eibert J. C. Tigchelaar, and A. S. van der Woude, eds. *Qumran Cave 11:II: 11Q2-18, 11Q20-31.* Oxford: Clarendon, 1998.

DJD 26   Philip S. Alexander and Geza Vermes, eds. *Qumran Cave 4:XIX, Serekh Ha-Yahad and Two Related Texts.* Oxford: Clarendon, 1998.

DJD 27   Hannah M. Cotton and Ada Yardeni, eds. *Aramaic, Hebrew and Greek Documentary Texts from Nahal Hever and Other Sites, with an Appendix Containing Alleged Qumran Texts (The Seiyâl Collection).* Oxford: Clarendon, 1997.

DJD 33   Dana M. Pike and Andrew C. Skinner, eds. *Qumran Cave 4:XXIII, Unidentified Fragments.* Oxford: Clarendon, 2001.

DJD 35   Joseph M. Baumgarten et al., eds. *Qumran Cave 4:XXV, Halakhic Texts.* Oxford: Clarendon, 1999.

DJD 36   Stephen J. Pfann, *Cryptic Texts,* and Philip Alexander et al., eds., *Miscellanea, Part 1: Qumran Cave 4:XXVI.* Oxford: Clarendon, 2000.

DJD 39   Emanuel Tov, et al., eds. *The Texts from the Judaean Desert: Indices and an Introduction to the* Discoveries in the Judaean Desert *Series.* Oxford: Clarendon, 2002.

Methods and Theories

Abrams, Dominic, and Michael A. Hogg, eds. *Social Identity Theory: Constructive and Critical Advances.* New York: Springer, 1990.

Adam, A. K. M., ed. *Handbook of Postmodern Biblical Interpretation.* St. Louis: Chalice, 2000.

Austin, J. L. *How To Do Things with Words.* William James Lectures 1955. Cambridge, MA: Harvard University Press, 1962.

Bell, Catherine. *Ritual: Perspectives and Dimensions.* Oxford: Oxford University Press, 1997.

———. *Ritual Theory, Ritual Practice.* Oxford: Oxford University Press, 1992.

Bitzer, Lloyd F. "The Rhetorical Situation." *Philosophy and Rhetoric* 1 (1968) 1-14.

Black, Edwin. *Rhetorical Criticism: A Study in Method.* Madison: University of Wisconsin Press, 1978.

Boettner, Loraine. *The Reformed Doctrine of Predestination.* Phillipsburg, NJ: Presbyterian and Reformed, 1932.

Bolle, Kees W. "Fate." *ER,* 5:290-97.

Burke, Kenneth. *On Symbols and Society.* Ed. Joseph R. Gusfield. Chicago: University of Chicago Press, 1989.

——. *A Rhetoric of Motives.* Berkeley: University of California Press, 1969.

——. "Synthetic Freedom." *New Republic* 89 (20 January 1937) 364.

Christ, Carol P. "Mircea Eliade and the Feminist Paradigm Shift." *JFSR* 7 (1991) 75-94.

Chwe, Michael Suk-Young. *Rational Ritual: Culture, Coordination, and Common Knowledge.* Princeton: Princeton University Press, 2001.

Condor, Susan. "Social Identity and Time." In Robinson, *Social Groups and Identities,* 285-315.

Conrad, C. "Social History." In *International Encyclopedia of the Social & Behavioral Sciences,* ed. Neil J. Smelser and Paul B. Baltes, 21:14299-306. Amsterdam: Elsevier, 2001.

Cunningham, Lawrence S., and John Kelsay. *The Sacred Quest: An Invitation to the Study of Religion.* 5th ed. Upper Saddle River: Prentice Hall, 2010.

Deutsch, David. *The Fabric of Reality: The Science of Parallel Universes — and Its Implications.* London: Penguin, 1997.

Dozois, Gardner, and Stanley Schmidt, eds. *Roads Not Taken: Tales of Alternate History.* New York: Del Ray, 1998.

Eliade, Mircea, ed. *The Encyclopedia of Religion.* 16 vols. New York: Macmillan, 1987.

Ferguson, Niall, ed. *Virtual History: Alternatives and Counterfactuals.* London: Picador, 1997.

Fitzgerald, Timothy. *The Ideology of Religious Studies.* New York: Oxford University Press, 2000.

Fogel, Robert. *Railroads and American Economic Growth: Essays in Econometric History.* Baltimore: Johns Hopkins University Press, 1964.

Geertz, Clifford. "Thick Description: Toward an Interpretive Theory of Culture." In *The Interpretation of Cultures,* 3-30. New York: Basic Books, 1973.

Hawthorne, Geoffrey. *Plausible Worlds: Possibility and Understanding in History and the Social Sciences.* Cambridge: Cambridge University Press, 1991.

Heath, Robert L. *Realism and Relativism: A Perspective on Kenneth Burke.* Macon: Mercer University Press, 1986.

James, William. *The Will to Believe, and Other Essays in Popular Philosophy.* New York: Dover, 1956.

Kreinrath, Jens, Jan Snoek, and Michael Stausberg, eds. *Theorizing Rituals: Classical Topics, Theoretical Approaches, Analytical Concepts.* SHR 114. Leiden: Brill, 2006.

Lebow, Richard Ned. "What's So Different about a Counterfactual?" *World Politics* 52 (2000) 550-85.

Levi, Giovanni. "On Microhistory." In *New Perspectives on Historical Writing,* ed. Peter Burke, 93-113. Cambridge: Polity, 1991.

McCann, Carole R., and Seung-Kyung Kim, eds. *Feminist Theory Reader: Local and Global Perspectives.* 2nd ed. New York: Routledge, 2010.

McCutcheon, Russell T. *Manufacturing Religion: The Discourse on Sui Generis Religion and the Politics of Nostalgia.* New York: Oxford University Press, 1997.

————, ed. *The Insider/Outsider Problem in the Study of Religion: A Reader.* London: Cassell, 1999.

MacKay, Bradley. "Counterfactual Reasoning in Strategy Context." Diss., St. Andrews, 2004.

Marcoulesco, Ileana. "Free Will and Determinism." *ER*, 5:419-21.

Mudge, Mark, Michael Ashley, and Carla Schroer. "A Digital Future for Cultural Heritage." http://www.c-h-i.org/events/CIPA_2007.pdf.

Pink, Thomas. *Free Will: A Very Short Introduction.* Oxford: Oxford University Press, 2004.

Robinson, W. Peter., ed. *Social Groups and Identities: Developing the Legacy of Henri Tajfel.* Oxford: Butterworth-Heinemann, 1996.

Schmunck, Robert B. Uchronia. http://www.uchronia.net/

Scott, Joan Wallach. *Gender and the Politics of History.* Rev. ed. New York: Columbia University Press, 1999.

Smith, Jonathan Z. "'Narratives into Problems': The College Introductory Course and the Study of Religion." *JAAR* 56 (1988) 727-39.

Squire, J. C., ed. *If It Had Happened Otherwise.* 2nd ed.. London: Sidgwick & Jackson, 1972. 1st ed. *If; or, History Rewritten.* New York: Viking, 1931.

Stark, Rodney, and William Sims Bainbridge. *The Future of Religion: Secularization, Revival, and Cult Formation.* Berkeley: University of California Press, 1985.

————. *A Theory of Religion.* Toronto Studies in Religion 2. New York: Lang, 1987.

Tajfel, Henri, ed. *Differentiation between Social Groups: Studies in the Social Psychology of Intergroup Relations.* London: Academic, 1978.

Taylor, Mark C., ed. *Critical Terms for Religious Studies.* Chicago: University of Chicago Press, 1998.

Tetlock, Philip E., and Aaron Belkin, eds., *Counterfactual Thought Experiments in World Politics: Logical, Methodological, and Psychological Perspectives.* Princeton: Princeton University Press, 1996.

Turner, John C. "Henri Tajfel: An Introduction." In Robinson, *Social Groups and Identities*, 1-24.

————, and Richard Y. Bourhis. "Social Identity, Interdependence and the Social Group: A Reply to Rabbie *et al.*" In Robinson, *Social Groups and Identities*, 25-63.

Turtledove, Harry, with Martin H. Greenberg, eds. *The Best Alternate History Stories of the 20th Century.* New York: Del Ray, 2001.

Vatz, Richard E. "The Myth of the Rhetorical Situation." In *Contemporary Rhetorical Theory*, ed. John Louis Lucaites, Celeste Michelle Condit, and Sally Caudill, 226-31. New York: Guilford, 1999.

Vinikas, Vincent. *Soft Soap, Hard Sell: American Hygiene in an Age of Advertisement*. Ames: Iowa State University Press, 1992.

Wallace, Dewey D., Jr. "Free Will and Predestination." *ER*, 422-27.

Weber, Max. *The Protestant Ethic and the Spirit of Capitalism*. Trans. Talcott Parsons. London: Routledge, 1992 (German ed. 1904-5).

―――. *The Sociology of Religion*. Trans. Ephraim Fischoff. Boston: Beacon, 1963 (German ed. 1922).

White, James Boyd. *When Words Lose Their Meaning: Constitutions and Reconstitutions of Language, Character, and Community*. Chicago: University of Chicago Press, 1994.

Wilson, Bryan R. *Magic and the Millennium: A Sociological Study of Religious Movements of Protest among Tribal and Third-World Peoples*. London: Heinemann, 1973.

―――. *Religion in Sociological Perspective*. Oxford: Oxford University Press, 1982.

―――. *The Social Dimensions of Sectarianism: Sects and New Religious Movements in Contemporary Society*. Oxford: Clarendon, 1990.

Scrolls, Scriptures, and Related Studies

Abegg, Martin G. "A Concordance of Proper Nouns in the Non-Biblical Texts from Qumran." DJD 39, 229-84.

―――. "The Hebrew of the Dead Sea Scrolls." In Flint and VanderKam, *The Dead Sea Scrolls after Fifty Years*, 1:325-58.

―――. *Qumran Sectarian Manuscripts: Qumran Text and Grammatical Tags*. Accordance QUMRAN, version 2.8. Altamonte Springs, FL: OakTree Software, 2006.

Albani, Matthias. *Astronomie und Schöpfungsglaube: Untersuchungen zum astronomischen Henochbuch*. WMANT 68. Neukirchen-Vluyn: Neukirchener, 1994.

―――. "Die lunaren Zyklen im 364-Tage-Festkalendar von 4QMischmerot/ 4QS^c." Kirchliche Hochschule Leipzig *Forschungsstelle Judentum, Mitteilungen und Beiträge* 4 (1992) 28-43.

Alexander, Philip S. "The Redaction-History of *Serekh ha-Yaḥad*: A Proposal." *RevQ* 17 (1996) 437-53.

―――. "Rules." *EDSS*, 2:800.

Allegro, John M. "'The Wiles of the Wicked Woman': A Sapiential Work from Qumran's Fourth Cave." *PEQ* 96 (1964) 53-55, Pl. XIII.

Avigad, Nahman. "The Palaeography of the Dead Sea Scrolls and Related Documents." In Rabin and Yadin, *Aspects of the Dead Sea Scrolls*, 56-87.

Barkay, Gabriel, Andrew G. Vaughn, Marilyn J. Lundberg, and Bruce Zuckerman.

"The Amulets from Ketef Hinnom: A New Edition and Evaluation." *BASOR* 334 (2004) 41-71.

————, Marilyn J. Lundberg, Andrew G. Vaughn, Bruce Zuckerman, and Kenneth Zuckerman. "The Challenges of Ketef Hinnom: Using Advanced Technologies to Reclaim the Earliest Biblical Texts and Their Context." *NEA* 66 (2003) 162-71.

Barton, John. "Redaction Criticism: Old Testament." *ABD*, 5:644-47.

————. "Source Criticism: Old Testament." *ABD*, 6:162-65.

Baumgarten, Albert I. *The Flourishing of Jewish Sects in the Maccabean Era: An Interpretation.* JSJSup 55. Leiden: Brill, 1997.

————. "Who Cares and Why Does it Matter? Qumran and the Essenes Once Again." *DSD* 11 (2004) 174-90.

————. "The Zadokite Priests at Qumran: A Reconsideration." *DSD* 4 (1997) 137-56.

Baumgarten, Joseph M. "The Cave 4 Versions of the Qumran Penal Code." *JJS* 43 (1992) 268-76.

————. "On the Testimony of Women in 1QSa." *JBL* 76 (1957) 266-69.

————. "4Q502, Marriage or Golden Age Ritual?" *JJS* 34 (1983) 125-35.

Bejon, Jane Elizabeth. "A Study of the Recensional Position, the Style and the Translation Technique of the Syriac Translation of Judith." Diss., Sheffield, 1976.

Bernstein, Moshe J. "Introductory Formulas for Citation and Re-citation of Biblical Verses in the Qumran Pesharim: Observations on the Pesher Technique." *DSD* 1 (1994) 30-70.

————. "Pentateuchal Interpretation at Qumran." In Flint and VanderKam, *The Dead Sea Scrolls after Fifty Years,* 1:128-59.

————. "Pesher Psalms." *EDSS*, 2:656.

————, and D. R. Schwartz. "Damascus Document (CD)." In *Damascus Document, War Scroll, and Related Documents,* 4-57. PTSDSSP 2. Tübingen: Mohr Siebeck and Louisville: Westminster John Knox, 1995.

Berrin, Shani L. *The Pesher Nahum Scroll from Qumran: An Exegetical Study of 4Q169.* STDJ 53. Leiden: Brill, 2004.

Betz, Otto. *Offenbarung und Schriftforschung in der Qumransekte.* WUNT 6. Tübingen: Mohr, 1960.

Brock, Sebastian P. "Syriac and Greek Hymnography: Problems of Origin." In *Studies in Syriac Christianity: History, Literature and Theology,* 77-81. Aldershot: Variorum, 1992.

Brooke, George J. "The Qumran Scrolls and the Demise of the Distinction Between Higher and Lower Criticism." In Campbell, Lyons, and Pietersen, *New Directions in Qumran Studies,* 26-42.

————. "The Rewritten Law, Prophets and Psalms: Issues for Understanding the Text of the Bible." In Herbert and Tov, *The Bible as Book,* 31-40.

Brooten, Bernadette. "Early Christian Women and Their Cultural Context: Issues of Method in Historical Reconstruction." In *Feminist Perspectives on Biblical Scholarship,* ed. Adela Yarbro Collins, 66-91. SBLBSNA 10. Chico: Scholars, 1985.

Bruce, F. F. *Biblical Exegesis in the Qumran Texts.* Grand Rapids: Wm. B. Eerdmans, 1959.

Campbell, Jonathan G., William John Lyons, and Lloyd K. Pietersen, eds. *New Directions in Qumran Studies.* LSTS 52. London: T. & T. Clark, 2005.

Cancik, Hubert, Hermann Lichtenberger, and Peter Schäfer, eds. *Geschichte — Tradition — Reflexion: Festschrift für Martin Hengel zum 70. Geburtstag.* 3 vols. Tübingen: Mohr Siebeck, 1996.

Carmignac, Jean. "Poème allégorique sur la secte rivale." *RevQ* 5 (1965) 361-74.

Carr, David M. *Writing on the Tablet of the Heart: Origins of Scripture and Literature.* Oxford: Oxford University Press, 2005.

Chalcraft, David J., ed. *Sectarianism in Early Judaism: Sociological Advances.* London: Equinox, 2007.

Chambon, Alain. "Catalogue des blocs d'architecture localisés ou erratiques." In Humbert and Gunneweg, *Khirbet Qumran et 'Ain Feshkha II,* 445-65.

Charlesworth, James H. "John the Baptizer and the Dead Sea Scrolls." In *The Bible and the Dead Sea Scrolls,* 3: *The Scrolls and Christian Origins,* 1-35.

———. *The Odes of Solomon: The Syriac Texts.* SBLTT 13. SBLPS 7. Missoula: Scholars, 1977.

———. *Papyri and Leather Manuscripts of the Odes of Solomon.* Dickerson Series of Facsimiles of Manuscripts Important for Christian Origins 1. Durham: International Center for the Study of Ancient Near Eastern Civilizations and Christian Origins, Duke University, 1981.

———, ed. *The Bible and the Dead Sea Scrolls.* 3 vols. Waco: Baylor University Press, 2006.

———, et al., eds. *The Dead Sea Scrolls: Hebrew, Aramaic, and Greek Texts with English Translations.* Vol. 1: *Rule of the Community and Related Documents.* PTSDSSP 1. Tübingen: Mohr Siebeck and Louisville: Westminster John Knox, 1994.

———. Vol. 2: *Damascus Document, War Scroll, and Related Documents.* PTSDSSP 2. Tübingen: Mohr Siebeck and Louisville: Westminster John Knox, 1995.

Collins, John J. *Apocalypticism in the Dead Sea Scrolls.* The Literature of the Dead Sea Scrolls 1. London: Routledge, 1997.

———, and Robert A. Kugler, eds. *Religion in the Dead Sea Scrolls.* SDSSRL. Grand Rapids: Wm. B. Eerdmans, 2000.

Crawford, Sidnie White. "Not According to Rule: Women, the Dead Sea Scrolls and Qumran." In *Emanuel: Studies in Hebrew Bible, Septuagint, and Dead Sea Scrolls in Honor of Emanuel Tov,* ed. Shalom M. Paul, et al., 127-50. VTSup 94. Leiden: Brill, 2003.

————. *Rewriting Scripture in Second Temple Times.* SDSSRL. Grand Rapids: Wm. B. Eerdmans, 2008.

Crenshaw, James L. *Old Testament Wisdom: An Introduction.* 3rd ed. Louisville: Westminster John Knox, 2010.

Cross, Frank Moore. *The Ancient Library of Qumran and Modern Biblical Studies.* Garden City: Doubleday, 1958; 2nd ed., 1961.

————. "The Development of the Jewish Scripts." In *The Bible and the Ancient Near East: Essays in Honor of William Foxwell Albright,* ed. G. Ernest Wright, 133-202. Garden City: Doubleday, 1965.

————. "The Evolution of a Theory of Local Texts." In *1972 Proceedings of the International Organization for Septuagint and Cognate Studies,* ed. Robert A. Kraft, 108-26. SBLSCS 2. Missoula: Scholars, 1972. Repr. in Cross and Talmon, *Qumran and the History of the Biblical Text,* 306-20.

————. "Palaeography and the Dead Sea Scrolls." In Flint and VanderKam, *The Dead Sea Scrolls after Fifty Years,* 1:379-402.

————, and Esther Eshel. "Ostraca from Khirbet Qumran." *IEJ* 47 (1997) 17-28.

————, and Shemaryahu Talmon, eds. *Qumran and the History of the Biblical Text.* Cambridge, MA: Harvard University Press, 1975.

Davies, Philip R. *The Damascus Covenant: An Interpretation of the "Damascus Document."* JSOTSup 25. Sheffield: JSOT, 1983.

————. "Halakhah at Qumran." In *A Tribute to Géza Vermès: Essays on Jewish and Christian Literature and History,* ed. Davies and Richard T. White, 37-50. JSOTSup 100. Sheffield: JSOT, 1990.

————. "Sects from Texts: On the Problems of Doing a Sociology of the Qumran Literature." In Campbell, Lyons, and Pietersen, *New Directions in Qumran Studies,* 69-82.

————, and Joan E. Taylor. "On the Testimony of Women in 1QSa." *DSD* 3 (1996) 223-35.

Davila, James R. *The Provenance of the Pseudepigrapha: Jewish, Christian, or Other?* JSJSup 105. Leiden: Brill, 2005.

Dimant, Devorah. "The Qumran Manuscripts: Contents and Significance." In *Time to Prepare the Way in the Wilderness: Papers on the Qumran Scrolls by Fellows of the Institute for Advanced Studies of the Hebrew University, Jerusalem, 1989-1990,* ed. Dimant and Lawrence H. Schiffman, 23-58. STDJ 16. Leiden: Brill, 1995.

Donceel-Voûte, Pauline. "Les ruines de Qumran réinterprétées." *Archéologia* 298 (1994) 24-35.

Doudna, Gregory L. "Dating the Scrolls on the Basis of Radiocarbon Analysis." In Flint and VanderKam, *The Dead Sea Scrolls after Fifty Years,* 1:430-71.

————. "The Legacy of an Error in Archaeological Interpretation: The Dating of the Qumran Cave Scroll Deposits." In Galor, Humbert, and Zangenberg, *Qumran, The Site of the Dead Sea Scrolls,* 147-57.

Duhaime, Jean. "Determinism." *EDSS*, 1:194-98.

———. "L'instruction sur les deux esprits et les interpolations dualistes à Qumran (1QS III,13-IV,26)." *RB* 84 (1977) 566-94.

———. *The War Texts: 1QM and Related Manuscripts*. CQS 6. London: T. & T. Clark, 2004.

Eisenman, Robert H., and James M. Robinson, eds. *A Facsimile Edition of the Dead Sea Scrolls: Prepared with an Introduction and Index*. 2 vols. Washington: Biblical Archaeology Society, 1991.

———, and Michael O. Wise, eds. *The Dead Sea Scrolls Uncovered: The First Complete Translation and Interpretation of 50 Key Documents Withheld for Over 35 Years*. Shaftesbury: Element, 1992.

Epstein, Isidore. *The Babylonian Talmud*. 35 vols. London: Soncino, 1935-1948.

Eshel, Esther. "*4Q471*[b]: A Self-Glorification Hymn." *RevQ* 17 (1996) 175-203.

Eshel, Hanan, and Ze'ev Safrai. "Economic Life." *EDSS*, 1:228-33.

Fagan, Brian M., ed. *The Oxford Companion to Archaeology*. New York: Oxford University Press, 1996.

Fitzmyer, Joseph A. *The Genesis Apocryphon of Qumran Cave 1 (1Q20): A Commentary*. 3rd ed. BibOr 19A. Rome: Pontifical Biblical Institute, 2004.

Flint, Peter W. *The Dead Sea Psalms Scrolls and the Book of Psalms*. STDJ 17. Leiden: Brill, 1997.

———, and James C. VanderKam, eds. *The Dead Sea Scrolls after Fifty Years: A Comprehensive Assessment*. 2 vols. Leiden: Brill, 1998-99.

Freedman, David Noel, ed. *The Anchor Bible Dictionary*. 6 vols. New York: Doubleday, 1992.

Galor, Katharina, Jean-Baptiste Humbert, and Jürgen Zangenberg, eds. *Qumran, The Site of the Dead Sea Scrolls: Archaeological Interpretations and Debates*. STDJ 57. Leiden: Brill, 2006.

García Martínez, Florentino. "Calendarios en Qumran (I)." *EstBib* 54 (1996) 327-48.

———, and Mladen Popović, eds. *Defining Identities: "We," "You" and "the Others" in the Dead Sea Scrolls*. STDJ 70. Leiden: Brill, 2007.

———, and Eibert J. C. Tigchelaar. *The Dead Sea Scrolls Study Edition*. 2 vols. Leiden: Brill and Grand Rapids: Wm. B. Eerdmans, 1997.

———, and J. Trebolle Barrera. *The People of the Dead Sea Scrolls*. Trans. W. G. E. Watson. Leiden: Brill, 1995.

———, and A. S. van der Woude. "A 'Groningen' Hypothesis of Qumran Origins and Early History." *RevQ* 14 (1990) 521-41.

Gigante, Marcello. *Philodemus in Italy: The Books from Herculaneum*. Trans. Dirk Obbink. Ann Arbor: University of Michigan Press, 1995.

Glessmer, Uwe. "Calendars in the Qumran Scrolls." In Flint and VanderKam, *The Dead Sea Scrolls After Fifty Years*, 2:213-78.

———. *Die ideale Kultordnung: 24 Priesterordnungen in den Chronikbüchern, den kalendarischen Qumrantexten und in synagogalen Inschriften.* Habilitation, Hamburg, 1995.

―――. "Investigation of the Otot-text [4Q319] and Questions about Methodology." In Wise et al., *Methods of Investigation of the Dead Sea Scrolls and the Khirbet Qumran Site,* 429-40.

―――. "Der 364-Tage-Kalendar und die Sabbatstruktur seiner Schaltungen in ihrer Bedeutung für den Kult." In *Ernten, was man sät: Festschrift Klaus Koch zu seinem 65. Geburtstag,* ed. Dwight R. Daniels, Uwe Glessmer, and Martin Rösel, 379-98. Neukirchen-Vluyn: Neukircherner, 1991.

Golb, Norman. *Who Wrote the Dead Sea Scrolls?* New York: Scribner, 1995.

Goshen-Gottstein, Moshe H. "The Psalms Scroll (11QPs^a): A Problem of Canon and Text." *Textus* 5 (1966) 22-33.

Grossman, Maxine L. "From Text to History: Some Methodological Observations." http://www.st-andrews.ac.uk/divinity/grossman_lecture_05.html.

―――. "Reading for Gender in the Damascus Document." *DSD* 11 (2004) 212-39.

―――. *Reading for History in the Damascus Document: A Methodological Study.* STDJ 45. Leiden: Brill, 2002. Repr. Atlanta: SBL, 2009.

―――, and Catherine M. Murphy, eds. "The Dead Sea Scrolls in the Popular Imagination." *DSD* 12 (2005).

Gunkel, Hermann, *Die Psalmen übersetzt und erklärt.* HAT. 6th ed. Göttingen: Vandenhoeck & Ruprecht, 1989.

Haines-Eitzen, Kim. *Guardians of Letters: Literacy, Power, and the Transmitters of Early Christian Literature.* Oxford: Oxford University Press, 2000.

Hakola, Raimo. "Social Identities and Group Phenomena in Second Temple Judaism." In *Explaining Christian Origins and Early Judaism: Contributions from Cognitive and Social Science,* ed. Petri Luomanen, Ilkka Pyysiäinen, and Risto Uro, 259-76. Biblical Interpretation 89. Leiden: Brill, 2007.

Harris, William V. *Ancient Literacy.* Cambridge, MA: Harvard University Press, 1989.

Hauptman, Judith. *Rereading the Rabbis: A Woman's Voice.* Boulder: Westview, 1998.

Hempel, Charlotte. *The Damascus Texts.* CQS 1. Sheffield: Sheffield Academic, 2000.

―――. "The Earthly Essene Nucleus of 1QSa." *DSD* 3 (1996) 253-67.

―――. "Emerging Communal Life and Ideology in the S Tradition." In García Martínez and Popović, *Defining Identities,* 43-61.

―――. *The Laws of the Damascus Document: Sources, Tradition, and Redaction.* STDJ 29. Leiden: Brill, 1998. Repr. Atlanta: SBL, 2006.

―――. "The Literary Development of the S Tradition — A New Paradigm." *RevQ* 22 (2006) 389-401.

―――. "The Penal Code Reconsidered." In *Legal Texts and Legal Issues: Proceedings of the Second Meeting of the International Organization for Qumran*

Studies, Published in Honour of Joseph M. Baumgarten, ed. Moshe Bernstein, Florentino García Martínez, and John Kampen, 337-48. STDJ 23. Leiden: Brill, 1997.

————. "Vielgestaltigkeit und Verbindlichkeit: Serekh ha-Yachad in Qumran." In *Qumran und der biblische Kanon,* ed. Jörg Frey and Michael Becker. Biblisch-Theologische Studien 92. Neukirchen: Neukirchener Verlag, forthcoming.

Hendel, Ronald. "The Oxford Hebrew Bible: Prologue to a New Critical Edition." *VT* 58 (2008) 324-51.

Hengel, Martin. *Judaism and Hellenism: Studies in Their Encounter in Palestine during the Early Hellenistic Period.* Trans. John Bowden. Minneapolis: Fortress, 1974.

Herbert, Edward D., and Emanuel Tov, eds. *The Bible as Book: The Hebrew Bible and the Judaean Desert Discoveries.* London: British Library and New Castle: Oak Knoll in association with Grand Haven: Scriptorium, 2002.

Hezser, Catherine. *Jewish Literacy in Roman Palestine.* TSAJ 81. Tübingen: Mohr Siebeck, 2001.

Hirschfeld, Yizhar. *Qumran in Context: Reassessing the Archaeological Evidence.* Peabody: Hendrickson, 2004.

Hopkins, Keith. "Christian Number and Its Implication." *JECS* 6 (1998) 185-226.

Horgan, Maurya P., and Paul J. Kobelski. "The Hodayot (1QH) and New Testament Poetry." In *To Touch the Text: Biblical and Related Studies in Honor of Joseph A. Fitzmyer, S.J.,* 179-93. New York: Crossroad, 1989.

Horsley, Richard A. "The Dead Sea Scrolls and the Historical Jesus." In Charlesworth, *The Bible and the Dead Sea Scrolls,* 3: *The Scrolls and Christian Origins,* 37-60.

Hossfeld, Frank-Lothar, and Erich Zenger. *Die Psalmen: Psalm 1-50.* NEchtB 29. Würzburg: Echter, 1993.

Howard, George. "Frank Cross and Recensional Criticism." *VT* 21 (1971) 440-50.

Humbert, Jean-Baptiste, and Alain Chambon, eds. *The Excavations of Khirbet Qumran and Ain Feshkha: Synthesis of Roland de Vaux's Field Notes.* Trans. and rev. Stephen J. Pfann. NTOA Series Archaeologica 1B. Fribourg: University and Göttingen: Vandenhoeck & Ruprecht, 2003.

————. *Fouilles de Khirbet Qumrân et de Ain Feshkha I.* NTOA Series Archaeologica 1. Fribourg: Editions Universitaires and Göttingen: Vandenhoeck & Ruprecht, 1994.

Humbert, Jean-Baptiste, and Jan Gunneweg. *Khirbet Qumran et 'Ain Feshkha II.* NTOA Series Archaeologica 2. Fribourg: Academic and Göttingen: Vandenhoeck & Ruprecht, 2003.

Ilan, Tal. "Appendix: The Dead Sea Sect." In *Integrating Women into Second Temple History,* 38-42. TSAJ 76. Tubingen: Mohr Siebeck, 1999.

Jaffee, Martin S. *Torah in the Mouth: Writing and Oral Tradition in Palestinian Judaism, 200 BCE–400 CE.* Oxford: Oxford University Press, 2001.

Jassen, Alex P. "Religion in the Dead Sea Scrolls." *Religion Compass* 1 (2007) 1-25.

Jokiranta, Jutta. *Identity on a Continuum: Constructing and Expressing Sectarian Social Identity in Qumran* Serakhim *and* Pesharim. STDJ. Leiden: Brill, forthcoming.

———. "Learning from Sectarian Responses: Windows on Qumran Sects and Emerging Christian Sects." In *Echoes from the Caves: Qumran and the New Testament,* ed. Florentino García Martínez, 177-201. STDJ 85. Leiden: Brill, 2009.

———. "'Sectarianism' of the Qumran 'Sect': Sociological Notes." *RevQ* 78 (2001) 223-39.

———. "Social Identity Approach: Identity-Constructing Elements in the Psalms Pesher." In García Martínez and Popović, *Defining Identities,* 85-109.

Josephus, Flavius. *Josephus.* 10 vols. Trans. H. St. J. Thackeray, et al. New York: Putnam and Cambridge, MA: Harvard University Press, 1926-1981.

Kister, Menahem. "A Common Heritage: Biblical Interpretation at Qumran and Its Implications." In *Biblical Perspectives: Early Use and Interpretation of the Bible in Light of the Dead Sea Scrolls. Proceedings of the First International Symposium of the Orion Center, 12-14 May 1996,* ed. Michael E. Stone and Esther G. Chazon, 101-11. STDJ 28. Leiden: Brill, 1998.

Kittel, Bonnie Pedrotti. *The Hymns of Qumran.* SBLDS 50. Chico: Scholars, 1981.

Klawans, Jonathan. "Josephus on Fate, Free Will and Ancient Jewish Types of Compatibilism." *Numen* 56 (2009) 44-90.

Knibb, Michael A. "Rule of the Community." *EDSS,* 2:793-97.

———. "Teacher of Righteousness." *EDSS,* 2:918-21.

Korpel, Marjo C. A., and Josef M. Oesch. *Delimitation Criticism: A New Tool in Biblical Scholarship.* Pericope 1. Assen: Van Gorcum, 2000.

Kraemer, Ross Shepard. *Her Share of the Blessings: Women's Religions Among Pagans, Jews, and Christians in the Greco-Roman World.* New York: Oxford University Press, 1992.

———, ed. *Women's Religions in the Greco-Roman World: A Sourcebook.* Rev. ed. New York: Oxford University Press, 2004.

Kraus, Hans-Joachim. *Psalms 1–59: A Commentary.* CC. Minneapolis: Augsburg, 1988.

Kugler, Robert A. "Hearing 4Q225: A Case Study in Reconstructing the Religious Imagination of the Qumran Community." *DSD* 10 (2003) 81-103.

———. "Making All Experience Religious: The Hegemony of Ritual at Qumran." *JSJ* 33 (2002) 131-52.

———, and Eileen Schuller. *The Dead Sea Scrolls at Fifty: Proceedings of the Society of Biblical Literature Qumran Section Meetings.* SBLEJL 15. Atlanta: Scholars, 1999.

Kutscher, Eduard Y. *A History of the Hebrew Language.* Jerusalem: Magnes, 1982.

———. *The Language and Linguistic Background of the Isaiah Scroll (1QIsaᵃ).* STDJ 6. Leiden: Brill, 1974.

Lange, Armin. *Weisheit und Prädestination: Weisheitliche Urordnung und Prädestination in den Textfunden von Qumran.* STDJ 18. Leiden: Brill, 1995.

———. "Wisdom and Predestination in the Dead Sea Scrolls." *DSD* 2 (1995) 340-54.

———, and Ulrike Mittmann-Richert. "Annotated List of the Texts from the Judaean Desert Classified by Content and Genre." DJD 39, 115-64.

Lauffer, Siegfried, ed. *Diokletians Preisedikt.* Berlin: de Gruyter, 1971.

LeFebvre, Michael. *Collections, Codes, and Torah: The Re-characterization of Israel's Written Law.* LHB/OTS 451. New York: T. & T. Clark, 2006.

Levin, Christoph. "Das Gebetbuch der Gerechten: Literargeschichtliche Beobachtungen am Psalter." *ZTK* 90 (1993) 355-81.

Lewis, Naphtali. *Papyrus in Classical Antiquity.* Oxford: Clarendon, 1974.

Lieberman, Saul. "The Discipline in the So-called Dead Sea Manual of Discipline." *JBL* 71 (1952) 199-206.

Lim, Timothy H. "Eschatological Orientation and the Alteration of Scripture in the Habakkuk Pesher." *JNES* 49 (1990) 185-94.

———. *Holy Scripture in the Qumran Commentaries and Pauline Letters.* Oxford: Clarendon, 1997.

———. *Pesharim.* CQS 3. London: Sheffield Academic, 2002.

———, ed., in consultation with Philip S. Alexander. *The Dead Sea Scrolls Electronic Reference Library.* 3 vols. Oxford: Oxford University Press and Leiden: Brill, 1997.

Lundberg, Marilyn, and Bruce Zuckerman. "New Aramaic Fragments from Qumran Cave One." *The Comprehensive Aramaic Lexicon Newsletter* 12 (1996) 1-5.

Magen, Yitzhak. "Jerusalem as a Center of the Stone Vessel Industry during the Second Temple Period." In *Ancient Judaism Revealed,* ed. Hillel Geva, 244-56. Rev. ed. Jerusalem: Israel Exploration Society, 2000.

Magen, Yizhak, and Yuval Peleg. *The Qumran Excavations 1993-2004: Preliminary Report.* Jerusalem: Israel Antiquities Authority, 2007.

Magness, Jodi. *The Archaeology of Qumran and the Dead Sea Scrolls.* SDSSRL. Grand Rapids: Wm. B. Eerdmans, 2002.

———. *Debating Qumran: Collected Essays on Its Archaeology.* Leuven: Peeters, 2004.

———. Review of Galor, Humbert, and Zangenberg, *Qumran, The Site of the Dead Sea Scrolls. RevQ* 23 (2007) 641-64.

———. Review of Y. Hirschfeld, *Qumran in Context: Reassessing the Archaeological Evidence. RBL* 8/27/2005. http://www.bookreviews.org/BookDetail.asp?TitleId=4500.

————. Review of J.-B. Humbert and A. Chambon, *The Excavations of Khirbet Qumran and Ain Feshkha: Synthesis of Roland de Vaux's Field Notes. DSD* 13 (2006) 262-66.

McDonald, Lee M., and James A. Sanders, eds. *The Canon Debate.* Peabody: Hendrickson, 2002.

Maier, Johann. "Ritual of Marriage." *EDSS*, 2:783.

Martin, Malachi. *The Scribal Character of the Dead Sea Scrolls.* Louvain: Publications universitaires, 1958.

Mason, Steve. *Flavius Josephus on the Pharisees.* StPB 39. Leiden: Brill, 1991.

Meier, John P. "Is There *Halaka* (the Noun) at Qumran?" *JBL* 122 (2003) 150-56.

Mendels, Doron. "Hellenistic Utopia and the Essenes." *HTR* 72 (1979) 207-22. Repr. in *Identity, Religion and Historiography: Studies in Hellenistic History,* 420-39. JSPSup 24. Sheffield: Sheffield Academic, 1998.

Merrill, Eugene H. *Qumran and Predestination: A Theological Study of the Thanksgiving Hymns.* STDJ 8. Leiden: Brill, 1975.

Metso, Sarianna. "Constitutional Rules at Qumran." In Flint and VanderKam, *The Dead Sea Scrolls after Fifty Years,* 1:186-210.

————. "Creating Community Halakhah." In *Studies in the Hebrew Bible, Qumran, and the Septuagint: Presented to Eugene Ulrich,* ed. Peter W. Flint, Emanuel Tov, and James C. VanderKam, 279-301. Leiden: Brill, 2005.

————. "Methodological Problems in Reconstructing History from Rule Texts Found at Qumran." *DSD* 11 (2004) 315-35.

————. "The Primary Results of the Reconstruction of 4QS^e." *JJS* 44 (1993) 303-8.

————. *The Serekh Texts.* CQS 9. LSTS 62. London: T. & T. Clark, 2007.

————. *The Textual Development of the Qumran Community Rule.* STDJ 21. Leiden: Brill, 1997.

Metzger, Bruce M. *The Canon of the New Testament: Its Origin, Development, and Significance.* Oxford: Clarendon, 1987.

Meyers, Eric M., ed. *The Oxford Encyclopedia of Near Eastern Archaeology.* 5 vols. New York: Oxford University Press, 1997.

Milgrom, Jacob. *Leviticus 17–22.* AB 3A. New York: Doubleday, 2000.

Milik, J. T., ed., with the collaboration of Matthew Black. *The Books of Enoch: Aramaic Fragments of Qumrân Cave 4.* Oxford: Clarendon, 1976.

Moore, George Foot. "Fate and Free Will in the Jewish Philosophies According to Josephus." *HTR* 22 (1929) 371-89.

Morawe, Günter. *Aufbau und Abgrenzung der Loblieder von Qumrân: Studien zur gattungsgeschichtlichen Einordnung der Hodajôth.* Theologische Arbeiten 16. Berlin: Evangelische Verlaganstalt, 1961.

————. "Vergleich des Aufbaus der Danklieder und hymnischen Bekenntnislieder (1QH) von Qumran mit dem Aufbau der Psalme in Alten Testament und im Spätjudentum." *RevQ* 4 (1963) 323-56.

Muraoka, Takamitsu. "An Approach to the Morphosyntax and Syntax of Qumran

Hebrew." In *Diggers at the Well: Proceedings of a Third International Symposium on the Hebrew of the Dead Sea Scrolls and Ben Sira,* ed. Muraoka and J. F. Elwolde. STDJ 36. Leiden: Brill, 2000.

Murphy, Catharine M. *Wealth in the Dead Sea Scrolls and in the Qumran Community.* STDJ 40. Leiden: Brill, 2002.

Murphy-O'Connor, J. "Community, Rule of the (1QS)." *ABD,* 1:1110-12.

———. "An Essene Missionary Document? CD II,14–VI,1." *RB* 77 (1970) 201-29.

———. "La genèse littéraire de la *Règle de la Communauté." RB* 76 (1969) 528-49.

Nedungatt, George. "The Covenanters of the Early Syriac-Speaking Church." *OCP* 39 (1973) 191-215, 419-44.

Newsom, Carol A. "Response to 'Religious Exclusivism': A World View Governing Some Texts Found at Qumran." In *George W. E. Nickelsburg in Perspective: An Ongoing Dialogue of Learning,* ed. Jacob Neusner and Alan J. Avery-Peck, 162-75. JSJSup 80. Leiden: Brill, 2003.

———. "'Sectually Explicit' Literature from Qumran." In *The Hebrew Bible and Its Interpreters,* ed. William Henry Propp, Baruch Halpern, and David Noel Freedman, 167-87. Winona Lake: Eisenbrauns, 1990.

———. *The Self as Symbolic Space: Constructing Identity and Community at Qumran.* STDJ 52. Leiden: Brill, 2004.

Nitzan, Bilhah. *Qumran Prayer and Religious Poetry.* STDJ 12. Leiden: Brill, 1994.

Obbink, Dirk. "Craft, Cult, and Canon in the Books from Herculaneum." In *Philodemus and the New Testament World,* ed. John T. Fitzgerald, Obbink, and Glenn S. Holland, 73-84. NovTSup 111. Leiden: Brill, 2004.

Orlinsky, Harry M. "Studies in the St. Mark's Isaiah Scroll, IV." *JQR* 43 (1952-53) 329-40.

Osten-Sacken, Peter von der. *Gott und Belial: Traditionsgeschichtliche Untersuchungen zum Dualismus in den Texten aus Qumran.* SUNT 6. Göttingen: Vandenhoeck & Ruprecht, 1969.

Porter, Stanley E., and Craig A. Evans, eds. *The Scrolls and the Scriptures: Qumran Fifty Years After.* JSPSup 26. Sheffield: Sheffield Academic, 1997.

Pouilly, Jean. *La Règle de la Communauté de Qumrân: Son évolution littéraire.* CahRB 17. Paris: Gabalda, 1976.

Puèch, Émile. "Remarques sur l'écriture de 1QS VII-VIII." *RevQ* 10 (1979) 35-43.

Qimron, Elisha. *The Hebrew of the Dead Sea Scrolls.* HSS 29. Atlanta: Scholars, 1986.

———. "Improving the Editions of the Dead Sea Scrolls." *Meghillot* 1 (2003) 135-45. (Hebrew)

Rabin, Chaim, and Yigael Yadin. *Aspects of the Dead Sea Scrolls.* ScrHier 4. Jerusalem: Magnes, 1958.

Reed, Stephen A. *The Dead Sea Scrolls Catalogue: Documents, Photographs and Museum Inventory Numbers.* Ed. Marilyn J. Lundberg, with the collaboration of Michael B. Phelps. SBLRBS 32. Atlanta: Scholars, 1994.

Regev, Eyal. *Sectarianism in Qumran: A Cross-Cultural Perspective.* Religion and Society 45. Berlin: de Gruyter, 2007.

Reich, Ronny. *"Miqwa'ot* (Jewish Ritual Baths) in the Second Temple, Mishnah and Talmud Periods." Diss., Hebrew University, 1990. (Hebrew)

Reicke, Bo. "Remarques sur l'histoire de la forme (Formgeschichte) des textes de Qumran." In *Les manuscrits de la mer Morte: Colloque de Strasbourg, 25-27 Mai 1955,* ed. Jean Daniélou, 38-44. Paris: Presses universitaires, 1957.

Richardson, H. Neil. "Some Notes on 1QSa." *JBL* 76 (1957) 108-22.

Ringgren, Helmer. *The Faith of Qumran: Theology of the Dead Sea Scrolls.* Expanded ed. by James H. Charlesworth. New York: Crossroad, 1995.

Rodrigues Pereira, A. S. *Studies in Aramaic Poetry (c. 100 B.C.E.–c. 600 C.E.).* SSN 34. Assen: Van Gorcum, 1997.

Rothstein, David. "Women's Testimony at Qumran: The Biblical and Second Temple Evidence." *RevQ* 21 (2004) 597-614.

Sanders, E. P. *Paul and Palestinian Judaism: A Comparison of Patterns of Religion.* Minneapolis: Fortress, 1977.

Satlow, Michael L. "4Q502 A New Year Festival?" *DSD* 5 (1998) 57-68.

Schams, Christine. *Jewish Scribes in the Second Temple Period.* JSOTSup 291. Sheffield: Sheffield Academic, 1998.

Schiffman, Lawrence H. "The Eschatological Community and the Stages of Sectarian Life." In *Eschatological Community,* 11-27.

―――. *The Eschatological Community of the Dead Sea Scrolls: A Study of the Rule of the Congregation.* SBLMS 38. Atlanta: Scholars, 1989.

―――. *From Text to Tradition: A History of Second Temple and Rabbinic Judaism.* Hoboken: Ktav, 1991.

―――. *The Halakhah at Qumran.* SJLA 16. Leiden: Brill, 1975.

―――. "Legal Texts and Codification in the Dead Sea Scrolls." In *Discussing Cultural Influences: Text, Context and Non-text in Rabbinic Judaism,* ed. Rivka Ulmer, 1-39. Lanham: University Press of America, 2006.

―――. "The New Halakhic Letter (4QMMT) and the Origins of the Dead Sea Sect." *BA* 53 (1990) 64-73.

―――. *Reclaiming the Dead Sea Scrolls: The History of Judaism, the Background of Christianity, the Lost Library of Qumran.* ABRL. New York: Doubleday, 1995.

―――. "Women in the Scrolls." Pp. 127-43 in *Reclaiming the Dead Sea Scrolls.*

―――, Emanuel Tov, and James C. VanderKam, eds. *The Dead Sea Scrolls Fifty Years after Their Discovery.* Jerusalem: Israel Exploration Society and Shrine of the Book, Israel Museum, 2000.

―――, and James C. VanderKam, eds. *Encyclopedia of the Dead Sea Scrolls.* 2 vols. Oxford: Oxford University Press, 2000.

Schuller, Eileen. "Petitionary Prayer and the Religion of Qumran." In Collins and Kugler, *Religion in the Dead Sea Scrolls,* 29-45.

———. "Women in the Dead Sea Scrolls." In Flint and VanderKam, *The Dead Sea Scrolls after Fifty Years,* 2:117-44.

Segal, Michael. "4QReworked Pentateuch or 4QPentateuch?" In Schiffman, Tov, and VanderKam, *The Dead Sea Scrolls Fifty Years after Their Discovery,* 391-99.

Segal, Moshe Tzvi. *Sefer Ben Sira ha-Shalem.* 2nd ed. Jerusalem: Mossad Bialik, 1958.

Sheridan, Susan G. "Scholars, Soldiers, Craftsmen, Elites? Analysis of the French Collection of Human Remains from Qumran." *DSD* 9 (2002) 199-248.

———, and Jaime Ullinger. "A Reconsideration of the French Qumran Collection." In Galor, Humbert, and Zangenberg, *Qumran, The Site of the Dead Sea Scrolls,* 195-212.

Skehan, Patrick W. "A Liturgical Complex in 11QPs^a." *CBQ* 34 (1973) 195-205.

———. "Qumran and Old Testament Criticism." In *Qumran: Sa piété, sa théologie et son milieu,* ed. M. Delcor, 163-82. Paris: Duculot and Leuven: Leuven University Press, 1978.

———, and Alexander A. Di Lella. *The Wisdom of Ben Sira: A New Translation.* AB 39. New York: Doubleday, 1987.

Steck, Odil Hannes. *Die erste Jesajarolle von Qumran (1QIsa): Schreibweise als Leseanleitung.* Stuttgarter Bibelstudien 173/1. Stuttgart: Katholisches Bibelwerk, 1998.

Stegemann, Hartmut. "Methods for the Reconstruction of Scrolls from Scattered Fragments." In *Archaeology and History in the Dead Sea Scrolls: The New York University Conference in Memory of Yigael Yadin,* ed. Lawrence H. Schiffman, 189-220. JSPSup 8. Sheffield: JSOT, 1990.

Steudel, Annette. "Assembling and Reconstructing Manuscripts." In Flint and VanderKam, *The Dead Sea Scrolls after Fifty Years,* 1:516-34.

Stoekl Ben Ezra, Daniel. "Old Caves and Young Caves: A Statistical Reevaluation of a Qumran Consensus." *DSD* 14 (2007) 313-31.

Strugnell, John. "Notes en marge du volume V des 'Discoveries in the Judaean Desert of Jordan.'" *RevQ* 7 (1970) 163-276.

Sutcliffe, Edmund F. "The First Fifteen Members of the Qumran Community: A Note on 1QS 8:1ff." *JSS* 4 (1959) 134-38.

Talmon, Shemaryahu. "Anti-Lunar-Calendar Polemics in Covenanters' Writings." In *Das Ende der Tage und die Gegenwart des Heils: Begegnungen mit dem Neuen Testament und seiner Umwelt, Festschrift für Heinz-Wolfgang Kuhn zum 65. Geburtstag,* ed. Michael Becker and Wolfgang Fenske, 29-40. AGJU 44. Leiden: Brill, 1999.

———. "Between the Bible and the Mishnah: Qumran from Within." In Talmon, ed., *Jewish Civilization in the Hellenistic-Roman Period,* 214-57.

———. "Calendar Controversy in Ancient Judaism: The Case of the 'Community of the Renewed Covenant.'" In *The Provo International Conference on the*

Dead Sea Scrolls: Technological Innovations, New Texts, and Reformulated Issues, ed. Donald Parry and Eugene Ulrich, 379-95. STDJ 30. Leiden: Brill, 1999.

———. "The Calendar Reckoning of the Sect from the Judean Desert." In Rabin and Yadin, *Aspects of the Dead Sea Scrolls,* 162-99.

———. "The Community of the Renewed Covenant: Between Judaism and Christianity." In Ulrich and VanderKam, *The Community of the Renewed Covenant,* 3-24.

———. "The Emergence of Jewish Sectarianism in the Early Second Temple Period." In *King, Cult, and Calendar in Ancient Israel,* 165-201. Repr. in *Ancient Israelite Religion: Essays in Honor of Frank Moore Cross,* ed. Patrick D. Miller, Paul D. Hanson, and S. Dean McBride, 587-616. Philadelphia: Fortress, 1987.

———. "The Essential 'Community of the Renewed Covenant': How Should Qumran Studies Proceed?" In Cancik, Lichtenberger, and Schäfer, *Geschichte — Tradition — Reflexion,* 323-52.

———. "The Internal Diversification of Judaism in the Early Second Temple Period." In Talmon, ed., *Jewish Civilization in the Hellenistic-Roman Period,* 16-43.

———. *King, Cult, and Calendar in Ancient Israel: Collected Studies.* Jerusalem: Magnes, 1986.

———. "The New Covenanters of Qumran." *Scientific American* 225/5 (1971) 73-81.

———. "The Old Testament Text." In Cross and Talmon, *Qumran and the History of the Biblical Text,* 1-41.

———. "Oral Tradition and Written Transmission, or the Heard and the Seen Word in Judaism of the Second Temple Period." In *Jesus and the Oral Gospel Tradition,* ed. Henry Wansbrough, 121-58. JSNTSup 64. Sheffield: Sheffield Academic, 1991.

———. "Pisqah Be'emṣaʿ Pasuq and 11QPsᵃ." *Textus* 5 (1966) 11-21.

———. "The Textual Study of the Bible — A New Outlook." In Cross and Talmon, *Qumran and the History of the Biblical Text,* 321-400.

———. "The Transmission History of the Text of the Hebrew Bible in the Light of Biblical Manuscripts from Qumran and Other Sites in the Judean Desert." In Schiffman, Tov, and VanderKam, *The Dead Sea Scrolls: Fifty Years After Their Discovery,* 40-50.

———. "Types of Messianic Expectation at the Turn of the Era." In *King, Cult and Calendar in Ancient Israel,* 202-24.

———. "Waiting for the Messiah: The Spiritual Universe of the Qumran Covenanters." In *Judaisms and Their Messiahs at the Turn of the Christian Era,* ed. Jacob Neusner, William Scott Green, and Ernest S. Frerichs, 111-37. Cambridge: Cambridge University Press, 1987.

————. ed. *Jewish Civilization in the Hellenistic-Roman Period.* JSPSup 10. Sheffield: Sheffield Academic, 1991.

————, ed. *Masada VI: Hebrew Fragments from Masada.* Jerusalem: Israel Exploration Society, 1999.

Testuz, Michel. "Greek *Ode of Solomon.*" In *Papyrus Bodmer X-XII,* 49-69. Cologny: Bibliotheca Bodmeriana, 1959.

Tigchelaar, Eibert. "Annotated List of Overlaps and Parallels in the Non-biblical Texts from Qumran and Masada." DJD 39, 285-322.

————. "Lady Folly and Her House in Three Qumran Manuscripts: On the Relation between *4Q525* 15, *5Q16*, and *4Q184* 1." *RevQ* 23 (2008) 371-81.

————. "'These are the names of the spirits of . . .'": A Preliminary Edition of 4QCatalogue of Spirits (4Q230) and New Manuscript Evidence for the Two Spirits Treatise (4Q257 and 1Q29a)." *RevQ* 21 (2004) 529-47.

Tov, Emanuel. "The Biblical Texts from the Judaean Desert: An Overview and Analysis of All the Published Texts." In Herbert and Tov, *The Bible as Book,* 139-66.

————. "Further Evidence for the Existence of a Qumran Scribal School." In Schiffman, Tov, and VanderKam, *The Dead Sea Scrolls: Fifty Years After Their Discovery,* 199-216.

————. "Hebrew Biblical Manuscripts from the Judaean Desert: Their Contribution to Textual Criticism." *JJS* 39 (1988) 5-37.

————. "The Many Forms of Scripture: Reflections in Light of the LXX and 4QReworked Pentateuch." In *From Qumran to Aleppo: A Discussion with Emanuel Tov about the Textual History of Jewish Scriptures in Honor of His 65th Birthday,* ed. Armin Lange, Matthias Weigold, and József Zsengellér, 11-28. FRLANT 230. Göttingen: Vandenhoeck & Ruprecht, 2009.

————. "The Nature of the Greek Texts from the Judean Desert." *NovT* 43 (2001) 1-11.

————. "The Orthography and Language of the Hebrew Scrolls Found at Qumran and the Origin of These Scrolls." *Textus* 13 (1986) 31-57.

————. *Revised Lists of the Texts from the Judean Desert.* Leiden: Brill, 2010.

————. "Scribal Practices." *EDSS,* 2:827-30.

————. *Scribal Practices and Approaches Reflected in the Texts Found in the Judean Desert.* STDJ 54. Leiden: Brill, 2004.

————. "Scribal Practices Reflected in the Paleo-Hebrew Texts from the Judean Desert." *Scripta Classica Israelica* 15 (1996) 268-73.

————. "The Socio-Religious Background of the Paleo-Hebrew Biblical Texts Found at Qumran." In Cancik, Lichtenberger, and Schäfer, *Geschichte — Tradition — Reflexion,* 1:333-74.

————. *Textual Criticism of the Hebrew Bible.* 2nd ed. Minneapolis: Fortress and Assen: Van Gorcum, 2001.

————. "The Writing of Early Scrolls: Implications for the Literary Analysis of

Hebrew Scripture." In *L'Ecrit et l'Esprit: Etudes d'histoire du texte et de théologie biblique en hommage à Adrian Schenker,* ed. Dieter Böhler, Innocent Himbaza, and Philippe Hugo, 355-71. Fribourg: Academic and Göttingen: Vandenhoeck & Ruprecht, 2005. In abbreviated form, "The Writing of Early Scrolls and the Literary Analysis of Hebrew Scripture." *DSD* 13 (2006) 339-47.

————, ed., with the collaboration of Stephen J. Pfann. *Companion Volume to The Dead Sea Scrolls Microfiche Edition.* 2nd ed. Leiden: Brill, 1995.

————. *The Dead Sea Scrolls on Microfiche: A Comprehensive Facsimile Edition of the Texts from the Judean Desert.* Leiden: Brill, 1993.

Trever, John. "Completion of the Publication of Some Fragments from Qumran Cave I." *RevQ* 5 (1964-66) 323-44.

Ulrich, Eugene. "The Bible in the Making: The Scriptures at Qumran." In Ulrich and VanderKam, *The Community of the Renewed Covenant,* 77-93. Repr. in *The Dead Sea Scrolls and the Origins of the Bible,* 17-33.

————. "The Biblical Scrolls from Qumran Cave 4: An Overview and a Progress Report on Their Publication." In *The Texts of Qumran and the History of the Community: Proceedings of the Groningen Congress on the Dead Sea Scrolls [20-23 August 1989],* ed. Florentino García Martínez, vol. 1: *Biblical Texts,* 207-28. Paris: Gabalda, 1989 = *RevQ* 14/2 (54-55).

————. "The Dead Sea Scrolls and the Biblical Text." In Flint and VanderKam, *The Dead Sea Scrolls after Fifty Years,* 79-100.

————. *The Dead Sea Scrolls and the Origins of the Bible.* SDSSRL. Grand Rapids: Wm. B. Eerdmans and Leiden: Brill, 1999.

————. "Double Literary Editions of Biblical Narratives and Reflections on Determining the Form to Be Translated." In *Perspectives on the Hebrew Bible: Essays in Honor of Walter J. Harrelson,* ed. James L. Crenshaw, 101-16. Macon: Mercer University Press, 1988. Repr. in *The Dead Sea Scrolls and the Origins of the Bible,* 34-50.

————. "From Literature to Scripture: The Growth of a Text's Authoritativeness." *DSD* 10 (2003) 3-25.

————. "Multiple Literary Editions: Reflections Toward a Theory of the History of the Biblical Text." In *Current Research and Technological Developments on the Dead Sea Scrolls,* ed. Donald W. Parry and Stephen D. Ricks, 78-105. STDJ 6. Leiden: Brill, 1996. Repr. in *The Dead Sea Scrolls and the Origins of the Bible,* 99-120.

————. "The Non-attestation of a Tripartite Canon in 4QMMT." *CBQ* 65 (2003) 202-14.

————. "The Notion and Definition of Canon." In McDonald and Sanders, *The Canon Debate,* 21-35.

————. "Qumran and the Canon of the Old Testament." In *The Biblical Canons,*

ed. J.-M. Auwers and H. J. de Jonge, 57-80. Colloquium Biblicum Lovani-
ense LI. BETL 163. Leuven: Leuven University Press, 2003.

―――. "The Qumran Biblical Scrolls — The Scriptures of Late Second Temple
Judaism." In *The Dead Sea Scrolls in Their Historical Context,* ed. Timothy H. Lim, et al., 67-87. Edinburgh: T. & T. Clark, 2000.

―――. "The Text of the Hebrew Scriptures at the Time of Hillel and Jesus." In
Congress Volume Basel 2001, ed. André Lemaire, 85-105. VTSup 92. Leiden:
Brill, 2002.

―――, and James C. VanderKam, eds. *The Community of the Renewed Covenant:
The Notre Dame Symposium on the Dead Sea Scrolls.* Notre Dame: University of Notre Dame Press, 1994.

Urbach, Ephraim E. *The Sages, Their Concepts and Beliefs.* Jerusalem: Magnes,
1975.

VanderKam, James C. *Calendars in the Dead Sea Scrolls: Measuring Time.* London:
Routledge, 1998.

―――. "Questions of Canon Viewed through the Dead Sea Scrolls." In McDonald
and Sanders, *The Canon Debate,* 91-109.

―――. "The Wording of Biblical Citations in Some Rewritten Scriptural Works."
In Herbert and Tov, *The Bible as Book,* 41-56.

Van Seters, John. *The Edited Bible: The Curious History of the "Editor" in Biblical
Criticism.* Winona Lake: Eisenbrauns, 2006.

Vaux, Roland de. *Archaeology and the Dead Sea Scrolls.* Schweich Lectures 1959.
Rev. ed. London: British Academy, 1973.

Vermes, Geza. *The Complete Dead Sea Scrolls in English.* New York: Allen Lane,
1997. Rev. ed. London: Penguin, 2004.

―――. *The Dead Sea Scrolls Forty Years On: The Fourteenth Sacks Lecture.* Oxford: Oxford Centre for Postgraduate Hebrew Studies, 1987.

―――. *The Dead Sea Scrolls: Qumran in Perspective.* 3rd ed. London: SCM, 1994.

―――. "Historiographical Elements in the Qumran Writings: A Synopsis of the
Textual Evidence." *JJS* 58 (2007) 121-39.

―――, and Martin D. Goodman, eds. *The Essenes According to the Classical
Sources.* Sheffield: JSOT, 1989.

Wassen, Cecilia. *Women in the Damascus Document.* Academia Biblica 21. Leiden:
Brill, 2005.

―――, and Jutta Jokiranta. "Groups in Tension: Sectarianism in the Damascus
Document and the Community Rule." In Chalcraft, *Sectarianism in Early Judaism,* 205-45.

Webster, Brian. "Chronological Index of the Texts from the Judaean Desert." DJD
39, 351-446.

Weinfeld, Moshe. *The Organizational Pattern and the Penal Code of the Qumran
Sect: A Comparison with Guilds and Religious Associations of the Hellenistic-
Roman Period.* NTOA 2. Göttingen: Vandenhoeck & Ruprecht, 1986.

Weitzman, Steven. "Revisiting Myth and Ritual in Early Judaism." *DSD* 4 (1997) 21-54.

Werner, Eric. "Hebrew and Oriental Christian Metrical Hymns: A Comparison." *HUCA* 23 (1950-51) 397-432.

Winston, David. *The Wisdom of Solomon: A New Translation with Introduction and Commentary.* AB 43. Garden City: Doubleday, 1979.

Winter, Paul. "Ben Sira and the Teaching of 'Two Ways.'" *VT* 5 (1955) 315-18.

Wise, Michael O. "Dating the Teacher of Righteousness and the *Floruit* of His Movement." *JBL* 122 (2003) 53-87.

———, Martin Abegg, Jr., and Edward Cook. *The Dead Sea Scrolls: A New Translation.* San Francisco: HarperCollins, 1996.

———, Norman Golb, John J. Collins, and Dennis G. Pardee, eds. *Methods of Investigation of the Dead Sea Scrolls and the Khirbet Qumran Site: Present Realities and Future Prospects.* Annals of the New York Academy of Sciences 722. New York: New York Academy of Sciences, 1994.

Wright, Benjamin G. *No Small Difference: Sirach's Relationship to Its Hebrew Parent Text.* SBLSCS 26. Atlanta: Scholars, 1989.

Wright, William. *Catalogue of Syriac Manuscripts in the British Museum Acquired since the Year 1838.* 3 vols. London: British Museum, 1870-72.

Yadin, Yigael. *Tefillin from Qumran (XQPhyl 1-4).* Jerusalem: Israel Exploration Society, 1969.

Yardeni, Ada. *The Book of Hebrew Script: History, Paleography, Script Styles, Calligraphy, and Design.* Jerusalem: Carta, 1997. (Hebrew)

———. "A Draft of a Deed on an Ostracon from Khirbet Qumran." *IEJ* 47 (1997) 233-37.

Zias, Joseph E. "The Cemeteries of Qumran and Celibacy: Confusion Laid to Rest?" *DSD* 7 (2000) 220-53.

———. "Qumran Archaeology: Skeletons with Multiple Personality Disorders and Other Grave Errors." *RevQ* 21 (2003) 83-98.

Zuckerman, Bruce. "Bringing the Dead Sea Scrolls Back to Life: A New Evaluation of the Photographic and Electronic Imaging of the Dead Sea Scrolls." *DSD* 3 (1996) 178-207.

———. "Every Dot and Tiddle: A Consideration of the Limitation of Computer Imaging for the Study of Dead Sea Scrolls." In *Double Takes: Thinking and Rethinking Issues of Modern Judaism in Ancient Contexts,* ed. Zev Garber and Bruce Zuckerman, 183-96. Studies in the Shoah 26. Lanham: University Press of America, 2004.

———. "Working with a Little More Data: New Finds in the Twentieth Century; The Semitic Languages of the Ancient World." In *Semitic Linguistics: The State of the Art at the Turn of the Twenty-First Century,* ed. Shlemo Izre'el, 481-97. IOS 20. Winona Lake: Eisenbrauns, 2002.

————, and Lynn Swartz Dodd. "Pots and Alphabets: Refractions of Reflections on Typological Method." *Maarav* 10 (2003) 89-133.

————, and Kenneth Zuckerman. "Photography of Manuscripts." *OEANE* 4:336-47.

————. "Photography and Computer Imaging." *EDSS* 2:669-75.

Index of Subjects

Aemilius Scaurus, 123
Alexander Jannaeus, 122-23
Anachronism, 11, 14, 15, 115, 148, 149, 157, 165, 183, 184, 194
Androcentrism, 8, 230-31, 233, 239, 241-42, 244
Antiochus IV Epiphanes, 122, 205, 247
Apocrypha, 131, 142-43, 190
Archaeological method, 92, 94-98, 100
Aristobulus II, 123

Bar Kokhba, 114
Ben Sira (Sirach), 131, 134, 139, 146, 150, 267-71, 276, 282-83
Biblical Hebrew (BH), 52, 53, 57, 58, 61-63, 66, 158. *See also* Qumran Hebrew

Cairo Genizah, 53, 117, 202-3
Calendar, 2, 97, 104, 184, 215-20, 223-24, 227
Canon, 6, 13, 115, 133, 145-50, 152, 157, 161, 188-92, 197
Carbon dating, 4, 49-51, 95-97, 100, 116
Caves. *See* Qumran caves.
Cemetery. *See* Qumran cemetery.
Chaos theory, 130
Christianity, 1, 8, 23, 121, 124, 134-35, 137, 141, 146, 151, 161, 222, 238, 249-50, 264, 274, 277-83
Codex, 149, 188, 191
Codex Nintriensis, 136-38
Coins, 6, 93, 95, 98-100, 104, 110, 114, 120-21, 127, 158
Compatibilism, 8, 270, 271, 275, 278, 281-83
Conspiracy theories, 90
Counterfactual history, 128-32, 136, 142-44
Covenant, 15, 17, 20, 141, 173, 174, 184, 206, 209, 211, 213, 220, 226, 227, 233, 243, 244, 252, 253, 259, 260, 261, 275, 276

Dead Sea Sect (sectarian movement), 8, 15, 20, 90, 104, 106, 108, 111, 112, 122-25, 132, 200-202, 206-10, 214, 231, 232-33, 256, 260, 265, 267, 269-71, 279-83
Delimitation criticism, 167
Demetrius III, 122-23
Digital imaging (digitization), 49, 69-75, 81, 84-88, 186
Ductus (scribal ductus), 85-86

Epicureans, 126

Index of Ancient Texts and Manuscripts